TRANSITIONAL JURISPRUDENCE AND THE EUROPEAN CONVENTION ON HUMAN RIGHTS

The European Convention on Human Rights has been a standard-setting text for transitions to peace and democracy in states throughout Europe. This book analyses the content, role and effects of the jurisprudence of the European Court relating to societies in transition. It features a wide range of transitional challenges, from killings by security forces in Northern Ireland to property restitution in Central and Eastern Europe, and from political upheaval in the Balkans to the position of religious minorities and Roma. Has the European Court developed a specific transitional jurisprudence? How do politics affect the ways in which the Court's judgments are implemented? Does the Court's case-law itself become woven into narratives of struggle in transitional societies? This book seeks to answer these questions by highlighting the unique role of Europe's main guardian of human rights, the Court in Strasbourg. It includes a comparison with the Inter-American and African human rights systems.

ANTOINE BUYSE is Associate Professor and Senior Researcher at the Netherlands Institute of Human Rights (SIM), Utrecht University.

MICHAEL HAMILTON is Associate Professor at the Legal Studies Department of Central European University, Budapest, and Senior Lecturer at the Transitional Justice Institute, University of Ulster.

TRANSITIONAL JURISPRUDENCE AND THE EUROPEAN CONVENTION ON HUMAN RIGHTS

Justice, Politics and Rights

Edited by

ANTOINE BUYSE

MICHAEL HAMILTON

CAMBRIDGE UNIVERSITY PRESS
Cambridge, New York, Melbourne, Madrid, Cape Town,
Singapore, São Paulo, Delhi, Tokyo, Mexico City

Cambridge University Press
The Edinburgh Building, Cambridge CB2 8RU, UK

Published in the United States of America by Cambridge University Press, New York

www.cambridge.org
Information on this title: www.cambridge.org/9781107003019

First published 2011

Printed in the United Kingdom at the University Press, Cambridge

A catalogue record for this publication is available from the British Library

Library of Congress Cataloguing in Publication data
Transitional jurisprudence and the European Convention on Human Rights / [edited by]
Antoine Buyse, Michael Hamilton.
p.   cm.
Includes bibliographical references and index.
ISBN 978-1-107-00301-9
1. European Court of Human Rights.   2. Convention for the Protection of
Human Rights and Fundamental Freedoms (1950)   3. Civil rights–Europe–
Cases.   4. Human rights–Europe–Cases.   I. Buyse, Antoine C.
(Antoine Christian), 1977–   II. Hamilton, Michael, 1975–
KJC5138.T73 2011
342.408′5–dc22
2011016714

ISBN 978-1-107-00301-9 Hardback

CONTENTS

Foreword   vii
RUTI TEITEL

Acknowledgements   xi

1   Introduction   1
MICHAEL HAMILTON AND ANTOINE BUYSE

2   Transitional emergency jurisprudence: derogation
and transition   24
FIONNUALA NÍ AOLÁIN

3   Rights and victims, martyrs and memories: the
European Court of Human Rights and political
transition in Northern Ireland   52
KRIS BROWN

4   Confronting the consequences of authoritarianism
and conflict: the ECHR and transition   81
CHRISTOPHER K. LAMONT

5   Freedom of religion and democratic transition   103
JAMES A. SWEENEY

6   The truth, the past and the present: Article 10 ECHR
and situations of transition   131
ANTOINE BUYSE

7   Transition, political loyalties and the order of the state   151
MICHAEL HAMILTON

8   Transition, equality and non-discrimination   185
ANNE SMITH AND RORY O'CONNELL

9   Closing the door on restitution: the European Court of
    Human Rights   208
    TOM ALLEN AND BENEDICT DOUGLAS

10 The Inter-American human rights system and
    transitional processes   239
    DIEGO RODRÍGUEZ-PINZÓN

11 The 'transitional' jurisprudence of the African
    Commission on Human and Peoples' Rights   267
    GINA BEKKER

12 Conclusions   286
    ANTOINE BUYSE AND MICHAEL HAMILTON

    Index   301

FOREWORD

RUTI TEITEL

We are in a 'global' phase of transitional justice, marked by the proliferation of accountability mechanisms and processes at and across different levels – international, regional and domestic.[1] What all of this means theoretically and practically is the central theme of this probing book. This is a work that questions prevailing assumptions, in particular regarding the European Court of Human Rights, through cross-cutting comparative research.

The point of departure is the current state of the field of transitional justice. The global phase has three dimensions: the globalization of the context; the concern for actors and interests beyond the state, both public and private; and the expansion, entrenchment and normalization of accountability as a response to conflict, wherever it occurs and whatever its forms. Moreover, this is a time in which courts are increasingly the institutions called upon to respond to conflict. The purposes of and hopes for transitional justice are extended beyond state building to advance the promotion and maintenance of human security.

Through a comparative lens, the book aims to engage with the jurisprudence of regional tribunals. It interrogates the parameters of transitional justice and it looks to the law that has emerged to assess its form – the relevant modality. What distinguishes this jurisprudence? What might we learn about the rule of law in transitional times and, given the permanency of these judicial structures and their principles of jurisdiction, what relation might these precedents bear to ordinary times?

More specifically – what techniques are employed and what means of supervision exist in the European region? Here, the book explores the central principles which recur in judicial review such as the margin of

Ruti Teitel is Ernst C. Stiefel Professor of Comparative Law, New York Law School; author, *Transitional Justice* (New York: Oxford University Press, 2000).

[1] See R. Teitel, 'Transitional Justice Globalized', *International Journal of Transitional Justice* (2009).

appreciation – a principle of judicial deference; proportionality – implicating a closer look at means–ends analysis; and yet another engagement with 'militant democracy', i.e. of closer scrutiny in instances where certain democracy related rights are under threat but where the end somehow justifies the means of limited rights restriction – all in the name of preserving other orders.[2] In this regard, the volume's contributors emphasize the role of the oldest such regional court – the European Court of Human Rights which enforces the European Convention – but also include perspectives from the Americas and Africa.

The canon of human rights jurisprudence has itself been shaped by the confrontation with transition and related problems. What exactly might this mean? To what extent are transitional responses becoming entrenched? Here, one can see that the term transition does a lot of work, in some instances concerning adjudication relating to states undergoing political change in the here and now, such as *Sejdić and Finci* v. *Bosnia and Herzegovina* where the European Court of Human Rights sets limits on discriminatory transitional arrangements. In other instances, the term involves issues of regional transformation, i.e. supervision of states in processes of European accession.[3] Here one might consider recent case law involving Turkey. A third such understanding might be where questions of regional transformation are linked to the performance of unaddressed duties regarding transitional justice, e.g. concerning Serbia or Hungary.[4] A fourth such role is one involving the normative entrenchment of rights guarantees, deriving from challenges in times of emergency, as in the European Court of Human Rights' role regarding derogations in the United Kingdom.[5] Sometimes the phenomena seem to present a combination of these, such as the Greek derogation regime, claimed shortly after its authoritarian reversion.

Of course, there is a risk in the use of the concept of transition regarding all of these moments of judicial review. For example, considering the Court's role in rubberstamping findings of the Turkish state as to whether it is in justifiable derogation of the human rights regime. What connection

---

[2] R. Teitel, 'Militating Democracy', *Michigan Journal of International Law* 29 (2007).

[3] ECtHR, *Sejdić and Finci* v. *Bosnia and Herzegovina*, 22 December 2009 (Appl. nos. 27996/06 and 34836/06).

[4] See ECtHR, *Korbely* v. *Hungary*, 19 September 2008 (Appl. no. 9174/02).

[5] *McCann and others* v. *United Kingdom*, 27 September 1995 (Appl. no. 18984/91); see Chapter 2, this volume. See also O. Gross, 'The Normless and Exceptionless Exception: Carl Schmitt's Theory of Emergency Powers and the "Norm-Exception" Dichotomy', *Cardozo Law Review* 21 (2000) 1825.

might findings in such transitional times of emergency play regarding judicial deference in ordinary times, e.g. in the Welfare Party case?[6]

The book further shows how the judgments of these regional courts may well catalyse reform at the national level, influence the strategies employed by domestic actors and help settle contested histories. But conclusions as to evaluation seem a daunting proposition given the diversity of regions and judicial players and varying interests and purposes at issue.

There are many interesting questions raised here: what distinguishes the institutions of regional tribunals as opposed to national and/or international judiciaries? To what extent are there continuities or affinities across regions? Here, one might observe common practices across the regional tribunals. Another question goes to law's relation to politics and political development. What the Inter-American Court does may well differ from others such as the older European Court doing supervision now of human rights issues in states acceding to membership of the Council of Europe and, indeed, the European Union. Indeed, there may be some tension between the transitional priorities of states and the transitional goals of supra-national actors.

These are difficult issues as they go to the question of how effectively targeted courts can really be in insuring such normative change. To what extent is this really a transitional jurisprudence? And insofar as this term is used here beyond the transition, is there a risk in the entrenchment of such precedents? More particularly, how successful have strategies such as the margin of appreciation been? We have seen more and less progressive interpretations of this principle raising serious questions about the role of courts in protecting minority rights. But if one assumes dynamic rather than static understandings, then how exactly does the deference to the state work? To what extent do such principles imply deference to static or dynamic understandings of democratic majorities?[7]

What is the relation of regional compared to global transitional justice? Might different courts be more transitional at different times? More or less supervisory? Here, the compendium raises the potential role of the passage of time, as one factor of concern to the courts. But, of course, we know from the development of the field that rarely are societal responses speedy; and we might even detect tensions and contradictions regarding

---

[6] See *Refah Partisi (Welfare Party)* v. *Turkey*, 13 February 2003 (Appl. nos. 41340/98, 41342/98, 41343/98 and 41344/98) paras. 267, 269.
[7] R. Teitel, 'Militating Democracy', *Michigan Journal of International Law* 29 (2007).

the passage of time where state crimes are at issue and where the role of time may well be paradoxical.[8]

In evaluating between the regions, there may be less awareness of the European Court as fulfilling a transformative role than the role of the Inter-American Court whose adjudication docket was launched at the time of the major transitions out of military grip in Latin America, and moreover whose jurisprudence has ended up defining policy regarding the transition. This happened most famously in its first landmark case ruling in which the Inter-American Court held that there must be a minimum level of investigation and reparation (the *Velasquez Rodriguez* decision).[9]

On this question, the book contributes to an existing debate, i.e. one between this author and Martin Krieger, Wojciech Sadurski and other observers of the East European transitions who explore the relationship of transitional justice to law as it is in ordinary times, and from their critical perspective, offer the view that there is always normative decision-making and some degree of transformation and not always in a liberal direction. There can be, for example, derogation even in ordinary times. But we know that this is always a question of degree; and moreover that the continuum is informed by culture, legal tradition (common law versus civil law) and ultimately by the degree of commitment to transformation.

This book moves deftly between laying out the case law and the basic principles of human rights law and of transitional justice to further probe the nature of this jurisprudence. Bringing this case law together is itself an important accomplishment. Beyond this, the book also entertains two related profound questions about what distinguishes this jurisprudence and what it is actually advancing.

---

[8] R. Teitel, *Transitional Justice* (New York: Oxford University Press, 2000) 138–145, 182–185.

[9] See IACtHR, *Velazquez-Rodriguez* v. *Honduras*, 29 July 1988 (Series C no. 4); see also IACtHR, *Case of Barrios Altos* v. *Peru*, 14 March 2001 (Series C no. 75) (concurring opinion of Judge Trindade) para. 26.

ACKNOWLEDGEMENTS

Transitions are long-term processes, in which the road ahead is often full of trials and tribulations. Societies emerging from armed conflict or authoritarian rule face the difficult challenge of re-inventing themselves in a constant process of adaptation. The experience of editing this book has left us with an unmistakable feeling that edited collections have many features in common with transitions: they take time, involve many actors and require continual re-adjustment. Nonetheless, we did not have to face directly the horrors of war or the terror of dictators. Rather benignly, we were haunted only by deadlines and competing academic responsibilities. And in the process, we enjoyed and benefited greatly from the expertise, collaboration and friendship of many. The transition from tentative idea to tangible result is marked with the publication of the present volume.

The possibility of this project was first floated at an away-day at the Rural College and Derrynoid Centre in Draperstown – a secluded oasis halfway between the University of Ulster's Magee and Jordanstown campuses. It evolved and developed under the flag of the Transitional Justice Institute (TJI) at the University of Ulster. Not only are several of the book's contributors researchers or visiting scholars at TJI, the Institute provided the perfect intellectual space, and the collegial and financial support, for us to discuss and develop the themes at the core of this book. In March 2010, at something of a mid-point, we organised a roundtable seminar for the book's authors. This event was funded by TJI and proved indispensable to the further crystallisation of ideas and cross-cutting themes. For all of this, we remain truly indebted to Professors Christine Bell, Colm Campbell and Fionnuala Ní Aoláin – and also to David Kretzmer during his time in residence at TJI – for their mentoring, encouragement and support along the way. Also at TJI, we want to thank Lisa Gormley, Elaine McCoubrey and Emer Carlin for their immeasurable help throughout the book's gestation. And at Utrecht University, we are sincerely grateful to the encouragement and support of the director of the Netherlands Institute of Human Rights SIM, Professor Jenny Goldschmidt.

We are particularly indebted to those experts from beyond Ulster and Utrecht who directly contributed to this volume: Tom Allen, Benedict Douglas and James Sweeney from Durham University Law School; Diego Rodríguez-Pinzón from Washington College of Law; and Ruti Teitel (whose 1997 *Yale Law Journal* article inspired the book's title) from New York University. In addition, our warm acknowledgements go to Brice Dickson and Rory O'Connell from Queen's University Belfast who read and commented on specific chapters, and to Helen Fenwick of Durham University with whom we discussed our initial idea and who connected us with Durham's transition specialists.

The passage of this collection into its present form was greatly facilitated by the anonymous reviewers whose helpful comments guided our thoughts. Ultimately, the book was made possible by Sinéad Moloney and Richard Woodham at Cambridge University Press, and we owe them a huge debt for all of their advice and assistance.

Friends and colleagues at the Netherlands Institute of Human Rights (SIM) of Utrecht University, and at the Legal Studies Department of Central European University in Budapest, have provided an inspiring atmosphere for us to work on this project, and for this we are truly grateful.

Finally, a special word of thanks goes to our families and friends for all their patience, love and support. In particular, Kirsten McConnachie and Ward Rennen for reminding us of the things that truly matter in life. We dedicate this book to them.

Michael Hamilton and Antoine Buyse

Introduction

MICHAEL HAMILTON AND ANTOINE BUYSE

This book is concerned with the role and contribution of the permanent regional judicial mechanisms – in Europe, Africa and the Americas – to improving human rights compliance in societies emerging from conflict or authoritarian rule. Many studies have contrasted the approaches of constitutional courts in such settings,[1] or the ad hoc and sometimes quasi-judicial mechanisms instituted to navigate transitional obstacles.[2] With few exceptions, however, there has so far been little recognition that the jurisprudence of these regional institutions is profoundly shaping and enriching the law of transitional justice.[3] As critical sites of transitional normativity, the case law of the regional commissions and courts – particularly the European Court of Human Rights – deserves close attention.

The very emergence of the European system was intimately bound up with transition from abusive pasts. As Fionnuala Ní Aoláin suggests in

---

[1] See R. Teitel, 'Post-Communist Constitutionalism: A Transitional Perspective', *Colum. Hum. Rts. L. Rev.* 26 (1994–1995) 167 at 186, cf. W. Sadurski, 'Transitional Constitutionalism: Simplistic and Fancy Theories', in A. Czarnota, M. Krygier and W. Sadurski (eds.) *Rethinking the Rule of Law after Communism* (Budapest: CEU Press, 2005) 9–24 at 18–19. See also R. Uitz, *Constitutions, Courts and History: Historical Narratives in Constitutional Adjudication* (Budapest and New York: CEU Press, 2005) at 204–224; A. Czarnota, 'Lustration, Decommunisation and the Rule of Law', *Hague Journal on the Rule of Law* 1 (2009) 307–336; and H. Schwartz, *The Struggle for Constitutional Justice in Post-Communist Europe* (University of Chicago Press, 2000) at 102. Also, A. Sajó, 'Militant Democracy and Transition Towards Democracy', in A. Sajó (ed.) *Militant Democracy* (Utrecht: Eleven International Publishing, 2004) 209 at 218–220 and 223–230; and S. Issacharoff, 'Constitutionalizing Democracy in Fractured Societies', *Tex. L. Rev.* 82 (2003–2004) 1861–1893.

[2] See, for example, P. Haynor, *Unspeakable Truths: Transitional Justice and the Challenge of Truth Commissions*, 2nd edn (New York and London: Routledge, 2010).

[3] Exceptions include L. Viaene and E. Brems, 'Transitional Justice and Cultural Contexts: Learning from the Universality Debate', *Netherlands Quarterly of Human Rights* 28(2) (2010) 199, 200–201; and P. Engstrom and A. Hurrell, 'Why the Human Rights Regime in the Americas Matters', in M. Serrano and V. Popovski, *Human Rights Regimes in the Americas* (Tokyo, New York and Paris: United Nations University Press, 2010) at 29–55.

Chapter 2 – examining the overlap between situations of transition and emergency – 'transition can be viewed as a motif for the early history of the Convention' which itself 'can be understood as a transitional legal instrument'. Similarly, Tony Allen and Benedict Douglas (in Chapter 9) note that 'the majority of members ratified the Convention after emerging from a period of military conflict or authoritarian government or both' and that 'the Convention itself was seen as a restoration of the legal traditions of the member states'.

With contributors from various disciplinary backgrounds, the book examines the ways in which law, leveraged from this external vantage-point, brings (or, in some cases, fails to bring) human rights norms to bear on situations where national legal institutions have either been complicit in, or powerless to halt, violations of core rights. The overarching question is whether such external human rights scrutiny can assist in refounding domestic rule of law commitments. Within this project, however, are three further subsidiary themes which we set out briefly in this introductory chapter.

First, there is a need to widen the scope of 'transitional justice' analysis beyond the dialectic of 'peace versus justice'. Transitional justice entails a much more expansive legal frame demanding analysis of human rights interpretation both within and between transitional and non-transitional settings, and across multiple rights issues. This, however, is not to promote only a 'thin' or 'legalistic' conception of transitional justice.[4] The narratives of individual applicants that come to the fore in these chapters provide a much fuller picture of the myriad challenges that confront transitional policy-makers. More fundamentally, these narratives pointedly illustrate the equivocal and contingent nature of the concepts of harm, responsibility, victimhood and justice during periods of transition.

Second, the book overviews the parameters and internal coherence of this regional 'transitional jurisprudence'.[5] The key question here is whether (and if so, how) the 'evolutive jurisprudence'[6] of regional mechanisms

---

[4] K. McEvoy, 'Letting Go of Legalism: Developing a "Thicker" Version of Transitional Justice', in K. McEvoy and L. McGregor (eds.) *Transitional Justice From Below* (Oxford and Portland, Oregon: Hart Publishing, 2008).

[5] R. Teitel, 'Transitional Jurisprudence: The Role of Law in Political Transformation', *Yale L. J.* 106 (1997) 2009.

[6] The President of the European Court of Human Rights, for example, has argued that 'the leitmotiv of the Court's case law has been continuity in the framework of an evolutive jurisprudence'. Speech by Mr Luzius Wildhaber, President of the European Court of Human Rights, on the Occasion of the Opening of the Judicial Year, 20 January 2006, in *European Court of Human Rights, Annual Report 2005*, at 20.

can remain true to the rule of law whilst also meaningfully recognising the acute social, economic and political exigencies which characterise periods of transition (for example, when successor governments are held accountable for the abuses of previous regimes).[7] With regard to the latter, we attempt to distil what the concept of 'transition' itself means for the regional courts. How does 'transition' differ, or intersect with, declared states of emergency, situations of armed conflict, or other extant threats to 'effective political democracies'? Given that transitional settings are often characterised by systemic and structural deficiencies, do the regional courts have capacity to provide normative guidance across political, economic and legal spheres? Moreover, in assessing the legitimacy and/or necessity of measures tailored to manage the fallout of transition, how does the case law acknowledge the significance of passing time, or delimit transition start and endpoints? Central to this jurisprudential analysis is the degree of deference afforded to national authorities. Indeed, the deference question opens a number of further lines of inquiry – how precisely are arguments from transition used to determine the appropriate degree of deference afforded? And at what point in judicial reasoning does such deference have bite? In one way or another, all the chapters assess whether the regional mechanisms succeed in mediating between maximal and minimal poles of norm compliance, and ultimately, whether this results in a *sui generis* transitional jurisprudence.

Third, the book addresses the role and wider impact of regional judicial mechanisms. By contrasting the three regional systems – paying particular attention in this regard to the book's two comparator chapters on the Inter-American (Chapter 10) and African (Chapter 11) systems by Diego Rodríguez-Pinzón and Gina Bekker respectively – we seek to highlight the alternative ways in which regional mechanisms can meet transitional challenges. The remoteness of these regional courts from the situations under review gives rise to two specific challenges – evidential fact-finding and reliance upon recognised expertise, and the delivery of judgments when the issues at stake are time-sensitive. These issues also link to the nature of the relationship between the regional and national courts. Specifically, they raise the question of whether the regional mechanisms

---

[7] See, for example, ECtHR, *Kononov* v. *Latvia* [GC], 17 May 2010 (Appl. no. 36376/04) para. 241. Similarly, Gina Bekker in Chapter 11 of this volume welcomes the African Commission's approach in situations where regime change has occurred and the Commission – expressly drawing upon international law – has 'strictly adhered to the principle of the continuity of the state'.

exist as a fourth-instance court or de facto court of appeal (or indeed, as some have suggested, a regional constitutional court).

These three sub-themes – narratives of transition, the contours and coherence of transitional jurisprudence and the roles of regional review – provide the structure for this brief introduction. We aim here simply to precis the key arguments that resurface in the chapters that follow.

Narratives of transition

Perhaps most clearly, this book illustrates the ways in which narratives of transition are refracted and constructed through individual human rights complaints. The cases involve individuals from widely different backgrounds with the uniting factor being that enjoyment of their rights has been diminished in the course of, or more pertinently, because of, the transition process. The cases evince the human dimension at the heart of every transitional claim – individual quests for justice, exoneration, amnesty, truth, inclusion, equality, representation, protection, restitution or compensation. These claims underscore the breadth of remedial measures necessary to fully consolidate transitional gains. They also illustrate how regional courts are frequently confronted with the nuances of identity politics. The chapters by James Sweeney (Chapter 5) and by Anne Smith and Rory O'Connell (Chapter 8), for example, recount stories of those whose traditional influence has been affected by transition (such as established churches) and those who have been structurally excluded from public life (including the Roma and LGBT communities, and minority religious groups).

Far from being epiphenomenal in the reconstructive process, the constitutive role of law is clearly demonstrated in Kris Brown's examination (in Chapter 3) of how Strasbourg judgments are integrated into the narratives of non-state combatants in Northern Ireland. Brown's analysis provides powerful empirical evidence of the role of transitional jurisprudence in legitimating particular understandings of the past (and of struggle and victimhood) and thereby also shaping the conflict resolution agenda. Several key Strasbourg judgments (regarding the state's failure to meet its positive obligations when using lethal force to counter attacks by Republican paramilitaries in Northern Ireland) not only vindicated campaigns for justice by victims' relatives, but helped authenticate the Irish Republican account of the causes of the conflict – among them, the 'mis-rule of British law' – and served to instigate reforms by the British government.[8] The transitional case law can thus posit normative referents for movements seeking to mobilise support in their struggle for recognition. In the same way that legal developments in other jurisdictions can provide human rights advocates with greater leverage when addressing domestic justice deficits,[9] the judgments of regional courts can create 'structural openings' that influence the strategies employed by different actors in the context of transition.[10] As Paul Schiff Berman has argued, 'the very existence of multiple systems can at times create openings for contestation, resistance and creative adaptation'.[11]

The precariousness of history, and the possibility of judicial revisionism, is also well illustrated by the case of *Kononov* v. *Latvia* (2010).[12] As described in Chapter 6 by Antoine Buyse, this case concerned the prosecution of Vasiliy Kononov for his role during the Second World War in the 1944 killing of inhabitants of a village who were alleged to have collaborated with the Nazis. The period in question recalls the 'dual occupation' of Latvia (first, in 1940 by the USSR, then in 1941 by Nazi Germany). Kononov, a Latvian, was called up to the Soviet army in 1942 and soon became the leader of a commando unit. In his trial, his defence was that the attack was one of liberation in the face of German aggression (which had earlier forced the retreat of Soviet forces from the Baltic states).

The alternative view though, and that ultimately given credence by the Grand Chamber's ruling, was that he had committed war crimes

---

[8] See, for example, the Council of Europe, Committee of Ministers, Interim Resolution, CM/ResDH(2009)44, 'Action of the Security Forces in Northern Ireland' (Case of *McKerr* against the United Kingdom and five similar cases): Measures taken or envisaged to ensure compliance with the judgments of the European Court of Human Rights: Adopted on 19 March 2009 at the 1051st Meeting of the Ministers' Deputies. For analysis of the 'package of measures' introduced by the British government, see, P. Lundy, 'Commissioning the Past in Northern Ireland', *Review of International Affairs* LX, 1138–1139 (2010) 101–133.

[9] See, for example, E. Lutz and K. Sikkink, 'The Justice Cascade: The Evolution and Impact of Foreign Human Rights Trials in Latin America', *Chi. J. Int'l. L.* 2 (2001) 1.

[10] See further C. Hilson, 'New Social Movements: The Role of Legal Opportunity', *Journal of European Public Policy* 9(2) (April 2002) 238; B. M. Wilson and J. C. Rodríguez Cordero, 'Legal Opportunity Structures and Social Movements: The Effects of Institutional Change on Costa Rican Politics', *Comparative Political Studies* 39(3) (April 2006) 325; and E. Anderson, *Out of the Closets and Into the Courts: Legal Opportunity Structure and Gay Rights Litigation* (University of Michigan Press, 2006).

[11] P. S. Berman, 'Global Legal Pluralism', *S. Cal. L. Rev.* 80 (2006–2007) 1158 at 1159.

[12] The vulnerability of historical record is particularly striking given that in some of the most significant transitional rulings of the European Court, the Grand Chamber has overturned the previous ruling of the Chamber (see, for example, the cases of ECtHR, *Ždanoka* v. *Latvia*, 16 March 2006 (Appl. no. 58278/00), and ECtHR, *Kononov* v. *Latvia*, 17 May 2010 (Appl. no. 36376/04)).

which had been sufficiently foreseeable as such in 1944. Overruling the
Chamber judgment (which found that his prosecution violated Article 7
– the ECHR's prohibition on retrospective sanctions),[13] the majority of
the Grand Chamber concluded that there was no violation of Article 7
ECHR.[14] The successful prosecution of the applicant arguably cast the
Soviet occupation itself as unlawful (thus comporting with Latvia's
post-independence narrative).[15] Aside from demonstrating the complex
prosecutorial issues that arise when injustice is facilitated by unjust law,
Kononov illustrates how law can inscribe the actions of individuals and
groups during momentous events with either valour or treachery.[16] In
this sense, the jurisprudence serves a fixative role – the finality of legal
judgment helping to settle contested histories. As Buyse observes in
Chapter 6, the judgments produce 'different narratives of the oppressor
and oppressed, about the significance of key events and persons, and
more broadly, about right and wrong'. Indeed, in addition to their contribution to the historical record, these alternative accounts are not without
consequence. As Károly Bárd noted prior to the Grand Chamber judgment in *Kononov*:

> [A] decision of no-violation by Latvia could result in branding the USSR
> as an occupying power which, in turn, could justify Latvia's claim for
> compensation ... [and] induce descendents of Jews murdered by Latvian
> subunits during World War II to make claims for compensation ... [A]
> finding that Kononov's conviction ... was in line with the ECHR could

---

[13] Article 7(1) provides that 'No one shall be held guilty of any criminal offence on account
of any act or omission which did not constitute a criminal offence under national or international law at the time when it was committed. Nor shall a heavier penalty be imposed
than the one that was applicable at the time the criminal offence was committed'.

[14] The three dissenting judges included the Court's President.

[15] See the 1996 'Declaration on the Occupation of Latvia' which referred to the annexation
of Latvian territory by the USSR in 1940 as a 'military occupation' and an 'illegal incorporation', and its repossession after the Second World War as the 're-establishment of an
occupying regime'. See ECtHR, *Kononov* v. *Latvia*, 17 May 2010 (Appl. no. 36376/04)
para. 29.

[16] See also ECtHR, *Streletz, Kessler and Krenz* v. *Germany*, 22 March 2001 (Appl. nos.
34044/96, 35532/97 and 44801/98) – the East German Border Guards case – and ECtHR,
Korbely v. *Hungary*, 19 September 2008 (Appl. no. 9174/02) – in which the applicant
was prosecuted for his part in putting down the anti-communist uprising in Budapest
in 1956. Both cases concern the actions of individuals decorated as heroes by regimes
that were themselves subsequently discredited (respectively, the German Democratic
Republic, and Hungary under Soviet rule). See also, Teitel, 'Transitional Jurisprudence',
2022–2026; P. Quint, 'Judging the Past: The Prosecution of East German Border Guards
and the GDR Chain of Command', *The Review of Politics* 61(2) (1999) 303 at 327. See also
the Hart-Fuller-Radbruch debate as discussed in Chapter 9, this volume.

result in repercussions for the Russian minority of Latvia and could provide support for the argument that the role the Soviet Union had played in
World War II should be revisited.[17]

In the words of Rodríguez-Pinzón (Chapter 10), the regional jurisprudence speaks of 'civil society's continuous struggle to achieve justice'.
Inevitably though, it captures only partial narratives. Christopher
Lamont, in Chapter 4, points out that since Croatia only became subject to the ECHR's contentious jurisdiction in 1997, all judgments delivered by the ECtHR occurred after the collapse of the Tudjman regime.
As he notes, this blindspot is all the more striking in relation to Serbia
given the relatively small number of cases heard since Serbia belatedly
ratified the Convention in 2003. The resulting jurisprudential gap is
also noted by Allen and Douglas (Chapter 9) – the denial of temporal
jurisdiction by Strasbourg has precluded the admission of complaints
regarding property that was lawfully confiscated before Article 1 of
Protocol 1 came into force.[18] Such temporal markers help us begin to
understand the manner in which 'transition' itself is conceptualised by
regional courts.

Transitional jurisprudence: contours, endpoints and coherence

Initially, this project sought to identify whether a *sui generis* transitional jurisprudence existed – a task eliciting Eric Posner and Adrian
Vermeule's contention that 'legal and political transitions lie on a continuum, of which regime transitions are merely the endpoint'.[19] Posner
and Vermeule doubt that transition is really 'a distinctive topic present-
ing a distinctive set of moral and jurisprudential dilemmas',[20] suggesting
instead that 'the problems are at most overblown versions of ordinary
legal problems'.[21]

---

[17] K. Bárd, 'The Difficulties of Writing the Past Through Law – Historical Trials Revisited at
the European Court of Human Rights', *International Review of Penal Law* 81 (2010) 27 at
28, citing 'Ex-Soviet partisan Vasily Kononov fights his last battle'.
[18] Whereas prior *unlawful* deprivation of property is sometimes regarded by the Court as a
continuing act which it has been willing to scrutinise.
[19] E. Posner and A. Vermeule, 'Transitional Justice as Ordinary Justice', *Harv. L. Rev.* 117
(2004) 761, 763.
[20] *Ibid.*, at 764. [21] *Ibid.*, at 765.

The contours of 'transitional jurisprudence'

We fully accept that the line between transitional and non-transitional settings is evanescent. The challenge of ensuring free and fair elections, for example, is common to all democracies (more or less difficult according to any number of institutional and demographic variables). Moreover, 'transitional jurisprudence' encompasses both human rights violations directly connected to (occurring because of) transition and those which simply coincide with (occurring in the course of) transition. The difficulty in distinguishing between these categories, given both indirect causes and cumulative harms, is further heightened because of transitional posturing by individual applicants[22] and (more frequently) respondent states.[23] Both have sought to capitalise on the rhetorical capital of 'transition'. Indeed, the invocation of arguments from transition may even serve courts well by providing a 'constitutive fiction' which enables seeming fidelity to rule of law ideals whilst deferring to transitional pressures.[24]

In light of the narratives of transition outlined above, we favour the view that the 'abusive paradigms' implicated in transition do actually pose distinct dilemmas and are not merely extreme cases of ordinary problems.[25] Nonetheless, we also believe that the question of whether transition gives rise to an entirely unique problem set (and thus a *sui generis* jurisprudence) is something of a distraction. There are clear synergies and divergences between transitional and non-transitional cases, but little is achieved by honing in on the question of whether a particular application is, or is not, truly 'a transition case'. Often, transition is recognised by the Court as a valid consideration in determining the proportionality of a particular restriction or the scope of the margin of appreciation, but it may not be the only or decisive factor. In some cases, as Marton Varju has

---

[22] For example, Tatjana Ždanoka's (unsuccessful) argument that a constitutional diarchy existed in which diverging opinions regarding Latvia's future (specifically those favouring a return to Soviet rule) should have been protected. ECtHR, *Ždanoka* v. *Latvia* [GC], 16 March 2006 (Appl. no. 58278/00). See further Chapter 7 in this volume.

[23] For example, in seeking to expand its margin of appreciation, the Bulgarian government (unsuccessfully) sought to capitalise on the existence of communal tensions in order to restrict the commemorative activities of the United Macedonian Organisation, ILINDEN. See ECtHR, *Stankov and the United Macedonian Organisation Ilinden* v. *Bulgaria*, 2 October 2001 (Appl. nos. 29221/95 and 29225/95) para. 73.

[24] J. Přibáň, *Dissidents of Law: On the 1989 Velvet Revolutions, Legitimations, Fictions of Legality and Contemporary Version of the Social Contract* (Aldershot: Ashgate, 2002) 4–5.

[25] For further discussion of 'abusive paradigms', see D. C. Gray, 'Extraordinary Justice', *Ala. L. Rev.* 62 (2010).

highlighted elsewhere, 'the inappropriateness of the impugned measure' is simply 'more relevant than the uniqueness of the transition'.[26] Indeed, even judgments which place heavy emphasis on arguments from transition can often be read as employing straightforward consequentialist reasoning given the contextual risk of political regression.[27]

Furthermore, to classify as 'transitional jurisprudence' only those cases that develop a uniquely transitional conception of justice would itself be problematic. James Sweeney (in Chapter 5) helpfully points to the distinction in the Strasbourg jurisprudence between what the Court deems *legitimate* and what is *proportionate*. He argues that the former, since it embodies the Court's conception of justice, should not be varied or diluted by the application of the margin of appreciation since this would undermine both the vanguard role of the Court and its claim to universality. Sweeney's observation that there is 'a notable absence of consistency in the stage at which the transitional context … is considered', makes it all the more important to analyse *how* transition arguments influence the regional mechanisms, and the coherence of these arguments. In this regard, it is undoubtedly the case that the proportionality of restrictions is often assessed differently in transition cases. By way of illustration, in one notable case relating to post-transition property restitution, the Court expressly ruled that:

> In complex cases as the present one, which involve difficult questions in the conditions of transition from a totalitarian regime to democracy and rule of law, a certain 'threshold of hardship' must have been crossed for the Court to find a breach of the applicants' Article 1 Protocol No. 1 rights.[28]

On occasion, the regional jurisprudence thus deals directly with the traditional concerns and modalities of transitional justice. This is most evident in the non-European chapters. Bekker (in Chapter 11), for example, recalls a Sudanese case where the African Commission recommended the

---

[26] M. Varju, 'Transition as a Concept of European Human Rights Law', *European Human Rights Law Review* 2 (2009) 170–189, 183.

[27] See G. Letsas, *A Theory of Interpretation of the European Convention on Human Rights* (Oxford University Press, 2007) at 125.

[28] ECtHR, *Velikovi and Others* v. *Bulgaria*, 15 March 2007 (Appl. nos. 43278/98, 45437/99, 48014/99, 48380/99, 51362/99, 53367/99, 60036/00, 73465/01 and 194/02) paras. 192 and 235, finding no violation of Article 1 of Protocol 1 on this basis. The applications in both *Padalevičius* v. *Lithuania*, 7 July 2009 (Appl. no. 12278/03) and *Pavlinović and Tonić* v. *Croatia*, 3 September 2009 (Appl. nos. 17124/05 and 17126/05) were declared inadmissible since this threshold of hardship had not been reached.

establishment of a National Reconciliation Forum and that the government refrain from adopting amnesty laws. In addition, the first case heard by the new African Court on Human and Peoples' Rights raised issues of the relationship between criminal proceedings and truth commissions, although the Court ultimately held that it lacked jurisdiction in the case. Diego Rodríguez-Pinzón's chapter examining the Inter-American system similarly demonstrates how this 'hemispheric laboratory' has been traditionally associated with the fight against impunity (Chapter 10).[29]

Paradigmatic transitional concerns have also arisen in the European system. Even though 'the ECHR is not a system or a jurisprudence ... noted for confronting situations of gross and systematic violations of rights'[30] and the ECHR does not deal explicitly with prosecution or amnesty, it does 'prohibit the underlying violations, and provide a right to a remedy (in general terms), and to a hearing before a competent tribunal for violations of rights'.[31] Moreover, as James Sweeney's chapter highlights, the Council of Europe has dealt directly with transitional preoccupations in its Resolution 1096 (1996) on 'Measures to dismantle the heritage of former communist totalitarian systems'.[32] Buyse's discussion of the case of *Kenedi* v. *Hungary* (2009) also shows how the search for historical truths is increasingly underpinned by legal norms which derive from the right to freedom of expression and its corollary, the right to receive information.[33] Finally, and also relating to the attenuated Hungarian transition, Ní Aoláin notes that the 2008 *Korbely* case 'raises

---

[29] In reviewing situations such as the dictatorships in the southern cone, the civil wars in Central America, the 'democratic' dictatorship of the Fujimori regime, and the protracted war still affecting Colombia.

[30] See F. Ní Aoláin, 'The Fractured Soul of the Dayton Peace Agreement: A Legal Analysis', *Mich. J. Int'l L.* 19 (1998) 957 at 977–978.

[31] C. Bell, 'The New Law of Transitional Justice', in K. Ambos, J. Large and M. Wierda (eds.) *Building a Future on Peace and Justice: Studies on Transitional Justice, Peace and Development* (Berlin and Heidelberg: Springer-Verlag, 2009) 105, 108. See also, EComHR, *Asociación de Aviadores de la Republica* v. *Spain*, 11 March 1985 (Appl. no. 10733/84) in which the applicants argued that amnesty provisions enacted in the post-Franco period were, *inter alia*, discriminatory because they did not apply similarly to members of the Republican armed forces and to civilian public servants. The Commission found the complaint to be inadmissible on several grounds (both *ratione materiae* and *ratione temporis*), including that 'where the person concerned has already been convicted, any dispute concerning the existence or extent of an amnesty falls outside the scope of Article 6 of the Convention since the dispute has ceased to involve a criminal charge against the applicant within the meaning of Article 6.'

[32] Reiterated a decade later in Resolution 1481 (2006) on the 'Need for international condemnation of crimes of totalitarian communist regimes'.

[33] Similarly, see ECtHR, *Chauvy and Others* v. *France*, 29 June 2004 (Appl. no. 64915/01).

characteristic transitional justice elements involving a reckoning with the past, the compatibility of addressing past injustice with principles of fairness with due notice to the defendant(s) and … the proper scope for international courts to interfere with the process of political and legal transition (including accountability) taking place in the domestic sphere'. That said, Ní Aoláin points out that the Court has demonstrated a 'clear unwillingness' to clarify the relationship between humanitarian and human rights norms and the complementarity of these two legal frames.

Beyond these paradigmatic examples, the case law also catalogues the endless variation in transition start-points. In answering the question, 'transition *from what?*', the cases described in each of the contributions survey a range of economic, political and legal contexts. The following examples provide just a flavour of those later discussed.

In relation to the *legal* context of transition, the Article 7 case law – including the East German border guard cases – most starkly highlights the challenges presented by the wholesale transition from one legal system to another.[34] Such legal transitions may also give rise to uncertainty regarding *which* laws from the old system remain in force (and are thus sufficiently 'prescribed by law').[35] In a similar vein, Lamont's chapter chronicles the implications of a seriously weakened legal system in Croatia and the state's corresponding failure to provide effective remedies.[36] Introducing a further dimension, Fionnuala Ní Aoláin examines the overlap between situations of emergency and situations of transition, arguing that derogation measures often compound already existing legal (and human rights) deficits in transitional contexts. Given such legal dysfunctionality, Teitel's original insight into the nature of law in transitional jurisprudence remains highly apposite for our examination of the regional case law:

> In transitional jurisprudence, the conception of law is partial, contextual, and situated between at least two legal and political orders. Legal norms are necessarily multiple, the idea of justice always a compromise.

---

[34] For example, in ECtHR, *Streletz, Kessler and Krenz v. Germany*, 22 March 2001 (Appl. nos. 34044/96, 35532/97 and 44801/98), the Court noted (para. 52) that 'one special feature of the present case is that its background is the transition between two States governed by two different legal systems'.

[35] See, for example, ECtHR, *Mkrtchyan v. Armenia*, 11 January 2007 (Appl. no. 6562/03) paras. 39–43.

[36] Delay in domestic court proceedings is frequently encountered in societies in transition and is not a problem unique to Croatia. See also, for example, *Lukenda v. Slovenia*, 6 October 2005 (Appl. no. 23032/02) para. 91.

> In transitional jurisprudence, the nature and role of law centers upon
> its paradigmatic use in the normative construction of the new political
> regime.[37]

Clearly, transition is a multi-layered concept which must be analysed through other lenses besides law. Many countries – particularly in Central and Eastern Europe – experienced economic liberalisation alongside political democratisation. In this regard, the Strasbourg Court has recognised that transition from centrally planned to market oriented economies is 'fraught with difficulties'.[38] Issues relating to social housing, authenticating property ownership and demands for restitution perhaps demonstrate most sharply how tectonic shifts in the economy give rise to uniquely transitional claims under the Convention. The tension between property restitution and the transitional imperative of economic stability is analysed in depth by Tom Allen and Benedict Douglas in Chapter 9. Examining principally those cases in which the Strasbourg Court denied the restitution sought, they conclude that the Court has offered a prospective and distributive rather than a corrective form of justice.

Socio-economic obstacles are by no means unique to the transitions in Europe. In relation to the African system, Gina Bekker points to socio-economic rights violations which characterised the transitional backdrop in Nigeria. She cites the example of environmental degradation in the Niger Delta region in which the previous military government had been complicit. Given the serious impact on the living conditions and health of the Ogoni people, the African Commission on Human Rights held the new government accountable for multiple rights violations, notwithstanding that some efforts had already been undertaken to redress the situation.

Transition goals and endpoints

One defining characteristic of the transitional jurisprudence lies in its articulation of transitional goals or endpoints (albeit sometimes implicitly). At one level, this goal is simply to ensure that 'the attenuation of past injustices [or old injuries] does not create [disproportionate] new wrongs'.[39] Beyond this, however, it becomes clear that the concept of 'democracy' is,

---

[37] Teitel, 'Transitional Jurisprudence', 2016.
[38] ECtHR, *Schirmer* v. *Poland*, 21 September 2004 (Appl. no. 68880/01) para. 38.
[39] For example, ECtHR, *Bečvář and Bečvářová* v. *the Czech Republic*, 14 December 2004 (Appl. no. 58358/00) para. 69; ECtHR, *Padalevičius* v. *Lithuania* (admissibility decision), 7 July 2009 (Appl. no. 12278/03) para. 67; *Pincová and Pinc* v. *Czech Republic*, 5 November 2002 (Appl. no. 36548/97) para. 58.

in itself, insufficiently prescriptive. The chapters by Fionnuala Ní Aoláin and Diego Rodríguez-Pinzón each highlight that democracy alone is no guarantee against rights abuse: Rodríguez-Pinzón's compelling account of the Inter-American jurisprudence (explicitly referring to 'democratic-ally elected despots') parallels Ní Aoláin's critique of derogation measures in the European system. Similarly, Gina Bekker's overview of political transitions on the African continent highlights the 'neo-authoritarian' shift that occurred in many African countries in the 1990s and was char-acterised only by a 'limited opening up of the political process'.

Of course, the nexus between rights protection and democracy is not straightforward. Chapters 6 and 7 by Buyse and Hamilton respectively examine how expressive rights (under Article 10), and associative rights and the obligation upon states to hold free elections (under Article 11 and Article 3, Protocol 1) have been utilised to instantiate a particular form of inclusive, pluralist democracy. This end goal is most explicitly recognised in the speech regulation cases reviewed by Buyse. While acknowledg-ing that the experience of authoritarianism leaves in its wake social and psychological traumas which may be reopened by provocative speech, the best remedy is not to severely limit political discourse and foreclose the possibility of an inclusive post-transition pluralism.[40] Together, these chapters demonstrate that the Strasbourg Court has sought to demarcate transition endpoints by declaring the restriction of historically sensitive speech and symbols[41] or unduly protracted lustration programmes[42] to be no longer justified and thus in violation of individual rights.

Anne Smith and Rory O'Connell's examination of 'equality in tran-sition' cases (Chapter 8) emphasises that while transitional priorities can relegate enduring inequalities to the political backburner, substan-tive (rather than procedural) equality is needed to challenge previously accepted distinctions and deepen commitment to democratic values.

---

[40] For example, the Court's judgment in ECtHR, *Balsytė-Lideikienė* v. *Lithuania*, 4 November 2008 (Appl. no. 72596/01) to combat hate speech, sought to 'protect the pre-carious ethnic pluralism in Lithuanian society'.

[41] See Buyse, Chapter 6, citing the Court's judgments in ECtHR, *Lehideux and Isorni* v. *France*, 23 September 1998 (Appl. no. 24662/94); ECtHR, *Vajnai* v. *Hungary*, 8 July 2008 (Appl. no. 33629/06), and ECtHR, *Orban and others* v. *France*, 15 January 2009 (Appl. no. 20985/05).

[42] See Hamilton, Chapter 7, citing the three Lithuanian cases of *Sidabras and Džiautas*, 27 July 2004 (Appl. nos. 55480/00 and 59330/00); *Rainys and Gasparavičius*, 7 April 2005 (Appl. nos. 70665/01 and 74345/01); and *Zickus*, 7 April 2009 (Appl. no. 26652/02). Also, ECtHR, *Ādamsons* v. *Latvia*, 24 June 2008 (Appl. no. 3669/03) and ECtHR, *Tănase* v. *Moldova* [GC], 27 April 2010 (Appl. no. 7/08).

They focus on the Roma in the context of transition, noting their 'double minority status' and include analysis of the significant Grand Chamber judgment in *Oršuš* v. *Croatia* (2010).[43] This chapter not only demonstrates that the elimination of discrimination needs to be an integral transitional goal, but also that institutional racism – which persists in both the policing and education systems – must be addressed if rights protections are ever to be realised. As with Lamont's chapter which focuses on the imperative of improving the criminal justice system, institutional reform in these spheres is critical to the consolidation of transition. That said, in their chapter describing unremedied confiscations of property, Tom Allen and Benedict Douglas sound a cautionary note about the 'modernist faith in new institutions' to prevent a recurrence of the past.

The coherence of the jurisprudence

One important conclusion that we can reach in relation to the coherence of this regional transitional jurisprudence, is that the Strasbourg Court has in many cases developed an impressively nuanced approach to transitional dilemmas. In determining the breadth of the margin of appreciation to be afforded to the domestic authorities, or in assessing the proportionality of specific restrictions, a number of chapters signpost the Court's recognition of three guiding principles – the passage of time, the need for individualised assessment and the need to consider whether other safeguards exist to mollify the impact of transitional measures.

The passage of time generally serves to diminish the import of transitional pleading. Buyse's analysis of several freedom of expression cases (*Lehideux and Isorni* v. *France* (1998), *Vajnai* v. *Hungary* (2008) and *Orban* v. *France* (2009)) well captures this point. Passing time serves to temper the permissible legal reactions to transitional harms, and its reification as a jurisprudential rule-of-thumb suggests a clear expectation that transitional societies must come to terms with their past.[44] Relatedly, the Court has asserted that while sweeping rights restrictions may be justified in the initial phase of a transition, as time passes there is a need for increased individualisation in the assessment of specific restrictions. Hamilton (in Chapter 7), for example, highlights this approach in relation to electoral

---

[43] ECtHR, *Oršuš* v. *Croatia*, 16 March 2010 (Appl. no. 15766/03). This emphasised not only the vulnerability of the Roma but also the consequent positive obligation of special protection.

[44] For further discussion of the moral significance of time, see J. Coleman and A. Sarch, *Blameworthiness and Time*, Yale Law School Research Paper 214 (2010). Available at: http://papers.ssrn.com/abstract#1646949.

rights.[45] Similarly, though, in relation to those affected by property confiscations, the Court has sought to distinguish those who acquired bona fide third party interests from others whose acquisition was through the abuse of power or in breach of the law. Thus, in several cases concerning restitution laws in Bulgaria and the Czech Republic, the Court has stressed that:

> [T]he legislation should make it possible to take into account the particular circumstances of each case, so that persons who acquired their possessions in good faith are not made to bear the burden of responsibility which is rightfully that of the State which once confiscated those possessions.[46]

Finally, the provision of adequate safeguards which limit the potential for abuse of exceptional measures has frequently been decisive in the Court's assessment of proportionality. As Smith and O'Connell point out in the *Oršuš* (Roma education) case, a monitoring procedure enabling individual assessment of pupils' competency in the Croatian language might have been sufficient to prevent a finding of a violation of the right to non-discrimination. Taken together, these three factors help limit the scope for 'rights instrumentalism'[47] during fraught periods of transition. They thus serve to reduce the risk of undermining law's normative legitimacy and its capacity to catalyse progressive change.[48]

The role of regional supervision

The jurisprudential approach of the regional institutions to 'transition' strikes at the core of vital questions about their role. While it has been argued that court trials are 'generally ill suited to illuminate a period of history or deal with subtleties of facing a past marked by collective violence and other forms of atrocity',[49] constitutional and human rights

---

[45] In the cases of ECtHR, *Ādamsons* v. *Latvia*, 24 June 2008 (Appl. no. 3669/03) and ECtHR, *Tănase* v. *Moldova*, 27 April 2010 (Appl. no. 7/08).

[46] ECtHR, *Pincová and Pinc* v. *the Czech Republic*, 5 November 2002 (Appl. no. 36548/97). Similarly, ECtHR, *Velikovi and Others* v. *Bulgaria*, 15 March 2007 (Appl. nos. 43278/98, 45437/99, 48014/99, 48380/99, 51362/99, 53367/99, 60036/00, 73465/01 and 194/02) para. 246. Applied in many subsequent cases such as ECtHR, *Madzharov* v. *Bulgaria*, 2 September 2010 (Appl. no. 40149/05).

[47] See, for example, J. Waldron, *Law and Disagreement* (Oxford University Press, 1999) 54.

[48] Y. Ghai, 'The Role of Law in the Transition of Societies: The African Experience', *J. Afr. L.* 25 (1991) 8.

[49] A. Chapman, 'Truth Finding in the Transitional Justice Process', in H. Van Der Merwe, V. Baxter and A. R. Chapman (eds.) *Assessing the Impact of Transitional Justice: Challenges for Empirical Research* (Washington: USIP, 2009) 93, citing M. Minow, *Between Vengeance and Forgiveness: Facing History after Genocide and Mass Violence* (Boston: Beacon Press, 1998) 51 and 58.

jurisprudence, in contrast, has yielded 'new normative principles and values' which have served to guide transition processes.[50] James Sweeney (in Chapter 5) goes so far as to suggest that the European Court has become an 'embodiment of an international form of transitional justice: the human rights counterpart to international criminal responses'.

Governments are often reminded that '[b]y joining the regime, European states have invited external authority structures into their domestic politics'.[51] As Sweeney argues, '[b]y joining the Council of Europe, and signing and ratifying the ECHR, it may be that states have thereby disbarred themselves from employing some transitional policies, in favour of a "human rights based approach" to transition'. Wojciech Sadurski has suggested that this elite 'self-binding' might have been the very outcome intended: 'To put it sharply, an "intervention from Strasbourg" was seen as an important and highly appreciated additional guarantee of the correct path and irreversibility of the democratic transition.'[52]

Ostensibly then, the role of the European Court of Human Rights is simply to hold the new Council of Europe member states to their human rights commitments. Whilst acknowledging the economic and political hurdles facing transitional states, the Court has argued that 'these difficulties and the enormity of the tasks facing legislators having to deal with all the complex issues involved in such transition do not exempt the Member States from the obligations stemming from the Convention or its Protocols'.[53] This argument chimes with the claim that a rights framework should provide both symbolic and systemic anchorage during times of political flux.[54] Indeed, it is also supported by the Court's judgment in the case of *Sejdić and Finci* v. *Bosnia and Herzegovina* (2009) which is examined in more detail in the chapters by both Hamilton and Sweeney.[55] Jakob Finci, speaking about his challenge to the prohibition under the

---

[50] M. Safjan, 'Transitional Justice: The Polish Example, the Case of Lustration', *European Journal of Legal Studies* 1(2) (2007) 1, 4.

[51] S. D. Krasner, *Sovereignty: Organized Hypocrisy* (Princeton University Press, 1999) 119.

[52] W. Sadurski, 'Partnering with Strasbourg', *Human Rights Law Review* 9(3) (2009) 397, 437 and 451.

[53] See ECtHR, *Schirmer* v. *Poland*, 21 September 2004 (Appl. no. 68880/01) para. 38.

[54] See, for example, N. Krisch, 'The Open Architecture of European Human Rights Law', *Modern Law Review* 71 (2008) 82, at 87–88 (in relation to Spain). Similarly, Sadurski, 'Partnering with Strasbourg', 408 (in relation to the accession of Portugal in 1976 and Spain in 1977, and the return of Greece in 1974): 'one should not under-estimate the role of the ECHR system in affecting consolidation of democracy and human rights in those post-authoritarian states.'

[55] ECtHR, *Sejdić and Finci* v. *Bosnia and Herzegovina*, 22 December 2009 (Appl. nos. 27996/06 and 34836/06).

terms of the Dayton Peace Accord which prevented him from standing for election to the parliament and Presidency because of his ethnicity, said: 'In [a] situation when [the] national judicial system is not able to overcome a problem, [the] last chance for individuals is [the] Court in Strasbourg, and thank God that such institution exists.'[56]

The accession of Central and East European states to the Council of Europe has impacted on the Strasbourg Court's role. This has changed 'from a fine-tuning role to that of the scrutiniser of failing legal and political systems'[57] with an accompanying change in the nature of the cases being heard 'both in terms of the severity of the violations and the systemic nature of the challenged deficiencies'.[58] It is often discussed, though, whether this 'front-line' position[59] means that the regional mechanisms are (or ought to be) a fourth instance court or de facto court of appeal (as Lamont, in Chapter 4, claims it has been in respect of Croatia), or even a quasi-constitutional body.

Rodríguez-Pinzón's discussion of the Fourth Instance Formula developed by the Inter-American Commission clearly distinguishes it from the Strasbourg model. He also cites the Inter-American Court's decision in *Barrios Altos* v. *Peru* (2001)[60] – which found the Peruvian Amnesty Law to be incompatible with the Convention and thus to lack legal effect – as evidencing 'a significant legal step towards a monist approach in regional international law'.

By way of contrast, the Secretary General of the Council of Europe has expressly cautioned against viewing the ECHR as a 'European Constitution', noting that 'it is difficult to see how the Court could become like any existing national constitutional court'.[61] The competence of the European Court, and its interaction with domestic authorities, is formally governed by the subsidiarity principle.[62] On this basis, and due to its

---

[56] Amnesty International, 'What the European Court of Human Rights Means to Me', 18 February 2010. See www.amnesty.org.

[57] Sadurski, 'Partnering with Strasbourg', 401.

[58] *Ibid.*, 402.

[59] R. Harmsen, 'The European Convention of Human Rights after Enlargement', *International Journal of Human Rights* 5(4) (2001) 18, 29.

[60] IACtHR, *Case of Barrios Altos* v. *Peru*, 14 March 2001, IACtHR, Series C no. 75.

[61] Contribution of the Secretary General of the Council of Europe to the Preparation of the Interlaken Ministerial Conference, 18 December 2009, at para. 28. Available at www.coe. int.

[62] Article 1 ECHR squarely places the protective obligation under the Convention upon High Contracting Parties (and this is reinforced through the requirement to exhaust domestic remedies under Article 35 ECHR). See also ECtHR *Handyside* v. *UK*, 7 December 1976 (Appl. no. 5493/72) para. 48; *Schenk* v. *Switzerland*, 12 July 1988 (Appl. no. 10862/84) para. 45, cited in ECtHR, *Streletz, Kessler and Krenz* v. *Germany*, 22 March

remoteness (both physical and temporal), the Court has refused 'to deal with errors of fact or law allegedly committed by national courts unless and in so far as they may have infringed rights and freedoms protected by the Convention'.[63] Nonetheless, while Sweeney argues that 'it remains important not to cast the European Court in the role of a dispenser of transitional justice itself', the Court appears sometimes to overstep this line (as the dissenting opinion in *Korbely* v. *Hungary* (2008) laments).[64] In her recent book, Sonja Grover remarks that, in *Korbely*:

> [T]he Grand Chamber took it upon itself to reinterpret facts in such a way that its interpretation contradicted the findings of fact of the domestic courts which actually heard from witnesses and experts on the stand and via written submissions. In this way, the European Court departs from its usual tact and, it may be argued, infringes its own self-described jurisdictional boundaries.[65]

Yet, it is precisely in such historical cases that the traditional justifications for deferring to the national courts are less persuasive.[66] One way in which the Court has sought to reduce its distance from situations of transition is by hearing third party evidence and referencing external research. Hamilton notes the Court's extensive reliance on the opinions of the Venice Commission, and the chapters by Buyse and Ní Aoláin each highlight cases in which the Court has drawn extensively on expert testimony.[67] Indeed, pointing to the landmark Grand Chamber judgment *DH* v. *Czech Republic* (2008), Smith and O'Connell suggest that one of the most important developments in the Court's transitional jurisprudence 'is the willingness to use reports by international organisations to assess

---

2001 (Appl. nos. 34044/96, 35532/97 and 44801/98) para. 49. See also, George Letsas' distinction between the 'substantive' and 'structural' conceptions of the margin of appreciation. See Letsas, *A Theory of Interpretation*, 80–81. See further, H. van der Wilt and S. Lyngdorf, 'Procedural Obligations Under the European Convention on Human Rights: Useful Guidelines for the Assessment of "Unwillingness" and "Inability" in the Context of the Complementarity Principle', *International Criminal Law Review* 9 (2009) 39–75.

[63] See, for example, *Streletz, Kessler and Krenz; Kononov* v. *Latvia* [GC], 17 May 2010 (Appl. no. 36376/04) para. 197; ECtHR, *Korbely* v. *Hungary*, 19 September 2008 (Appl. no. 9174/02) para. 72.

[64] Dissenting opinion of Judges Lorenzen, Tulkens, Zagrebelsky, Fura-Sandström and Popović.

[65] S. C. Grover, *The European Court of Human Rights as a Pathway to Impunity for International Crimes* (Berlin and Heidelberg: Springer-Verlag, 2010) at 244–245.

[66] Bárd, 'The Difficulties of Writing the Past Through Law', 34.

[67] For example, the Court looked at evidence from a psychologist, historian, political scientist and library scientist, all of which were heard in domestic proceedings, in the freedom of expression case of *Balsytė-Lideikienė* v. *Lithuania*, 4 November 2008 (Appl. no. 72596/01).

the general context in which the specific individual cases occur' (here, to substantiate evidence of discrimination against the Roma community).[68] Clearly this is an area in which there are significant differences between the practice and working methods of the three regional systems. Fact-finding, for example, is used relatively rarely by the European Court,[69] whereas Rodríguez-Pinzón concludes that such political powers of the Inter-American Commission have enabled it 'to closely follow evolving transitional processes almost in "real-time"'.

The relative absence of a 'real-time' jurisprudence in the European context (apart from the issuing of interim measures), may be partly explained by the Strasbourg Court's ever burgeoning case load which has been well documented.[70] Alec Stone Sweet and Helen Keller, for example, have noted that the typical delay between application and judgment on the merits is over five years.[71] As Kris Brown's chapter highlights, the formative impact of the right to life rulings in Northern Ireland was undoubtedly limited by the lengthy delays in bringing cases to Strasbourg. This can be directly contrasted with the causal role played by an Inter-American Commission report (following an on-site visit to Peru in 1998) in Fujimori's decision to resign his Presidency (see further, Chapter 10).

Recent changes to the Strasbourg machinery pave the way for more timely and, one hopes, a more effective approach to addressing systemic rights violations. The reforms – including the introduction of the pilot judgment procedure – are in no small part due to the transitions in East-Central Europe and the enlargement of the Council of Europe.[72]

In addition to calls for further translation and dissemination of leading judgments in national languages, the Action Plan adopted at the Interlaken

---

[68] See Viaene and Brems, 'Transitional Justice and Cultural Contexts', 222–223, citing the *Escué Zapata* case of the Inter-American Court of Human Rights and discussing the role of legal and cultural anthropologists.

[69] See P. Leach *et al.*, *International Human Rights and Fact-Finding* (2009). Available at: www.londonmet.ac.uk. Compare Article 52 ECHR, with the African Commission's system of Special Rapporteurs and Working Groups, and with the promotional role of the Inter-American Commission (Article 41, see further www.cidh.oas.org/publi.eng.htm).

[70] See, for example, 'Memorandum of the President of the European Court of Human Rights to the States with a view to preparing the Interlaken Conference', 3 July 2009. Available at: www.echr.coe.int. Also, A. Mowbray, 'The Interlaken Declaration: The Beginning of a New Era for the European Court of Human Rights?', *Human Rights Law Review* 10(3) (2010) 519, 520 and 522 (citing Thorbjorn Jagland).

[71] A. Stone Sweet and H. Keller, *A Europe of Rights: The Impact of the ECHR on National Legal Systems* (Oxford University Press, 2008) at 12.

[72] See, for example, D. Harris, M. O'Boyle, E. Bates and C. Buckley (eds.) *Law of the European Convention on Human Rights*, 2nd edn (Oxford University Press, 2009) 851.

Conference in February 2010 urged state parties to have regard to judgments involving other states experiencing similar problems as those in their own legal systems.[73] As James McAdams has argued, identifying similarities among cases is 'a more demanding task than pointing to differences'.[74] We therefore hope that this volume can contribute to future developments by beginning to systematise the Court's transitional jurisprudence.

Conclusion: a double legal legacy

As noted at the outset, the regional systems have, until now, been largely neglected as a source of transitional normativity. This book aims to help fill that gap with its analysis of supra-national human rights interpretation during periods of transition towards pluralist democratic rule. By laying bare systemic failures[75] or statutory injustices,[76] regional human rights cases have become vital, even totemic, staging posts in the negotiation of new political and legal dispensations. Despite the remoteness of regional mechanisms, the chapters in this collection demonstrate that the jurisprudence can exert an important steer on the direction of transition processes, and thus enable and sustain significant shifts in power.

The transitional cases bequeath a double legal legacy. First, they are read into domestic judicial reasoning and thereby inform and shape political and legal agendas at the national level. What the regional jurisprudence might lose in immediacy, it undoubtedly gains in traction. The regional institutions serve to extend law's normative reach in addressing and remedying past injustice. Second, though, the transition cases have also led to a realignment of the Strasbourg Court's ordinary jurisprudence and a more bold articulation of the state's positive obligations. Transitional cases have fundamentally strengthened the jurisprudence of the Inter-American system, and clear examples can also be identified in the European Court's case law.[77] Just as regional jurisprudence has helped

---

[73] Mowbray, 'The Interlaken Declaration', 526.

[74] A. J. McAdams, 'Transitional Justice After 1989: Is Germany so Different?', *GHI Bulletin* 33 (Fall 2003) 53, 54.

[75] See, for example, ECtHR, *Broniowski* v. *Poland*, 22 June 2004 (Appl. no. 31443/96) paras. 189–194, and ECtHR, *Hutten-Czapska* v. *Poland*, 22 February 2005 (Appl. no. 35014/97).

[76] See, for example, ECtHR, *Streletz, Kessler and Krenz* v. *Germany* and ECtHR, *K.-H. W.* v. *Germany*, 22 March 2001 (Appl. no. 37201/97) referring to 'a system so contrary to justice'. See also Teitel 'Transitional Jurisprudence', 2023–2024.

[77] For example, ECtHR, *Oršuš* v. *Croatia*, 16 March 2010 (Appl. no. 15766/03) and ECtHR, *McCann* v. *United Kingdom*, 27 September 1995 (Appl. no. 18984/91).

to shape societies in transition, experiences of transition have also shaped the jurisprudence of the regional human rights mechanisms.

Bibliography

Anderson, E., *Out of the Closets and Into the Courts: Legal Opportunity Structure and Gay Rights Litigation* (University of Michigan Press, 2006).

Bárd, K., 'The Difficulties of Writing the Past Through Law – Historical Trials Revisited at the European Court of Human Rights', *International Review of Penal Law* 81 (2010) 27–44.

Bell, C., 'The New Law of Transitional Justice', in Ambos, K., Large, J. and Wierda, M. (eds.) *Building a Future on Peace and Justice: Studies on Transitional Justice, Peace and Development* (Berlin and Heidelberg: Springer-Verlag, 2009) 105–126.

Berman, P. S., 'Global Legal Pluralism', *S. Cal. L. Rev.* 80 (2006–2007) 1158–1237.

Chapman, A., 'Truth Finding in the Transitional Justice Process', in Van Der Merwe, H., Baxter, V. and Chapman, A. R. (eds.) *Assessing the Impact of Transitional Justice: Challenges for Empirical Research* (Washington: USIP, 2009) 91–114.

Coleman, J. and Sarch, A., *Blameworthiness and Time*, Yale Law School Research Paper 214 (2010). Available at http://papers.ssrn.com/abstract#1646949.

Council of Europe, *Democracy in Europe: Crisis and Perspectives*, Report of the Council of Europe, Parliamentary Assembly's Political Affairs Committee, 7 June 2010. Available at: assembly.coe.int.

Czarnota, A., 'Lustration, Decommunisation and the Rule of Law', *Hague Journal on the Rule of Law* 1 (2009) 307–336.

Engstrom, P. and Hurrell, A., 'Why the Human Rights Regime in the Americas Matters', in Serrano, M. and Popovski, V. (eds.) *Human Rights Regimes in the Americas* (Tokyo, New York and Paris: United Nations University Press, 2010) at 29–55.

Ghai, Y., 'The Role of Law in the Transition of Societies: The African Experience', *J. Afr. L.* 25 (1991) 8–20.

Gray, D. C., 'Extraordinary Justice', *Ala. L. Rev.* 62 (2010).

Grover, S. C., *The European Court of Human Rights as a Pathway to Impunity for International Crimes* (Berlin and Heidelberg: Springer-Verlag, 2010).

Harmsen, R., 'The European Convention of Human Rights after Enlargement', *International Journal of Human Rights* 5(4) (2001) 18–43.

Harris, D., O'Boyle, M., Bates, E. and Buckley, C. (eds.) *Harris, O'Boyle and Warbrick: Law of the European Convention on Human Rights*, 2nd edn (Oxford University Press, 2009).

Haynor, P., *Unspeakable Truths: Transitional Justice and the Challenge of Truth Commissions*, 2nd edn (New York and London: Routledge, 2010).

Hilson, C., 'New Social Movements: The Role of Legal Opportunity', *Journal of European Public Policy* 9(2) (April 2002) 238–255.

Issacharoff, S., 'Constitutionalizing Democracy in Fractured Societies', *Tex. L. Rev.* 82 (2003–2004) 1861–1893.

Krasner, S. D., *Sovereignty: Organized Hypocrisy* (Princeton University Press, 1999).

Krisch, N., 'The Open Architecture of European Human Rights Law', *Modern Law Review* 71 (2008) 183–216.

Leach, P., Paraskeva, C. and Uzelac, G., *International Human Rights and Fact-Finding*, online report, 2009. Available at: www.londonmet.ac.uk.

Letsas, G., *A Theory of Interpretation of the European Convention on Human Rights* (Oxford University Press, 2007).

Lundy, P., 'Commissioning the Past in Northern Ireland', *Review of International Affairs* LX, 1138–1139 (2010) 101–133.

Lutz, E. and Sikkink, K., 'The Justice Cascade: The Evolution and Impact of Foreign Human Rights Trials in Latin America', *Chi. J. Int'l. L.* 2 (2001) 1–34.

McAdams, A. J., 'Transitional Justice After 1989: Is Germany so Different?', *GHI Bulletin* 33 (Fall 2003) 53–64.

McEvoy, K., 'Letting Go of Legalism: Developing a "Thicker" Version of Transitional Justice', in McEvoy, K. and McGregor, L. (eds.) *Transitional Justice From Below* (Oxford and Portland, Oregon: Hart Publishing, 2008).

Mowbray, A., 'The Interlaken Declaration: The Beginning of a New Era for the European Court of Human Rights?', *Human Rights Law Review* 10(3) (2010) 519–528.

Ní Aoláin, F., 'The Fractured Soul of the Dayton Peace Agreement: A Legal Analysis', *Mich. J. Int'l L.* 19 (1998) 957–1004.

Posner, E. and Vermeule, A., 'Transitional Justice as Ordinary Justice', *Harv. L. Rev.* 117 (2004) 761–825.

Přibáň, J., *Dissidents of Law: On the 1989 Velvet Revolutions, Legitimations, Fictions of Legality and Contemporary Version of the Social Contract* (Aldershot: Ashgate, 2002).

Quint, P., 'Judging the Past: The Prosecution of East German Border Guards and the GDR Chain of Command', *The Review of Politics* 61(2) (1999) 303–329.

Sadurski, W., 'Partnering with Strasbourg: Constitutionalization of the European Court of Human Rights, the Accession of Central and East European States to the Council of Europe and the Idea of Pilot Judgments', *Human Rights Law Review* 9(3) (2009) 397–453.

'Transitional Constitutionalism: Simplistic and Fancy Theories', in Czarnota, A., Krygier, M. and Sadurski, W. (eds.) *Rethinking the Rule of Law after Communism* (Budapest: CEU Press, 2005) 9–24.

Safjan, M., 'Transitional Justice: The Polish Example, the Case of Lustration', *European Journal of Legal Studies* 1(2) (2007) 1–20.

Sajó, A., 'Militant Democracy and Transition Towards Democracy', in Sajó, A. (ed.) *Militant Democracy* (Utrecht: Eleven International Publishing, 2004) 209.

Schwartz, H., *The Struggle for Constitutional Justice in Post-Communist Europe* (University of Chicago Press, 2000).

Stone Sweet, A. and Keller, H., *A Europe of Rights: The Impact of the ECHR on National Legal Systems* (Oxford University Press, 2008).

Teitel, R., 'Post-Communist Constitutionalism: A Transitional Perspective', *Colum. Hum. Rts. L. Rev.* 26 (1994–1995) 167–190.

'Transitional Jurisprudence: The Role of Law in Political Transformation', *Yale L. J.* 106 (1997) 2009–2080.

Uitz, R., *Constitutions, Courts and History: Historical Narratives in Constitutional Adjudication* (Budapest and New York: CEU Press, 2005).

Van der Wilt, H. and Lyngdorf, S., 'Procedural Obligations Under the European Convention on Human Rights: Useful Guidelines for the Assessment of "Unwillingness" and "Inability" in the Context of the Complementarity Principle', *International Criminal Law Review* 9 (2009) 39–75.

Varju, M., 'Transition as a Concept of European Human Rights Law', *European Human Rights Law Review* 2 (2009) 170–189.

Viaene, L. and Brems, E., 'Transitional Justice and Cultural Contexts: Learning from the Universality Debate', *Netherlands Quarterly of Human Rights* 28(2) (2010) 199–224.

Waldron, J., *Law and Disagreement* (Oxford University Press, 1999).

Wilson, B. M. and Rodríguez Cordero, J. C., 'Legal Opportunity Structures and Social Movements: The Effects of Institutional Change on Costa Rican Politics', *Comparative Political Studies* 39(3) (April 2006) 325–351.

2

Transitional emergency jurisprudence: derogation and transition

FIONNUALA NÍ AOLÁIN

International law recognises and accommodates the fact that in times of political, economic or social crisis the state may be required to limit the extent of protection resulting from consentingly entered into treaty obligations protecting individual rights. The derogation provisions of the international human rights instruments including Article 15 of the European Convention contain the politically and legally mandated processes whereby states can suspend their international obligations protecting individual rights in time of emergency or crisis. Given that the Council of Europe (and the Convention as its primary legal instrument) was born out of a massive transition from war to peace on the European continent, transition can be viewed a motif for the early history of the Convention. In this sense, the Convention itself constitutes a response to the devastating human rights violations of the Second World War, and can be understood as a transitional legal instrument.[1] With that background in mind, this chapter explores the extent to which an extensive jurisprudence of emergency powers in the European system contains recognition of or interfaces with the thematic and structural aspects of transitional justice discourse.

In one sense the resort to the exceptional state of emergency constitutes a transition in itself, a move from norm to exception.[2] In this broader conceptual framework, the European Court of Human Rights has recognised

Professor Fionnuala Ní Aoláin, Dorsey and Whitney Chair in Law University of Minnesota Law School and Professor of Law Transitional Justice Institute, University of Ulster (Northern Ireland). My thanks to K. T. Farley for research assistance on this chapter.

[1] See generally, B. A. Simpson, *Human Rights and the End of Empire: Britain and the Genesis of the European Convention* (Oxford University Press, 2004).

[2] See O. Gross, 'The Normless and Exceptionless Exception: Carl Schmitt's Theory of Emergency Powers and the "Norm-Exception" Dichotomy', *Cardozo Law Review* 21 (2000) 1825.

the significance of the move involved – and, at least in theory, the aberrational nature of the shift is affirmed through judicial language emphasising temporality, exception and the need to revert to a status quo ante. The first part of the chapter starts by conceptualising transition and introduces the extent to which a broad notion of transition (a move 'from' and 'to') can be adduced from the Court's jurisprudence on exceptionality. The second part then turns to assess the more common frame of reference for transitional justice, namely its overlap with the shift from either repressive or authoritarian forms of governance and/or the move from violence to peaceful co-existence in societies that have experienced political violence or armed conflict within the definitions of international humanitarian law.[3] Here the chapter examines how transitional sites have a high degree of overlap with states of emergency, both during the period leading up to transition and throughout the transitional political process itself. In this context, transitions and emergency often cohabit in legal and political space, though this chapter argues that the cohabitation and its implications are frequently ignored. In this there is a silo effect in play, the effects of which will be explored at some length. The third part of the chapter follows by examining how the legal norms regulating armed conflict have been utilised (or not) by the European Court of Human Rights, linking the limits of transitional jurisprudence in conflicted societies to this dearth of analysis. The final section explores the specific case study of Northern Ireland and the way in which, despite an agreed peace treaty and transition, derogation continues to play a role in the legal life of the transitioning state. In doing so, I articulate concerns about the extent to which the need for rule of law reform and confidence building in the transitional phase can be undercut by continuing to resort to exceptionality through derogation.

Conceptualising transition

While much of the analysis in this volume is concerned with transitions from conflict to peace or authoritarian transitions, I pause to give some reflection to the notion of transition more generally conceived. A number of authors have described the emergence of the field of transitional

---

[3] See F. Ní Aoláin and C. Campbell, 'The Paradox of Democratic Transition', *Human Rights Quarterly* 27 (2005) 172, noting that the paradigmatic transition is the repressive to more liberal forms of governance model, and only relatively recently has the war/peace axis been grafted onto transitional justice frameworks of analysis.

justice from its early beginnings in Latin American states (including Argentina, Uruguay, Guatemala and Brazil) to more recent incarnations in South Africa, Northern Ireland and Eastern European states.[4] In all of these settings societies facing the difficult process of political transition have addressed large-scale human rights violations meted out during the prior regime. Doing so has involved the use of criminal sanction nationally and internationally, the utilisation of truth recovery processes and more recently other restorative justice processes. Using the term 'transitional justice' to capture the various locales and legal responses to atrocity has been challenged, on the basis that there is a problem with '[i]mputing ideas about "transitional justice" to actors who, presumably, were unlikely to have held them, particularly in their discussions of the immediate post-World War II era'.[5] This problem immediately faces us in the context of tracing the interface between the European Convention and the field of transitional justice. We could start with the Convention's inception and impute contemporary notions of transition and presume their relevance to conversations and negotiations held in the late 1940s. There are concerns of intellectual overreach with this approach. Equally to ignore the extent to which the Convention constituted a key legal and political response to the atrocities that had taken place within states during the Second World War and Holocaust is to miss something captured by the qualities of the Convention and of the views of states concerning the nature of their treaty obligations. Under-appreciating the extent to which the Convention when created marked a clear point of departure and distinction for its contracting states is to mistakenly presume that only by using the word transition do we mark the legal and political space in which lines are drawn around systematic human rights violations. To ignore the Convention as a form of line-drawing on the human rights and humanitarian law violations of the Second World War is to under-appreciate subject-matter reach of the treaty.[6]

---

[4] See P. Arthur, 'How "Transitions" Reshaped Human Rights: A Conceptual History of Transitional Justice', *Human Rights Quarterly* 31 (2009) 321; R. Teitel, 'Transitional Justice Genealogy', *Harvard Human Rights Journal* 16 (2003) 69; C. Bell, 'Interdisciplinarity and the State of the "Field" or "Non-Field"', *International Journal of Transitional Justice* 3 (2008) 5.

[5] Arthur, 'How "Transitions" Reshaped Human Rights', 328.

[6] This analysis shortcuts literature and debates on the meaning and use of language in political contexts. See generally Q. Skinner, 'Meaning and Understanding in the History of Ideas', in J. Tully (ed.) *Meaning and Content: Quentin Skinner and His Critics* (Cambridge University Press, 1988) 29–67.

As Campbell and I have articulated elsewhere there has been a tendency in transitional justice theorising to concentrate on the paradigmatic transition at the expense of seeing broader practices and locales of transition.[7] This paradigmatic transition primarily sees a shift from an authoritarian state structure (whether conflicted or not) to peaceful democracy as its frame of reference. Analyses of paradigmatic transition tended implicitly to conflate movement towards democracy with that towards peace. This view has obscured the reach of transitional justice by presuming it applies only to situations generally involving democracy shifts, and has tended to leave the democratic state out of the equation of analysis.[8] In particular it misses the democratic state experiencing internal conflict, or a transition from conflict through peace agreements or other negotiated settlements. This blind spot has quite significant implications for analysis of the Council of Europe system, where the requirements of democratic credentials for membership may presume or render irrelevant engagement with transitional discourses – particularly when the state is an established member of the system.

More wholesale criticism has also emerged of the transitional justice 'field',[9] questioning the specificity of transition as a framing device;[10] or has developed as a response to the perceived 'top-down' approach to transitional justice at odds with a broader democratic 'bottom-up' approach.[11] As recent work by Viaene and Brems explains,[12] the approach making essentialist distinctions between 'bottom-up' versus 'top-down' transition is frequently overarching in nature and takes a somewhat black and white method to what is 'in practice' a far more complex phenomena.

As introduced above, the general use of emergency powers is potentially a site of transitionary analysis at a meta-level. The concept of emergency is conceptually rooted in the notion of a sudden and unexpected occurrence, the effects of which are to make necessary unusual legal and

---

[7] Ní Aoláin and Campbell, 'The Paradox of Democratic Transition', 205.

[8] See generally, C. Campbell and F. Ní Aoláin, *The Paradox of Democratic Transition* (under review with Oxford University Press, 2012).

[9] As Arthur points out '[s]ome have dismissed the relevance of the word "transitional" as a kind of syntactical error'. Arthur, 'How "Transitions" Reshaped Human Rights', 325.

[10] E. Posner and A. Vermeule, 'Transitional Justice as Ordinary Justice', *Harvard Law Review* 117 (2004) 761.

[11] P. Lundy and M. McGovern, 'The Role of Community in Participatory Criminal Justice', in K. McEvoy and L. McGregor (eds.) *Transitional Justice from Below: An Agenda for Research, Policy and Practice* (Oxford and Portland, Oregon: Hart, 2008) 99–120.

[12] L. Viaene and E. Brems, 'Transitional Justice and Cultural Contexts Learning from the Universality Debate', *Netherlands Human Rights Quarterly* 28 (2010) 199.

political responses. This shift from the normal to an exceptional legal regime responding to particular challenges is at the core of the transition captured within the concept of derogation clauses enshrined in human rights treaties.

In reality, this idea of the unexpected nature of the emergency is at odds with the regularity of emergency experiences for many states. In fact, crisis and emergency are not sporadic episodes in the lives of many nations. They are permanent fixtures in the unfolding story of humanity. For example, as early as 1978 a key study estimated that at least 30 of the 150 countries then existing were under a state of emergency.[13] At that time and since, a substantial number of states have entered a formal derogation notice under Article 4(3) of the International Covenant on Civil and Political Rights, indicating that they were experiencing a situation of emergency. This number does not include states that are not signatories to the international human rights monitoring system or states which experience de facto emergencies because governments have failed to officially proclaim and notify a particular state of emergency. Nor does this figure take account of those states that have routinised and institutionalised emergency measures within their ordinary legal system. Moreover, not only has emergency expanded to an ever-greater number of nations, but also within the affected nations, it has extended its scope and strengthened its grip. Observations that '[e]mergency government has become the norm'[14] cannot be dismissed out of hand. The observation is all the more pertinent as we take account of the legal responses in many states to the events of 9/11.

Despite the propensity to crisis in many states, the legal and political rhetoric and practices accompanying emergency fixates on the unusual nature of both the threat faced and the *sui generis* nature of the response. Exceptionality may be the normatively right frame of analysis and practice here, given the propensity of states to abuse and normalise the use of exceptional powers and the illiberal tendencies that follow in political systems that concentrate executive powers in response to perceived or actual threat. In theory, the European system is locked into an exceptionality model by virtue of a derogation mechanism that requires the state to specify its opt-out from specific treaty measures, and offers the possibility of external scrutiny and measurement for such action. It is relevant to this

---

[13] See D. O'Donnell, 'States of Exception', *International Commission of Jurists Review* 21 (1978) 52–53.

[14] *A Brief History of Emergency Powers in the United States*, Working Paper Prepared for the Special Committee on National Emergencies and Delegated Emergency Powers, US Senate, 93rd Cong., 2nd sess., at v.

analysis that the states resorting to exceptional powers are generally those states that have experienced (or continue to experience) internal armed conflict and/or threats by violent actors whether external or internal – including Cyprus, the United Kingdom, Italy, Spain, Turkey and Russia. For most of these states, justifications for emergency are located in its articulation as a shift from the normal to the exceptional, and holding out the possibility that emergency powers themselves are the means to facilitate a shift back – a circular capacity to transition as it were. Two other categories of derogation are relevant but not discussed in this analysis. They include post-9/11 derogations entered on the basis of the 'war on terror' (envisaging long-term and indefinite derogation based on a threat with no conceived end),[15] and derogations occasionally entered by states arising from public order concerns.

Transition and emergency overlaps

The derogation provision of the European Convention, like many other international human rights treaties, stipulates that certain rights are non-derogable and cannot be limited or suspended under any circumstances.[16] In theory, the right of derogation is limited and has a number of procedural requirements attached to it, including notification and proportionality requirements. Derogations are not open-ended. Rather, they are intended to facilitate specific responses by the state to a particular set of challenges for which other measures are not sufficient. Clearly the very fact of external treaty (and Court) oversight signals that a state's resort to exceptional measures is not a blank cheque. Oversight is a fundamental aspect of the derogation system, exercised both as a result of the requirement that derogations are notified to the Council of Europe (a reporting requirement) and as a result of the Court's capacity to exercise review (a substantive oversight) on the state resort to derogation where persons challenge the infringement of rights that follows.

As the introduction asserts, one way to view the derogation regime of the European Convention is as a transition regime, facilitating the move from one legal status and one set of legal obligations to another (quite different) set of obligations for the state. The *Lawless* v. *Ireland* case, the

---

[15] Derogation entered by the United Kingdom (18 December 2001).
[16] The ECHR includes as non-derogable the right to life, freedom from torture, slavery, and freedom from *ex-post facto* laws.

very first case before the European Court and Commission, illustrates this thematic approach well. The *Lawless* case exhibits the dynamics of a new supra-national court anxious to establish its legitimacy, offer a meaningful review of states' actions while anxious not to overstep the boundaries of state consent to be subject to external oversight.[17] While the Court demonstrates a willingness to establish the theoretical boundaries on the state's determination as to whether an emergency exists, its decision also shows an unwillingness to articulate a negative assessment of the state's action that was clearly sustainable on the facts before it. Arguably in this case the Court remains vigilant about the negative capacity of derogation to facilitate backsliding on human rights obligations with the recent history of the Second World War looming large. In essence, then, derogation is a means for states to remain in suspension of human rights obligations temporarily and to transition back to full observance of treaty obligations. This 'to and from' notion is key to why derogation was considered a short-term solution for challenges experienced by states, and why permanent derogation is inherently inconsistent with the Convention's notion of a transition back to normality and full human rights protection.

These key themes are evident in the *Lawless* decision. Here, the European Court was asked to examine the validity of a derogation entered by the Irish government.[18] Gerard Lawless, an Irish citizen, was arrested on 11 July 1957, in the Republic of Ireland on suspicion of membership of the illegal Irish Republican Army (IRA). He was detained without trial from 13 July to 11 December 1957, in a military detention camp. On 20 July, the Irish Minister for External Affairs sent a letter to the Secretary-General of the Council of Europe, informing him of the entry into force of the special powers of arrest and detention that served as the legal basis for Lawless' detention and notifying him of a derogation to that extent under the provisions of Article 15 of the European Convention.[19] Lawless filed a complaint with the European Commission of Human Rights alleging numerous violations of his rights under the Convention. Both the Commission and the Court found that detaining Lawless without trial for a five-month period violated the obligations of the Irish government under the European

---

[17] ECtHR, *Lawless* v. *Ireland* (No.3), 1 July 1961 (Appl. no. 332/57).
[18] *Ibid.*, at para. 15.
[19] EComHR, *Lawless* v. *Ireland*, 19 December 1959 (Appl. no. 332/57) para. 72. For a description of the factual basis of the case, see para. 56; and ECtHR, *Lawless* v. *Ireland* (No.3), 1 July 1961 (Appl. no. 332/57) paras. 15–25.

Convention.[20] Thus, it became necessary to examine whether the detention could be justified under the derogation clause.

Lawless is the first critical judicial step taken towards placing the resort to emergency powers by states within an international review framework. The Irish government had contested the right of the European Court (and Commission) of Human Rights to scrutinise the government's actions – arguing effectively that while the government used the framework of derogation it was nonetheless entirely at its discretion to determine that a state of 'public emergency' existed and what measures were needed to overcome the exigency and in what proportion. The Court paid close attention to the need for a thorough procedural examination of the claim before it. It stated categorically, 'it is for the Court to determine whether the conditions laid down in Article 15 for the exercise of the exceptional right of derogation have been fulfilled'.[21] In doing so, the Court set out core concepts that define the state of exception in international law – and frames a particular legal setting for emergencies – namely proportionality, temporariness and limitations on the exercise of certain rights.

Thus, defining 'public emergency' for the purposes of Article 15, the European Court declared that: '[I]n the general context of Article 15 of the Convention, the natural and customary meaning of the words "other public emergency threatening the life of the nation" is sufficiently clear ... they refer to an exceptional situation of crisis or emergency which affects the whole population and constitutes a threat to the organised life of the community of which the State is composed.'[22] Here we see the Court going some way towards developing criteria to evaluate whether a situation of emergency could be said to exist. The Court based its judgment on three factual elements that validated in the Court's opinion the Irish government's resort to the mechanism of derogation under Article 15: the

---

[20] The Court held that the detention violated the provisions included in Articles 5 and 6 of the European Convention but did not conflict with Article 7. See ECtHR, *Lawless* v. *Ireland* (No.3), 1 July 1961 (Appl. no. 332/57) paras. 8–22.

[21] *Ibid.*, para. 22, at 55. The European Commission of Human Rights had previously established its competence to review and rule on the compliance of a derogating state with its obligations under Article 15. See EComHR, *Greece* v. *United Kingdom* [report], 26 September 1958 (Appl. no. 176/56).

[22] ECtHR, *Lawless* v. *Ireland* (No.3), 1 July 1961 (Appl. no. 332/57) para. 28. In his concurring opinion, Judge Maridakis wrote that: 'By "public emergency threatening the life of the nation" it is to be understood a quite exceptional situation which imperils or might imperil the normal operation of public policy established in accordance with the lawfully expressed will of the citizens, in respect alike of the situation inside the country and of relations with foreign Powers.'

existence of an illegal and secret military organisation operating within the territory of the Irish Republic that resorted to violent actions to further its goals; the detrimental impact of this organisation's operations on the foreign relations of the Republic due to its activities in Northern Ireland; and finally, the 'steady and alarming' escalation in the intensity and scale of its terrorist campaign from the autumn of 1956 through the first six months of 1957.[23] The Court's cursory analysis here is problematic both with respect to the particular facts presented in this case and, more significantly, for its long-term effects on the jurisprudence under Article 15. It is questionable whether, on the facts of the case, the Court's answer to the primary question as to the existence of a public emergency in Ireland could be sustained.[24] The decisions of both the Commission and the Court reflect strong deference to the government's assessment of crisis. Although they have not completely abdicated their judicial review responsibility to decide a derogation case on its merits, both the Commission and the Court adopted a markedly deferential attitude towards the national governments as to whether a 'public emergency' existed, employing (and extending) for this purpose the 'margin of appreciation' doctrine.[25] This deference, as we will see later, substantially affects the application and review of emergency powers in transitional states and the willingness of the Court to challenge the use of derogation notwithstanding variable domestic conditions.[26] In *Lawless*, the Commission extended the notion of a measure of discretion, applying it not only to the question of whether the measures taken by the government were 'strictly required' by the exigencies but also to the determination of whether a 'public emergency threatening the life of the nation' existed. Thus, the Commission stated:

---

[23] *Ibid.*, para. 28.

[24] Oren Gross, 'Once More unto the Breach: The Systemic Failure of Applying the European Convention on Human Rights to Entrenched Emergencies', *Yale Journal International Law* 23 (1998) 437 at 462–464.

[25] EComHR, *Greece v. United Kingdom* [report Vol.II], 26 September 1958 (Appl. no. 176/56) para. 318. This doctrine was initially formulated by the Commission in the (first) *Cyprus* case when it stated that a state exercising the derogation power under the European Convention enjoyed 'a certain measure of discretion in assessing the extent strictly required by the exigencies of the situation'. See also, ECtHR, *Lawless v. Ireland* (No.3), 1 July 1961 (Appl. no. 332/57) para. 28.

[26] EComHR, *The Greek Case*, 5 November 1969 (*Denmark v. Greece*, Appl. no. 3321/67; *Norway v. Greece*, Appl. no. 3322/67; *Sweden v. Greece*, Appl. no. 3323/67; *Netherlands v. Greece*, Appl. no. 3344/67) paras. 180–184 (Commission member Eustathiades, dissenting).

> [H]aving regard to the high responsibility which a government has to its people to protect them against any threat to the life of the nation, it is evident that a certain discretion – a certain margin of appreciation – must be kept to the Government in determining whether there exists a public emergency which threatens the life of the nation and which must be dealt with by exceptional measures derogating from its normal obligations under the Convention.[27]

As we evaluate the system's effectiveness in *Lawless* there is value in affirming the right to oversee, but hidden in that message was a clear arena of lax accountability achieved by giving deference to the state calling the state of emergency in the first place. Interestingly, as the Council of Europe system has increased its membership, an evident concern of some states (and judges) has been that the margin of appreciation doctrine as applied to transitional, post-communist states would lead to an erosion of the integrity and coherence of rights protection within the system.[28] As Judge Martens pointed out in his concurrence in the *Brannigan* derogation case:

> The 1978 view of the Court as to the margin of appreciation under Article 15 was, presumably, influenced by the view that the majority of the then members of the Council of Europe might be assumed to be societies which … had been democracies for a long time … Since the accession of Eastern and Central European States that assumption has lost its pertinence.[29]

I return to this issue below.

Lawless is the starting point for the Court's multiple interactions with states on derogation in the decades that follow. It can be viewed as a case that sets the litmus test on derogation for states, confirms the exceptionality of the derogation regime, and places limits on the state's exclusive rights to declare its own perception of threat as binding externally. The judicial footprint set out in *Lawless* is the framework within which subsequent derogation assessments by the Court are broadly located.

---

[27] EComHR, *Lawless* v. *Ireland*, 19 December 1959 (Appl. No. 332/57) para. 90. A minority of the Commission members adamantly rejected the margin of appreciation doctrine, arguing that evaluation of the existence of a public emergency ought to be based solely on existing facts without regard to any 'account of subjective predictions as to future development'. *Ibid.*, para. 92, at 94 (Commission member Eustathiades, dissenting).

[28] W. Sadurski, 'Partnering with Strasbourg: Constitutionalization of the European Court of Human Rights, the Accession of Central and East European States to the Council of Europe and the Idea of Pilot Judgments', *Human Rights Law Review* 9 (2009) 397, 430–431.

[29] ECtHR, *Brannigan and McBride* v. *United Kingdom*, 25 May 1993 (Appl. nos. 14553/89; 14554/89), concurring opinion of Judge Martens at para. 3.

Moving beyond a general motif of derogation as a more abstract variety of transition and regarding cases in which derogation was being Court reviewed for states sliding to less liberal/more authoritarian forms of governance or as a stated means to address conflict transitions, the Court (and Commission's) judicial record is thinner. Prior to the Eastern European transitions derogation practice and jurisprudence was confined to a small and select group of states. This group can be divided into two broad categories. The first group includes those states experiencing long-term internal conflict (specifically Northern Ireland and Turkey). In these states there was a notable overlap between the state response to terrorism, the experience of conflict and the deployment of the legal systems to manage the conflict and/or the terrorist threat. These states could be described as repeat players in the derogation system.

The second group of states can be described as sporadic players in the derogation system, invoking derogation in specific and often one-off situations. They include, for example, Greece and Cyprus. After the wave of political transitions in Eastern European states and the rush to join the Council of Europe system, an interesting and relevant question for this study is whether the Convention system is seeing an emerging or different pattern in the resort to derogation from states whose democratic credentials are still consolidating and many of which are still striving to embed democratic practices in local political cultures long honed in a different political environment. I return to this question below.

The most notable transition case under Article 15 came early on in the Convention's history and involved an authoritarian reversion. The case taken against Greece was significant in that there were serious and systematic human rights violations in play. An illiberal military government had overthrown a democratic regime, and the derogation process was being used by the military government as a means to justify its aberrational human rights record. In April 1967, a group of military officers carried out a successful *coup d'état* in Greece. In the name of 'The National Revolution' constitutional guarantees protecting human rights were suspended. Mass arrests, purges of the intellectual and political community, censorship and martial law followed. Clearly due process rights alone were not the sole or most significant response in the arsenal of the authoritarian regime. In May 1967, the new government informed the Secretary-General of the Council of Europe that it was invoking Article 15 of the European Convention to allow for the suspension of certain constitutional rights, arguing that a 'public emergency threatening the life of the nation' existed in Greece due to the threat of a violent communist overthrow of the military government, a crisis of constitutional government and a crisis of public order. Subsequently, a case was brought to the European Commission by Denmark, Sweden, Norway and the Netherlands against Greece, on 2 October 1967.

At first blush, the decision by the European Commission – determining that no public emergency existed in Greece at the time derogation occurred – is unusual, but this case was until relatively recently (and the accession of the transitional Eastern European states) viewed as an anomaly. Its outcome was explained by the need of the Council of Europe (and by implication its judicial organs) to self-define politically in terms of democratic identity and institutions. The imposition of an authoritarian military regime in Greece was a direct challenge to that political self-identity and was therefore met by a staunch judicial response. The overwhelming consensus was that the transition in Greece was an illegitimate and backwards move, and that view was reflected in the strong legal (and political) response of the Commission. The eventual consequence of that response to the Greek derogation was the withdrawal of Greece from the Council of Europe, a result that might not have been unintended by the Commission's own reasoning.[30] The case reflects the capacity to generate transitional jurisprudence in real time, as the human rights violations were recent and ongoing at the time when the Commission's decision was released.

In contrast to *Lawless* the Commission assessed both procedurally and substantively whether a state of emergency actually existed in Greece at the relevant time. It concluded that the evidence supplied by the Greek government was not persuasive. Thus, for example, after carefully reviewing the facts, the Commission found that not only did the Greek government not show that the threat of a communist coup was imminent, but rather the evidence actually indicated that a violent takeover was 'neither planned at that time, nor seriously anticipated by either the military or police authorities'.[31]

---

[30] The case never came before the European Court as the Greek government denounced the European Convention and withdrew its membership in the Convention after the Commission's Report was made public.

[31] *The Greek Case*, para. 159. The Commission similarly rejected the Greek government's claim that the circumstances prevailing in Greece at the relevant time constituted a constitutional crisis that put public order in serious jeopardy. *Ibid.*, paras. 126–132; paras. 163–164. Similarly, while acknowledging that great tension existed in Athens and Salonica, particularly among students and building workers, the Commission nonetheless found that 'there [was] no evidence that the police were not in both cities fully able to cope with the situation; there [was] no indication that firearms were used or their use planned and still less was there any suggestion that the army should be called in to assist the police'. *Ibid.*, para. 149. Thus, the government 'was in effective control of the situation'. *Ibid.*, para. 160.

Although the Commission paid its rhetorical respect to the 'constant juris-prudence' concerning the margin of appreciation doctrine, it did not grant any such margin to the Greek revolutionary government in what consti-tuted a virtual *de novo* review of the factual basis of the case and the Greek government's submissions.[32] The case demonstrates the capacity to assess the fundamental legitimacy of the derogation question based on the cri-teria developed by the Court and Commission. This capacity was further strengthened by an emphasis on independent fact-finding, a key element when addressing systematic human rights violations.[33] The Commission's approach in this case was characterised by objective assessment, non-defer-ence to state justification and the streamlining of categories within which to assess state action. It set a positive example of robust international judicial oversight. However, this approach has not been adopted in relation to other assessments of valid derogations and it has been typecast by many as simply a response to the anti-democratic character of the Greek government.[34] The non-democratic nature of the Greek government enabled the Commission to assume an uncompromising stance: not only would such a decision enjoy moral and political support, but it would be easily distinguishable from any future case involving a democratic regime, thus alleviating member states' fears that a strong decision might be used against them in the future. Insofar as the Commission's decision opposed the self-proclaimed interests of the Greek junta, it was all the more palatable to established regimes, as it worked against an unconstitutional overthrow of a lawful government. The clear signal was that the use of the Convention and its processes to legitim-ate usurping the democratic order was intolerable. The Convention would not be an instrument used to transition democracies to less liberal forms of governance.

As outlined above, when ostensibly democratic states have engaged in the suspension of certain rights guaranteed under the Convention, the Commission and Court have been less exacting in their oversight require-ments.[35] In practice, cases coming to the Court testing the derogations exercised by democratic states involve either situations of internal armed

---

[32] C. S. Feingold, 'The Doctrine of Margin of Appreciation and the European Convention on Human Rights', *Notre Dame Law Review* 53 (1977) 90 at 91–94.

[33] J. F. Hartman, 'Derogation from Human Rights Treaties in Public Emergencies', *Harvard International Law Journal* 22 (1981) 41.

[34] J. Beckett, '*The Greek Case* before the European Human Rights Commission', *Human Rights* 1 (1970–1971) 91 at 113.

[35] O. Gross and F. Ní Aoláin, *Law in Times of Crisis: Emergency Powers in Theory and Practice* (Cambridge University Press, 2006).

conflict, terrorism challenges or a mixture of both. In conflict related derogation of most interest to this study, the use of derogation is occurring in tandem with significant and systematic human rights violations. In theory, given the *raison d'être* of the Convention, one might expect a fairly robust response by the Court to such violations. Instead, at least insofar as ostensibly democratic states are concerned, the challenges have been more muted. An interesting and relevant question is how this jurisprudential baggage will be carried by the Court as transitional Eastern European states respond to internal armed conflicts or resort to the use of derogation to quell domestic political dissent? One relevant pattern of the conflict related derogations was their overlap with long-term or permanent emergencies. The nexus is most evidently shown in contexts where democratic states introduced temporary legislation limiting rights protection in order to confront finite crises, but subsequently allowed such legislation to become entrenched and survive as an integral component of the state's legal regulation.[36] It is notable that these long emergencies also overlap with negotiations to end conflicts, sometimes with ongoing and deeply problematic exclusions of minority groupings from full and equal participation in the political system and with political and legal phases that are transitional in nature and substance. The continuous or overlapping application of derogation through the transitional phase has its own complexities and dynamic that has received little academic attention. In assessing the effectiveness of the Court's oversight of these consolidated democratic derogations having an armed conflict nexus, some preliminary observations can be made. Positively, oversight clearly limited the state's room for manoeuvre in terms of the scope and extent of specific rights limited – illustrated most clearly by the *Brogan* and *Brannigan and McBride* cases from Northern Ireland.[37] On the broader issue as to the Court's effect on systematic patterns of human rights violations (including violations of the right to life) in internal armed conflict situations, the evidence of significant effect is less convincing. As the chapter will explore further below, the very exclusion of armed conflict and its applicable norms may operate to create a blind spot in accountability, or at least to obscure the methods and means being utilised by state and non-state actors as they confront one another in violent encounters.

[36] *The Prevention of Terrorism (Temporary Provisions) Act* 1974, 48 Halsbury Stat. 972 (3rd edn, 1978) is the classic example of this phenomenon.

[37] ECtHR, *Brogan and Others* v. *United Kingdom*, 29 November 1988 (Appl. nos. 11209/84; 11234/84; 11266/84; 11386/85); ECtHR, *Brannigan and McBride* v. *United Kingdom*, 25 May 1993 (Appl. nos. 14553/89; 14554/89).

The most notable site of derogation distinction is a comparison between the approach of the Court in relation to Turkey and its approach to cases involving the United Kingdom. Both states experienced long-term internal conflict, and both have to varying degrees flirted with or sought to negotiate an end to conflict. There were, and remain, salient differences between the response of the Court to derogation cases coming from both jurisdictions – a difference that suggests a difference in approach to established democracies and states with a more inconsistent tradition. While one state is currently undergoing conflict transition (UK) and one is not (Turkey), for a period both had very similar profiles in terms of derogations, rights violations and state responsiveness. In both contexts the Court was/is generally deferential on the key question of the legitimacy of the emergency itself, unwilling to second-guess the state on its resort to emergency powers, but on the attendant questions of measures taken there are notable differences in the application of legal tests and their outcomes.

A common thread of the Turkish cases is the allegations of ongoing human rights violations by Turkish security forces in the context of the bloody armed struggle against the Kurdistan Workers Party. Turkish security forces allegedly committed extensive and systematic human rights violations – including forcible displacement of civilian non-combatants, deaths in detention as a result of excessive force, 'mystery killings' and killings by 'execution squads', disappearances and torture during detention or interrogation – during their fighting against Kurdish guerrillas. Criticism also has focused on Turkey's suspension of civil and political rights, especially those of the Kurdish minority. Turkey invoked Article 15 derogations for more than 77 per cent of the period between June 1970 and July 1987, including a continuous stretch of almost seven years from September 1980 to May 1987. Since 1987, most of the provinces of south-eastern Turkey have been continuously subjected to an emergency regime. After 1987 a further derogation covered the period August 1990 to January 2002, and another from January 1991 to January 2002. There has been little if any progress on advancing a political settlement with the PKK,[38] the Kurdish separatist organisation whose activities have been the stated focus for the curtailment of rights (though clearly broadly defined autonomy and status demands by the Kurdish minority underpin the violent and ongoing conflict).

---

[38] A brief ceasefire was agreed in September 2010 for the month of Ramadan but devoid of any broader political settlement (see www.cbsnews.com/stories/2010/09/20/ap/world/main6883484.shtml).

The Turkish cases highlight a number of relevant issues. First, these cases demonstrate that the Court can be fairly robust when it comes to measuring the necessity and proportionality of particular measures taken by a derogating state. These patterns auger reasonably well for expanded use by newly democratised states. Second, the Court demonstrates a markedly more activist jurisprudence when faced with a recalcitrant state whose democratic credentials are suspect. Third, the cases reveal a structural inability to deal credibly with permanent emergencies. Finally, due process rights (as well as core non-derogable rights) remain consistently and flagrantly violated by states resorting to emergency powers and practices, whether they are derogating formally from their treaty obligations or not. These rights remain at risk whether the state is in open conflict with non-state actors, in transition, or some time away from the formal end of hostilities. Some cases below illustrate the point.

In *Aksoy* v. *Turkey*, the Commission and the Court examined the validity of the Turkish derogation from Article 15 in the context of the applicant's detention and alleged ill-treatment in custody for approximately fourteen days in November 1992.[39] The derogation in place was limited to Article 5 protections only. Both the Commission and Court demonstrated again their reluctance to examine substantively the emergency justification question.[40] The Court ruled that 'in the light of all the material before it ... the particular extent and impact of PKK terrorist activity in South East Turkey has undoubtedly created, in the region concerned, a "public emergency threatening the life of the nation"'.[41] The Court repeated its consistent assertion that states had a 'wide margin of appreciation' in deciding whether they were facing a public emergency.[42] It did not second-guess the state's call that an emergency was in play, nor seek to tease out the role of the state versus the role of non-state actors (if any) in the circumstances that created the emergency. This approach is striking

---

[39] EComHR, *Aksoy* v. *Turkey* [report] 23 October 1995 (Appl. no. 21987/93); ECtHR, *Aksoy* v. *Turkey*, 18 December 1996 (Appl. no. 21987/93) para. 78. There was dispute as to the length of detention time. The Commission based on its fact-finding mission to the region concluded that the applicants were held for at least fourteen days. *Ibid.*, at para. 23.

[40] EComHR, *Aksoy* v. *Turkey* [report], 23 October 1995 (Appl. no. 21987/93) para. 179. Thus, the Commission briefly disposed of the question, concluding that: 'There is no serious dispute between the parties as to the existence of a public emergency in South-East Turkey threatening the life of the nation. In view of the grave threat posed by terrorism in this region, the Commission can only conclude that there is indeed a state of emergency in South-East Turkey which threatens the life of the nation.'

[41] ECtHR, *Aksoy* v. *Turkey*, 18 December 1996 (Appl. no. 21987/93) para. 70.

[42] *Ibid.*, at para. 173.

when contrasted with three other elements of the Court's decision. First, the Court asserted that in exercising its supervision over states' actions, it 'must give appropriate weight to such relevant factors as the nature of the rights affected by the derogation and the circumstances leading to, *and the duration of*, the emergency situation'.[43] Second, discussing the Turkish government's compliance with the notification requirements of Article 15(3), the Court pointed out that it was competent to examine this issue of its own motion, although none of those appearing before it had contested that Turkey's notice of derogation complied with the formal requirements of Article 15(3).[44] Finally, as regards the secondary question of proportionality of measures the Court was markedly more interventionist. Reiterating its view that seven-day detention accompanied by derogation (the *Brannigan and McBride* situation) was within the bounds permissible under the European Convention, it went on to state that fourteen-day detention was outside that perimeter.[45] Thus, an Article 5 violation was upheld notwithstanding the state's derogation.

Regarding the difference of approach towards democratic states and those with more suspect credentials the *Sakik and Others* v. *Turkey* case is instructive.[46] The case concerned the arrest and detention of six former members of the Turkish National Assembly who were prosecuted in a national security court. At issue was extended detention (fourteen days) and all the detainees had been charged with terrorist offences. The Court showed a markedly less deferential stance to the state's views than was evident in the Northern Ireland cases. The applicable derogation had been submitted in August 1990. The notice was highly specific both in its geographical scope of application and the rights affected (Article 5).

The judgment is particularly illuminating as the Court made some substantial inroads on meaningfully assessing the question of emergency justification. The Court reviewed whether the derogation in force at the time of the alleged violation was in fact applicable to the facts of the case. It found that the derogation applied only to the region where a state of emergency had been proclaimed, and did not include the city of Ankara (where the applicants were arrested, detained and subjected to trial). Thus, the Court forcefully held that it would be working against the purpose of

---

[43] *Ibid.*, at para. 68 (emphasis added).
[44] Though notably the Court stated that it was competent to judge whether the Turkish derogation met the formal requirements of Article 15(3). *Ibid.*, at paras. 85–86, 90.
[45] *Ibid.*, at para. 84.
[46] ECtHR, *Sakik and Others* v. *Turkey*, 26 November 1997 (Appl. nos. 23878/94; 23879/94; 23880/94).

Article 15 if the territorial scope of the provision were to be extended judicially to a part of the state not explicitly named in the notice of derogation. The Court here was working through and applying spatial distinctions to the exercise of emergency powers and, on some level, seeking to make legally meaningful the political and legal characteristics held by the state itself which maintained that two legal regimes could be contemporaneously applied within the territory controlled by the state. In this case, the Court held that Article 15 did not apply to the facts of the case.

What does this snapshot of derogation jurisprudence tell us about the likely significance and application of derogation jurisprudence to contemporary transitional states? To start, our data set is limited and requires some segregation. Following Sadurski, one might start by making a core distinction between two groups of Central and Eastern European states, namely the group of states where 'consolidation' after transition was the *mot d'ordre*,[47] and for which joining the Council of Europe system was a way to prevent any backslide into nationalistic or populist authoritarianism. For this group, the resort to derogation may be inherently problematic, giving rise to the dangers of political conflation with previously rule-deficient and exceptional regimes. By contrast, another group of late joiners, most prominently Russia, underscore the fragility of transition. The flagrant and systematic violation of rights from members of this group (again Russia) calls into question the authenticity of the transitional paradigm and its application.[48] States that have derogated include Georgia, which entered a derogation to the Convention in November 2007, and Armenia which derogated from the Convention in a series of communications with the Council in March 2008.[49] Notably, in respect of its actions in Chechnya, Russia has not entered any derogations, claiming

---

[47] Sadurski, 'Partnering with Strasbourg', 435.

[48] Illustrated, for example, by Article 100(1)(18) of the Constitution of the Republic of Belarus which provides that a 'state of emergency' may be introduced 'in the event of a natural disaster, a catastrophe, or unrest involving violence or the threat of violence on the part of a group of persons or organizations that endangers peoples' lives and health or jeopardises the territorial integrity and existence of the State'. Article 100(1)(25) provides that a 'state of martial law' may be imposed 'in the event of a military threat or attack'.

[49] See further, Council of Europe Parliamentary Assembly, *The Protection of Human Rights in Emergency Situations: Report of the Committee on Legal Affairs and Human Rights* (Doc. 11858; 9 April 2009), Rapporteur: Mr. Holger Haibach; and Council of Europe Parliamentary Assembly, Recommendation 1865 (2009) *The Protection of Rights in Emergency Situations: Reply from the Committee of Ministers*, adopted at the 1081st meeting of the Ministers' Deputies on 31 March 2010 (Doc. 12204; 16 April 2010). Available at:http://assembly.coe.int/Documents/WorkingDocs/Doc09/EDOC11858.pdf and http://assembly.coe.int/Documents/WorkingDocs/Doc10/EDOC12204.pdf.

the conflict to be a 'counter-terrorist operation'.[50] As a result, as cases have started to trickle through to the Court, the justices have considered that they should judge military operations (including aerial bombardment and artillery shelling) 'against a normal legal background'.[51] The overlap between transition, human rights and humanitarian law is taken up in more detail in the following section.

Humanitarian law, transition and human rights dimensions

Until relatively recently the relationship between international human rights law and international humanitarian law was delineated on the basis of the classic distinction between the law of war and the law of peace.[52] A growing body of law has made significant inroads on the theory and practice of the distinction, in essence concluding that human rights protections continue throughout armed conflict, no matter what the scale of its intensity. Increased judicial recognition of this overlap creates significant challenge for the European Convention system and for the Court in particular. The significance of overlap and the primacy of legal regimes have particular relevance in one class of cases considered here, namely situations in which a state is experiencing or transitioning from conflict. What norms apply if a state does not derogate but is experiencing significant internal conflict? If the state acknowledges a conflict context is it bound by human rights norms and are they modified in any way? To what extent should the European Court take the transition from a situation of conflict to peace into account as it accounts for systematic human rights violations?

A notable feature of the European Convention's jurisprudence has been its past unwillingness to concede or simultaneously undertake a review of the contemporaneous application of humanitarian law norms with human rights standards. On one general level the position is a principled and not spurious one. The European Court and Convention are founded in human rights law norms and practice. Where norms have evolved they have done so consistent with developments in the domestic jurisprudence and practice of states.[53] In a universe dominated by human rights norms

---

[50] P. Leach, 'The Chechen Conflict: Analysing the Oversight of the European Court of Human Rights', *EHRLR* 6 (2008) 732, 733.

[51] ECtHR, *Isayeva v. Russia*, 24 February 2005 (Appl. no. 57950/00) para. 191.

[52] G. Verdirame, 'Human Rights in Wartime: A Framework for Analysis', *EHRLR* 6 (2008) 689.

[53] S. Greer, *The European Convention on Human Rights: Achievements, Problems and Prospects* (Cambridge University Press, 2007).

and values it may appear ill-advised to bring a different legal regime, namely international humanitarian law, into play. Yet, a clean break between these two legal regimes is not always possible nor in the best interests of justice nor the rights of victims. In situations where the state experiences internal and/or communal violence the two legal regimes may be equally, simultaneously and/or sequentially in play in the same jurisdiction. In such context, to view the violations of rights solely in the context of international human rights law norms may be to impoverish judicial and state understandings of the nature of their legal obligations, as well as the specific kinds of violations that can and should be sustained in such circumstances. I suggest in this part of the chapter that issues of regime overlap and regime interplay are particularly relevant in transitional contexts, and that the Court has only recently started to traverse the terrain.

A textual examination of Article 15 demonstrates that the notion of 'war' was recognised in the formal language of the Convention. It states '[i]n time of war or other public emergency ...'. A black letter reading here would indicate that the context of 'war' gives a bona fide basis to the state to limit the exercise of rights contained in the Convention. The more vexing question is what constitutes 'war' for the purpose of the Convention. Over the years, as previously noted, states generally relied on the 'public emergency' designation to activate the Article 15 provisions. Democratic states may have done so in part because to admit to a state of internal armed conflict on their territory has both a factual and a political dimension – it concedes the political and territorial fragility of the state in ways that may undermine the capacity of the state to politically address the source of armed conflict without considerable restraint and/or scrutiny being imposed upon it. Moreover the public emergency category allows for the conceptual space of 'transition' to be occupied, namely it signals a period of extremis for the state but inherently transmits the notion of a temporary aberration as I have outlined above.

Despite the Court's reluctance to examine directly the issues of armed conflict and human rights regime overlap in both the cases relating to Northern Ireland and those relating to Turkey, the issue has been cast in a more direct light by the series of cases coming to the Court as a result of the Chechen conflict. Because Russia considers the issue a counter-terrorism operation, neither a state of emergency nor a situation of martial law has been declared since the inception of the conflict. As noted above, the Court has taken a formalist approach and maintained that a normal

legal assessment applies.[54] This description clearly does not do justice to
the reality of the experiences on the ground, and demonstrates the clear
unwillingness of the Court to 'delve into the question of complementarity
of human rights and humanitarian law'.[55] The Chechen cases are notable
for their lack of express reference to humanitarian law and principles. One
view of this approach is that it may be more 'victim-friendly', because the
overall scope of human rights protections provides a greater shield to those
whose rights have been violated, by excluding such notions as 'military
necessity' and collateral damage from the judicial balancing exercise. The
European Court also provides an avenue of legal redress in a society where
the rule of law is barely functional and remedies are entirely unavailable
to persons who have experienced serious human rights violations. On the
other hand, the lack of recognition for an armed conflict, when the threshold and scale of violence is clearly not within normal confines, provides a
political shield to the state – when the existence of an acknowledged armed
conflict would potentially bring greater political attention to bear. This
political dynamic might ultimately be the key element to placing limits on
the state's use of force, and bringing other legal instruments (such as the
United Nations Charter) more clearly into play, thereby forcing conflict
end and ultimately a transitional process.

Interestingly while the Russian cases have not forced an interface
around legal regimes in conflict zones the Eastern European transitions
have forced some interesting conversations. A key decision by the Court
in this regard is the *Korbely* v. *Hungary* decision. It originated in an
action by a Hungarian national who alleged that he had been convicted
of a crime which did not constitute an offence at the time it was committed, violating the principle of *nullum crimen sine lege*.[56] The events
in question took place at the outbreak of the Hungarian revolution in
Budapest in October 1956, when the applicant was a serving military
officer. During the course of demonstrations the applicant, with a group
of military officers under his command, was charged to regain control
of a building at a military school. Significant factual dispute surrounded
the sequence of events that resulted in the military regaining control of
the building, but it was not disputed that a number of insurgents were
killed and injured during the operation. Proceedings in respect of these
deaths were activated in 1993 when the Hungarian Parliament passed an

[54] ECtHR, *Isayeva* v. *Russia*, 24 February 2005 (Appl. no. 57950/00) para. 191.
[55] Leach, 'The Chechen Conflict', 734.
[56] ECtHR, *Korbely* v. *Hungary*, 19 September 2008 (Appl. no. 9174/02).

act providing that certain acts committed during the 1956 uprising were not subject to statutory limitation (a classical transitional piece of legislation). The applicant was charged with a crime against humanity under the Fourth Geneva Convention as subsequently proclaimed by Hungarian law. After various domestic legal proceedings at the Budapest Regional Court, followed by various appearances before the Constitutional Court, the case came to the European Court of Human Rights. The case raises characteristic transitional justice elements involving a reckoning with the past, the compatibility of addressing past injustice with principles of fairness and finally the proper scope for international courts to interfere with the process of political and legal transition (including accountability) taking place in the domestic sphere. All these are generally interesting matters but a key and relevant question in the case was the relationship between Common Article 3 of the four Geneva Conventions (1949) and applicable human rights standards. The Court was forced to address the relationship between a core provision of the laws of war and the scope of the European Convention's protections. The question it had to assess was whether, from the standpoint of Article 7(1) of the Convention (*nullum crimen sine lege*), the applicant's act, at the time it was committed, constituted an offence defined with sufficient 'accessibility and foreseeability by domestic or international law'.[57]

The case is instructive on the level of textual analysis as a group of human rights experts grapple with the meaning and scope of Common Article 3, as well as the characteristics of a crime against humanity.[58] The Court does not shy away from that task. While the decision does not produce any kind of synthesis on the overlap between human rights norms generally and humanitarian law, it provides substantive analysis of humanitarian standards in 'backwards looking' legal settings and the degree to which they must comport with human rights norms. This co-existence of norms is not the most straightforward or seamless, yet it provides transitional societies with a set of markers on the Court's willingness to make the European Convention meaningful and applied in such settings. Anticipating ongoing engagement from former Soviet states in this regard, as well as with the long-term fallout of the Russian engagement in Chechnya, this case at least demonstrates the capacity of

---

[57] *Ibid.*, para. 73.
[58] E.g. *ibid.*, at para. 78, concluding that: 'It follows that the Court must satisfy itself that the act in respect of which the applicant was convicted was capable of constituting, at the time when it was committed, a crime against humanity under international law.'

the Court to engage with the complexity of legal regimes, though it may very well be that it is the past-focused context that makes it possible.

Some concluding reflections on transition in context – Northern Ireland

Northern Ireland has a long history of derogations on the grounds of crisis or threat from the European Convention on Human Rights. The derogations date back to the very inception of the conflict and were resorted to cyclically as various pieces of emergency legislation were deployed by the state to respond to paramilitary threats. I have argued elsewhere that the resort to derogation resulted from the management of conflict through legal means and was a decisive if inconsistently successful strategy for the state.[59] While as general matter derogation jurisprudence has been relative to the particular circumstances of each contracting state, a relevant question for this chapter is whether the political realties of transition affect the substance and interpretation of derogation. A suitable site for exploring this question of differentiation is Northern Ireland.

On 31 August 1994 the Irish Republican Army (IRA) declared a complete cessation of military operations following decades of violent conflict. On 14 October 1994 the Combined Loyalist Military Command responded by declaring its own ceasefire. The Irish National Liberation Army (INLA) declared a 'tactical rather than permanent' ceasefire in a statement issued on 1 May 1995. Ultimately, after much stop and start, including an abandonment of the ceasefire commitments, a comprehensive framework agreement was established and signed in 1998 by almost all of the major political parties in the jurisdiction.[60] The Good Friday/ Belfast Agreement is composed of three strands: Strand One – internal political arrangements within Northern Ireland; Strand Two – bilateral relationships between Northern Ireland and the Republic of Ireland; and Strand Three – multilateral relationships between Northern Ireland, the United Kingdom and the Irish Republic. These are variously set out in a political agreement reached between the negotiating parties, and in a treaty binding in international law between the two state parties.[61]

---

[59] F. Ní Aoláin, *The Politics of Force: Conflict Management and State Violence in Northern Ireland* (Belfast: Blackstaff Press, 2000).
[60] *Agreement Reached in the Multi-Party Negotiations* Report (Cm. 3883, 1998).
[61] See also *Belfast Agreement: Implementation Bodies* Report (Cm. 4293, 1999); *Belfast Agreement: British Irish Council* Report (Cm. 4296, 1999); *Belfast Agreement: North/South Ministerial Council* (Cm. 4294, 1999); *Belfast Agreement: Intergovernmental Conference.*

Throughout the course of the negotiations, during periods of ceasefire by paramilitary groupings and following the signing of the Belfast peace agreement, derogation provisions were in place limiting the protection of due process rights in the jurisdiction (Article 5, ECHR). Arguably, whatever limited justification may have existed for the use of emergency powers prior to these ceasefires was removed by the absence of a sustained campaign of violence in the United Kingdom and by the subsequent agreement on a permanent peace agreement with a variety of domestic legislative and structural provisions. A number of international and domestic observers contended that the use of extensive crisis powers in that time was in direct violation of international legal standards on the maintenance and termination of states of emergency.[62] The ongoing use of derogation beyond the peace negotiations and maintained well into the transitional period raises hard questions about the appropriateness of the use of extensive emergency powers requiring derogation from international human rights treaty obligations.

In a way the jurisdiction (as well as others in the Council of Europe system including Bosnia-Herzegovina and Turkey) experiencing or transitioning from conflict is a litmus test for the willingness of democratic states to conform to the full requirements of international law. An important point to recall is that many transitional states struggle with rule of law deficits. Specifically for states transitioning from violent conflict a lack of confidence in the impartiality of law and legal institutions is prevalent – sometimes confined to specific minority or social groups within the states, sometimes more widespread. Where law and legal institutions have been a core element in the arsenal of the state to respond to conflict, limitations on the exercise of rights supported by the legal mechanism of derogation on the international plane have facilitated the state's approach and are complicit in the rule of law deficits. The pathways laid down in the legal system when the limitations on rights facilitate structural short-cuts by law enforcement agencies are often embedded and tricky to undo. Transition implies a notion of move 'from' and 'to', and in many transitional societies reconstruction of confidence in the rule of law and legal institutions is a critical dimension of the confidence-building process. However, this chapter suggests that many states – for reasons of expediency, and related to the rule of law short circuits that develop

---

[62] For example, the Lawyers Committee for Human Rights (now, Human Rights First); Human Rights Watch.

during the course of conflict and periods of repression – often fail to fully or adequately dismantle their emergency law arsenal in the aftermath. Rather, as in the United Kingdom, there was an evident unwillingness to let go of these extraordinary and wide-ranging powers. In the years following the Belfast Agreement (and prior to the events of 9/11) the state undertook a review of emergency legislation, which within its terms of reference sought to and ultimately proposed permanent counter-terrorist (emergency) legislation as part of the ordinary law of the state. The result was a permanent set of counter-terrorism laws with significant impact on civil liberties enshrined in the ordinary law of the United Kingdom and Northern Ireland.

The Council of Europe's supervision of the emergency law framework before, during and after the peace negotiations and their implementation has been limited. As outlined above, the number of derogation cases reaching the Court throughout the decades of conflict was relatively few in number. During this period, the response of the Court could be characterised as anaemic to the issues before it. Since the signing of the Belfast Agreement no derogation cases have been taken to the Court, though challenges remain in play concerning the ongoing use of non-jury courts based on the non-judicial certification of the Director of Public Prosecutions (DPP) as to terrorist link.[63] The reasons for this are varied. Case-load barriers for the Convention system, the availability of suitable cases (and the willingness of lawyers to bring them from the domestic jurisdiction) and the particular effects of the Human Rights Act on domestic proceedings in the United Kingdom all play a role. What is also clear is that in practice derogation provisions still stand, and have been utilised on an ongoing basis in the transitional setting. Empirical analysis by Campbell and Connolly focused on the deployment of the Diplock Court system and its attendant emergency detention processes since 1998, demonstrates that many of the patterns that were salient features of the emergency regime throughout the conflict are still in play in the post-conflict setting.[64] The use of extended detention remains a point of criticism and concern for human rights bodies, most recently articulated by the Northern Ireland

---

[63] See, for example, *In Re Brian and Paula Arthurs* (Judicial Review of the certification made by the DPP that the trial of the defendants be conducted without jury), Judgment delivered 30/6/10 (Queens Bench Division).

[64] C. Campbell and I. Connolly, 'A Model for the "War Against Terrorism"? Military Intervention and the 1970 Falls Curfew', *Journal of Law and Society* 30(3) (2003) 341–375.

Human Rights Commission.[65] If ameliorating rule of law deficits is a core goal of the transitional period to prevent a sliding back to violence or to support civil society and liberal political elements, then its neglect poses significant challenges to the integrity of the transitional process itself.

Conclusion

Derogation and transition have territorial overlap to a greater or lesser degree in multiple state settings. The core of this overlap pertains to those states resorting to derogation when armed conflict or transition to more liberal governance is being undertaken. Derogation makes an interesting site for assessing the Court's role and effectiveness in situations of transition because many of the states transitioning have had long-standing resort to derogation and some remain in derogation throughout the process of the transition itself. However, close analysis of the derogation jurisprudence reveals a cautious Court, one that maintains a right to review, but rarely has strongly reigned in the limitations placed on the exercise of rights by states in derogation. These precedents have direct translation to the transitional setting. In general, states understand that derogation jurisprudence broadly leans in their favour (accepting some differences based on the perceived depth of democratic compliance) and that even in transition such balances are not likely to have profound recalibration. Shifts in derogation practice during transition are far more likely to result from broader rule of law reforms and political confidence building rather than resulting from the Court's robust stance on derogation because a transition is in play.

In closing, this chapter argues that, in general, a vigorous derogation jurisprudence would be an augmentation of the Court's overall effectiveness. Recall that many of the most serious human rights violations take place in the context of derogation. Derogation is a fraught arena for rights protection and is thus a locale in which higher and not lower scrutiny should apply. This observation has particular resonance in situations of armed conflict. Here, the Court's unwillingness to systematically address

---

[65] Note that following recent dissident Republican activity a significant number of individuals were arrested and held under extended detention provisions of the Terrorism Act 2000. Some were minors or persons with chemical dependencies. The Human Rights Commission strongly protested the use of extended detention in a number of these cases. Their intervention and visits to sites of detention resulted in release. Based on interview with Monica McWilliams Chief Commissions NIHRC, 13 August 2010 (notes on file with author).

the reality of armed conflict on the territory of its contracting states points to both the ineffectiveness and the hollowness of the Convention's capacity to capture the complexity it operates within. While defensible on narrow legalistic grounds, I argue that ignoring humanitarian law and principles tends to produce a jurisprudence that has little real connection with the lived reality of victims on the ground, the causes of their harms and the scale of institutional reform (and political will) that may be required to change the ongoing conditions producing violent conflict. A transition from conflict to peace requires a recognition that a conflict exists in the first place. Without the conditions conducive to transition being set by key political and legal actors – including the European Court of Human Rights – transformations are likely to be limited in those states where violent conflict is a normalised reality.

Bibliography

Arthur, P., 'How "Transitions" Reshaped Human Rights: A Conceptual History of Transitional Justice', *Human Rights Quarterly* 31 (2009) 321.

Beckett, J., '*The Greek Case* before the European Human Rights Commission', *Human Rights* 1 (1970–1971) 91.

Bell, C., 'Interdisciplinarity and the State of the "Field" or "Non-Field"', *International Journal of Transitional Justice* 3 (2008) 5.

Campbell, C. and Connolly, I., 'A Model for the "War Against Terrorism"? Military Intervention and the 1970 Falls Curfew', *Journal of Law and Society* 30(3) (2003) 341–375.

Campbell, C. and Ní Aoláin, F., *The Paradox of Democratic Transition* (under review with Oxford University Press, 2012).

Council of Europe Parliamentary Assembly, Recommendation 1865 (2009) *The Protection of Rights in Emergency Situations: Reply from the Committee of Ministers*, adopted at the 1081st meeting of the Ministers' Deputies on 31 March 2010 (Doc. 12204; 16 April 2010). Available at: http://assembly.coe. int/Documents/WorkingDocs/Doc10/EDOC12204.pdf.

Council of Europe Parliamentary Assembly, *The Protection of Human Rights in Emergency Situations: Report of the Committee on Legal Affairs and Human Rights* (Doc. 11858; 9 April 2009), Rapporteur: Haibach, H. Available at: http://assembly.coe.int/Documents/WorkingDocs/Doc09/EDOC11858. pdf.

Feingold, C. S., 'The Doctrine of Margin of Appreciation and the European Convention on Human Rights', *Notre Dame Law Review* 53 (1977) 90.

Greer, S., *The European Convention on Human Rights: Achievements, Problems and Prospects* (Cambridge University Press, 2007).

Gross, O., 'The Normless and Exceptionless Exception: Carl Schmitt's Theory of Emergency Powers and the "Norm-Exception" Dichotomy', *Cardozo Law Review* 21 (2000) 1825.

'Once More unto the Breach: The Systemic Failure of Applying the European Convention on Human Rights to Entrenched Emergencies', *Yale Journal International Law* 23 (1998) 437.

Gross, O. and Ní Aoláin, F., *Law in Times of Crisis: Emergency Powers in Theory and Practice* (Cambridge University Press, 2006).

Hartman, J. F., 'Derogation from Human Rights Treaties in Public Emergencies', *Harvard International Law Journal* 22 (1981) 41.

Leach, P., 'The Chechen Conflict: Analysing the Oversight of the European Court of Human Rights', *EHRLR* 6 (2008) 732.

Lundy, P. and McGovern, M., 'The Role of Community in Participatory Criminal Justice', in McEvoy, K. and McGregor, L. (eds.) *Transitional Justice from Below: An Agenda for Research, Policy and Practice* (Oxford and Portland, Oregon: Hart, 2008) 99–120.

Ní Aoláin, F., *The Politics of Force: Conflict Management and State Violence in Northern Ireland* (Belfast: Blackstaff Press, 2000).

Ní Aoláin, F. and Campbell, C., 'The Paradox of Democratic Transition', *Human Rights Quarterly* 27 (2005) 172.

O'Donnell, D., 'States of Exception', *International Commission of Jurists Review* 21 (1978) 52–53.

Posner, E. and Vermeule, A., 'Transitional Justice as Ordinary Justice', *Harvard Law Review* 117 (2004) 761.

Sadurski, W., 'Partnering with Strasbourg: Constitutionalization of the European Court of Human Rights, the Accession of Central and East European States to the Council of Europe and the Idea of Pilot Judgments', *Human Rights Law Review* 9 (2009) 397.

Simpson, B. A., *Human Rights and the End of Empire: Britain and the Genesis of the European Convention* (Oxford University Press, 2004).

Skinner, Q., 'Meaning and Understanding in the History of Ideas', in Tully, J. (ed.) *Meaning and Content: Quentin Skinner and His Critics* (Cambridge University Press, 1988) 29–67.

Teitel, R., 'Transitional Justice Genealogy', *Harvard Human Rights Journal* 16 (2003) 69.

Verdirame, G., 'Human Rights in Wartime: A Framework for Analysis', *EHRLR* 6 (2008) 689.

Viaene, L. and Brems, E., 'Transitional Justice and Cultural Contexts Learning from the Universality Debate', *Netherlands Human Rights Quarterly* 28 (2010) 199.

3

Rights and victims, martyrs and memories: the European Court of Human Rights and political transition in Northern Ireland

KRIS BROWN

Introduction

In Loughgall in 1987, eight members of the IRA were killed by members of the British Army's elite unit the Special Air Service whilst attacking a police station (a civilian passer-by was also gunned down by the unit); in Gibraltar in 1988, three unarmed members of the IRA were also killed by the SAS. In 1995 and 2001 the European Court of Human Rights issued judgments which found against the British government in violating Article 2 of the Convention in the case of both sets of killings; the judgments were much welcomed within the Irish Republican constituency – and fed into a process of re-calibrating political legitimacy and deconstructing hierarchies of victimhood undertaken by Irish Republicans in post-conflict memory practices. To bring this process into clearer focus, it will be necessary to undertake a close reading of the text of the Court's judgments as the basis for examining their confluence with post-conflict memory practices and accommodation by Irish Republicans in a transitional setting. As an intensely political constituency, the latter sought to legitimise the memory of its struggle, undercut the legitimacy of its state opponents, and strip away the perceived 'demonisation' of the Republican dead and grieving relatives. Legal judgments and memory practices each played a part in this.

For Savelsberg and King,[1] more research, particularly in the form of case studies, is needed to unpick the interactions of legal narratives with

Kris Brown, Post-Doctoral Research Fellow, Transitional Justice Institute, Ulster University. Grateful thanks are due to Michael Hamilton and Fionnuala Ní Aoláin for their comments and suggestions in drafting this piece.

[1] J. Savelsberg and R. King, 'Law and Collective Memory', *Annual Review of Law and Social Science* 3 (2007) 189–211.

other social forms of memory. This study of politically charged collective memories, their blending with judicial decisions, and their development against a backdrop of a divided society in transition, provides a useful lens with which to examine those interactions.

In examining this confluence through the contexts of legitimacy and victimhood, it will be necessary to critically engage with manifest tensions in this process – particularly between simultaneous projections of victimhood and support for human rights on one hand, and martial valorisation of the dead combatants on the other. In showing how these tensions resolve themselves rather than establish political dissonance, this case study will contribute to an understanding of how the language and norms of human rights, and judgments by supra-state bodies, are understood by non-state combatants in transitional processes and worked into evolving narratives of both struggle and adherence to human rights. It is a process which partly follows the vernacular interpretation of human rights norms as examined by Merry; one in which there is both tension and exchange between differing political cultures.[2]

Law and the memory of conflict

Collective memory is a term first used by the sociologist Maurice Halbwachs and indicates communal or social remembrance established by means of collective acts of ritual, symbolic display and marking of space. It references something more than a simple assemblage of individual memory; instead it is a process which uses ritual commemoration and sites of memorialisation to pass information about a given event through society or along generations. Law can form part of this process. McEvoy crystallises the point: 'Resort to law itself may be viewed as an attempt to fix historical meaning, to shape how events are to be remembered. This "memorializing" capacity of law has been described as one of its most important functions.'[3] Legal documents and legal decisions may also serve as reservoirs of collective memories. Savelsberg and King describe it thus:

> Law and collective memory are reciprocally associated. Law steers collective memory, directly but selectively, as trials produce images of the past through the production and presentation of evidence in ritual practices

[2] S. E. Merry, 'Transnational Human Rights and Local Activism: Mapping the Middle', *American Anthropologist* 108(1) (2006) 38–51.
[3] K. McEvoy, 'Law, Struggle, and Political Transformation in Northern Ireland', *Journal of Law and Society* 27 (2000) 562.

and public discourse … Simultaneously, collective memory is preserved
and activated by carrier groups to inform lawmaking and law enforcement; and memories of past atrocities serve as analogical devices that,
under certain conditions, influence law.[4]

Law forms an 'especially powerful institution for the creation of collective memory' because it involves 'highly effective rituals' which in a
Durkheimian sense elevate the authority of legal deliberations and decisions. They not only place narratives firmly in public discourse, but provide
a sacralising sheen. The ritual sacralising process may run thus – evidence
has been rigorously gathered, sworn statements made, documents placed
on record and judgment openly given after learned deliberation. There is
an assumption that law's emphasis in building a narrative is on recording
a definitive account of events as they occurred.[5] Accuracy and objectiv-
ity underlie this goal and thus become jealously sought for the sheen of
authenticity they may bring to the construction of collective memory.

Memory and Irish Republicanism

Irish Republicanism, whether in its political form of Sinn Féin, or its military wing, the Irish Republican Army, was engaged from 1970 in fighting
by both ballot box and 'armed struggle' to force a British withdrawal from
the six north-eastern counties of Ireland, Northern Ireland, and secure
their unification with the rest of the island. The conflict, euphemistically
known as the 'Troubles', resulted in more than 3,500 dead; the Provisional
IRA, it is calculated, is responsible for almost 1,800 of these fatalities.[6] The
IRA, together with its political expression Sinn Féin, themselves made
up 364 of the casualties of this low intensity conflict. Republicans were
fastidious in commemorating their dead throughout the conflict, with
memorial parades and militarised, politicised funerals; similarly, a material culture of political memory typically featuring wall murals and monuments is peppered across the urban and rural landscape of Republican
areas.[7] The mourning of friends, relations and comrades plays a large

---

[4] Savelsberg and King, 'Law and Collective Memory', 189.
[5] P. Brooks and P. D. Gerwitz, *Law's Stories: Narrative and Rhetoric in the Law* (New Haven: Yale University Press, 1996).
[6] D. McKittrick, *Lost Lives: The Stories of the Men, Women, and Children who Died as a Result of the Northern Ireland Troubles* (Edinburgh: Mainstream, 1999) 1534.
[7] K. Brown and E. Vigianni, 'Performing Provisionalism – Republican Commemorative Practice as Political Performance', in L. Fitzpatrick (ed.) *Performing Violence in Contemporary Ireland* (Dublin: Carysfort Press, 2009).

part in Republican memory practice, but these expressions of a collective memory have a potent political utility and symbolism. Despite several
violent breaches of its ceasefire, modern mainstream Irish Republicanism
has been a willing and capable participant in the Northern Ireland peace
process. This has paid electoral dividends as the adoption of a purely political path has led to Sinn Féin's dominance within Irish nationalist politics
in Northern Ireland. But this political project also entailed the hollowing
out of more traditionalist forms of Republican ideology and rhetoric, and
the gradual dissolution of the military capability of its armed wing. This
brought with it attendant pressures. There was the possibility that the
re-calibration of Republican ideology and political activity would mean a
de-legitimisation of its years of 'armed struggle'. This, in turn, could further buttress the creation of victim hierarchies within the out-workings of
the political process. The 'meta conflict', the conflict about the meaning of
the conflict, is an overhanging presence through the peace process[8] and,
as Henry Patterson puts it, '[t]he "war" has in part, been transferred into
a clash of conflicting narratives of who was to blame for the Troubles and,
in particular, for its thousands of victims'.[9]

   Questions of legitimacy and the status of victims were obvious zones of
contestation. Memory practices, and law, would serve as instruments of
challenge and counter-challenge.

Commemoration: spotlighting state injustice and shielding from criminalisation

Republicans in a very specific manner have drawn on history, as water
is drawn from a well in order to douse criticism of their political project
from contemporary opponents.

   Republicans interpreted attacks on them as a part of the new phase of
the struggle, 'the battle of ideas and the battle for truth about the armed
conflict' and memorialisation provided a useful platform to deflect these
attacks and echo one's own historical interpretation. At the commemoration for hunger striker Kieran Doherty, Sinn Féin representative

---

[8] C. Campbell, F. Ní Aoláin and C. Harvey, 'The Frontiers of Legal Analysis: Reframing the
   Transition in Northern Ireland', *The Modern Law Review* 66(3) (2003) and C. Bell, *On the
   Law of Peace: Peace Agreements and the Lex Pacificatoria* (Oxford University Press, 2008)
   13, 201, 256.
[9] H. Patterson, 'The Republican Movement and the Legacy of the Troubles', in I. Honohan
   (ed.) *Republicanism in Ireland: Confronting Theories and Traditions* (Manchester
   University Press, 2009) 149.

Caoimhghin O Caelian wove a typical narrative of state criminality and Republican assertion of rights:

> The opponents of Sinn Féin are attempting to place the responsibility for 25 years of conflict on the shoulders of Irish Republicans. They do so in an effort to thwart the growth of Sinn Féin. But the tide of history is running against them. They cannot conceal the responsibility of the British government … Basic demands for civil rights were met with violence. Homes, communities and lives were wrecked by the British state. Was it therefore a criminal conspiracy when young people took up arms to resist all this? Any such claim is a lie – the very lie that Kieran Doherty exposed by his heroic sacrifice.[10]

As Republicanism seeks to expand electorally north and south, underlining the legitimacy of the now historic armed struggle is an important goal. Memorialisation and commemoration play a key role in this, providing a platform to expound the Republican view and counter any attempts to portray Republicanism as a violent and dysfunctional aberration; links with historic struggles, sanctified by the passage of time, and the continually stressed sacrifice of the fallen, provide an emotive appeal against charges of criminality.

A plethora of Republican memory sites have been created since the ceasefire of 1994,[11] and memorial sites have served as public stages for the performance of politics, acting as focal points in time and space around which group members gather together to convey a common sense of social identification and belonging

War memorialisation and commemoration has often formed an instrumental, *post facto* expression for the legitimisation of force, as an expression of the national will, patriotic feeling and the moral nature of a given community's struggle.[12] Even if collective remembrance cannot ensure a war is viewed as a *just* war, it at the very least elevates the status of those who fought in it. Soldiers are commemorated, whilst criminals are not. Legitimising narratives thus have real currency, especially if bolstered by appeals to law, or the illegality of enemy action.

---

[10] Author unknown, 'Establishment Politicians Slammed at Cavan Commemoration', *An Phoblacht/Republican News* (Belfast: 1 September 2005).

[11] For information on the growth of memorialisation in Belfast in recent years see Elisabetta Viggiani's database 'Public Forms of Memorialisation to the Victims of the Northern Irish "Troubles" in the City of Belfast' at http://cain.ulst.ac.uk/viggiani/introduction.htm.

[12] B. Anderson, *Imagined Communities: Reflections on the Origins and Spread of Nationalism* (London: Verso, 1983) 17–18.

One of the largest categories of content within the pages of the movement's newspaper *An Phoblacht/Republican News* is that of commemoration;[13] some see in the commemorative diligence of Republicanism a kind of civil religious aspect, in which commemorative piety plays an important part in explaining the movement's durability.[14]

But it can have a strongly political function. Metress and Metress,[15] in their study of Republican funerary practice, underline its usefulness as part of a psychological battle, noting how it was used to increase the social bonds between Irish Republicanism and the wider Nationalist community, and was a zone of political (and physical) conflict between Republicans and the security forces of the state. Ritual commemoration could be another front in the 'war'. There is more current evidence for this viewpoint too. Martin McGuinness has written of 'the importance of remembering and periodically renewing the memory process as a way of reaffirming, acknowledging and making a valuable contribution to advancing the Republican cause'.[16] This reveals crucial strands within the Republican commemorative calendar.

As Kertzer has argued, anti-state groups may find the public ritual displays even more useful than state elites might. In his study, he delineates how ritual commemorative displays may provide a basis for communication and social bonding, can aid the de-legitimising of the power relations of the status quo, can help foster emotive resistance, and can even allow movement leaderships to replenish or refashion themselves.[17] Rather than appearing epiphenomenal and backwards facing, collective memory practices can provide instruments with which to reinforce political communities.

Legitimacy in the new dispensation: the role of memory

The 1998 Belfast Agreement created new challenges for Republicanism; the new political dispensation brought with it a devolved Assembly,

[13] R. G. Picard, 'How Violence is Justified: Sinn Féin's An Phoblacht', *Journal of Communication* 41(4) (1991) 98.

[14] M. O'Doherty, *The Trouble with Guns: Republican Strategy and the Provisional IRA* (Belfast: Blackstaff Press, 1998) 22.

[15] S. Metress and E. Metress, 'The Communal Significance of the Irish Republican Army Funeral Ritual', Unpublished paper (1993). Accessed in Northern Ireland Political Collection, Linen Hall Library.

[16] M. McGuinness, 'Introduction', in *Unforgotten Sacrifice – A Tribute to Fallen Comrades* (Belfast: Twinbrook and Poleglass Commemoration Committee, 1999) 2.

[17] D. I. Kertzer, *Ritual, Politics, and Power* (New Haven: Yale University Press, 1988) 169–172.

traditionally a partitionist anathema to Sinn Féin; it also brought recognition of the need to acknowledge the pain of victims of the conflict.[18] This latter proposition was a potential Achilles heel for Provisional Republicans, to be exploited by political opponents, given that they had killed the single largest number of people in the conflict, whilst they had also benefited from prison releases in the wake of the Agreement. Commemoration too can play a role in redefining narratives of conflict. Whilst taking a seat in a partitionist Assembly was once derided as heresy, it could now be redefined as a means of advancing the conflict, even of symbolic re-occupation. Accordingly, Sinn Féin have instituted commemorative ceremonies in the devolved Northern Ireland legislature itself.

However, the question of recognising the suffering of victims as a necessary means of healing and reconciliation, and the need to defend the historic legitimacy of armed struggle, was a thorny one. An important consideration for Republicans was the need to avoid a concept of a hierarchy of victims, in which paramilitaries might appear at the bottom of the metaphorical casualty list, so de-legitimising their role in the preceding conflict. Armed struggle had to continue to be presented as a strategy whose time had passed, but which had been historically necessary; it could not be allowed to be presented as a 'dirty, squalid terrorist war' as David Trimble had said the day after the signing of the Belfast Agreement.[19] Speeches by Sinn Féin representatives and draft resolutions proposed by grassroots at *ard fheisanna* (party conferences) had noted the need to recognise that the strong position republicans now enjoyed had been because of the sacrifice of volunteers.[20] Republicans had to be seen as taking their rightful place in the new dispensation but could not countenance any criminalisation of the last three decades of struggle. Republican ex-prisoner groups have been concerned that the stigma of criminalisation and the construction of a hierarchy of victims had been wielded as a club by anti-agreement unionism to attack the early release programme, and to obfuscate the circumstances that drove people to engage in armed activity.[21]

---

[18] For the Belfast Agreement see www.nio.gov.uk/agreement.pdf (accessed June 2010).
[19] See BBC News, 'Union Stonger-Trimble', http://news.bbc.co.uk/1/hi/events/northern_ireland/latest_news/770Two6.stm.
[20] Author unknown, 'Dublin Volunteer Remembered', *An Phoblacht/Republican News* (Belfast: 21 July 2005) and Sinn Féin, *Ard Fheis '06 Clár* (Dublin: Sinn Féin, 2006) 8, Resolution 30.
[21] See Republican ex-prisoner umbrella group *Coiste na n-Iarchimí*-web article www.coiste.ie/articles/ritchie/equality.htm.

Taking their place in this dispensation therefore involved asserting their claim to have also been victims of the conflict, on the same plane as everyone else. Commemorations served as high-profile platforms for this assertion of the equality of suffering, and the point was underlined by the Republican leadership at events such as the *Tírghrá* commemorative dinner for the families of dead volunteers,[22] and most forcefully in Gerry Adams' speech at the re-burial of Tom Williams:

> If there is truly to be a healing process, then there has to be an understanding of the equivalence of grief. To pretend, as elements of the media and the political establishment does, that republican Volunteers do not have families, do not have loved ones, have not got feelings, is part of the open wound that has yet to be healed as part of any conflict resolution process.[23]

Commemoration and remembrance were a means to ensure that equal victimhood could be continually stressed lest an incremental, historical de-legitimisation be allowed to isolate or embarrass Republicans. Republicans needed to ensure their equal place in the new dispensation; if the memory of the dead were granted no legitimacy in this dispensation, then opponents could pick at the seams of a narrative of Republican struggle progressing, with ideological continuity, from military campaign through to solely political means. And more bluntly, if the Republican dead could not be assured equality, what of the Republican living?

The European Court and counter-state narrative

In the years prior to the peace process, the conflict had been marked by a decided change in gear. During the late 1980s, the conflict between Irish Republicanism and the British state had entered into a new phase, one of increased counterinsurgency by the state[24] and the intensification and broadening of armed activity by the IRA.[25] Two of the most high-profile encounters between the IRA and the British state involved the 'set piece' killings of IRA activists in Loughgall in 1987 and Gibraltar in 1988. When an armed active service unit of the IRA attacked a small police station in

---

[22] Author unknown, 'Sinn Féin Honours IRA Dead at Dublin Event', *Irish Times* (Dublin: 15 April 2002) 6, and A. McIntyre, 'Last Supper', *The Blanket* online magazine, 21 April 2002, viewable at www.phoblacht.net/lastsupper.html.

[23] Author unknown, '50,000 Honour Williams', *An Phoblacht/Republican News* (Belfast: 27 January 2000).

[24] F. Ní Aoláin, *The Politics of Force: Conflict Management and State Violence in Northern Ireland* (Belfast: Blackstaff Press, 2000) 58–64.

[25] E. Moloney, *A Secret History of the IRA* (New York: W. W. Norton, 2003).

the village of Loughgall in County Armagh, they were ambushed by the elite regiment the SAS, who had received intelligence and were lying in wait. The IRA unit detonated a bomb damaging the police station, and fired off dozens of rounds, but they were completely outgunned by the waiting security forces, and all members of the unit were killed. Two civilians were also shot by the security forces, who had mistaken them as paramilitaries. One died, the other was badly injured.[26] The killings in Gibraltar of three members of an IRA active service unit, Daniel McCann, Máiread Farrell and Sean Savage, also involved an intelligence operation by the British state. The three were planning a bomb attack on Gibraltar, but had been under intense surveillance for a period of time before they entered the British overseas territory. The three were shot dead by under-cover SAS soldiers, who believed that the suspects were about to detonate their bomb. All three were unarmed, and later investigation showed that the bomb had not yet been planted, and that the three were still engaging in planning and reconnaissance.

Both cases were intensely controversial. Accusations that these oper-ations amounted to a policy of 'shoot to kill', of extrajudicial killing, were levelled at the British government. Republicans argued that these actions exposed the undemocratic and hypocritical nature of British counter-insurgency – these were not operations in which arrest was an option, nor were they about defending the rule of law. Instead they saw them as proof of a policy of assassination exemplifying a de facto dirty war. For the British, the shootings represented a robust, but lawful policy of coun-ter-terrorism, in which ruthless criminals had been thwarted in their attempts to perpetrate mass killings. But against the inevitable backdrop of political contestation, questions continued to circulate about the degree of force used and the investigation of the killings. The families of the dead sought legal redress, and both the Loughgall and Gibraltar killings were eventually considered by the European Court of Human Rights, in 2001 and 1995 respectively. In each case the Court found a breach of Article 2 by the United Kingdom.

The Gibraltar case, *McCann* v. *United Kingdom*,[27] had a particular impact on the developing jurisprudence of the Court. Before *McCann*, the Court had developed virtually no jurisprudence relating to the right to life, and complaints submitted tended to be filtered out by the Commission

---

[26] Those killed were Patrick Kelly, Patrick McKearney, Declan Arthurs, Seamus Donnelly, Eugene Kelly, Michael Gormley, Gerard O'Callaghan, James Lynagh and the civilian Antony Hughes.

[27] ECtHR, *McCann* v. *United Kingdom*, 27 September 1995 (Appl. no. 18984/91).

before reaching the Court itself.[28] The Court's decision in *McCann* significantly broadened understanding of obligations under Article 2, and underlined a distinct procedural component to the right to life. Its ruling held that states must plan, organise and supervise law enforcement operations in a manner which would respect the right to life of those who are the subjects of law enforcement activity. The window of legal scrutiny was thus greatly widened. If lethal force was used, the moment of pulling the trigger was no longer the only frame of legal review. The Court decided that focusing on the actions in the seconds leading up to the killings was too narrow an approach; instead 'all the surrounding circumstances including such matters as the planning and control of the actions under examination' would be subject to scrutiny.[29] This telescoping backwards of the period of scrutiny rested on a particularly strong re-affirmation of Article 2 protections.

As the Commission has pointed out, the text of Article 2, read as a whole, demonstrates that paragraph 2 does not primarily define instances where it is permitted intentionally to kill an individual, but describes the situations where it is permitted to 'use force' which may result, as an unintended outcome, in the deprivation of life. The use of force, however, must be no more than 'absolutely necessary'. In this respect the use of the term 'absolutely necessary' in Article 2(2) indicates that a stricter and more compelling test of necessity must be employed from that normally applicable when determining whether State action is 'necessary in a democratic society' under paragraph 2 of Articles 8 to 11 of the Convention. In particular, the force used must be strictly proportionate to the achievement of the aims set out in sub-paragraphs 2 (a), (b) and (c) of Article 2.[30]

The Court underscored that given the importance of the right to life in a functioning democracy, it was compelled to 'subject deprivations of life to the most careful scrutiny'.[31] Under this more exacting benchmark of review, and within a much widened window of procedural reference, the Court decided that the United Kingdom's use of force against the three IRA members had breached Article 2, paragraph 2. The Court spotlighted three errors of procedure in the British state's command and control of the law enforcement operation. In the first instance, the Court criticised the security forces' decision not to arrest the suspects as they

---

[28] C. K. Connolly, 'Seeking the Final Court of Justice: The European Court of Human Rights and Accountability for State Violence in Northern Ireland', *San Diego International Law Journal* 9(1) (2007/2008) 93.

[29] *McCann*, para. 150.   [30] *Ibid.*, para. 149.   [31] *Ibid.*, para. 150.

entered Gibraltar, but rather to let them proceed in their activity.[32] The Court also highlighted the security forces had been operating from a series of 'working hypotheses' and assessments which failed to take into consideration 'alternative possibilities' and a 'margin of error'.[33] Instead, assumptions were made, which were on at least one occasion based on 'cursory' examination. The Court decided that this was inappropriate given the deployment of armed officers, and that '[a]gainst this background, the authorities were bound by their obligation to respect the right to life of the suspects to exercise the greatest of care in evaluating the information at their disposal'.[34] The final procedural error highlighted by the Court related to the decision to deploy the SAS, a military force with a markedly different trained response to potential threats, one which it suggested was incompatible with the duties of law enforcement in a liberal democracy:

> Their reflex action in this vital respect lacks the degree of caution in the use of firearms to be expected from law enforcement personnel in a democratic society, even when dealing with dangerous terrorist suspects, and stands in marked contrast to the standard of care reflected in the instructions in the use of firearms by the police which had been drawn to their attention and which emphasised the legal responsibilities of the individual officer in the light of conditions prevailing at the moment of engagement.[35]

Again highlighting the command and control procedural aspect of their review, the Court did not hold that the individual servicemen had violated any right to life, but rather that their military training, combined with the 'worst case' intelligence that they had received, almost inevitably led to the fatal shootings.[36] A rough, but useful, approximation might be to say that at the moment of firing, they were considered almost as stimulus response automata. For the Court, the critical points of review stretched back through the timeline and thus, perhaps, up the chain of command (a point not lost on Irish Republicans).

The Loughgall shootings also formed an important part of developing Article 2 jurisprudence, one which related to procedures of investigation following the use of lethal force by the state. The Loughgall case, *Kelly and others* v. *United Kingdom*,[37] was joined by the Court to several other similar cases resulting from disputed killings in Northern Ireland, and

---

[32] *Ibid.*, para. 203.   [33] *Ibid.*, paras. 209–211.   [34] *Ibid.*, para. 211.
[35] *Ibid.*, para. 212.   [36] *Ibid.*, paras. 210–212, 213.
[37] ECtHR, *Kelly and others* v. *United Kingdom*, 4 May 2001 (Appl. no. 30054/96).

consequently the proceedings in the case would be conducted simultaneously with those in the cases of *Jordan* v. *United Kingdom*, *McKerr* v. *United Kingdom* and *Shanaghan* v. *United Kingdom*.[38] Each of the cases underscored broadly similar problems and failings in relation to killings by the state; and in each case the Court decided that the right to life had been breached by the failure of the state to properly investigate the circumstances of the killing, which was held to be an important procedure with which to protect against arbitrary state killing.[39] Once again emphasising that Article 2 is a fundamental right from which other rights flow, the Court stated that it 'enshrines one of the basic values of the democratic societies making up the Council of Europe'. Therefore the circumstances in which state killing might 'be justified must therefore be strictly construed'[40] and subject to 'some form of effective official investigation';[41] indeed, when deaths were solely in the control of the state 'the burden of proof may be regarded as resting on the authorities to provide a satisfactory and convincing explanation'.[42]

The *Kelly* judgment also criticised the ability of investigative procedures in Northern Ireland to piece together a credible, reliable narrative in the wake of the killings. The judgment was critical of the Coroner's inability to compel attendance by those responsible for the killings, and of the fact that proceedings did not convene promptly. The judges also highlighted that the procedure did not make allowance for any verdict or findings which could feed into a prosecution in respect of any criminal offence. Indeed the Northern Ireland inquest procedure 'could play no effective role in the identification or prosecution of any criminal offences which may have occurred and, in that respect, falls short of the requirements of Article 2'.[43] The judgment also noted the lack of independence of investigating police officers from the security forces involved in the shootings, and was critical of the non-disclosure of witness statements prior to inquest, which prejudiced the families' ability to participate and led to a stopstart process.[44]

This was an important point. As Ní Aoláin asserts, the Court laid 'weighty emphasis on the involvement of the next-of-kin' in the investigative process.[45] In the Court's view:

---

[38] ECtHR, *Jordan* v. *the United Kingdom*, 4 May 2001 (Appl. no. 24746/94) and ECtHR, *McKerr* v. *the United Kingdom*, 4 May 2001 (Appl. no. 28883/95) and ECtHR, *Shanaghan* v. *the United Kingdom*, 4 May 2001 (Appl. no. 37715/97).

[39] *Kelly*, para. 94.   [40] *Ibid.*, paras. 91–92.

[41] *Ibid.*, para. 94.   [42] *Ibid.*, para. 92.

[43] *Ibid.*, para. 124.   [44] *Ibid.*, para. 136.

[45] F. Ní Aoláin, 'Truth Telling, Accountability and the Right to Life in Northern Ireland', *European Human Rights Law Review* 5 (2002) 585.

The inability of the families to have access to witness statements before the appearance of the witness must be regarded as having placed them at a disadvantage in terms of preparation and ability to participate in questioning. This contrasts strikingly with the position of the RUC and army (Ministry of Defence) who had the resources to provide for legal representation and had access to information about the incident from their own records and personnel. The Court considers that the right of the family of the deceased whose death is under investigation to participate in the proceedings requires that the procedures adopted ensure the requisite protection of their interests, which may be in direct conflict with those of the police or security forces implicated in the events. The Court is not persuaded that the interests of the applicants as next-of-kin were fairly or adequately protected in this respect.[46]

These decisions of the Court had a great impact on the expansion of the jurisprudence in relation to Article 2, and they also influenced Republican memory practices and narratives in the post-violence transitional setting. The decisions helped feed into a 'meta conflict' within the contested areas of legitimacy and victimhood. Republicans wished to bolster legitimacy surrounding their own actions, delegitimise their British opponents, and resist the creation of hierarchies of victimhood which would push their dead into the outer darkness of criminality. The ways in which the Court's decisions aided Republican memory practice can be conceptualised in several ways. First, they provided some authentication of the *Mis-Rule of Law*. *McCann* and *Kelly* (and the conjoined judgments of *Jordan et al.*) allowed the high-profile formation of a narrative that the United Kingdom had veered from the highest standards of a democratic state, either by allowing a disproportionate use of force or by failing to investigate multiple killings adequately. Second, the Court's decisions facilitated a *Public Widening of Narrative*, the better to critique British security policy. *McCann* projected the state's responsibility for protecting the right to life back from the feverish moments of gunplay, and deeper into the timeline of tactical command and control, which in itself would allow for closer probing into the state's security policy itself. Similarly, *Kelly* (and *Jordan et al.*) would allow this narrative extension to be strengthened by calls for proper investigation into killings. The third concept, of *Equality of Victimhood*, has been part buttressed by the Court's assertion that the deceased's status as a member of an illegal organisation does not have a bearing on their rights under Article 2. As Ní Aoláin notes:

---

[46] *Kelly*, para. 128.

The Court underscored the significance of the right to life in a democratic society. The emphasis on the role of the right in the democratic order, also signalled an equality approach, whereby the status of the victims, in this case as terrorists, was not a means to lessen the value of the right to them per se.[47]

This is important as, during the conflict, a hierarchical process appeared to have been in-built, and it could seem 'that suspicion or actual membership of a proscribed organisation in Northern Ireland weaken[ed] the right to life of the suspected'.[48] Similarly, the emphasis the Court put on the rights and fair treatment of the families, also ensured that any projection of the IRA dead purely as violent ciphers, or of the families as a lower tier of grieving victim, could also be better resisted.

Finally, the nature of the Court's remit itself provided a particular strength in the building of Republican narrative – aiding a *Critical Examination of State Policy*. Savelsberg and King[49] have noted the often individualising effects of legal action in dealing with issues of politicised violence – legal processes such as trials tended to target individuals, but left groupings, structures or social processes free from the closest examination. By providing a forum in which a collective entity might be judged, and allowing for critical, authoritative examination of its procedures, any default defence by the state that it was individual action or inaction which resulted in killings could be undercut.

'Challenged before the world': law, legitimacy, victimhood and the court

McEvoy, in a conceptually strong piece of research,[50] has demarcated several phases in the Irish Republican use of law. Initially taken up as an opportunistic means of launching 'symbolic' attacks, it soon came to be used as a means of scoring material victories too, as the politicisation of the Republican movement progressed. Legal challenge, particularly in the higher courts and supra-national bodies, came to be seen as a means to embarrass and expose British policy, to internationalise the conflict and break out of a policy of encapsulation that sought to contain the Irish question within the parameters of state policy. The European Court of Human Rights in particular was a most effective forum in which Republicans

---

[47] Ní Aoláin, 'Truth Telling', 576.   [48] Ní Aoláin, *Politics of Force*, 64.
[49] Savelsberg and King, 'Law and Collective Memory', 194.
[50] K. McEvoy, 'Law, Struggle, and Political Transformation in Northern Ireland'.

'raised the political stakes' and could induce 'howls of outrage' from British representatives, whilst offering their own competing narratives.[51]

Crucially, for McEvoy, this process was not a purely instrumental one. As Irish Republicans used the law and engaged with the state in a variety of non-violent ways, the legal 'tactic' developed its own constitutive properties – legal activity was shaping Republican strategy and outlook; using the courts was softening edges and broadening political horizons. Appealing to 'external objective sources' such as the European Court and human rights organisations, meant that political modification (and the pursuance of a rights agenda) came more and more to be seen as a 'defining characteristic' of the Republican approach.[52] It would be putting too much weight on the utility of the legal approach to say that the availability of a supra-national forum was a decisive reason to shift away from the use of political violence, but within the developing peace process, it added incremental momentum to a political strategy which sought other avenues of challenging the state and legitimising its own narrative. As McEvoy has argued this legal process was not simply a convenient stick with which to thrash the state, but was also part of a process of developing engagement, that shifted political conflict into other institutional arenas. Continuing political violence might simply be a distraction or a hindrance; and if terrorism had served in part as armed propaganda, this role might be superseded by the media and moral value of victories in distinguished settings such as the Court.

Republican utilisation of the European Court of Human Rights judgment in the case of *McCann* focused on de-legitimising British state policy (and thus legitimising Republican response), by underlining the *Mis-Rule of Law* and *Publicly Widening the Narrative*. British policy was to be presented as inimical to liberal democratic law, and its hidden ideological positions spotlighted in terms of a Republican analysis. In these terms, legal means would be used to tear away the veil of legal niceties that Britain had constructed for itself, and reveal armed conflict. Or to put it in Republican terms, that Britain was waging war in, and on, Ireland. This had real value in struggles over legitimacy.

Following the *McCann* verdict, Irish Republican reportage took great pleasure in the perceived international exposure of Britain's position:

> Now the government which boasts of its adherence to the 'rule of law' is dismissing the European Court judgment. But the ruling stands and not since the court's judgment on torture in internment camps in the

---

[51] *Ibid.*, 557–558.   [52] *Ibid.*, 568.

Six Counties in the 70s has Britain been so exposed internationally. The Gibraltar killings were just three of nearly four hundred carried out by British forces in their Irish war. Only a handful of those forces have ever been prosecuted, let alone convicted. Now the entire military and legal apparatus which has been used to fight Britain's war has been challenged before the world.[53]

By showing that Britain was fighting a dirty war, Republicans would show that it was a *real* war, not a problem of a state invoking the law against criminality.

It would appear that those who claim to uphold the law see themselves as above the law. In reality, the British have never operated according to legal norms in Ireland. They have fought a war and where necessary used the law as a means of war. British courts have repeatedly supported their right to operate a shoot to kill policy in their dirty war in Ireland. Now when the law catches up with them, they will simply ignore it.[54]

The *McCann* ruling energised further campaigns; as Republican writing gleefully acknowledged, 'the redundancy of British "justice" has been exposed on the international stage' and so the verdict would 'provide an added impetus to all those campaigning around the many other cases of disputed killings which have taken place during the past 20 years'.[55] Several notable campaigners, who would take their cases to the Court in years to come, underlined the utility of the supra-national verdict in the Republican press. Mairéad Kelly felt that the verdict would strengthen her case regarding the Loughgall shootings, whilst Hugh Jordan, father of IRA member Pearse Jordan shot dead by police in 1992, argued that the 'only way to ensure justice was through the channels of the European Court'.[56]

British reaction: a further enticement?

British government reaction to the Gibraltar ruling was practically incandescent and felt that the Court's decision directly challenged its own narrative of a state engaged in the lawful protection of its citizens against an armed terrorist conspiracy. Downing Street felt that the judgment

---

[53] Author unknown, 'Justice at Last – Britain Guilty Over Gibraltar', *An Phoblacht/ Republican News* (Belfast: 28 September 1995).

[54] Author unknown, 'Editorial', *An Phoblacht/Republican News* (Belfast: 28 September 1995).

[55] Author unknown, 'Gibraltar Verdict Vindicates Other Relatives', *An Phoblacht/ Republican News* (Belfast: 5 October 1995).

[56] *Ibid.*

overturning verdicts favourable to Britain in lower courts, 'defied common sense' and was 'incomprehensible' – a reaction which was echoed by ministerial comment emerging from the Northern Ireland Office. But the principal critique was made by Michael Heseltine, the deputy Prime Minister, who felt that the judgment would not impact on British counter-terrorist policy in any shape or form:

> We shall do absolutely nothing at all. We will pursue our right to fight terrorism, to protect innocent people wherever we have jurisdiction. We will not be swayed or deterred in any way by this ludicrous decision. If we were faced with similar circumstances as those in Gibraltar, I have not the slightest doubt that the same decisions would be taken.[57]

This bullish defence precipitated a series of sniping exchanges with the British Labour Party then in opposition, in which Heseltine accused the Labour response of supporting the judgment as an 'encouragement to the terrorist mentality' that was 'part of a process that has seen a whole range of people sympathetic to the terrorists, coming out with statements, encouraging full enquiries'.[58] There was however a significant amount of bluster around the British government position, which whilst hinting that Britain would consider withdrawing recognition of the European Convention on Human Rights, and would stonewall on paying the Gibraltar families' costs, in fact quietly paid the £40,000 to the relatives of the three IRA members within the three-month deadline.[59]

Irish Republicanism exhibited a political *schadenfreude* at the shrill British response and Republican reportage spotlighted the emotionalism of the British tabloids' anger and ministerial discomfiture.[60] The supranational verdict had demonstrated an immense symbolic value on the political stage, and more than this had shown that legal challenges could be an effective picador's blade with which to jab at the flesh of British security policy. In the wake of the Gibraltar ruling Barry McIlduff, the Sinn Féin legal affairs spokesperson, said that his party would now press for further investigations into disputed security force killings in Northern Ireland.[61]

---

[57] Author unknown, 'Outrage over Death on the Rock Verdict by Euro Court', *The Times* (London: 28 September 1995).

[58] *Ibid.*

[59] Author unknown, '40,000 Paid to Death on Rock Families', *The Times* (London: 27 December 1995).

[60] Author unknown, 'Hard Tabloid to Swallow', *An Phoblacht/Republican News* (Belfast: 5 October 1995).

[61] Author unknown, 'Partisan Reaction from Northern Politicians', *Irish Times* (Dublin: 28 September 1995).

The verdict spotlighted a point of opportunity for Republicans to press home their own viewpoint on the legitimacy of their political resistance, by challenging the legitimacy of state actions.

Memory, violence and legitimacy

The legitimacy of those resisting the state is underlined by one of the principal 'carrier groups' of the memory of Republican opposition – the families of those Republicans killed. As one of the relatives of those killed at Loughgall puts it:

> Yes, within our community there was an understanding of the reasons behind the actions people took. People felt they were fighting a just war, were fighting against an oppressive state, and I think that the story needs to be told in that context, so that people can understand that it was not some deviant criminal act.[62]

Indeed for those socialised within particular areas, the conduct of the dead IRA men would have been exemplary:

> For a lot of people within the communities we come from, what our loved ones were doing that night would be seen as legitimate activity. The activities of the IRA would have been supported and they would have been seen as people to be looked up to within the community.[63]

In these terms there is thus a need to put the story behind their deaths in a wider political context, that reveals the abuse of law. As the brother of one of those killed in Gibraltar states:

> But what really appals is that the British continue to live the lie that they are honest brokers in the conflict. They have no right to claim the moral high ground and it is only by establishing the truth can this situation be rectified. So the conflict has to be examined in the public forum in its broader historical context: the whys and the wherefores surrounding the creation and maintenance of the corrupt northern statelet.[64]

The Loughgall relatives echo this call for a deepening of the narrative. They counterpose a 'context determined by the British' with the 'real political context and the real underlying issues' which 'rarely get talked about'.

[62] Loughgall Truth and Justice Campaign, *The Unequal Victims* (Newtownabbey, County Antrim: Island Publications, 2001) 8.
[63] *Ibid.*
[64] B. Rolston, *Unfinished Business: State Killings and the Quest for Truth* (Belfast: Beyond The Pale, 2000) 174.

That context, in part facilitated by the *Public Widening of the Narrative* flowing from the activity of the Court, chimes directly with the notion of the *Mis-Rule of Law*:

> [T]hat context corrupted whatever normal activities a police force would usually have, the British system was corrupted, their legal system was corrupted completely, so many institutions in society became subject to the war effort against the IRA and the only way out of that, the only way to undo the effects of that corruption, is first of all admit that certain things happened as part of this war effort. For example with regard to telling the truth about the extrajudicial killings that happened in Loughgall, if they were to put their hands up and say: look we killed these people, because this was part of a war effort and we saw it as a necessary evil.[65]

By showing the underhand side to the conflict, and pulling aside some of the legal defences of the state, agents of memory such as activists and family members hope to expose the 'war like' aspects of the conflict, and thus legitimise the actions of those killed. Explaining and thus helping legitimise the IRA members' motivation entails showing a broader, more complex context. By stretching back the timeline of responsibility, and noting the flawed investigational procedures of the state, the decisions of the Court can assist the memory practices of Republicanism by indicating that substantial sections of the conflict narrative have not been fully addressed. Mairéad Kelly, sister of one of those killed at Loughgall, argued that the decision in the four conjoined cases of which *Kelly* was a part, were 'not just about these four incidents'; rather it amounted to the first chippings at an unexcavated narrative: 'Over 360 people have been killed by British Crown forces. 74 of them children and this opens the way for their families to take a similar course of action.'[66] For Hugh Jordan, the father of an IRA member shot in disputed circumstances in 1992, the Court's decision reversed the moral compass of the usual state narrative: 'the next time I see a British minister on TV accusing other countries of being terrorist states, I would like to ask the question, "are they a terrorist state?"'[67]

The Court's judgments are thus used to create a grand authentication of the Republican narrative within the 'meta conflict' – one of legal misrule:

> So there we have it, the European Court upheld what we have all suspected and long maintained. The British government has been systematically

---

[65] Loughgall Truth and Justice Campaign, *Unequal Victims*, 11.
[66] Author unknown, 'Shoot to Kill Relatives Win in European Court of Human Rights', *An Phoblacht/Republican News* (Belfast: 10 May 2001).
[67] *Ibid.*

engaged in obscuring the truth and denying justice to Irish Citizens killed by British forces of occupation. There has been a cover up, that much has been established.[68]

More recent Republican reportage has also considered other cases brought before the Court as a means of underpinning the Republican narrative of a less than liberal state masking a dirty war.[69] The cases *Brecknell* v. *United Kingdom* and *Finucane* v. *United Kingdom*[70] helped to maintain a focus on allegations of state collusion in killings, a perennial and significant critique within the Republican narrative, and the cases furthered the maintenance of political momentum to continue to hold the state to book. The Court's decision in *Brecknell* underlined the lack of independence in the Royal Ulster Constabulary's initial investigations, thereby assisting a counter-state narrative of a wayward and partisan state trying to deflect attention from its activities. The Court's decision in *Brecknell* also illustrates how its jurisprudence need not automatically clog the wheels of transition, even if its decisions may be used in a meta conflict of 'dealing with the past'. Fortuitously for both the state and the majority of Irish Republicans who now support the reformed Police Service of Northern Ireland, the Court concluded that the new police force was institutionally distinct from the Royal Ulster Constabulary.[71] The Court may not simply provide material to further the conflict over history, but may play a crucial role in helping to set its temporal boundaries. The timing of moves can also be key in any meta conflict; and the lengthy delays in the Court's hearing of the *Finucane* case (the application was in 1993, the judgment in 2003) perhaps limited the role of the Court in providing sustenance for the Republican narrative of widespread collusion. However, *Finucane* and *Brecknell*, whilst providing further support for a state critical narrative, could not form part of a proper Republican narrative, as neither case involved Republican activists. This was part of a deeper story of possible state malfeasance.

Of course, Republican use of the Court's judgments often involves a series of over-simplifications, and instances of 'amnesia'. These are tactical choices inherent in the political construction of any collective

---

[68] *Ibid.*
[69] Author unknown, 'Allow the Truth to be Told', *An Phoblacht/Republican News* (Belfast: 3 July 2003) and Author unknown, 'European Court Rules in Favour of Families of Collusion Victims', *An Phoblacht/Republican News* (Belfast: 29 November 2007).
[70] ECtHR, *Brecknell* v. *the United Kingdom*, 27 November 2007 (Appl. no. 32457/04) and ECtHR *Finucane* v. *the United Kingdom*, 1 July 2003 (Appl. no. 29178/95).
[71] *Brecknell*, para. 76.

memory. In the *Kelly* case, the assertion of the relatives that Article 14 had been violated in that 'there was a discriminatory use of lethal force and a lack of legal protection vis-à-vis a section of the community on grounds of national origin or association with a national minority', was not upheld by the Court.[72] There was no mention of this failed challenge within the Republican narrative. In a similar vein, the fact that the Court produced a narrow, split decision in the *McCann* case is also eclipsed. Furthermore, in the Court's judgment on *McCann*, the word 'terrorist' is repeatedly used to describe the three killed, and the Court characterises the IRA as a ruthless body, which 'judged by its actions in the past, had demonstrated a disregard for human life, including that of its own members',[73] but again these de-legitimising terms are fit only for the memory-hole. Instead, judgments critical of the state are spotlighted to provide a legitimising sheen.

Shifts in language? Political violence and the Court's terminology against the backdrop of a peace process

In transitional settings, the transmission belt between local and international political cultures may be two-way. The terminology used by the Court in describing those killed is also suggestive of the impact the burgeoning peace process may have had on the political lens through which the Court may have examined these cases. Just as the Court may have helped shape approaches within the wider Republican family, so too may have the peacemaking in Northern Ireland moulded the language which the Court chose to use. The word 'terrorist' or 'terrorists' appears sixty-four times in the 1995 *McCann* judgment in relation to those killed, but only seven times (and one of these is a direct quote from the *McCann* case) in *Kelly*, delivered in 2001. Instead, the language in *Kelly* plumps for more neutral terms such as 'IRA members' (four references), 'IRA men' (two references), 'gunmen' (four references), or 'hooded' or 'armed' men (twenty-three references in total). Given that the Northern Ireland political process had entered a post-Good Friday Agreement phase, this may indicate a sensitivity around the use of language in political transitions. A word such as 'terrorist' has certain ideological, 'othering', or criminal meanings and is suggestive of fanaticism and militancy – of being beyond the pale. This may have been regarded as a poor semantic fit for the newly emergent dispensation. The different use of language between *McCann*

---

[72] *Kelly*, paras. 146–149.   [73] *McCann*, para. 193.

and *Kelly* is all the more marked when one considers that the Gibraltar three were completely unarmed and engaged in a reconnaissance exercise, whereas those IRA members killed at Loughgall were masked, heavily armed with assault weapons and explosives and engaged in attacking a police station. This re-moulding of language would have a particular attraction for Republicans in buttressing their own positions in 'legacy' battles over the legitimacy of 'armed struggle'.

Loughgall and Gibraltar – the practice of memory

Memory practices by Irish Republicans in relation to the Gibraltar and Loughgall killings dovetail with this underlining of legitimacy in the overall narrative surrounding the events as described above. Material culture such as exhibitions and memorial statuary underlines the martial activity of the 'Loughgall Martyrs', as do commemorative lectures, pamphlets and websites. They are lionised as soldiers fighting a war; yet ultimately they are presented as victims too – David against Goliath, but with Goliath triumphant. The official website commemorating the 'Loughgall Martyrs' is peppered with militaristic terms and imagery, but also contains sections tapping directly into legal frameworks, providing the full text of the Court judgment in *Kelly*, and a long article detailing the families' legal campaigns and challenges.[74] Fieldwork undertaken during the twentieth anniversary of the Loughgall shootings provides a case study throwing into sharp relief the means by which these narratives are woven through the social fabric of the Irish Republican constituency. Commemorative activity takes numerous forms, suiting many levels of individual commitment. There are sporting events such as Gaelic football, a tour of the dead men's graves, a religious service in the form of a Mass, a commemorative parade, the production and screening of a documentary film, together with an exhibition and a well attended lecture. Overall, the commemorative narrative emphasises the weight of fire thrown against the men, the foreknowledge of the enemy and the ruthlessness of an occupying illegitimate force. The lecture sought to put the Loughgall shootings in their proper 'military context',[75] that which emphasised 'the strategy of foreign occupying powers and the tactics and propaganda used to keep natives of

---

[74] The site is now archived. See http://web.archive.org/web/20080408014731; www.loughgall20.com.

[75] *Ibid.*

an occupied country under control and in a constant state of fear'.[76] The framing of this narrative is one which seeks to castigate the state as prosecuting a hidden war of extrajudicial executions and repression, whilst also lionising the martial ability of the men.

> The Brits were upping the ante big time in the '80s in terms of loyalist death squads and their own death squads. They were executing people left, right and centre. The Volunteers killed in the ambush had been prosecuting a very strong war against the Brits and the Brits saw them as a threat.[77]

The veteran Republican Brian Keenan re-iterated and emphasised this narrative as he gave the keynote twentieth anniversary oration in 2007:

> The lads they wouldn't have expected any quarter nor did they get any ... you only get quarter from democratic forces, from legitimate governments and of course the British had no legitimacy in this country ... they [the IRA men] knew what they were doing, they were out to [sic] a very simple objective, they were involved in a war of national liberation.[78]

The martial approach is in part a function of the 'path dependency' of collective memory, today's collective memories must take previous forms into account for fear of breaking certain conventions and causing reputational damage.[79] But it also represents less a militarism, than a 'pseudo-militarism'. Just as the use of law has had a softening constitutive effect on Republicanism (as argued by McEvoy), other swingeing ideological changes have meant a hollowing out of Republicanism as a site of radical resistance. Republicanism becomes identity politics, and the 'organisational charisma' of former military structures simply helps create a 'Republican heritage' to help legitimate their politics in the present.[80] This Loughgall narrative is less a case of militant separatists 'hostaging' victimhood, than a transformed political project pursuing a rights agenda whilst trailing pseudo-militarist bunting. The Court's judgment is lauded for having 'put pressure on the British Government to address

---

[76] See L. Jefferson, 'Loughgall: 20 Years on', www.irishdemocrat.co.uk/news/2007/loughgall-20-years-on.

[77] Author unknown, 'Loughgall Martyrs 20th Anniversary', *An Phoblacht/Republican News* (Belfast: 5 April 2007).

[78] Field recording, 20th Anniversary Loughgall Martyrs, Cappagh, Northern Ireland, 7 May 2007.

[79] J. K. Olick, 'Genre Memories and Memory Genres: A Dialogical Analysis of May 8, 1945 Commemorations in the Federal Republic of Germany', *American Sociological Review* 64 (1999) 381–402.

[80] K. Bean, *The New Politics of Sinn Féin* (Liverpool University Press, 2007) 128.

the concerns of the families that the incident has not been properly or adequately addressed' and the fact that 'the Committee of Ministers has been monitoring the UK government's response to the findings by the European Court that the government was in breach of Article 2 of the ECHR' is also noted with approval in the commemorative narrative.[81] Whereas the pseudo-militarism points to a 'war situation' in the past, fostering historical legitimacy, whilst also playing up to identity politics in the present. This creation of a 'militarised' victim is facilitated by the developing jurisprudence of the Court, which provided 'confirmation that situations of emergency do not discharge states of their obligations to protect the right to life' and that the right to life even of 'acknowledged terrorists was still given value and required guardianship'.[82]

Victimhood and the resistance of the imposition of hierarchies on the Troubles dead is a second contested zone in the 'meta conflict'. The jurisprudence of the Court, as well as the memory practices in relation to both the Gibraltar and Loughgall killings, has facilitated the defence against these hierarchies. For the Loughgall relatives, this state-created hierarchy serves an instrumental purpose, rather than simply expressing a moral position, as 'the state especially has a continuing need to dehumanise the Republican struggle, to rob it of any legitimacy'.[83] Therefore a process takes place in which the IRA men are presented as 'monsters', with no consideration of their human qualities as individuals and family members, and as such are 'demonised out of recognition'. For the Loughgall relatives the hierarchical imperative did not end with the dead:

> We were also constantly presented in the media as 'IRA Relatives' it was like using a dirty word to describe us. They wouldn't see us simply as bereaved relatives – that didn't suit many people, we had to be presented as something more than that, something evil. Throughout the last thirty years whole families have been criminalised.[84]

For the relatives, a widening and deepening of the conflict narrative is what is needed. A Gibraltar relative argues for a process of recovering truth, the better to 'level the political playing pitch' which would mean that the 'hierarchy of victimhood which has seen the victims of state

---

[81] 'Loughgall – a Search for the Truth', http://web.archive.org/web/20071128040312/www. loughgall20.com.

[82] F. Ní Aoláin, 'The Evolving Jurisprudence of the European Convention Concerning the Right to Life', *Netherlands Quarterly on Human Rights* 19 (2001) 21, 30.

[83] Loughgall Truth and Justice Campaign, *Unequal Victims*, 10.

[84] *Ibid.*, 4–5.

violence marginalised, would vanish'.[85] For the Loughgall relatives the question is even blunter, 'what is it that turns a world upside down and makes ordinary people, coming from ordinary homes do extraordinary things? That's the story that needs to be told and accepted'.[86]

Commemoration by Republican activists and the families works towards putting a human face back on to the dead, and showing something of their quotidian lives. The Loughgall exhibition, aiming to provide a 'touching insight into these normal families living in abnormal conditions' displays artefacts such as childhood toys and holiday photographs of the dead men, personal letters to their loved ones, diaries, teenage clothes, religious medals and the documentary accumulation of a life from sporting certificates to club memberships. Their paramilitary activity is not blurred out. The everyday objects sit in jarring, unsettling, but not impossible conjunction with the tools of their paramilitary life – masks, boiler suits and gloves worn to minimise forensics, and deactivated weaponry of the type they used.[87] For the Gibraltar Three the representation is less martial, but a series of events and publications laud them as motivated, principled individuals who should serve as models for a present generation. Painted murals and 'cut outs' adorned walls with smiling portraits of the slain IRA members, depicting them as ordinary human beings. Religious services, parades and candlelit vigils attracted hundreds or thousands at a time, whilst orations underlined the repressive nature of the state at this time. Literature also formed part of the social memory of the occasion, and the darkly satirical poem *Gib, A Modest Exposure* was re-published as part of the commemoration. The mock epic poem itself specifically engages in a human rights discourse tweaked with a barbed Swiftian satire of the British state's commitment to the rule of law. It references the European Court of Human Rights' ability to pressure and embarrass the British political leadership.[88]

[85] Rolston, *Unfinished Business*, 174.
[86] Loughgall Truth and Justice Campaign, *Unequal Victims*, 12.
[87] For an online description of the exhibition, see www.cain.ulster.ac.uk/cgi-bin/htr/htr. pl?full=3.
[88] J. Mitchell, *Gib: A Modest Exposure* (Dublin: Fulcrum Press, 2008). See, for example, page 19: 'It's sickening to hear them jaw/Of human rights and rule of law;/Their favourite view of human rights/Is down a loaded Browning's sights;/And as for rule of law, by God/Whose law ordains a murder squad?' Similarly, Margaret Thatcher is metaphorically pictured as squirming under the light of the Court on page 36: 'The pressure's on; each time the split/Widens, Meg's towering fit/Of rage gets that bit shriller./It's then we recognise the killer./Picture her apoplectice face/Snarling under the disgrace/Of being exposed as a prison warder/By Europe's Court of Human Rights/Advised to put *her* house in order'.

In contrast, Republicans strove to confect a gendered rights discourse for themselves based around one of the IRA members killed. On the twentieth anniversary of the shootings, which fell on International Women's Day, Republicans marked both days by celebrating Mairéad Farrell not only as a fallen activist, but as an example of a 'strong inspirational woman who is still highly respected and held in high esteem'; the event attracted strong criticism from Unionists which was described by Republicans as an attempt to 'demonise Republicans and insult the children and the families of those murdered'.[89] Unionist ire was particularly strong as the event was to be held in a public gallery of the power-sharing Northern Ireland Assembly. Although this was thwarted, Republicans managed to procure a facility within the building, and so managed to tap into its politically legitimising public space.[90] A welter of commemorative publications and DVDs also presented the Loughgall and Gibraltar dead as ordinary people, albeit motivated to behave in 'exemplary' ways, as a result of extraordinary circumstances. The jurisprudence of the Court has part facilitated this process of resisting the creation of a victim hierarchy. As Christine Bell notes, 'Article 2's procedural aspect has, in cases where state actors have been involved, given families of these victims some leverage on a victims debate which has often relegated them to a low place'.[91] Ní Aoláin fleshes this observation out; the Court's framing of the right to life, with its accentuation 'that an equal standard of care is due to all transgressors, no matter the heinousness of their alleged activities', lies at the centre of its judgment in the McCann ruling.[92] The emphasis placed on the involvement of next-of-kin in the investigation of state killings has also partially worked against the demotion of families' status in the inevitable tussles over victim hierarchies.

Conclusion

In a transitional process which has seen political and ideological re-calibration of the Republican project, all set within a sporadically firing 'meta conflict' over the meaning of the 'Troubles' itself, questions

---

[89] Author unknown, 'Plans for IRA Commemoration Hang in Balance', *Belfast Newsletter* (Belfast: 25 February 2008).

[90] Author unknown, 'Republican Women Celebrated at Stormont', *An Phoblacht/ Republican News* (Belfast: 13 March 2008).

[91] C. Bell and J. Keenan, 'Lost on the Way Home? The Right to Life in Northern Ireland', *Journal of Law and Society* 32 (2005) 87.

[92] Ní Aoláin, *Politics of Force*, 202.

of legitimacy and victimhood have assumed a long-standing importance. Whilst for Republicans those remembered may have been driven,
principled men and women killed by a conniving and hypocritical state,
for many others in society they represented militants far too ready to
engage in acts of violence, and blind to its real effects. Memory work by
political activists and families play an enormous part in these tussles,
and a complex calendar of commemorative activity has mushroomed
within this meta conflict. But law acts as a carrier of collective memory too, and more than this, as a constitutive re-shaper of Republican
politics. The Article 2 decisions of the Court in terms of the Loughgall
and Gibraltar killings, have been adopted and adapted into the collective
memory of those events, and have facilitated processes in which these
killings have been used to project a concept of the *Mis-Rule of Law* and
the *Equality of Victimhood*. The procedural aspects of *Kelly* and the telescoping backwards of the state's responsibility to protect life evidenced
in *McCann* have also facilitated a *Public Widening of Narrative*, the better to challenge and unpick British security policy in public discourse.
The fact that the challenges took place in the supra-national entity of the
European Court of Human Rights also added weight to Republican critical approaches, expediting a *Critical Examination of State Policy*. The
collective entity of the British state itself could be challenged, and its procedures critiqued by an authoritative body. Policy and structure was on
trial, not 'rotten apples'.

The case studies of Loughgall and Gibraltar illustrate two developing
themes within Republican memory work and its public discourse. At one
level, it represents a curious dissolution of Republicanism into identity
politics, in which 'militant' memory is political heritage. On another,
it suggests how engagement with legal processes, and the internalisa-
tion of the messages flowing from judicial decisions, may have sped the
construction of a rights discourse within Republicanism. Both themes
have altered Republicanism as a political project. This agglomeration
or bundling together of militant memory and the discourse of human
rights, may at times be unwieldy, and indeed off-putting to several constituencies, but has been absorbed within the vernacular political culture of Republicanism, and in so doing has amended its own language
and methods of engagement. The reach of the Court is wide and has
extended into several zones of political or ethnic conflict. What might
further case studies of the intersection between Court jurisprudence,
legitimacy and memory tells us about transitions in other divided
societies?

Bibliography

An Phoblacht/Republican News (weekly political newsletter).

Anderson, B., *Imagined Communities: Reflections on the Origins and Spread of Nationalism* (London: Verso, 1983).

Bean, K., *The New Politics of Sinn Féin* (Liverpool University Press, 2007).

Bell, C., *On the Law of Peace: Peace Agreements and the Lex Pacificatoria* (Oxford University Press, 2008).

Bell, C. and Keenan, J., 'Lost on the Way Home? The Right to Life in Northern Ireland', *Journal of Law and Society* 32 (2005) 68–89.

Brooks, P. and Gerwitz P. D., *Law's Stories: Narrative and Rhetoric in the Law* (New Haven: Yale University Press, 1996).

Brown, K. and Vigianni, E., 'Performing Provisionalism – Republican Commemorative Practice as Political Performance', in Fitzpatrick, L. (ed.) *Performing Violence in Contemporary Ireland* (Dublin: Carysfort Press, 2009).

Campbell, C., Ní Aoláin, F. and Harvey, C., 'The Frontiers of Legal Analysis: Reframing the Transition in Northern Ireland', *The Modern Law Review* 66(3) (2003) 317–345.

Connolly, C. K., 'Seeking the Final Court of Justice: The European Court of Human Rights and Accountability for State Violence in Northern Ireland', *San Diego International Law Journal* 9(1) (2007/2008) 81–134.

Kertzer, D. I., *Ritual, Politics, and Power* (New Haven: Yale University Press, 1988).

Loughgall Truth and Justice Campaign, *The Unequal Victims* (Newtownabbey, County Antrim: Island Publications, 2001).

McEvoy, K., 'Law, Struggle, and Political Transformation in Northern Ireland', *Journal of Law and Society* 27 (2000) 542–571.

McEvoy, K. and Conway, H., 'The Dead, the Law, and the Politics of the Past', *Journal of Law and Society* 31 (2004) 539–562.

McGuinness, M., 'Introduction', in *Unforgotten Sacrifice – A Tribute to Fallen Comrades* (Belfast: Twinbrook and Poleglass Commemoration Committee, 1999).

McKittrick, D., *Lost Lives: The Stories of the Men, Women, and Children who Died as a Result of the Northern Ireland Troubles* (Edinburgh: Mainstream, 1999).

Merry, S. E., 'Transnational Human Rights and Local Activism: Mapping the Middle', *American Anthropologist* 108(1) (2006) 38–51.

Metress, S. and Metress, E., 'The Communal Significance of the Irish Republican Army Funeral Ritual', Unpublished paper (1993) Accessed in Northern Ireland Political Collection, Linen Hall Library.

Mitchell, J., *Gib: A Modest Exposure* (Dublin: Fulcrum Press, 2008).

Moloney, E., *A Secret History of the IRA* (New York: W. W. Norton, 2003).

Ní Aoláin, F., 'The Evolving Jurisprudence of the European Convention Concerning the Right to Life', *Netherlands Quarterly on Human Rights* 19 (2001) 21–42.

The Politics of Force: Conflict Management and State Violence in Northern Ireland (Belfast: Blackstaff Press, 2000).

'Truth Telling, Accountability and the Right to Life in Northern Ireland', *European Human Rights Law Review* 5 (2002) 572–590.

O'Doherty, M., *The Trouble with Guns: Republican Strategy and the Provisional IRA* (Belfast: Blackstaff Press, 1998).

Olick, J. K., 'Genre Memories and Memory Genres: A Dialogical Analysis of May 8, 1945 Commemorations in the Federal Republic of Germany', *American Sociological Review* 64 (1999) 381–402.

Patterson, H., 'The Republican Movement and the Legacy of the Troubles', in Honohan, I. (ed.) *Republicanism in Ireland: Confronting Theories and Traditions* (Manchester University Press, 2009) 147–163.

Picard, R. G., 'How Violence is Justified: Sinn Féin's An Phoblacht', *Journal of Communication* 41(4) (1991) 90–103.

Rolston, B., *Unfinished Business: State Killings and the Quest for Truth* (Belfast: Beyond The Pale, 2000).

Savelsberg, J. and King, R., 'Law and Collective Memory', *Annual Review of Law and Social Science* 3 (2007) 189–211.

Tírghrá Committee, *Tírghrá – Ireland's Patriot Dead* (Dublin: Tírghrá Committee, 2002).

4

Confronting the consequences of authoritarianism and conflict: the ECHR and transition

CHRISTOPHER K. LAMONT

Introduction

On 6 November 1996 Croatia was formally admitted into the Council of Europe as the third former Yugoslav state to join the organization.[1] The Council of Europe's cautious expansion into the territories which formerly comprised the Socialist Federal Republic of Yugoslavia (SFRJ) expanded the geographic application of the European Convention of Human Rights to include states emerging from both conflict and authoritarianism. From the perspective of aspirant former Yugoslav states, membership in the Council of Europe constituted an achievable foreign policy goal for states seeking integration into Euro-Atlantic institutions.[2] Indeed, Croatia's

Christopher Lamont, Assistant Professor in International Relations, Department of International Relations and International Organization, University of Groningen.

[1] Slovenia became the first former Yugoslav state to join the Council of Europe in 1993 and Macedonia joined in 1995. Bosnia and Herzegovina became a member of the Council of Europe on 24 April 2002, while the State Union of Serbia and Montenegro would not accede to the Council of Europe until 3 April 2003. Following Montenegro's declaration of independence in 2006, Montenegro was admitted to the Council as an independent state on 11 May 2007.

[2] While Croatia was excluded from enlargement processes undertaken by European regional organizations during the 1990s, namely the European Union and NATO, the Council of Europe proved an exception to the rule. See G. Pridham, 'Uneasy Democratizations – Pariah Regimes, Political Conditionality and Reborn Transitions in Central and Eastern Europe', *Democratization* 8(4) (2001) 65–94, 79. For a different set of reasons, namely a dispute with Greece over the use of the geographic term 'Macedonia' that had blocked the Republic of Macedonia from developing relations with the European Union, the Council of Europe proved uniquely receptive to Macedonian membership when the former Yugoslav republic applied in 1993. Macedonia would join the Council of Europe under the compromise name of 'the Former Yugoslav Republic of Macedonia'. In 1994, the Council of Europe also noted that membership was open to the Federal Republic of Yugoslavia, which at the time enjoyed no formal relationship with the organization. See Council of Europe, Parliamentary Assembly *Recommendation 1247*, 4 October 1994.

admission to the Council of Europe was, for Croatian president Franjo Tudjman, a primary focus of Croatian diplomatic efforts in the months following the 1995 Dayton Agreement.[3] To be sure, the extent to which Tudjman desired membership in the Council was illustrated by the fact that prior to Croatia's accession, Tudjman's illiberal government accepted numerous human rights commitments that extended beyond the scope of the Council's core human rights treaties.[4]

The accession of an illiberal state to the Council of Europe proved controversial both within Croatia and abroad. When Tudjman's foreign minister Mate Granic opened Croatia's membership signing ceremony in Strasbourg, a transnational advocacy group, Reporters without Borders, interrupted proceedings by pelting Granic with leaflets that bore the provocative image of Tudjman in bed with Serbian president Slobodan Milosevic.[5] This symbolic protest, which marked Croatia's admittance to the Council of Europe in 1996, three years prior to Tudjman's death, nicely captures the role of regional human rights systems and transnational civil society networks in providing a mechanism through which state authorities could be challenged both during authoritarianism and during periods of rapid political change.[6] This chapter will illustrate that the European Convention on Human Rights, which Croatia signed upon its accession to the Council of Europe, tied Croatia into a regional human rights regime that served to assist domestic and external actors challenging the Tudjman

---

[3] Although Zagreb was frozen out of EU and NATO accession processes following Croatia's 1995 Operation Storm and the consolidation of an increasingly authoritarian form of governance under Franjo Tudjman, Tudjman's government still professed a desire to integrate into Euro-Atlantic institutions. See I. Sanader, 'Osporavanje Franje Tuđmana osporavanje temelja Hrvatske države', in I. Sanader, *HDZ za Hrvatsku* (Zagreb: Hrvatska Demokratska Zajednica, 2001) 77.

[4] Prior to Croatia's signing of the European Convention on Human Rights in November 1996 and ratification of the Convention the following year in November 1997, Croatia committed to accepting additional obligations related to protecting media freedoms after Croatia's membership negotiations were suspended in May 1996. Nevertheless, despite Zagreb's symbolic concessions to the Council in terms of accepting human rights commitments, state encroachment on media freedom continued throughout 1996. See *Croatia Country Report on Human Rights Practice for 1996* (United States Department of State, 30 January 2007).

[5] Reporters without Borders activists had taken up the cause of the Split-based opposition newspaper *Feral Tribune*, which was under intense state harassment following a series of articles probing corruption and war crimes.

[6] For a broader discussion of theoretical models relating to the above see K. Sikkink and M. Keck, *Activists Beyond Borders: Advocacy Networks in International Politics* (Ithaca: Cornell University Press, 1998) and T. Risse, C. Ropp and K. Sikkink (eds.), *The Power of Human Rights: International Norms and Domestic Change* (Cambridge University Press, 1999).

government's consolidation of authoritarianism. Later, after Tudjman's death, transitional jurisprudence would guide Croatia through the process of transition with the European Court of Human Rights acting as a de facto high court in the context of Croatia's transitional failed judiciary.[7] Absent integration into a regional human rights system, Croatia's encounter with transition may have produced a very different outcome.

Beyond Croatia, it was within the former Yugoslavia that Europe's regional human rights systems were most tested by transition. All former Yugoslav states experienced multiple transitions during the years immediately following the collapse of the Socialist Federal Republic of Yugoslavia. For example, Croatia and Serbia experienced at least four transitions during the last two decades. The first transition saw the republics move from being constituent republics within the Socialist Federal Republic of Yugoslavia to newly independent states, second from single party communist governance to presidential authoritarianism, third from conflict to post-conflict, and fourth, from presidential authoritarianism to parliamentary democracy. In terms of Kosovo and Bosnia and Herzegovina, there was an addition transition. These two territories were brought under the administration of international actors in an effort to state-build post-conflict governance structures.[8]

Given the multi-dimensional nature of transitions within the former Yugoslav context, this chapter will begin with a discussion of the Yugoslav judiciary prior to transition. Although Croatia constitutes the core case study, reference will also be made to other former Yugoslav republics, such as Serbia,[9] which shared a similar transitional trajectory that included both violent conflict and presidential authoritarianism.[10]

---

[7] The term de facto high court is intentionally provocative, and is used to illustrate the high number of repetitive Article 6 judgments delivered by the Court against Croatia. I use the term 'failed judiciary' not as a pejorative, but rather simply to describe a domestic judiciary that was unable to provide effective and timely judicial remedies during transition.

[8] An examination of Kosovo and Bosnia and Herzegovina and the ECHR system would necessitate an exploration of the relationship between the ECtHR and international administrations, which is beyond the scope of this chapter. See Chapter 7, this volume, for a discussion of ECtHR, *Sejdić and Finci* v. *Bosnia and Herzegovina*, 22 December 2009 (Appl. nos. 27996/06 and 34836/06).

[9] Throughout the 1990s Serbia was a constituent republic within the Federal Republic of Yugoslavia, which was comprised of two former Yugoslav republics, Serbia and Montenegro.

[10] It is important to emphasize that unlike Bosnia-Herzegovina and Kosovo, post-conflict governance in Croatia was not directly administered by external actors. Furthermore, while Serbia's transitional experience bears many similarities with Croatia in terms of

The discussion of the Yugoslav pre-transition experience will be followed by a discussion of Croatia's negotiated entry into the Council of Europe during authoritarianism, but after violent conflict. Croatia constitutes a valuable case study to test causal assumptions in norm diffusion literature,[11] because unlike Slobodan Milosevic's Federal Republic of Yugoslavia,[12] Croatia acceded to the Council of Europe prior to its transition from presidential authoritarianism to parliamentary democracy. In addition, when turning to post-Tudjman Croatia, attempts to grapple with the legacy of violent conflict, while often almost exclusively defined in terms of individual accountability for violations of international humanitarian law in transitional justice literature on the former Yugoslavia,[13] have also been shaped by Strasbourg jurisprudence. Finally, it will be emphasised that confronted with multiple transitions, the Croatian judiciary found itself unable to provide effective legal remedies and therefore the European Court of Human Rights took on the role of a de facto high court.

Transitional antecedents

Before examining the integration of post-Yugoslav states into the ECHR system, it is important to first briefly outline the historic antecedent to former Yugoslav failed judiciaries. Until 1990 the Socialist Federal Republic of Yugoslavia was an authoritarian single party federal state governed by the League of Communists. Nevertheless, the SFRJ did establish a system of constitutional courts and judicial practice that exhibited features in common with that of Western judiciaries.[14] All contemporary former Yugoslav constitutional courts trace back their origins to two major

---

multiple transitions, Serbia's belated accession to the European Convention on Human Rights limits the extent to which comparisons can be drawn between the two states. For more on Serbia, Montenegro and Kosovo see R. Etinski, 'The European Convention on Human Rights in the Constitutional System of Serbia and Montenegro', *Transition Studies Review* 12(1) (2005) 175–183.

[11] For an introduction see Risse *et al.*, *The Power of Human Rights*.

[12] In November 2000, the Federal Republic of Yugoslavia submitted an application for membership and acceded as the State Union of Serbia and Montenegro in April 2003.

[13] See for example, J. Subotic, *Hijacked Justice: Dealing with the Past in the Balkans* (Ithaca: Cornell University Press, 2009).

[14] Mathew M. Getter, 'Yugoslavia and the European Economic Community: Is a Merger Feasible?', *University of Pennsylvania Journal of International Business Law* 11(4) (1990) 789–810.

periods of SFRJ constitutional reform.[15] In terms of the SFRJ's judiciary, the 1963 Constitution established judicial structures that would later be transformed into constitutional courts in post-independence SFRJ republics. The 1963 Constitution also enumerated rights and created a judicial mechanism through which individuals could seek remedy for violations of these rights. Although the 1963 Yugoslav Constitution contained an extensive bill of rights that included both civil and political rights alongside socio-economic rights,[16] Article 40 of the 1963 Constitution limited the exercise of these rights in a manner consistent with limitations placed on bills of rights in single party communist states across East-Central Europe.[17] Furthermore, it must be emphasized that the SFRJ did not seek integration into the Council of Europe system.

At the time the SFRJ established its constitutional court system constitutional courts were 'alien to socialist law'. The authority of constitutional courts to adjudicate on the constitutionality of federal and republican laws had the potential to create a constitutional court system would be analogous to constitutional courts in non-socialist jurisdictions. Yet, to be sure, Yugoslavia's constitutional courts were restricted in the sense that rather than functioning as an independent authority that could act as a check on legislation adopted by federal and republican governments, the courts in practice enjoyed a close relationship with legislative bodies and acted more in an advisory role.[18] Judicial deference to executives, particularly in cases that were politically salient,[19] would become a common characteristic of post-1990 constitutional courts in the former Yugoslavia, in particular in

---

[15] The Croatian Constitutional Court makes reference to the 1963 SFRJ Constitution as having established the Court. Likewise, the Serbian Constitutional Court notes it was 'founded in 1963'. For a brief history of the Croatian Constitutional Court, see 'Povijest Hrvatskog ustavnog sudovanja' available at: www.usud.hr. For the Serbian Constitutional Court, see 'Ustavni Sud Republike Srbije' available at: www.ustavni.sud.rs

[16] The Socialist Federal Republic of Yugoslavia signed the International Covenant on Civil and Political Rights and the International Covenant on Economic, Social and Cultural Rights on 8 August 1967 and ratified the ICCPR and the ICESCR on 2 June 1971.

[17] Article 40 notes, 'These freedoms shall not be used to overthrow the foundations of socialist and democratic order established by this constitution'.

[18] B. Peselj, 'Socialist Law and the New Yugoslav Constitution', *The Georgetown Law Journal* 51(4) (1963) at 700–701.

[19] The practice of constitutional courts under post-communist presidential authoritarianism bore similarities to the past practice of dispute settlement within the SFRJ where major disputes were settled within the framework of the governing party, and minor disputes were left to the court system. For a limited overview of Yugoslav era constitutional court jurisprudence see D. Kulic, 'The Constitutional Court of Yugoslavia in the Protection of Basic Human Rights', *Osgoode Hall Law Journal* 11(2) (1973) 275–284.

Croatia and Serbia where political change did not coincide with a trans-formation in judiciaries. Despite a constitutional separation of powers in 1990 post-Yugoslav constitutions, in practice judiciaries in both Croatia and Serbia failed to effectively challenge powerful executives.

Political change: from single party authoritarianism to presidential authoritarian pluralism

In 1990 the Socialist Federal Republic of Yugoslavia was paralysed by an internal political conflict among its constituent members. Paradoxically, despite political paralysis, in terms of Yugoslavia's highly developed legal system and economic pluralism, Yugoslavia was in 1990 best positioned to integrate into the European Economic Communities.[20] However, an increasingly vitriolic intra-republican conflict between Slovenia and Serbia, would soon fracture already fragile federal level institutions and contrib-ute to the outbreak of violent conflict in 1991. Moreover, in Croatia and Serbia presidential authoritarian regimes, under Tudjman and Milosevic respectively, forestalled nascent democratic transitions. While the causes of conflict in the former Yugoslavia are not the subject of this chapter, it is sufficient to point out that violent conflict resulted in massive devastation, which included the displacement of 200,000 people in Croatia and the obliteration of Croatia's neighbouring republic of Bosnia and Herzegovina. Indeed, Bosnia and Herzegovina would only survive the war in the form of an international protectorate. In the context of Croatia and Serbia, presi-dential authoritarianism left post-communist judicial reform delayed for a decade, and confronted post-Tudjman and post-Milosevic judiciaries with the task of rebuilding effective judicial structures in the aftermath of vio-lent conflict and authoritarianism.

Judicial reform and presidential authoritarianism

Croatia's 1990 Constitution established a semi-presidential system of gov-ernment;[21] however, in practice the Office of the Presidency would come to dominate all other branches of government. The concentration of pow-ers within the Office of the Presidency occurred during the context of

---

[20] In 1990, Getter observed, 'the economic and legal climates in Yugoslavia make a mer-ger with the EEC quite feasible'. See, Getter, 'Yugoslavia and the European Economic Community', 809.

[21] N. Zakosek, *Politički sustav Hrvastke* (Zagreb: Fakultet političkih znanosti, 2002) 111–112.

armed conflict, which will be discussed below. At this point, it should be pointed out that Croatia's Constitutional Court played an important role in facilitating this process through a June 1992 decision in which the Court confirmed upon the presidency the authority to determine whether or not a state of emergency existed without explicitly requiring the president to declare a state of emergency and to issue executive orders with the force of law.[22]

In terms of institutional change, while the Office of the Presidency was a new institution created through the 1990 Constitution and the Croatian parliament, the Sabor, also constituted a new institution that replaced a cumbersome three-chambered[23] communist era legislative body, the Croatian judiciary experienced comparatively little change following the 1990 electoral triumph of the Croatian Democratic Union over the Croatian League of Communists. Superficially, on 25 July 1990 the Constitutional Court of the Socialist Republic of Croatia had the word 'socialist' removed from its title and became known simply as the Constitutional Court of the Republic of Croatia. A year later Jadranko Crnic, former president of the socialist-era Constitutional Court, became the first president of the now newly independent Republic of Croatia's Constitutional Court. Crnic had served as a judge on the Constitutional Court since 1984, and served as president of the Court until 1999. In general, Tudjman was able to appoint loyal Croatian Democratic Union party functionaries to key judicial positions. For example, Milan Vukovic, a lawyer with no experience as a judge was appointed as President of the Supreme Court in November 1992. Vukovic's inability to engage in legal analysis, application of law in a 'flexible manner' that was in the interest of the ruling party, and public pronouncements on his belief in the inability of ethnic Croats to commit war crimes would eventually generate international pressure for his removal from office in 1995.[24]

---

[22] It must also be noted that a parallel system of military courts was established during the 1991–1995 war in Croatia. Although a military court system had initially been abolished in 1990 as having been incompatible with a new democratic order, the re-established military courts exercised wide jurisdiction over both military personnel and in some cases civilians. A. Uzelac, 'Hrvatsko pravosuđe u devedesetima: od državne nezavisnosti do institucionalne krize', *Politička misao* 38 (2001) 10–11.

[23] The three chambers included the Socio-Political Chamber, the Chamber of Regions and the Chamber of Collective Labour. Of the three chambers the Socio-Political Chamber was dominant. See C. Lamont, 'Explaining the Regeneration of the Croatian Democratic Union in Post-Presidential Authoritarian Croatia: Elites, Legacies, and Party Organization', *Balkanistica* 21 (2008) 65.

[24] With regard to war crimes, Vukovic observed, 'Croats cannot commit war crimes'. Uzelac, 'Hrvatsko pravosuđe u devedesetima', 23–26.

Throughout the 1990s the Croatian judiciary remained highly politicized,[25] and mimicked its communist era practice of acting in deference to political actors. To illustrate the extent to which the judiciary was marginalized it is helpful to recall that Tudjman's informal Council of Defence and National Security discussed and approved key judicial decisions in place of judicial institutions.[26] It was within the context of conflict and marginalization that Croatia's judiciary was also faced with an exodus of qualified personnel. In fact, 200 judges[27] resigned during 1991 to pursue more lucrative careers as private lawyers.[28] Far from post-communist change ushering in a decade of judicial reform, Tudjman's new government initiated a process of judicial dismantling that would lead Croatian legal scholar Alan Uzelac to lament, 'unfortunately, the era from 1990 to 1999, was a lost period for Croatia, despite the constant warnings of [legal] professionals'.[29]

The consequences of conflict

The consolidation of presidential authoritarianism occurred in the context of a violent conflict that predated Croatia's ratification of the European Convention on Human Rights. While the war in Croatia began in March 1991, with the seizure of territory on the part of the Croatian Serb minority, intervention on the part of the Yugoslav National Army would result in the Croatian Serb Republic of Serbian Krajina (RSK) extending its control to over one-third of Croatian territory.[30] As a result, Croatia was faced with providing refuge to over 100,000 ethnic Croat refugees who had either fled or been expelled from territories under the control of Croatian Serb authorities. In 1995, Croatia re-exerted government control over the RSK, first through Operation Flash, in which the Croatian Army reclaimed Western Slavonia and second through Operation Storm, in which the Croatian Army seized all remaining territory under the control of Croatian Serbs with the exception of Eastern Slavonia. The two

---

[25] Lamont, 'The Regeneration of the Croatian Democratic Union', 70.
[26] *Ibid.*
[27] The figure of 200 constitutes an estimated one-fifth to one-sixth of Croatian judges. Uzelac, 'Hrvatsko pravosuđe u devedesetima', 13.
[28] *Ibid.*
[29] Translated from Croatian by author. Uzelac, 'Hrvatsko pravosuđe u devedesetima', 40.
[30] While the Republic of Serbian Krajina established its own governing structures which included a judicial system, the RSK's existence was terminated in 1995.

1995 military offensives resulted in the displacement of between 150,000 and 250,000 Croatian Serbs.[31]

During the course of the 1991–1995 conflict, large numbers of refugees occupied newly vacated properties, and the Croatian government acted to facilitate the ability of ethnic Croat refugees to legalize their ownership of property in parts of the country that had been formerly under the control of the RSK.[32] In order to discourage the return of Croatian Serbs and legalize the property rights of ethnic Croats, the Croatian government adopted legislation that limited the ability of Croatian Serbs to return to post-war Croatia.[33] These pieces of legislation included:

The Law on Temporary Take-Over and Administration of Specified Property and Law on Lease of Apartments in Liberated Areas (1995). This law placed all abandoned property in formerly Serb controlled regions of Croatia under temporary state custody. Original owners were required to return and reclaim property within ninety days to prevent a property's transfer to the state. These two laws were replaced after significant international pressure was exerted upon Croatia to facilitate the return of Serbs by the *1998 Returns Programme*.[34]

The Law on Areas of Special State Concern (1996): LASSC facilitated the settlement of Bosnian Croats in formerly Serb controlled territory, often in homes vacated by ethnic Serbs. This legislation was amended in 2002.

The Amnesty Law (1996): in addition to excluding perpetrators of war crimes and crimes against humanity, individuals responsible for

---

[31] This was the estimate of displaced referenced in the International Criminal Tribunal for the former Yugoslavia's initial indictment of Croatian general Ante Gotovina. The *Prosecutor* v. *Ante Gotovina*, Indictment, Case No. IT-01-45-I, 21 May 2001.

[32] Indeed, the appropriation of property to ethnic Croats constituted part of the International Criminal Tribunal for the former Yugoslavia's alleged joint criminal enterprise for which Croatian generals Ante Gotovina, Ivan Cermak and Mladen Markac were indicted. Interestingly, the ECtHR made no reference to the ICTY's alleged joint criminal enterprise in its jurisprudence. For the appropriation of property and the Gotovina, Cermak and Markac indictments see *The Prosecutor* v. *Ante Gotovina*, Amended Indictment, Case No. IT-01-45, 19 February 2004 and *The Prosecutor* v. *Ante Gotovina, Ivan Cermak, and Mladen Markac*, Joinder Indictment, Case No. IT-06-90-PT, 21 July 2006.

[33] B. K. Blitz, 'Democratic Development, Judicial Reform and the Serbian Question', *Human Rights Review* 9 (2008) 129–130.

[34] International Crisis Group, *Breaking the Logjam: Refugee Returns to Croatia* (Report no. 49, 9 November 1998) 8–11.

criminal acts not committed in relation to the armed rebellion and individuals convicted *in absentia* prior to the Amnesty Law were not amnestied.[35] In March 1998, 13,575 individuals were amnestied for taking part in armed rebellion, which suggested to potential Serb returnees that only those whose names appeared on the list had been amnestied.[36]

Significantly, the above pieces of legislation were adopted during Croatia's accession to the Council of Europe. However, despite the above, the European Court of Human Rights afforded a wide margin of appreciation in the *Blečić* case for instances where local governments relied upon such legislation to deprive individuals of tenancy rights in accordance with domestic law.[37] Indeed, it must be emphasized that despite the 'hundreds' of legal proceedings in the domestic courts at the time of the *Blečić* judgment, the jurisprudence of the European Court of Human Rights has been overshadowed by international treaties,[38] which obligated Croatia to facilitate refugee returns, and later European Union conditionality, which has become the primary instrument through which Croatia has been encouraged to provide restitution to Croatian Serbs deprived of property and tenancy rights.[39] Therefore, as will be noted later, property restitution cases only make up a relatively small percentage of complaints brought to the Strasbourg Court against Croatia, despite the large numbers of individuals who were deprived of property during the conflict. However, before turning to post-2000 Croatia, it is first necessary to revisit Croatia's accession to the Council of Europe and the Tudjman regime's strategic adaptation of international human rights commitments.

---

[35] For an overview of the aforementioned pieces of legislation see Blitz, 'Democratic Development', at 129–130.

[36] International Crisis Group, *Breaking the Logjam*, at 6 and 7.

[37] ECtHR, *Blečić* v. *Croatia* [GC], 8 March 2006 (Appl. no. 59532/00). In a broader study of ECtHR jurisprudence on post-communist property restitution cases, Tom Allen observed that the Court failed to note that the *Blečić*'s termination of tenancy took place within a wider context of ethnic cleansing. T. Allen, 'Restitution and Transitional Justice in the European Court of Human Rights', *Columbia Journal of European Law* 13 (2006–2007) 14–15. However, it should be noted that in *Radanović* v. *Croatia*, the ECtHR found a violation had occurred and noted, 'the exercise of the State's discretion cannot entail consequences which are at variance with Convention standards'. See, ECtHR, *Radanović* v. *Croatia*, 21 December 2006 (Appl. no. 9056/02).

[38] In particular see the Dayton Agreement (1995) and the Erdut Agreement (1995).

[39] See for example, Croatia's National Action Plan for European Union accession.

Croatia and the Council of Europe: bargaining for membership

As part of Croatia's effort to secure international recognition as a sovereign state, Croatia pursued membership in a wide range of international and regional organizations.[40] Among these was the Council of Europe. In September 1992, in the midst of armed conflict, Croatia submitted an application for full membership into the Council of Europe. While the newly independent Croatian state sought integration into Euro-Atlantic institutions, the outbreak of violent conflict and the consolidation of presidential authoritarianism would force Zagreb to abandon hopes of EU and NATO accession. Given the doors to European Union and NATO membership were firmly shut to Croatia, the Council of Europe's receptiveness to Croatian accession provided Tudjman's government with a regional organization to which Croatia could potentially accede.

Beginning in 1992, Croatia would experience perhaps one of the most turbulent accession processes ever initiated by the Council. Initially, Croatia's deepening involvement in the war in neighbouring Bosnia and Herzegovina led to an early suspension of Croatia's application for Council of Europe membership. With the end of the wars in Croatia and Bosnia and Herzegovina in 1995 and parliamentary elections deemed 'free and fair' held in October 1995, the Council of Europe reopened Croatia's accession process.[41] Nevertheless, the Council remained deeply troubled by flagrant violations of media freedoms in Croatia and demanded reassurances on the part of Zagreb that Croatia would commit to protecting media freedoms.[42] On 15 March 1996 the Croatian government committed to sign the European Convention on Human Rights at the moment of accession and to recognize protocol 11. In May 1996, Croatia's membership process was frozen for six months because of the deteriorating human rights situation. That same month, the Council of Europe's Parliamentary Assembly noted:

> The Assembly notes with dismay that the Croatian authorities have since acted in blatant disregard of their commitments. The repressive

---

[40] During the 1990s Croatia became a member of the United Nations, the Organization for Security and Co-operation in Europe, the Council of Europe and the World Trade Organization.

[41] An overview of key events following Croatia's initial 1992 application to join the Council of Europe can be found in *Opinion No. 195 on Croatia's Request for Membership of the Council of Europe* (24 April 1996).

[42] Protecting media freedoms is among the commitments Croatia accepted in return for Council of Europe membership. See *Opinion No. 195* (1996).

measures taken against the media, and the dissolution of the Zagreb City
Assembly have cast severe doubt on their good faith. Moreover, concern
has arisen about the implementation of the law on co-operation with the
International Criminal Tribunal for the Former Yugoslavia.[43]

However, despite a temporary suspension of Croatia's accession, the process was unfrozen in October 1996 and Croatia was formally admitted to the Council only weeks later. On 6 November 1996 Croatia signed the European Convention of Human Rights and on 7 November 1997 Croatia ratified the Convention. Croatia also submitted itself to the European Court's individual complaints mechanism, which brought supra-national oversight to Croatia's judiciary.

At first glance, in the context of the aforementioned legalization of a domestic regime that sought to prevent the return of Croatian Serbs and facilitated the consolidation of an illiberal regime, Tudjman's enthusiastic pursuit of Council of Europe membership and Zagreb's willingness to ratify international human rights treaties defies rationalist understanding.[44] Indeed, the pursuit of membership into a regional human rights system on the part of regimes engaged in human rights abuses may appear paradoxical. However, among the states of the former Yugoslavia, membership in international and regional organizations was not only perceived as reaffirming the sovereignty of fragile states, but also served to legitimize governing authorities before a domestic audience.

Nevertheless, within Croatia human rights groups raised concerns about whether Tudjman's Croatia warranted membership in the Council. While the prospect of Council membership led Zagreb to sign and ratify a number of human rights treaties, Tudjman's government continued to acquire an increasingly authoritarian hue during the late 1990s. In particular presidential intervention in Zagreb's mayoral elections illustrated the extent to which Tudjman was prepared to undermine democratic

---

[43] *Council of Europe Parliamentary Assembly Resolution 1089*, 'On the implementation by Croatia of its commitments in the framework of the procedure of accession to the Council of Europe' (29 May 1996). In regard to the dissolution of the Zagreb City Assembly, Resolution 1089 also commended the Constitutional Courts decision to annul the government's intervention in the City Assembly as a 'positive sign of the functioning of the rule of law in Croatia'.

[44] For a broader insight into Tudjman's personal distaste for 'Western' conceptions of human rights see Miomir Zuzul's, a former senior diplomat in Tudjman's government, testimony at the International Criminal Tribunal for the former Yugoslavia at the Gotovina, Cermark and Markac trial, ICTY transcript, 9 June 2009, at 18369.

norms in the pursuit of maintaining the hegemonic position of his governing Croatian Democratic Union.[45] Moreover, far from fulfilling its commitment to protect media freedoms, Zagreb continued to intensify its campaign to force opposition media outlets to either submit to government control or halt operations. Operation Chameleon, an intelligence-led operation designed to undermine the activities of human rights NGOs, illustrates the extent to which Tudjman's government were prepared to use the apparatus of the state against potential challengers as late as 1999.[46]

In the short term the benefits of Council of Europe membership and Croatian ratification of the ECHR appeared minimal. Croatia's accession to the Council failed to dissuade Tudjman's government from continuing to obstruct refugee returns, harassment of independent media, or consolidating power within the Office of the Presidency. However, this chapter argues Croatia's integration into a regional human rights system was significant for three reasons: first, opposition media and human rights non-governmental organizations were able to point to Tudjman's violations of commitments made to the Council of Europe both at home and abroad.[47] As the leaflet incident that marked Croatia's accession to the Council of Europe demonstrated, transnational advocacy networks proved effective in ensuring human rights abuses in Croatia remained on the international agenda. Second, international actors also instrumentally used Croatia's membership in the Council of Europe as a means of highlighting Tudjman's most flagrant human rights abuses. In September 1997, the United States requested that the Council of Europe's Parliamentary Assembly suspend Croatian membership.[48] As Kearns observed, in October 1997 Tudjman's government was in the 'humiliating' position of defending itself from US led demands that Croatian membership in the Council be suspended because of Zagreb's ongoing human rights abuses.[49] In the face of growing international isolation by 1999, Tudjman's Croatian Democratic Union led government was in crisis as public opinion began to turn away from the autocratic party of power towards a six

---

[45] I. Kearns, 'Croatian Politics: Authoritarianism or Democracy?', *Contemporary Politics* 4(3) (1998) 250.

[46] C. Lamont, *International Criminal Justice and the Politics of Compliance* (Farnham: Ashgate, 2010), 46.

[47] See for example frequent references to the European Convention on Human Rights in the opposition newspaper *Feral Tribune* during the late 1990s.

[48] M. Granic, *Vanskji poslovi: Iza kulisa politike* (Zagreb: Algoritam, 2005) 159.

[49] Kearns, 'Croatian Politics', 248.

party coalition of opposition parties.[50] And finally, although judicial institutions and judicial practice were deeply flawed, Croatia's 1997 ratification of the European Convention on Human Rights necessitated constitutional amendments that were adopted shortly after the Convention's ratification to bring Croatia's Constitution into formal conformance with Convention obligations.[51]

From compliance conditionality to rebuilding a failed judiciary

Tudjman's death in December 1999 and the subsequent election of a coalition of reformist parties under the Social Democratic Party initiated Croatia's second major political transition in a decade. The importance of Croatia's membership in the Council of Europe also shifted in 2000. While in the 1990s, Croatia's ratification of the ECHR assisted in efforts to highlight human rights abuses on the part of Tudjman's government, in the 2000s the ECtHR's transitional jurisprudence would assist the domestic judiciary in reconstituting itself in post-conflict and post-authoritarian Croatia. Furthermore, in the context of Serbia, it can be argued the European Court of Human Rights carried out a similar role following Serbia's belated ratification of the European Convention on Human Rights in 2003.

Croatia's constitutional reforms adopted in 2000, transformed the Office of the Presidency from an institution that monopolized decision-making authority to a largely symbolic office and transferred governing authority to the Croatian parliament.[52] However, while the executive and legislative branches of government were rapidly transformed through constitutional amendments, Croatia's judiciary, which until this point had been deeply politicized to the extent that judges often deferred key decisions to political actors, proved to be a much more difficult target of reform. The dysfunctional state of the post-Tudjman legal system was noted in *Pibernik* v. *Croatia*, which admonished the domestic judiciary for its inability to execute its own orders:

---

[50] For more on the 2000 elections see Lamont, 'The Regeneration of the Croatian Democratic Union'.

[51] M. Matulovic, 'Europa, Hrvastki ustav i teorija ljudskih prava', paper presented at *The Constitution – Forced Change or a Change for Change? Roundtable*, Zagreb (9 April 2010).

[52] *Narodne novine* 'Change of the Constitution of the Republic of Croatia' No. 113/00 (16 November 2000).

[I]t is evident that the Contracting State did not show that it organised its legal system in such a way that it would prevent obstruction of the execution of the final judgments of its courts. Such a failure on the part of the Contracting State in the present case created or at least enabled a situation where the applicant was prevented from enjoying her home for a very long period of time.[53]

Interestingly, the vast proportion of complaints against Croatia brought to the ECtHR did not involve direct legacies of conflict, but rather centred on the inability of the Croatian courts to ensure proceedings took place within a 'reasonable' period of time, albeit many of these cases did initially involve complaints that were a result of the 1991–1995 conflict. As such, the ECtHR did not act as a final court of appeal for questions of national law,[54] but rather the ECtHR provided a final court of appeal for applicants whose cases faced prolonged delays or whose court orders were left unenforced. When it came to addressing the application of domestic law during the war in Croatia, the ECtHR granted Croatia a 'wide margin of appreciation' as mentioned in the *Blečić* case. Meanwhile, in the *Kutić* case, the ECtHR found the applicant's demand for compensation from the state for damage to property during armed conflict was stayed for an unreasonably long period of time.[55] In short, a vast proportion of the ECtHR's transitional jurisprudence relating to Croatia, and more recently Serbia, was a product of the inability of domestic judiciaries to cope with domestic case loads.[56] In regard to Croatia, the upheaval of armed conflict only exacerbated administrative failings.

In 2004 the OSCE highlighted 'repetitive decisions' on the part of the Court in relation to lack of access to domestic courts and delays in the execution of court verdicts.[57] One illustrative case was *Jelavić-Mitrović*

---

[53] ECtHR, *Pibernik* v. *Croatia*, 4 March 2004 (Appl. no. 75139/01).

[54] For more on the ECtHR's refusal to engage in acting as a final court of appeal for questions of national law see Chapter 9, this volume.

[55] The *Kutić* case references legislation passed by the Croatian parliament which 'stayed' all proceedings that sought compensation for wartime damage until new legislation was adopted. Six years later no legislation on this matter had been adopted, and legal proceedings remained 'stayed'. The ECtHR found this to violate Article 6 of the European Convention on Human Rights. See ECtHR, *Kutić* v. *Croatia*, 1 March 2002 (Appl. no. 48778/99). For a similar reasoning, which involved different legislation, see ECtHR, *Aćimović* v. *Croatia*, 9 October 2003 (Appl. no. 61237/00).

[56] A similar observation can be made with respect to Macedonia where 78 per cent of cases before the ECtHR where a violation had been found were Article 6 cases. *Statistics for the Former Yugoslav Republic of Macedonia*, European Court of Human Rights, 1 January 2009.

[57] *OSCE Background Report: ECHR Adopts Decisions in 123 Cases Involving Croatia by July 2004*. OSCE Mission to Croatia, Zagreb, 29 July 2004, at 1.

v. *Croatia*. The applicants argued that civil proceedings which were instituted on 21 October 1991 and ended on 15 June 2001 constituted an 'unreasonably long time'. Indeed, the Court noted:

> [P]rior to the entry into force of the Convention, the proceedings had already been pending before the domestic courts for some six years. Furthermore, in the period to be taken into consideration, the proceedings lasted for almost another four years. During that time it took the Supreme Court more than three years to decide on the applicants' case, whereas it only reviewed the case on points of law and did not take any evidence or perform any other procedural activity.[58]

Nevertheless, unlike the Court's earlier jurisprudence, the Court now sought to emphasize that the domestic legal system did provide the mechanisms to remedy violations and highlighted the continuing obligation on the part of applicants to exhaust domestic remedies in the first instance. In support of the above, the ECtHR has found that the practice of the Constitutional Court has, at times, rendered a potentially effective remedy ineffective through its dismissal of complaints relating to Article 6 violations:

> [T]he Court concludes that the practice of the Constitutional Court in the circumstances of the present case rendered an otherwise effective remedy ineffective. This conclusion does not, however, call into question the effectiveness of the remedy as such or the obligation to lodge a constitutional complaint under section 63 of the Constitutional Court Act in order to exhaust domestic remedies concerning complaints about the length of proceedings still pending.[59]

In *Debelić* v. *Croatia*, the Court carefully emphasized that the Constitutional Court did constitute an effective remedy, despite its practice of refusing to hear cases relating to complaints about the length of proceedings.

In sum, as of 2009, 45 per cent of cases brought against Croatia before the European Court of Human Rights in which a violation was found pertained to Article 6 violations in terms of length of proceedings. As of 2009, only 6 per cent of cases related to the protection of property.[60] Likewise, in regard to Serbia, which was also tasked with re-establishing a judiciary after the collapse of the Milosevic regime in 2000, ten of

---

[58] ECtHR, *Jelavić-Mitrović* v. *Croatia*, 13 January 2005 (Appl. no. 9591/02).
[59] ECtHR, *Debelić* v. *Croatia*, 26 May 2005 (Appl. no. 2448/03).
[60] *Statistics for Croatia on 1 January 2009*, European Court of Human Rights.

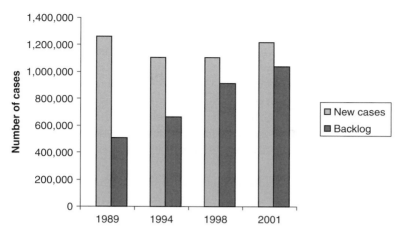

Figure 4.1 Cases before the Croatian courts

the sixteen judgments where a violation was found in 2008 were Article 6 cases.[61] However, as mentioned previously, Serbia's late entry into the European human rights system means that there is comparatively little supra-national jurisprudence when compared to Croatia.[62] In fact, the first judgment delivered in a case relating to Serbia was only delivered in September 2006.[63]

ECtHR jurisprudence highlighted the inability of the Croatian judiciary to cope with the consequences of the dual legacy of authoritarianism and violent conflict. As mentioned in *Debelić* v. *Croatia*, the tendency of the Constitutional Court to narrowly interpret its own jurisdiction combined with the large number of property case claims stemming from the armed conflict that remained before the domestic courts, resulted in a potentially effective remedy being rendered ineffective.[64] In 2002, the Croatian parliament attempted to provide further clarity in terms of the Constitutional Court's competencies and bring an end to the

---

[61] *Table of Violations 2009*, European Court of Human Rights, available at: www.echr. coe.int/NR/rdonlyres/E8F73EC8-AF6A-4205-BAF2-F6043F67F651/0/Tableau_de_ violations_2009_ENG.pdf.

[62] As of 2009, only twenty-six cases in which judgments were delivered involved Serbia, whereas, in relation to Croatia there were 151 cases.

[63] ECtHR, *Matijašević* v. *Serbia*, 19 September 2006 (Appl. no. 23037/04).

[64] It is estimated that a majority of Croatia's one million case backlog consists of property claim cases.

Constitutional Court's practice of failing to exercise jurisdiction in cases where it was obligated to do so. Croatia's 2002 Constitutional Law on the Constitutional Court specifically granted the Court the competence to decide on complaints for excessive delays in judicial proceedings.[65] While this legislation was a direct response to ECtHR judgments that found the Constitutional Court as not providing an effective remedy against excessive court delays,[66] the fact that *Debelić* post-dated the 2002 legislation illustrates that even when effective remedies exist under domestic law, the jurisprudence of national constitutional courts can continue to render these remedies ineffective.

In addition, Blitz pointed out that even after Tudjman's death, 'the judiciary and legislative branch have played a crucial role in the preservation of ethno-centric interest and the non-implementation of anti-discrimination legislation'.[67] In terms of the judiciary, the OSCE found that the Constitutional Court tended to dismiss human rights cases involving refugee returns and minorities and deferred to parliamentary legislation.[68] Moreover, when the Constitutional Court found that a human rights violation had occurred, the non-implementation of court orders on the part of the state served as an additional barrier to individuals seeking remedies through the domestic judiciary.[69] As late as 2007, the OSCE observed:

> The Constitutional Court (CC) continued to expand its role in ensuring respect for human rights, but gaps remain in its effectiveness as a court of last resort in human rights cases. As a result, the ECHR continues to serve as the primary remedy for some Croatian human rights concerns, including those affecting displaced persons, refugees, and minorities.[70]

Thus, the first decade of the 2000s was characterized by a judiciary that often failed to provide applicants with access to legal remedies, or when a judicial remedy was provided the judiciary proved unwilling to enforce its own orders. Despite the adoption of a new Constitutional Law on the Constitutional Court in 2002, which sought to create an effective domestic remedy for ECHR violations, the ECtHR's jurisprudence illustrated

---

[65] *OSCE Background Report* (2004) 2.
[66] *Ibid.*
[67] Blitz, 'Democratic Development', 132.
[68] *OSCE Background Report: ECHR Cases Involving Croatia as of August 2005.* OSCE Mission to Croatia, Zagreb, 12 August 2005, at 8.
[69] See, for example ECtHR, *Cvijetić* v. *Croatia*, 26 February 2004 (Appl. no. 71549/01).
[70] *OSCE Status Report No. 18 on Croatia's Progress in Meeting International Commitments since June 2006* (OSCE Mission to Croatia, Zagreb, 19 July 2007) 8.

that even when a domestic remedy existed, the practice of the domestic judiciary rendered an effective remedy ineffective. The extent to which the jurisprudence of the Constitutional Court would change would be subject to changes in judicial personnel. Indeed, 2007 proved a critical year for Constitutional Court reform given that the Croatian parliament's appointment of nine judges to the thirteen-member Court marked the first major post-Tudjman era round of judicial appointments.[71]

Finally, judicial reform cannot be discussed without touching on the impact of Croatia's pursuit of membership in the European Union. Just as property restitution was primarily encouraged by third party political actors, such as European Union member states and the OSCE, and not the ECtHR, it could be argued that Croatia's recent efforts to improve the functioning of its judiciary are also closely linked to Zagreb's pursuit of EU membership.[72] However, this is not meant to underplay the observation that the ECtHR's transitional jurisprudence proved crucial in both providing a remedy to applicants and providing jurisprudential guidance during Croatia's attempt to rebuild its 'failed judiciary'. Increasingly, Croatia's accession to the European Union has acted as a catalyst for judicial reform as Croatia's failed judiciary constituted a significant obstacle to membership negotiations. To be sure, Croatia's *Action Plan for Judicial Reform*, adopted by parliament in 2006 and revised in 2008, sought to address key deficiencies in the judiciary that had been identified through both ECtHR jurisprudence and the European Union.[73] One of the central aims of the *Action Plan* was to increase the efficiency of the judiciary, and from 2004 to 2007, Croatia appeared to have made significant progress in this respect. Overall, the total number of backlog cases was reduced from a 2004 high of 1,318,083 to 610,184 in 2007.[74] While serious concerns remain as to the quality of judicial decisions,[75] the reduction of Croatia's backlog of cases demonstrates a desire on the part of the Croatian government to restore the local judiciary's capability to act as a remedy in human rights cases. According to the 2008 *Action Plan*,

[71] *OSCE Status Report No. 18* (2007) 8–9.
[72] A. Uzelac, 'The Rule of Law and the Judicial System: Court Delays as a Barrier to Accession', in K. Ott (ed.), *Croatian Accession to the European Union*, vol. 2 (Institute of Public Finance, 2004) 105–130. In regard to refugee return in particular see, for example, 'Croatia: Reforms Come too Late for Most Remaining Ethnic Serb IDPs', Internal Displacement Monitoring Centre (18 April 2006) 172.
[73] *Action Plan of the Judicial Reform Strategy*, Republic of Croatia Ministry of Justice (Zagreb, 25 June 2008).
[74] *Action Plan of the Judicial Reform Strategy*, 2008.
[75] See, for example, Blitz, 'Democratic Development'.

Croatia hoped to be able to resolve all outstanding cases within a period of three years.[76]

Although as of May 2010 the judicial chapter of Croatia's accession negotiations has yet to be opened, EU concerns over the pervasiveness of corruption in the judiciary led Croatia to include specific transparency and anti-corruption provisions in the *Action Plan for Judicial Reform*. Given recent developments, the ECtHR's ability to step in to provide judicial remedy during Croatia's transitional period that followed Tudjman's death both highlighted the failings of Croatia's judiciary while acting as a de facto constitutional court for a failed domestic judiciary.

Conclusions

It is the ability of regional human rights systems to ensure adherence to human rights norms during processes of political transition and violent conflict that present a key test for the supra-national judicial oversight of states. In the context of transitional jurisprudence, Yugoslavia's violent collapse and the creation of new states during the 1990s constituted a fundamental test of not just the European Union's ability to respond to humanitarian crisis, but of the ECtHR's ability to ensure the protection of human rights norms in the aftermath of violent conflict and during transitions from authoritarianism.

This chapter examined the European Court of Human Rights in the context of the former Yugoslavia in order to explore both the ECtHR's impact in the former Yugoslavia and how the transitional jurisprudence shaped former Yugoslav encounters with transition. Croatia constitutes an important case study as Croatia came under ECtHR jurisdiction at a time when the local judiciary was confronted with rapid political change, which included a transition from presidential authoritarianism to parliamentary democracy, and an attempt to confront the legacy of violent conflict. It was noted that while the Tudjman regime's motivations for negotiating entry into the Council of Europe did not include a desire to adhere to ECHR human rights norms, Croatia's ratification of the ECHR facilitated both domestic and international attempts to highlight human rights abuses perpetrated by Tudjman's government. However, as Croatia only became subject to the ECtHR's individual complaint jurisdiction in 1997 all judgments delivered by the ECtHR occurred after the collapse of the Tudjman regime. Nevertheless, the

---

[76] *Action Plan of the Judicial Reform Strategy*, 2008.

ECtHR's transitional jurisprudence, while granting the state a 'wide margin of appreciation', exposed failings within the domestic legal system and provided a de facto high court for applicants confronted with a failed judiciary.

Bibliography

Allen, T., 'Restitution and Transitional Justice in the European Court of Human Rights', *Columbia Journal of European Law* 13 (2006–2007) 1–46.

Blitz, B. K., 'Democratic Development, Judicial Reform and the Serbian Question', *Human Rights Review* 9 (2008) 123–135.

Etinski, R., 'The European Convention on Human Rights in the Constitutional System of Serbia and Montenegro', *Transition Studies Review* 12(1) (2005) 175–183.

Getter, M., 'Yugoslavia and the European Economic Community: Is a Merger Feasible?', *University of Pennsylvania Journal of International Business Law* 11(4) (1990) 789–810.

Granic, M., *Vanjski poslovi: Iza kulisa politike* (Zagreb: Algoritam, 2005).

Kearns, I., 'Croatian Politics: Authoritarianism or Democracy?', *Contemporary Politics* 4(3) (1998) 147–258.

Kulic, D., 'The Constitutional Court of Yugoslavia in the Protection of Basic Human Rights', *Osgoode Hall Law Journal* 11(2) (1973) 275–284.

Lamont, C., 'Explaining the Regeneration of the Croatian Democratic Union in Post-Presidential Authoritarian Croatia: Elites, Legacies and Party Organization', *Balkanistica* 21 (2008) 57–86.

International Criminal Justice and the Politics of Compliance (Farnham: Ashgate, 2010).

Peselj, B. M., 'Socialist Law and the New Yugoslav Constitution', *The Georgetown Law Journal* 51(4) (1963) 651–705.

Pridham, G., 'Uneasy Democratizations – Pariah Regimes, Political Conditionality and Reborn Transitions in Central and Eastern Europe', *Democratization* 8(4) (2001) 65–94.

Risse, T., Ropp, C. and Sikkink, K. (eds.), *The Power of Human Rights: International Norms and Domestic Change* (Cambridge University Press, 1999).

Sanader, I., *HDZ za Hrvatsku: u novom veremenu pred novim izazovima* (Zagreb: Hrvatska Demokratska Zajednica, 2001).

Sikkink, K., and Keck, M., *Activists Beyond Borders: Advocacy Networks in International Politics* (Ithaca: Cornell University Press, 1998).

Subotic, J., *Hijacked Justice: Dealing with the Past in the Balkans* (Ithaca: Cornell University Press, 2009).

Uzelac, A., 'Hrvatsko pravosuđe u devedesetima: od državne nezavisnosti do institucionalne krize', *Politička misao* 38 (2001).

'The Rule of Law and the Judicial System: Court Delays as a Barrier to Accession',
in Ott, K. (ed.) *Croatian Accession to the European Union*, vol. 2 (Zagreb:
Institute of Public Finance, 2004) 105–130.

Zakosek, N., *Politički sustav Hrvatske* (Zagreb: Fakultet političkih znanosti,
2002).

5

Freedom of religion and democratic transition

JAMES A. SWEENEY

Introduction

Article 9 of the 1950 European Convention on Human Rights and Fundamental Freedoms (ECHR) protects the right to freedom of thought, conscience and religion. However the case law related to this right has only begun to develop quite recently, with the first judgment finding a violation of this article only delivered in 1993.[1] Since then a rich and often controversial jurisprudence has begun to develop,[2] including the two judgments on Turkish attempts to ban the wearing of Muslim headscarves in certain higher education establishments,[3] the fallout from the publication of cartoons of the prophet Muhammad in Denmark in 2005, and the Grand Chamber's reversal of the judgment backing a challenge to the display of the Christian crucifix in Italian state schools.[4] No doubt the Swiss attempt to ban the construction of new minarets will also give rise to some thought-provoking argumentation.[5]

James Sweeney, Senior Lecturer in Law and Convenor of the 'Law and Conflict at Durham' Research Group, Durham University, UK. An early version of this paper was presented at the Transitional Justice Institute, University of Ulster, on 23 March 2010. Thank you to the participants for their feedback. I would also like to show my appreciation for the undergraduate students on my Advanced Issues in Public Law class at Durham Law School in 2009/2010, on whom I tried out some of the ideas expressed in this paper and who responded with great aplomb and only occasional bafflement.

[1] ECtHR, *Kokkinakis* v. *Greece*, 25 May 1993 (Appl. no. 14307/88).

[2] See C. Evans, *Freedom of Religion under the European Convention on Human Rights* (Oxford University Press, 2001).

[3] ECtHR, *Leyla Şahin* v. *Turkey* [GC], 10 November 2005 (Appl. no. 44774/98) and discussed in K. Altiparmak and O. Karahanogullari, 'After Sahin: The Debate on Headscarves is Not Over', *European Constitutional Law Review* 2 (2006) 268 and T. Lewis, 'What Not to Wear: Religious Rights, the European Court, and the Margin of Appreciation', *ICLQ* 56 (2007) 395 and D. McGoldrick, *Human Rights and Religion: The Islamic Headscarf Debate in Europe* (Oxford: Hart, 2006).

[4] ECtHR, *Lautsi* v. *Italy*, [GC], 18 March 2011 (Appl. no. 30814/06).

[5] BBC, 'Swiss Minaret Appeal goes to European Court' (16.12.2009) available at: http://news.bbc.co.uk/1/hi/8417076.stm.

This chapter questions the approach of the European Court of Human Rights to freedom of religion in transitional societies – to what will be termed 'religion in transition' cases. The aim is to arrive at a legally sound and theoretically robust approach to these cases, which also fully respects the experiences of transitional democracies. In particular, the chapter examines the 'margin of appreciation' left to Contracting Parties where the Respondent State cites the centrality of religion to the process of democratic transition as a reason for restricting some religious freedoms in favour of protecting others. The central argument of the chapter is that the European Court must take the transitional context seriously, without itself dispensing 'transitional justice'.

Freedom of religion is protected in all the other major international and regional human rights instruments, including Article 18 of the Universal Declaration of Human Rights (UDHR), Article 18 of the International Covenant on Civil and Political Rights (ICCPR), Article 3 of the American Declaration of the Rights and Duties of Man (American Declaration), Article 12 of the American Convention on Human Rights (ACHR) and Article 8 of the African Charter on Human and Peoples' Rights (ACHPR). Throughout this chapter, some modest comparisons are made between the approach advocated to freedom of religion in the European system and these comparators.[6]

Democracy as a limit on restricting freedom of religion

Article 9 ECHR protects freedom of thought, conscience and religion. Articles 8–11 ECHR all enshrine rights in their first paragraph, and provide for possible qualifications to the right in their second paragraph. The qualifications to Article 9 are slightly different to the other personal freedoms since they pertain only to the manifestation of religion or belief (the *forum externum*), rather than the act or state of believing itself (the *forum internum*).

Interpreting the scope of Article 9(1) has been challenging and the European Commission's decision in *Arrowsmith* v. *UK*,[7] that not all actions motivated by religious belief fall within it,[8] has met with some

---

[6] For a more comprehensive comparison with the UN system see: P. M. Taylor, *Freedom of Religion: UN and European Human Rights Law and Practice* (Cambridge University Press, 2005).

[7] EComHR, *Arrowsmith* v. *UK*, 16 May 1977 (Appl. no. 7050/75).

[8] *Ibid.*, para. 71.

criticism.[9] Many of the concerns about this case and its progeny are about identifying exactly which practices are, in fact, sufficiently motivated by religious or other beliefs to gain protection under Article 9(1).

The key characteristic of Article 9 for our purposes is the extent to which the Court has recognised a strong link between religion and democratic society. According to the Court:

> freedom of thought, conscience and religion is one of the foundations of a democratic society within the meaning of the Convention. The pluralism indissociable from a democratic society, which has been dearly won over the centuries, depends on it.[10]

In this way, Article 9 will often need to be interpreted in the light of other Convention rights, such as the Article 11 right to freedom of association and peaceful assembly.[11] Thus, interferences with Article 9 rights may be examined not only as an impingement on the applicant's own religion or beliefs, but also as an indirect impingement on the democratic fabric of society. However, as we shall see in the next section, the relationship between religion and democracy cuts both ways.

In order for a restriction upon Article 9 to be justified, it must meet the conditions specified in Article 9(2). The restriction must be prescribed by law and be necessary in a democratic society in the interest of public safety, for the protection of public order, health or morals, or for the protection of the rights and freedoms of others. These specified 'interests' are more commonly referred to in the European jurisprudence as 'legitimate aims'.

At this stage it is important to note the approach of the other major international instruments to limiting freedom of religion. The argument below will hinge on the relationship between questions about the 'legitimacy' of restrictions and questions about their 'necessity', since these are distinct stages in the European system.

Article 18 of the UDHR does not contain a limitations clause but Article 29 states that:

> In the exercise of his rights and freedoms, everyone shall be subject only to such limitations as are determined by law solely for the purpose of securing due recognition and respect for the rights and freedoms of others and

---

[9] Evans, *Freedom of Religion under the European Convention on Human Rights*, 115f.
[10] ECtHR, *Hasan and Chaush* v. *Bulgaria*, 26 October 2000 (Appl. no. 30985/96) para. 60.
[11] *Ibid.*, para. 62.

of meeting the just requirements of morality, public order and the general welfare in a democratic society.

Likewise Article 3 of the American Declaration does not contain a limitation clause, but all of the rights enumerated by it are subject to a general limitation clause in Article 28, which states that:

> The rights of man are limited by the rights of others, by the security of all, and by the just demands of the general welfare and the advancement of democracy.

Both the UDHR and American Declaration thus recognise that any restriction must therefore pursue 'just requirements' or 'just demands' that, at least in the more specific formulation of the UDHR, are comparable to the ECHR's 'legitimate aims'.

Article 18(3) ICCPR and Article 12(3) ACHR are almost identical in their formulation to Article 9(2) ECHR, so that restrictions must pursue specified legitimate aims as well as be necessary.[12]

The African system is slightly different in this regard.[13] Article 8 ACHPR consists of only one clause, which in its second sentence contains the guarantee that, 'No one may, subject to law and order, be submitted to measures restricting the exercise of [freedom of religion]'. Article 27(2), in the section of the Charter on individual duties, states that, 'The rights and freedoms of each individual shall be exercised with due regard to the rights of others, collective security, morality and common interest'. The African Commission on Human Rights has held this to mean that:

> The reasons for possible limitations must be founded in a legitimate state interest and the evils of limitations of rights must be strictly proportionate with and absolutely necessary for the advantages which are to be obtained.[14]

In this way, the African system likewise separates the issue of 'legitimate state interest' from proportionality and necessity.

---

[12] On limitations to the ICCPR see: UN Commission on Human Rights, 'The Siracusa Principles on the Limitation and Derogation Provisions in the International Covenant on Civil and Political Rights', 28 September 1984, E/CN.4/1985/4; the non-derogable nature of these rights is acknowledged and discussed below.

[13] See generally, A. Allo, 'Derogations or Limitations? Rethinking the African Human Rights System of Derogation in Light of the European System', *Ethiopian Journal of Legal Education* 2(2) (2009) 21.

[14] AfComHPR, *Media Rights Agenda and Others* v. *Nigeria*, 1998 (no. 105/93, 128/94, 130/94 and 152/96) para. 69.

Restricting freedom of religion in order to promote democratic consolidation

Religious questions run behind many significant cases brought before the European Court of Human Rights involving transitional issues, but which do not necessarily hinge on Article 9 itself. In these cases, as well some involving Article 9, the relationship between religion and democracy may be used instrumentally in order to justify rights-restrictive measures.

A case in point would be the 2002 case of *Al-Nashif* v. *Bulgaria*.[15] This case involved the detention in Bulgaria and deportation to Syria of a stateless person of Muslim faith and Palestinian origin. The applicants in the case were Mr Al-Nashif and his two children, who remained in Bulgaria with their mother after their father's deportation. The European Court of Human Rights found violations of Articles 5(4), 8 and 13 ECHR. For our purposes, it is the argumentation on Article 8 that is interesting.

This element of the case centred on whether Al-Nashif's deportation to Syria constituted an unjustified interference with his and his children's right to family life, since the family had no real connection with that state, and there were economic and legal impediments to establishing a family life in Syria or in neighbouring Jordan (where the children's maternal grandparents were living). The Bulgarian government denied, inter alia, that there was an interference with family life at all due to one crucial fact: whilst living in Bulgaria Al-Nashif had entered into a second, religious, marriage with another woman.[16]

The European Court took the approach that the existence of 'family life' for the purposes of Article 8 is a question of fact. From the moment of their birth, children have a familial bond with their parents that only exceptional circumstances can change.[17] The Court held that despite the first applicant entering into a second religious, concurrent, and thereby polygamous, marriage there were no exceptional circumstances such as to break the bond between the first applicant and his children.[18]

This is undoubtedly an interesting case in terms of the apparent openness of the European Court to the suggestion that religious polygamous

---

[15] ECtHR, *Al-Nashif* v. *Bulgaria*, 20 June 2002 (Appl. no. 50963/99).

[16] The government also argued that Al-Nashif had not proven that his first marriage was lawful (*ibid.*, para. 107). One might argue that if polygamy was such a problem for the Bulgarian authorities, then questioning the validity of the 'first' marriage would work against their central argument; that by marrying a second woman the applicant was showing he did not have a family life with the first.

[17] *Ibid.*, para. 112.   [18] *Ibid.*, para. 113.

marriage does not necessarily disrupt family life as understood in the Convention sense.[19] To the extent that it involves one of the states that joined the Convention system after the end of the Cold War, it presents features that relate to the transitional issues discussed below: the government had (unsuccessfully) argued that even if Article 8 applied to the case, the decision to deport Al-Nashif because of his alleged extremist activities was proportionate in the light of the Balkan regional context, where 'measures of active protection of religious tolerance were critical',[20] and where in Bulgaria in particular,

> owing to a number of factors – such as disruptions in community traditions caused by decades of totalitarianism – the religious consciousness of the population was currently unstable and unsettled. Communities in general, and the Muslim community in particular, were therefore susceptible to influences. It was necessary to protect them against Islamic fundamentalism.[21]

This passage illustrates that the real issue for the study of 'religion in transition' cases is the appearance of cases where the role of religion in the transitional context is cited as a justifying factor, pursuing a wider aim of democratic consolidation.

Enlargement of the Council of Europe

The early 1990s saw a massive enlargement of the Council of Europe, the parent organisation of the European Convention system. This, in turn, brought a great many new Contracting Parties to the ECHR. The wisdom of the Council's rapid enlargement and the consequent extension of the jurisdiction of the European Court of Human Rights is not universally accepted. For example in 1993 Peter Leuprecht resigned as Deputy Secretary General of the Council of Europe, protesting that the standards of the Convention risked dilution with the admission of Russia into the

---

[19] This is particularly surprising given the European Court's now notorious assessment of Sharia law in the *Refah Partisi* case (discussed in a different context below), where it stated that, 'sharia is incompatible with the fundamental principles of democracy, as set forth in the Convention' (ECtHR, *Refah Partisi (the Welfare Party)* v. *Turkey* [GC], 13 February 2003 (Appl. nos. 41340/98, 41342/98, 41343/98 and 41344/98) para. 123). For a critique of this judgment, see D. McGoldrick, 'Accommodating Muslims in Europe: From Adopting Sharia Law to Religiously Based Opt Outs from Generally Applicable Laws', *Human Rights Law Review* 9(4) (2009) 603–612.

[20] *Ibid.*, para. 111.   [21] *Ibid.*, para. 111.

Council.[22] Several academic commentators expressed similar concerns.[23] Nevertheless, the Council of Europe took the view that participation in and supervision by the Convention system was better than exclusion from it.[24]

The Parliamentary Assembly of the Council of Europe (PACE) offered the new Member States advice on the transitional process in the form of Resolution 1096, on 'Measures to dismantle the heritage of former communist totalitarian systems'.[25] It identified four principles that should guide the transition process: demilitarisation, decentralisation, demonopolisation and debureaucratisation.[26] These general principles were accompanied by some more specific recommendations relating to criminal responsibility for acts carried out under the previous regime; the rehabilitation of people convicted of political offences under the former regime; the opening of secret service files; the restitution of property expropriated under the former regime; and the treatment of people who, whilst not the perpetrators of crimes under the former regime, held high positions within the communist apparatus and are singled out for special treatment in the new regime (such as restrictions on holding public office).[27] The 'best guarantee' of dismantlement of the former regimes was 'the profound political, legal and economic reforms in the respective countries, leading to the formation of an authentic democratic mentality and political culture'.[28] In this, the new Member States were not on their own: PACE called on consolidated democracies to 'step up' their aid and assistance to the emerging democracies.[29]

Resolution 1096 deals both with elements of what political scientists would recognise as democratic transition, and what lawyers would recognise as transitional justice. The broad theme of democratic transition

[22] P. Leuprecht, 'Innovations in the European System of Human Rights Protection: Is Enlargement Compatible with Reinforcement?', *Transnational Law and Contemporary Problems* 8 (1998) 313.

[23] E.g. M. Janis, 'Russia and the "Legality" of Strasbourg Law', *European Journal of International Law* 8 (1997) 93; R. Kay, 'The European Convention on Human Rights and the Authority of Law', *Connecticut Journal of International Law* 8 (1993) 217.

[24] See J. A. Sweeney, *The European Court of Human Rights in the Post-Cold War Era: Universality in Transition* (New York: Routledge, 2011) and J. A. Sweeney, 'Divergence and Diversity in Post-Communist European Human Rights Cases', *Connecticut Journal of International Law* 21 (2005) 1.

[25] PACE Resolution 1096 on 'Measures to dismantle the heritage of former communist totalitarian systems', text adopted by the Assembly on 27 June 1996 (23rd Sitting).

[26] *Ibid.*, para. 5.   [27] *Ibid.*, paras. 7–14.

[28] *Ibid.*, para. 16.   [29] *Ibid.*, para. 16.

is outside the scope of this chapter, suffice it to say that there is abundant literature on the 'waves' of democratic transition that have taken place throughout history,[30] and competing explanations as to the relationship between internal (domestic) and external (international) factors in successful transitions. Indeed the orthodoxy for much of the twentieth century was that internal factors, rather than external factors such as pressure from organisations like the Council of Europe, were the most significant.[31] It is therefore worth remembering that, as only one element of the Council of Europe, itself an external factor in each state's transitional process, the impact of the European Court of Human Rights' jurisprudence on the ultimate success or otherwise of the Contracting Parties' transition should be kept in perspective.

In addition to being part of the process of democratisation, the more specific recommendations of Resolution 1096 can be viewed within the paradigm of 'transitional justice'. Transitional justice is the 'conception of justice associated with periods of political change, characterised by legal responses to confront the wrongdoings of repressive predecessor regimes'.[32] Thus often when we think of the relationship between human rights and transitional justice we are concerned with looking at attempts to deal with the human rights violations of the previous regime. For example Teitel notes that, 'the most vigorous enforcement of human rights law occurs in transitional periods', citing the creation of ad hoc tribunals to prosecute human rights abusers from the Rwandan and Bosnian conflicts.[33] Likewise David Little's work on 'dealing with human rights violations in transitional societies' concentrates on the relationship

---

[30] In particular, S. Huntington, *The Third Wave: Democratisation in the Late Twentieth Century* (Norman: University of Oklahoma Press, 1991).

[31] P. Schmitter, 'An Introduction to Southern European Transitions from Authoritarian Rule: Italy, Greece, Portugal, Spain, and Turkey', in G. O'Donnell *et al.* (eds.) *Transitions from Authoritarian Rule: Southern Europe* (Baltimore: Johns Hopkins University Press, 1986) 5 and J. C. Pevehouse, *Democracy from Above: Regional Organisations and Democratization* (Cambridge University Press, 2005) 2.

[32] R. Teitel, 'Transitional Justice Genealogy', *Harvard Human Rights Law Review* 16 (2003) 69 and see also Teitel's *Transitional Justice* (New York: Oxford University Press, 2000). One might question whether the distinctive policies in Resolution 1096, employed to reckon with the past, in fact embody a modified conception of justice or, as Posner and Vermeule would argue, can be placed along a spectrum that would see them merely as distinctive, albeit fairly extreme, elements of 'ordinary justice'. It is the approach of this chapter that the measures in Resolution 1096 in fact are measures rooted in transitional justice: cf. E. Posner and A. Vermeule, 'Transitional Justice as Ordinary Justice', *Harvard Law Review* 117 (2004) 761.

[33] Teitel, *Transitional Justice*, 228.

between the opposing impulses of retribution and reconciliation in dealing with human rights offenders of the former regime.[34] In the European
Convention on Human Rights, and in this chapter, this is not what we are
necessarily looking at – we are looking not at the actions of the former
regime, but of the current one. Transitional measures taken by the new
Contracting Parties may themselves impact upon human rights.

It is important to note that from the text of Resolution 1096, and from
the general approach to transitional justice of Teitel and others, that special measures justified on grounds related to the particular role of religion in transitional societies (or such societies' susceptibility to religious
extremism) do not, in and of themselves, hold a privileged status as an
obvious element of the transitional process. Nevertheless, the support
of the Catholic Church and, in particular, Pope John Paul II, for Lech
Walesa's 'Solidarity' movement in Poland[35] shows that as an intermingled
internal and external factor religion may have played an organic role in at
least some of the Central and Eastern European transitions.

The 'religion in transition' cases

In the case of *Metropolitan Church of Bessarabia* v. *Moldova*[36] the religious
context was relevant both to the right at stake, Article 9, and to the reasons
for restricting it. The Moldovan government argued that their refusal to
register a religious association that they deemed a schismatic group within
the Church of Moldova was justified because Moldova 'had few strengths
it could depend on to ensure its continued existence, but one factor conducive to stability was religion'.[37] On this basis the government argued,
and the Court accepted, that 'having regard to the circumstances of the
case' the restriction pursued the legitimate aim of protecting public order
and public safety.[38] In other words, the transitional context contributed to
the 'legitimacy' of the aim. Nevertheless the European Court of Human
Rights found that the restriction was not necessary to meet its stated aim,
and therefore violated Article 9 ECHR. In this part of the judgment the
Court engaged with the Respondent State's arguments that the measure

---

[34] D. Little, 'A Different Kind of Justice: Dealing with Human Rights Violations in
Transitional Societies', *Ethics and International Affairs* 13 (1999) 65.

[35] J. Grugel, *Democratization: A Critical Introduction* (Basingstoke: Palgrave Macmillan,
2002) 200.

[36] ECtHR, *Metropolitan Church of Bessarabia* v. *Moldova*, 13 December 2001 (Appl. no.
45701/99).

[37] *Ibid.*, para. 111.   [38] *Ibid.*, para. 113.

was necessary in order to uphold Moldovan law and Moldovan constitutional principles; to prevent a threat to territorial integrity; and to protect social peace and understanding between believers.[39] The European Court did not, at this stage, engage any further with the issue of whether the transitional context amplified or even impacted at all on these arguments.

The Respondent State made similar arguments about the special role of religion during democratic transition in the January 2009 case of *Holy Synod of the Bulgarian Orthodox Church (Metropolitan Inokentiy) and Others* v. *Bulgaria*.[40] Again, in this case the religious context was relevant both to the right invoked and to the reason for restricting it. The case concerned a dispute arising from the first democratic Bulgarian government's attempts to replace the Patriarch imposed during the communist era (Patriarch Maxim), and the subsequent government's decision to reinstate him in order to end the ensuing confusion within the Bulgarian Orthodox Church. The government argued before the European Court that, 'the unity of the Bulgarian Orthodox Church was an important national goal of historical significance, with ramifications affecting the very fabric of the Bulgarian nation and its cultural identity', and therefore their reinstatement of Patriarch Maxim was necessary and proportionate.[41] The European Court of Human Rights disagreed, and found a violation of Article 9 ECHR interpreted in the light of Article 11.

In *Holy Synod of the Bulgarian Orthodox Church* the European Court more explicitly accepted that the transitional context was relevant both to the 'legitimacy' of the aim and to the 'necessity' of the measure.[42] However, although the Court engaged directly with the arguments about the centrality of the issue for the state of Bulgaria, it failed to distinguish clearly which legitimate aim or aims were at stake, or to separate their identification from answering the questions of necessity and proportionality.[43] The Court found that:

> [Taking] into account the margin of appreciation ... the Bulgarian authorities had legitimate reasons to consider some form of action with the aim of helping to overcome the conflict in the Church, if possible, or limiting its negative effect on public order and legal certainty.[44]

---

[39] *Ibid.*, paras. 123–127.
[40] ECtHR, *Holy Synod of the Bulgarian Orthodox Church (Metropolitan Inokentiy) and Others* v. *Bulgaria*, 22 January 2009 (Appl. no 412/03 and 35677/04).
[41] *Ibid.*, para. 143.   [42] *Ibid.*, para. 145.
[43] *Ibid.*, para. 159.   [44] *Ibid.*, para. 131.

This is intriguing at a doctrinal level because the margin of appreciation is normally said to attach to the question of whether a restriction is 'necessary', rather than 'legitimate'.[45] Moreover in earlier non-transitional cases that Court had explained that the width of the margin of appreciation in each case will relate to the legitimate aim put forward by the state.[46] If the Court is to apply the margin of appreciation doctrine coherently, it must therefore always first identify the aim at stake.

In *Holy Synod of the Bulgarian Orthodox Church*, and in relation to what the Court saw as the issue before it, namely 'whether the concrete measures chosen by the authorities could be accepted as lawful and necessary in a democratic society',[47] the Court did not invoke the margin of appreciation at all, and simply determined that:

> [The] legitimate aim of remedying the injustices inflicted by the unlawful acts of 1992 and the following years, could not warrant the use of State power, in 2003, 2004 and afterwards, to take sweeping measures, imposing a return to the *status quo ante* against the will of a part of the religious community.[48]

On the one hand both *Metropolitan Church of Bessarabia* and *Holy Synod of the Bulgarian Orthodox Church* raise issues about state neutrality in religious matters that had arisen in non-transitional cases as well.[49] The European Court has consistently held that measures favouring a particular leader of a divided religious community or seeking to force the community to place itself, against its will, under a single leadership, would constitute a violation of Article 9.[50] One of the leading cases in this respect is also a Bulgarian one: *Hasan and Chaush v. Bulgaria*. In this case, as we shall see below, the transitional context did not play a role either in

---

[45] See the discussion in Sweeney, 'Divergence and Diversity in Post-Communist European Human Rights Cases', 25.

[46] See, for example, ECtHR, *Sunday Times* v. *UK*, 26 April 1979 (Appl. no. 6538/74) para. 59, where the European Court compared the aims of 'maintaining the authority and impartiality of the judiciary' and 'the protection of health or morals', concluding that there would be a narrower margin of appreciation in relation to the former than the latter.

[47] *Ibid.*, para. 132.

[48] *Holy Synod of the Bulgarian Orthodox Church (Metropolitan Inokentiy) and Others* v. *Bulgaria*, para. 138.

[49] For example in ECtHR, *Hasan and Chaush* v. *Bulgaria*, 26 October 2000 (Appl. no. 30985/96).

[50] *Ibid.*, para. 78, and ECtHR, *Serif* v. *Greece*, 14 December 1999 (Appl. no. 38178/97) para. 52 and *Metropolitan Church of Bessarabia* v. *Moldova*, para. 117 and *Holy Synod of the Bulgarian Orthodox Church (Metropolitan Inokentiy) and Others* v. *Bulgaria*, para. 120.

the arguments put forward by the Respondent State or in the assessment of them by the Court. However, and on the other hand, the way in which the Respondent States argued their cases in *Metropolitan Church of Bessarabia* and *Holy Synod of the Bulgarian Orthodox Church* shows that there is something else here of relevance to the study of human rights in transitional societies. The Respondent States were making a claim that certain measures that impact upon freedom of religion are justifiable in the particular circumstances of democratic transition because of the special role of religion in fragile democracies. In this respect, they are similar to the *Al-Nashif* case.

'Legitimacy' and 'necessity' distinguished

The approach of the European Court of Human Rights to the Respondent States' claims that the 'religion in transition' cases should be treated differently is intriguing. There is a notable absence of consistency in the stage at which the transitional context, including the role of religion within it, is considered. It is particularly important to develop a coherent approach to the relationship between 'legitimacy' and 'necessity' in cases such as these. At this stage there are several routes the Court might take.

One route is to argue that transitional situations themselves simply do not present substantively different issues, and therefore the Respondent State's arguments about the special status of religion in the transition should be dismissed as normatively unfounded: the impugned measure or decision could be neither legitimate nor necessary. This approach can be rejected. Convincing work has demonstrated that transitional justice may operate, usefully, in a different way to ordinary justice.[51] The real question for the European Court is about what it, as an international body, and a judicial body, should do about national transitional policies, including those that seek to use religion instrumentally in order to stabilise the transition, or those that claim the particular susceptibility of transitional societies to religious extremism.

This is where the second route begins. It might be argued that the Court should alter its own conception of justice in cases from transitional states, since transitional justice measures always outweigh considerations of ordinary justice in transitional democracies. This would recognise that

---

[51] Teitel, *Transitional Justice*, but note that Teitel is concerned about the possible extension of transitional justice style thinking to non-transitional contexts; see Teitel, 'Transitional Justice Genealogy'.

the new Contracting Parties are not only undergoing a transition to democracy, but also a transition to full compliance with the European Convention. The European Court would become an embodiment of an international form of transitional justice: the human rights counterpart to international criminal responses.[52] The cases in which the transitional context goes to the 'legitimacy' of a rights-restrictive measure might suggest that the Court is already doing precisely this. The implication is that via the application of a transitional form of justice, certain otherwise 'illegitimate' actions could be deemed 'legitimate'.

The bestowal of 'legitimacy' upon a restrictive measure is significant, legally and politically, even where it is found not to be necessary. It is particularly questionable when the stated aim is not one that even the most ardent advocate of transitional justice would recognise as a common transitional policy, such as establishing unity around a state church. As suggested above, allowing a margin of appreciation on the legitimacy of the restrictive aim is inconsistent with a normal doctrinal understanding of the stage at which the margin of appreciation figures in the Court's reasoning. Moreover, as demonstrated in the work of Arai-Takahashi, in order for the margin of appreciation to operate properly it must be seen alongside the question of proportionality, which is clearly more relevant to the question of 'necessity' than 'legitimacy'.[53] Furthermore, and finally, it is the argument of this chapter that altering the conception of justice and thus legitimacy to be applied to transitional democracies, and condoning less than full compliance with the European Convention, would call into question the European Court's commitment to the universality of human rights.

Yet another, third, route would be to argue that although national policies founded on transitional justice have a normative pedigree, the European Court should not change its own conception of justice. It must apply its existing standards in such a way as to respond meaningfully to the factual matrix presented by cases emanating from transitional democracies without altering its general approach. The Court may check whether a transitional measure is compliant with the rule of law; that, in regard to its legitimacy, the transitional measure pursues one of the

---

[52] In 'Transitional Justice Genealogy' Teitel notes the displacement of national justice by international justice as a defining feature of post-Second World War transitional justice, with the Nuremberg Trials as its most recognised symbol: Teitel, 'Transitional Justice Genealogy', 70, 72.

[53] Y. Arai-Takahashi, *The Margin of Appreciation Doctrine and the Principle of Proportionality in the Jurisprudence of the ECHR* (Oxford: Intersentia, 2002).

legitimate aims specified in the Convention; and, if it does, it may proceed
to consider the necessity and proportionality of the measure in the transitional context via a detailed and coherent application of the margin of
appreciation doctrine.

In this model the transitional context is far more relevant to the basis
and width of the margin of appreciation than to the conceptual 'legitimacy' of the measure. This approach is preferred since, whilst the margin
of appreciation in respect of necessity allows for some modulation in the
Court's jurisprudence in recognition of the transitional context (as it does
in relation to the idiosyncrasies of older Contracting Parties), it does not
(need to) disturb the universality human rights.[54] It is tempting to think of
this as a 'transitional margin of appreciation', or similar, but this would be
misleading because it would imply that the transitional margin is different, conceptually, to the regular margin of appreciation. It is not. Instead,
the European Court should apply (and sometimes has applied) its regular,
even formulaic, approach to 'religion in transition' cases whilst remaining fully cognisant of the conceptual relationship between domestic transitional justice policies and the international supervision of human rights
protection. In order to understand this approach, it is now necessary to
revisit the key cases.

Revisiting the 'religion in transition' cases

The first stage in any of the transitional cases is to ensure compliance
with the formal rule of law. Whether a rights-restrictive measure inter-
feres with Article 9 rights or other Convention rights on the basis of a
claimed relationship between religion and democratic stability (or susceptibility to extremism), the Respondent State must demonstrate that it
is acting through law. Thus, in the *Al-Nashif* case introduced above, when
the European Court examined whether the interference was justified, it
found that the legal regime surrounding the applicant's deportation did
not meet the Convention's requirement of lawfulness,[55] so it did not need
to examine whether the interference pursued a legitimate aim or was
actually proportionate.[56] The impugned actions in the *Hasan and Chaush*

---

[54] J. A. Sweeney, 'Margins of Appreciation: Cultural Relativity and the European Court of
Human Rights in the Post-Cold War Era', *ICLQ* 54(2) (2005) 459.

[55] *Al-Nashif* v. *Bulgaria*, para. 128.

[56] *Al-Nashif* v. *Bulgaria*, para. 129.

case also fell at this first hurdle.[57] If a rights-restrictive transitional measure is to survive scrutiny from the European Court it must, at the very least, be 'prescribed by law'.

The second stage is legitimacy. This could be (and often is) a short step. For Articles 8–11, the legitimate aims are listed exhaustively in the Convention itself. For others that might be relevant in religion cases, such as Article 14 or Article 3 of Protocol 1, the Court has fashioned a slightly different approach, albeit one which still carries with it an assessment of whether the aim of the measure is legitimate. As an aside, it might be noted that the Court could perhaps be a little less taciturn in its assimilation of myriad national policies to the Convention's 'legitimate aims'. For the approach advocated here it is vital not to give the impression that the only reason a measure is held to be 'legitimate' is that it was imposed in the transitional context. Otherwise the impression could be created that an alternative, transitional, form of justice is being applied by the European Court. Instead, the national transitional policy should be shown to correspond clearly to a Convention 'legitimate aim', leaving the impact of the transitional context as a factor to be considered when assessing the means chosen to achieve the aim. Of course if the transitional policy did not correspond to a Convention legitimate aim then, whether or not it might have some stabilising effect in a fragile democracy, it would be in conflict with the Convention. By joining the Council of Europe, and signing and ratifying the ECHR, it may be that states have thereby disbarred themselves from employing some transitional policies, in favour of a 'human rights based approach' to transition.

The third and most important stage is necessity. It is here where the Court can engage with the question of whether a purportedly transitional measure is widely recognised as pursuing a necessary task in the transitional process. If not then there is no reason to treat it differently to any other rights-restrictive measure when it comes to the basis or width of the margin of appreciation. This is particularly important in the religion cases since we have established that 'stabilising the state around an established church', or similar, is not widely recognised as a classic transitional policy.

Where a rights-restrictive practice, which is purportedly justified by reference to the transitional context, is to be examined then the Court should, in the first place, enforce the Convention in such a way as to protect against 'naked, bad faith abuse of power'.[58] However much a state

---

[57] *Hasan and Chaush* v. *Bulgaria*, para. 86.
[58] P. Mahoney, 'Marvellous Richness of Diversity or Invidious Cultural Relativism', *Human Rights Law Journal* 19(1) (1998) 1, 4.

stressed a special relationship between religion and democratic transition in the context of a case brought against it, a measure that amounted to an unmitigated abuse of power could never be justified. There would be no question of it falling within the state's margin of appreciation since the margin only allows variations in *how*, and not *whether*, to comply with the Convention. This is the first, but not the only, level of protection offered by the Convention. It is (only) at a second level, when a rights-restrictive transitional measure is imposed in 'good faith', for example within the wider context of democratic consolidation, that the margin of appreciation should be considered.[59]

The key here is that only a rights-restrictive transitional measure that contributed towards *democratic* consolidation could benefit from a margin of appreciation.[60] To suggest otherwise would be to radically expand the scope of the margin of appreciation doctrine, provide inadequate supervision of the new Contracting Parties' democratic transition, and undermine the rule of law.

This aligns neatly with the approach taken in PACE Resolution 1096 where, in an effort to avoid complaints reaching the Strasbourg institutions, PACE cautioned that:

> [A] democratic state based on the rule of law must, in dismantling the heritage of former communist totalitarian systems, apply the procedural means of such a state. It cannot apply any other means, since it would

---

[59] *Ibid.*

[60] On democracy in the ECHR, see ECtHR, *United Communist Party of Turkey* v. *Turkey*, 30 January 1998 (Appl. no. 19392/92) para. 45, where the European Court held that 'Democracy is without doubt a fundamental feature of the European public order … That is apparent … firstly, from the Preamble to the Convention … [The Court] has pointed out several times that the Convention was designed to maintain and promote the ideals and values of a democratic society … In addition, Articles 8, 9, 10 and 11 of the Convention require that interference with the exercise of the rights they enshrine must be assessed by the yardstick of what is "necessary in a democratic society". The only type of necessity capable of justifying an interference with any of those rights is, therefore, one which may claim to spring from "democratic society". Democracy thus appears to be the only political model contemplated by the Convention and, accordingly, the only one compatible with it'. However note the contrasting views expressed in A. Mowbray, 'The Role of the European Court of Human Rights in the Promotion of Democracy', *Public Law* (1999) 703 and C. Gearty, 'Democracy and Human Rights in the European Court of Human Rights: A Critical Appraisal', *Northern Ireland Legal Quarterly* 51 (2000) 381 and see also S. Marks, 'The European Convention on Human Rights and its "Democratic Society"', *British Yearbook of International Law* (1995) 209 and R. O'Connell, 'Towards a Stronger Concept of Democracy in the Strasbourg Convention', *European Human Rights Law Review* (2006) 281 and S. Wheatley, 'Minorities under the ECHR and the Construction of "a Democratic Society"', *Public Law* (2007) 770.

then be no better than the totalitarian regime which is to be dismantled. A democratic state based on the rule of law has sufficient means at its disposal to ensure that the cause of justice is served and the guilty are punished ... A state based on the rule of law can also defend itself against a resurgence of the communist totalitarian threat, since it has ample means at its disposal *which do not conflict with human rights and the rule of law.*[61]

There is reason to suppose that the European Court itself is sympathetic to this approach. A point of principle can be extracted from the judgment in the *Holy Synod* case: that transitional societies' common need to remedy unlawful acts of the past cannot justify, in a democratic society, disproportionate state action and further unlawful acts.[62]

As the Court examines the question of necessity in the transitional cases, it should encourage and scrutinise arguments about the basis and, separately, the width of the margin of appreciation. The basis of the margin may relate to the robustness of the domestic mechanisms for verifying the material facts of the case, or to the policy expertise and legitimacy of elected legislatures. The width of the margin in particular cases will be tied to some combination of various factors, including the right at stake, the way that it is invoked, and the legitimate aim the restriction pursues.[63] It is conceded that for some commentators the width of the margin of appreciation is determined too haphazardly to play the role suggested in this chapter. Nevertheless, the various factors that are identified as commonly playing a role in determining its width can, it is submitted, provide a useful framework on which to hang discussion of whether a rights-restrictive measure in the 'religion in transition' case ultimately discloses a violation of the Convention.

---

[61] PACE Resolution 1096, para. 4 (emphasis added).
[62] ECtHR, *Holy Synod of the Bulgarian Orthodox Church*, para. 142.
[63] On the width of the margin of appreciation, including those with a critical perspective on the doctrine itself, such as Jones and Hutchinson, see: Arai-Takahashi, *The Margin of Appreciation Doctrine*, 206 and E. Brems, 'The Margin of Appreciation Doctrine in the Case Law of the European Court of Human Rights', *Zeitschrift fur Auslandisches offenthiches recht und volkerrecht* 56 (1996) 240, 256–293 and M. Hutchinson, 'The Margin of Appreciation Doctrine in the European Court of Human Rights', *ICLQ* 48 (1999) 638, 640 and T. Jones, 'The Devaluation of Human Rights Under the European Convention', *Public Law* (1995) 430, 438 and Mahoney, 'Marvellous Richness of Diversity', 5 and J. Schokkenbroek, 'The Basis, Nature and Application of the Margin of Appreciation Doctrine in the Case Law of the European Court of Human Rights', *Human Rights Law Journal* 19(1) (1998) 30, 34 and J. A. Sweeney, 'A "Margin of Appreciation" in the Internal Market: Lessons from the European Court of Human Rights', *Legal Issues of Economic Integration* 34(1) (2007) 27, 45.

If relevant and sufficient reasons were provided that such a rights-restrictive measure had support from the national legislature, as an appropriate response to that state's distinctive experience of transition, this would seem to be a reasonable place to recognise a margin of appreciation within which different transitional states might defensibly come to different conclusions.[64] Naturally, however, there would still be 'a European supervision' 'hand in hand' with this.[65] The point is not that the margin would allow states to diverge from the standards of the Convention, but that each national response to democratic transition is not expected to be identical.

Thus, the approach advocated here does not demand that transitional measures per se should benefit from a wide margin of appreciation, but that the transitional context provides further data relevant to the identification of the existing rationales for its basis and width on a case by case basis.

The application of this approach to the 'religion in transition' (and other transitional) cases is advantageous because there are at least two other techniques open to the European Court to respond to distinct and especially difficult issues arising in relation to the role of religion in the transitional context. These techniques, derogations and invocation of the idea of self-defending (or militant) democracy, are considered more fully elsewhere in this volume, thus the examination here will be both brief and pinned to the religious context.

Derogations

First, we know that in emergency situations, the Court has allowed a wide margin of appreciation under Article 15 ECHR.[66] Article 9 is, to use a double-negative, not a non-derogable right.[67] If a transitional democracy

---

[64] ECtHR, *Ždanoka* v. *Latvia* [GC], 16 March 2006 (Appl. no. 58278/00) para. 134, discussed further below.

[65] ECtHR, *Handyside* v. *UK*, 7 December 1976 (Appl. no. 5493/72) para. 49.

[66] See R. Higgins, 'Derogations Under Human Rights Treaties', *BYIL* 48 (1976–1977) 281 and Jones, 'The Devaluation of Human Rights under the European Convention'; M. O'Boyle, 'The Margin of Appreciation and Derogation under Article 15: Ritual Incantation or Principle', *Human Rights Law Journal* 19(1) (1998) 23, who all note that the margin is particularly, even unnecessarily, wide in relation to the existence of a public emergency.

[67] Arai-Takahashi, *The Margin of Appreciation*, 94, would argue that, in contrast to the manifestation of religion, the internal aspect of it may in fact be 'considered' non-derogable.

had to take measures under Article 15, then the Court's existing jurisprudence would apply. It might be argued that where a rights-restrictive
measure, including a measure restrictive of Article 9, is required in order
to capitalise on the alleged stabilising effect of religion in a particular
society (or its susceptibility to religious extremism), the Contracting
Party would have to file a derogation and consequently to show compliance with the conditions of Article 15.

This is unsatisfactory from two perspectives. First, it would be too high
a threshold for the rights-restrictive measure to pass, and it might result
in the Contracting Party not being able to take steps that are necessary.
Second, if the first problem were to be remedied by conceding a wide margin of appreciation on transitional grounds, either on the existence of an
emergency situation or the necessity of the measures taken in response
to it, the new Contracting Parties would be allowed to evade the scrutiny
of the Court too easily and the role of Article 15 would become warped.
Thus, although the possibility of a valid derogation in respect of measures on religious grounds remains, it would be in only the most serious
of circumstances and could not be responsive enough to the transitional
context without compromising the integrity of Article 15.

This advice is not as necessary in relation to two of the international
comparators because although Article 4 ICCPR and Article 27 ACHR
authorise derogations in times of public emergency, both prohibit derogation from the right to freedom of conscience and religion. The ACHPR
does not contain a derogation clause at all, leading to some debate as to
whether the system adequately distinguishes between peacetime limitations and derogations in times of war or other public emergency.[68] To the
extent that a clear distinction might emerge, the suggestion here would
be that derogations would be useful in 'religion in transition' cases, again,
only in quite extreme circumstances.

Self-defending democracy

Second, and without resorting to a derogation, a Respondent State in the
European system whose democratic transition was under real threat of
failure due to anti-democratic religious forces might be able to persuade
the European Court to accept the notion of self-defending (or militant)
democracy in order to justify rights-restrictive measures. In a series of

---

[68] See Allo, 'Derogations or Limitations?'

cases, the European Court has accepted that democracies whose existence is under imminent threat may take pre-emptive measures against
the forces working against it, for example by dissolving political parties
(albeit subject to strict scrutiny).

The case of *Refah Partisi* v. *Turkey*[69] is perhaps now the most notorious
of the cases on self-defending democracy. Here, the Court did not find a
violation of the Convention when a major political party with around four
million members, which was already part of a coalition government and
which was likely to form a government after the next general election, was
dissolved because of its aim of imposing Sharia law on Turkey. The Court
held that a political party that was animated by the moral values imposed
by a religion cannot be regarded as 'intrinsically inimical' to the fundamental principles of democracy.[70] However, Sharia was, bluntly, held by
the Chamber and Grand Chamber to be 'incompatible with the fundamental principles of democracy'.[71] Thus, although this case is steeped
in religious contextual factors, the reason for restriction was tied to the
preservation of democracy. Moreover, although it can be argued that
the historical evolution of the idea of self-defending democracy suggests
that it is a species of transitional justice, this does not seem to be how the
European Court used it in *Refah Partisi*, since Turkey has been a member
of the Council of Europe since 1949.[72]

The limits of self-defending democracy in general, and in the European
jurisprudence, are still unclear, and there are risks of abuse.[73] The value of
its continued use as a basis for the European Court's reasoning on peacetime limitations is questionable. Given this, there is fruitful debate to be
had on the relevance of the self-defending democracy principle to cases

---

[69] *Refah Partisi (The Welfare Party) v. Turkey.*
[70] *Ibid.*, para. 100.   [71] *Ibid.*, para. 123.
[72] Council of Europe, 'The Council of Europe in Brief – 47 Countries, one Europe', www.
coe.int/aboutCoe/index.asp; Turkey's participation in the Council of Europe was suspended after the military *coup d'état* in 1980 (see Pevehouse, *Democracy from Above*,
48), and arguably only transitioned back to democracy with the general election in 1983.
Pevehouse (*ibid.*, 204) would go so far as to classify Turkey as a 'failed case' of democratic
consolidation in which membership of international organisations has not created conditions conducive to the survival of democracy. However we should be alert to the distinction between programmatic supra-national efforts at democratic consolidation on
the one hand, and the judicial application of transitional justice on the other. Although
the Council of Europe may well still be working towards democratic consolidation in
Turkey, the European Court's approach to it in *Refah Partisi* was not dominated by questions about the transition itself.
[73] P. Macklem, 'Militant Democracy, Legal Pluralism, and the Paradox of Self-
Determination', *International Journal of Constitutional Law* 4(3) (2006) 488, 492.

from the new Contracting Parties.[74] The clearest example of how it might look was the decision of the Grand Chamber in *Ždanoka* v. *Latvia*. In this case the Grand Chamber upheld a restriction on the political activities of a member of the Communist Party of Latvia, in order to defend Latvia against the resurgence of communism during the transitional phase. The applicant was prohibited from standing for election to the Latvian national parliament in 2002, as a result of her active participation in the Communist Party of Latvia after 13 January 1991 (the date they had launched an attempted coup).[75] Despite citing *Refah Partisi* and confirming 'the legitimacy of the concept of a "democracy capable of defending itself"',[76] the substance of the judgment owes a lot more to the Court's appraisal of the transitional context.[77] The threat was of a very different scale to the threat in *Refah Partisi*: the election of one person as opposed to the election of a government. Indeed it might have been better not to have decided it as a self-defending democracy case at all.

The European Court's approach to self-defending democracy is relevant to the 'religion in transition' cases only where the religious organisation subjected to a rights-restrictive measure also has an anti-democratic agenda, and passes the *Refah Partisi* threshold of posing an imminent danger.[78] Where the religious organisation has no anti-democratic agenda, the fact that restricting or prohibiting its activities might be conducive to transitional stability cannot be justified using this body of law or theory. The *Refah Partisi* and *Ždanoka* line of jurisprudence would not shed any further light on *Al-Nashif* or *Holy Synod of the Bulgarian Orthodox Church*, although it *could* potentially have played a role in *Metropolitan Church of Bessarabia* v. *Moldova*.

The Inter-American Commission on human rights does not seem to have been influenced by the European Court's reasoning in *Refah Partisi*,[79] nor does it generally recognise the concept of self-defending

---

[74] See Chapter 7, this volume. See also, P. Harvey, 'Militant Democracy and the European Convention on Human Rights', *European Law Review* 29(3) (2004) 407 and R. Teitel, 'Militating Democracy: Comparative Constitutional Perspectives', *Michigan Journal of International Law* 29 (2007) 49.

[75] *Ždanoka* v. *Latvia* [GC], para. 22.

[76] *Ibid.*, para. 100.   [77] *Ibid.*, paras. 133–135.

[78] One might question whether the blunt equation of Sharia with wholesale incompatibility with the Convention is an appropriately thorough methodology to apply when examining the democratic credentials of a religiously affiliated political party, but the validity of the logical step remains. For a critical reading of the Court's assessment of Sharia in *Refah* see McGoldrick, 'Accommodating Muslims in Europe', 603.

[79] The Dissenting Opinion of Commissioner Zalaquett in IAComHR, *Statehood Solidarity Committee* v. *USA*, 29 December 2003 (Report No. 98/03, Case 11.294) para. 15 refers to

democracy. The Inter-American Court has been critical of the European approach and, in *Yatama* v. *Nicaragua*, it implied that the European Court had 'discounted' the importance of political parties as essential forms of association for the development and strengthening of democracy by its judgment in *Refah Partisi*.[80] The African Commission on Human and Peoples' Rights does not seem to have pursued the thesis of self-defending democracy either. Given the inherent risks of the concept, this is no bad thing.

Conclusion: religion, transition and universality

In the introduction it was suggested that this chapter would attempt to construct a legally sound and theoretically robust approach to the 'religion in transition' cases, which also fully respects the experiences of transitional democracies. In this chapter, we have seen how the existing jurisprudence of the Court can be used to respond to the complex factual matrix of the 'religion in transition' cases, without the Court altering its own conception of justice. A thorough approach to prescription by law, pursuit of a legitimate aim, and discussion of necessity and proportionality via the margin of appreciation doctrine, yields workable results. The main difference between the approach advocated here and 'business as usual' is that it not only recognises, but also strongly recommends, a space for meaningful engagement with the relationship between national transitional justice policies and international human rights.

Although this space, or margin, would allow a more detailed engagement with the realities of transitional democracies, it remains important not to cast the European Court in the role of a dispenser of transitional justice itself. It was suggested above that if the Court were to hold that the transitional context could render certain otherwise 'illegitimate' measures 'legitimate' it would be doing just this.

The approach advocated here would strongly caution against allowing a margin of appreciation in relation to legitimate aims not only on doctrinal grounds related to the proper role of the margin, but also on two related normative grounds: first that the European Court, as an international human rights court, should not explicitly apply transitional justice itself; and, second, that this is because, if it did so, it would undermine

---

the *Refah Partisi* case, but on the question of electoral rights more generally and not on the specific issue of self-defending democracy.
[80] IACtHR, *Yatama* v. *Nicaragua*, 23 June 2005 (Series C no. 127) para. 215.

the universality of human rights. This second, normative, point would apply equally to the international comparators, whether they do or do not recognise the margin of appreciation as a judicial tool (and most do not).[81] Translated across to the international comparators, the point would be that any 'flexibility' in the system should relate not to the conceptual legitimacy of the aim put forward by the transitional state, but to the necessity of the impugned restrictive measure. Again, to do otherwise, and for the judges of the European Court to dispense transitional justice themselves, would be injurious to the universality of human rights.

Ironically enough, in the early days of the Council of Europe's enlargement, similar concerns were expressed about allowing a margin of appreciation to the new Contracting Parties.[82] Thus, one might argue that the approach for Europe recommended here, which allows for discussion of the transitional context via necessity and the margin of appreciation rather than on the question of the legitimacy of the aim, is no better a guarantee against undermining the universality of human rights. Nevertheless, the hypothesis on which the approach to the 'religion in transition' cases advocated here is based is that because (when it is correctly applied), the margin of appreciation attaches to the reasons given for a measure being necessary, rather than to the definition of the right in question[83] (or to the

---

[81] In HRC (United Nations Human Rights Committee), *Hertzberg, Mansson, Nikula and Putkonen* v. *Finland*, 2 April 1982 (Communication No. R.14/61, UN Doc. Supp. No. 40 (A/37/40) CCPR/C/15/D/61/1979) para. 10.3 the Human Rights Committee of the ICCPR recognised a 'margin of discretion' on moral issues, but then appeared rather critical of the doctrine in made use of the margin of appreciation doctrine, but in HRC, *Länsman et al* v. *Finland*, 22 November 1996 (Communication No. 511/1992, UN Doc. CCPR/C/52/D/511/1992) para. 9.4. On the ACHR see Chapter 10, this volume, noting that whilst the Inter-American Court has once made reference to it in an Advisory Opinion, it has not since developed this line of reasoning. By contrast the African Commission on Human and Peoples' Rights explicitly recognised that the margin of appreciation informs the African Charter in AfComHPR, *Prince* v. *South Africa*, 31 October 2007 (Communiqué 255/2002), reprinted in African Commission on Human and Peoples' Rights, 'Eighteenth Activity Report', presented at the Sixth Ordinary Session of the African Union Executive Council 24–31 January 2005, EX.CL/167 (VI).

[82] See generally Sweeney, 'Margins of Appreciation: Cultural Relativity and the European Court of Human Rights in the Post-Cold War Era', discussing inter alia comments made in A. Lester, 'Universality versus Subsidiarity: A Reply', *European Human Rights Law Review* 1 (1998) 73, 76; P. Mahoney, 'Speculating on the Future of the Reformed European Court of Human Rights', *Human Rights Law Journal* 20 (1999) 1, 3.

[83] J. Gerards and H. Senden, 'The Structure of Fundamental Rights and the European Court of Human Rights', *International Journal of Constitutional Law* 7(4) (2009) 619, especially at 647; a notable exception to this is the judgment in ECtHR, *Vo* v. *France* [GC], 8 July 2004 (Appl. no. 53924/00) para. 82, where the European Court recognised a margin of

'legitimacy' of the restrictive aim), it does not undermine the conceptual universality of human rights.

The approach recommended here is important because in the three principal cases examined, *Al-Nashif, Metropolitan Church of Bessarabia* and *Holy Synod of the Bulgarian Orthodox Church*, the European Court paid only lip service to the conceptual validity of domestic transitional policies when it held that the measures could be 'legitimate'. On the crucial question of whether the measure was necessary, the Court largely ignored the Respondent States' arguments from a transitional perspective. On the one hand this aloofness from the realities of the new Contracting Parties could be described as 'dynamics of condescension' from Western to Eastern Europe.[84] If there is a good transitional reason why Bulgarian Muslims are more susceptible to extremism than Muslims in other states, then it should be put to the Court. If not, there is no guarantee that suspicion of Muslim preachers such as *Al-Nashif* is not motivated by sectarian concerns emanating from the Balkans' difficult recent history. On the other hand, the Court might have been too generous by finding that the measures in *Metropolitan Church of Bessarabia* and *Holy Synod of the Bulgarian Orthodox Church* were perfectly 'legitimate', but only lacking in 'necessity', since the Court failed to challenge whether the stated aim of the measures was generally thought of as a useful transitional policy.

The approach advocated here calls for international human rights enforcement bodies, including the European Court, to engage far more robustly with the difficult question of when, and in what circumstances, national transitional policies that might secure peace or democratic consolidation are trumped by international human rights concerns. Judge Bonello identified the existence of this dilemma in his dissenting Opinion in *Sejdić and Finci* v. *Bosnia and Herzegovina*, when he argued that the Court had 'canonised' the relevant Convention rights whilst 'discounting' the values of peace and reconciliation. These values were, he argued, 'at least' equally invaluable.[85] Whether his view that, in the particular context, discrimination against Jews and Roma did not violate the Convention is accepted, at least he identified the crux of the issue.

---

appreciation on the issue of when the right to life begins. See Gerards and Senden, *ibid.*, 648; Sweeney, 'A "Margin of Appreciation" in the Internal Market', 39.

[84] M. Dembour and M. Krzyzanowska-Mierzewska, 'Ten Years On: The Voluminous and Interesting Polish Case Law', *European Human Rights Law Review* 5 (2005) 517.

[85] ECtHR, *Sejdić and Finci* v. *Bosnia and Herzegovina* [GC], 22 December 2009 (27996/06 and 34836/06) dissenting Opinion of Judge Bonello.

The outcome of the three cases naturally depends on both the approach to transition *and* to the approach of the European Court to religion. The *Al-Nashif* case is potentially the odd one out here since it dealt with the presumed susceptibility of one religion, Islam, to extremist influences during the transition. The Court did not strictly need to determine the veracity of this presumption in order to decide whether there had been a violation of Article 8. *Metropolitan Church of Bessarabia* and *Holy Synod of the Bulgarian Orthodox Church* have in common that the rights-restrictive measure was based upon a presumed beneficial role of having a stable state church during periods of democratic transition. In its summary determination that the measure was 'legitimate' the Court did not sufficiently question whether this presumption was valid either.

One might even be slightly surprised by the Court's relatively easy acceptance that these measures were 'legitimate': Teitel has argued that the European Court has pursued an 'extreme concept of secularism' as an element of its vision of a democratic society,[86] citing *Sahin* v. *Turkey* in this regard (where the Grand Chamber upheld a prohibition upon wearing Islamic headscarves at university). The Chamber decision in *Lautsi* v. *Italy*, in which the Chamber found that displaying a crucifix in Italian schools violated the Convention rights of secular parents, seemed to follow in this line.[87] However, the decision of the Grand Chamber to reverse that finding, noted in the introduction above, certainly makes the Court's position more ambiguous.[88] Of course, since the European Court found that the measures were not necessary, the conclusion (if not all the reasoning) in both *Metropolitan Church of Bessarabia* and *Holy Synod of the Bulgarian Orthodox Church* would also broadly conform to the pattern seen in *Sahin* and *Lautsi*. In this way, the conclusions in *Metropolitan Church of Bessarabia* and *Holy Synod of the Bulgarian Orthodox Church* might owe as much to an emerging secular orthodoxy as they do to a lack of engagement with the relationship between domestic transitional justice measures and international human rights. To this extent, it is perhaps less likely that the other international mechanisms would be drawn down this route in their own 'religion in transition' jurisprudence, and might even be more receptive to the broad approach outlined here (minus explicit invocation of the margin of appreciation doctrine).

---

[86] Teitel, 'Militating Democracy: Comparative Constitutional Perspectives', 59 – discussing the judgment in *Sahin* v. *Turkey*.
[87] ECtHR, *Lautsi* v. *Italy*, 3 November 2009 (Appl. no. 30814/06).
[88] ECtHR, *Lautsi* v. *Italy* [GC], 18 March 2011 (Appl. no. 30814/06).

The relationship between an international human rights court's responses to cases from a transitional context and the universality of human rights is a fertile area of further research. One might argue that it is the universality of human rights, rather than the normative pedigree of transitional justice, which is the greatest brake on such courts' approval of national transitional policies via alterations of their own standards of justice. The extent to which the margin of appreciation in the European system really does square the circle, by responding meaningfully to the transitional context without compromising the universality of human rights, is a demanding and crucial question but, for the purposes of this chapter, it will have to remain only partially articulated.[89]

Bibliography

Allo, A., 'Derogations or Limitations? Rethinking the African Human Rights System of Derogation in Light of the European System', *Ethiopian Journal of Legal Education* 2(2) (2009).

Altiparmak, K. and Karahanogullari, O., 'After Sahin: The Debate on Headscarves is Not Over', *European Constitutional Law Review* 2 (2006).

Arai-Takahashi, Y., *The Margin of Appreciation Doctrine and the Principle of Proportionality in the Jurisprudence of the ECHR* (Oxford: Intersentia, 2002).

Brems, E., 'The Margin of Appreciation Doctrine in the Case Law of the European Court of Human Rights', *Zeitschrift fur Auslandisches offenthiches recht und volkerrecht* 56 (1996).

Dembour, M. and Krzyzanowska-Mierzewska, M., 'Ten Years On: The Voluminous and Interesting Polish Case Law', *European Human Rights Law Review* 5 (2005).

Evans, C., *Freedom of Religion under the European Convention on Human Rights* (Oxford University Press, 2001).

Gearty, C., 'Democracy and Human Rights in the European Court of Human Rights: A Critical Appraisal', *Northern Ireland Legal Quarterly* 51 (2000).

Gerards, J. and Senden, H., 'The Structure of Fundamental Rights and the European Court of Human Rights', *International Journal of Constitutional Law* 7(4) (2009).

Grugel, J., *Democratization: A Critical Introduction* (Basingstoke: Palgrave Macmillan, 2002).

Hamilton, M., 'Freedom of Assembly, Consequential Harms and the Rule of Law: Liberty-Limiting Principles in the Context of Transition', *Oxford Journal of Legal Studies* 27(1) (2007).

---

[89] Cf. Sweeney, *The European Court of Human Rights in the Post-Cold War Era*.

Harvey, P., 'Militant Democracy and the European Convention on Human Rights', *European Law Review* 29(3) (2004).

Higgins, R., 'Derogations Under Human Rights Treaties', *BYIL* 48 (1976–1977).

Huntington, S., *The Third Wave: Democratisation in the Late Twentieth Century* (Norman: University of Oklahoma Press, 1991).

Hutchinson, M., 'The Margin of Appreciation Doctrine in the European Court of Human Rights', *ICLQ* 48 (1999).

Janis, M., 'Russia and the "Legality" of Strasbourg Law', *European Journal of International Law* 8 (1997).

Jones, T., 'The Devaluation of Human Rights under the European Convention', *Public Law* (1995).

Kay, R., 'The European Convention on Human Rights and the Authority of Law', *Connecticut Journal of International Law* 8 (1993).

Lester, A., 'Universality versus Subsidiarity: A Reply', *European Human Rights Law Review* 1 (1998).

Leuprecht, P., 'Innovations in the European System of Human Rights Protection: Is Enlargement Compatible with Reinforcement?', *Transnational Law and Contemporary Problems* 8 (1998).

Lewis, T., 'What Not to Wear: Religious Rights, the European Court, and the Margin of Appreciation', *ICLQ* 56 (2007).

Little, D., 'A Different Kind of Justice: Dealing with Human Rights Violations in Transitional Societies', *Ethics and International Affairs* 13 (1999).

McGoldrick, D., 'Accommodating Muslims in Europe: From Adopting Sharia Law to Religiously Based Opt Outs from Generally Applicable Laws', *Human Rights Law Review* 9(4) (2009).

Human Rights and Religion: The Islamic Headscarf Debate in Europe (Oxford: Hart, 2006).

Macklem, P., 'Militant Democracy, Legal Pluralism, and the Paradox of Self-Determination', *International Journal of Constitutional Law* 4(3) (2006).

Mahoney, P., 'Marvellous Richness of Diversity or Invidious Cultural Relativism', *Human Rights Law Journal* 19(1) (1998).

'Speculating on the Future of the Reformed European Court of Human Rights', *Human Rights Law Journal* 20 (1999).

Marks, S., 'The European Convention on Human Rights and its "Democratic Society"', *British Yearbook of International Law* (1995).

Mowbray, A., 'The Role of the European Court of Human Rights in the Promotion of Democracy', *Public Law* (1999).

O'Boyle, M., 'The Margin of Appreciation and Derogation under Article 15: Ritual Incantation or Principle', *Human Rights Law Journal* 19(1) (1998).

O'Connell, R., 'Towards a Stronger Concept of Democracy in the Strasbourg Convention', *European Human Rights Law Review* (2006).

Pevehouse, J. C., *Democracy from Above: Regional Organisations and Democratization* (Cambridge University Press, 2005).

Posner, E. and Vermeule, A., 'Transitional Justice as Ordinary Justice', *Harvard Law Review* 117 (2004).

Schmitter, P., 'An Introduction to Southern European Transitions from Authoritarian Rule: Italy, Greece, Portugal, Spain, and Turkey', in G. O'Donnell, P. Schmitter and L. Whitehead (eds.), *Transitions from Authoritarian Rule: Southern Europe* (Baltimore: Johns Hopkins University Press, 1986).

Schokkenbroek, J., 'The Basis, Nature and Application of the Margin of Appreciation Doctrine in the Case Law of the European Court of Human Rights', *Human Rights Law Journal* 19(1) (1998).

Sweeney, J. A., 'Divergence and Diversity in Post-Communist European Human Rights Cases', *Connecticut Journal of International Law* 21 (2005).

The European Court of Human Rights in the Post-Cold War Era: Universality in Transition (New York: Routledge, 2011).

'A "Margin of Appreciation" in the Internal Market: Lessons from the European Court of Human Rights', *Legal Issues of Economic Integration* 34(1) (2007).

'Margins of Appreciation: Cultural Relativity and the European Court of Human Rights in the Post-Cold War Era', *ICLQ* 54(2) (2005).

Taylor, P. M., *Freedom of Religion: UN and European Human Rights Law and Practice* (Cambridge University Press, 2005).

Teitel, R., 'Militating Democracy: Comparative Constitutional Perspectives', *Michigan Journal of International Law* 29 (2007).

Transitional Justice (New York: Oxford University Press, 2000).

'Transitional Justice Genealogy', *Harvard Human Rights Law Review* 16 (2003).

Wheatley, S., 'Minorities under the ECHR and the Construction of "a Democratic Society"', *Public Law* (2007).

The truth, the past and the present: Article 10 ECHR and situations of transition

ANTOINE BUYSE

Introduction

'Frankly, I do not believe that the fascist organizations ... have any independent existence, outside the state apparatus', wrote senator Miguel Castells in a magazine published in the Basque Country in 1979.[1] Thirteen years later, as the Iron Curtain which had divided Europe for so long had for the most part been torn down, the European Court of Human Rights dealt with this case which touched upon a much less recent transition from authoritarianism to democracy.

In the article, Castells wrote about a series of unsolved murders in the Basque region. He claimed that the authorities refused to investigate who the murderers were and even asserted that the government was quite certainly behind these acts. It can be added that Castells' article was published in a period which also marked the apex of ETA terrorist activity. The Basque Country was in a situation of turmoil, whereas Spain itself was tentatively trying out democracy after the first multi-party elections and a newly approved constitution in the previous years. In this context the state apparently deemed the article by Castells, a senator for the opposition, so dangerous that it had him prosecuted. He was convicted for insulting the government, by a court mostly consisting of judges appointed during the Franco regime. Subsequently, he took his case to the European Convention institutions in Strasbourg. The European Court of Human Rights found a violation of his freedom of expression.

The Spanish government had contended during the proceedings in Strasbourg that attempts to discredit democratic institutions could

Antoine Buyse, Associate Professor and Senior Researcher at the Netherlands Institute of Human Rights (SIM), Utrecht University, the Netherlands.

[1] ECtHR, *Castells* v. *Spain*, 23 April 1992 (Appl. no. 11798/85).

endanger the security of the state itself. After all, according to Spain, Castells not only described the murders but also complained that the state was inactive or even complicit in them. Although the Court accepted that the prevention of disorder in the specific situation of Spain at the end of the 1970s could be a legitimate aim, it did not consider the punishment of Castells necessary in a democratic society.

The case is a famous example of the freedom of expression of elected politicians. However, the argument of political transition as a relevant aspect has not received as much attention. It is striking that the – then still existing – European Commission of Human Rights explicitly took the delicate phase in Spain's history into account when it assessed the case: Spain had barely shed the shackles of the Franco regime and was just establishing a still very fragile democracy.[2] Several dissenters within the Commission even deemed this context so important that they found that Spain's action had been justified. They explicitly referred to the responsibilities inherent in the freedom of expression of Article 10 ECHR. These responsibilities should be read in the context of 'certain historical developments in which freedom of the press and of expression were abused in order to destabilise the rule of law and democracy'.[3]

Both the Court and the Commission seemed to acknowledge that in a transition to democracy it may be legitimate to counter forms of speech which are extremely critical of the state. Neither of these ECHR institutions accepted though that the transition itself could be a reason for widening the margin of appreciation accorded to states in applying fundamental rights protection. One might question whether they should have done. As the Spanish judge in the case indicated in a concurring opinion, 'in a situation where politically motivated violence poses a constant threat to the lives and security of the population, it is particularly difficult to strike a fair balance between the requirements of protecting freedom of expression and the imperatives of protecting the democratic State'.[4]

This chapter will focus on a number of aspects of the Court's case law under Article 10 ECHR, on the freedom of expression, in relation to transitions. It will assess the salience of the argument of transition in the Court's jurisprudence in this context. Simultaneously it will look at the possible

---

[2] EComHR, *Castells* v. *Spain*, 8 January 1991 (Appl. no. 11798/85) para. 53.
[3] My own translation of the original French version: 'certains développements historiques où on a abusé de la liberté de la presse et de l'expression pour la déstabilisation de l'Etat de droit et de la démocratie': Dissenting opinion of Frowein and Hall, para. 1. They also referred to Article 17 ECHR which prohibits the abuse of rights.
[4] Concurring opinion of Judge Carrillo Salcedo to the Court's judgment.

effects the Court's case law can have on transitions. In order to do so, four different issues will be dealt with. First, the interpretation of symbols in transitional societies will be focused on. Second, the approach towards the past through historic debate will be scrutinised. Third, instances of hate speech will be evaluated. And finally, the question of access to information of historical importance will be assessed. For each of these different aspects relating to the freedom of expression, one or more leading Court judgments will form the basis of the analysis.[5]

Symbols of the past

One of the key aspects for a successful transition to democracy is a symbolic break with the past, as Elke Fein has argued in a comparative study of Central and Eastern European transitions.[6] She was referring to a broad societal consensus which can be given effect through specific laws and policies, ranging from trials to lustration. One might add that the ratification of international human rights treaties, such as the ECHR, equally represents such a break. By formally pledging allegiance to human rights standards, a clear and explicit distance is created to previous human rights violations.[7] These specific instances of a formal dealing with the past can be regarded as a symbolic reflection of a rupture with previous politics and systems. There is, however, a much more immediate and literal sense in which symbolic politics play a role in transitions: the use of symbols themselves. After all, not merely the acts of a prior regime but also the symbols representing it can keep old wounds open and may negatively affect victims. Whether it concerns the Nazi swastika or the communist hammer and cross, these symbolic representations of the old order have even been banned from the public sphere in some countries during periods of transition.

The use of symbols came to the fore in the case of *Vajnai* v. *Hungary* in which the European Court of Human Rights issued its judgment in 2008.[8]

---

[5] For practical reasons, this contribution will not focus on some other aspects of Article 10 and transitions, such as processes of lustration.

[6] E. Fein, 'Transitional Justice and Democratization in Eastern Europe', in R. A. May and A. K. Milton (eds.) *(Un)civil Societies* (Lanham: Lexington Books, 2005) 197–223, at 216.

[7] In addition, the state concerned submits itself to an international accountability system concerning potential future human rights violations.

[8] ECtHR, *Vajnai* v. *Hungary*, 8 July 2008 (Appl. no. 33629/06). The case also came before the European Court of Justice (case C-328/04, 6 October 2005), but that Court held that it had no jurisdiction over the issue.

Attila Vajnai was the Vice-President of the left-wing Workers' Party. During a public and authorised demonstration in Budapest in 2003 he was asked by police officers to remove a red star which he wore on his jacket. Later he was prosecuted and found guilty of wearing a totalitarian symbol in public. This conviction was based on a provision in Hungary's post-communist criminal code which forbade the dissemination and public use of 'a swastika, an SS-badge, an arrow-cross, a symbol of the sickle and hammer or a red star, or a symbol depicting any of those'.[9] Importantly, this provision dealt with the use of 'totalitarian symbols'. A decision of Hungary's Constitutional Court dealing with the constitutionality of the provision explained the reasoning underlying the ban.[10] First, it held that the ban did away with unjustified distinctions between different kinds of totalitarian symbols. Indeed, under the previous communist regime, only fascist and Nazi symbols had been prohibited. Second, both the fascist and communist regimes had committed large-scale human rights violations. Therefore, the use of the symbols of these regimes could engender feelings of fear among the population in general and the victims of these atrocities in particular. As the Constitutional Court stated:

> Allowing an unrestricted, open and public use of the symbols concerned would, in the recent historical situation, seriously offend all persons committed to democracy who respect the human dignity of persons and thus condemn the ideologies of hatred and aggression, and would offend in particular those who were persecuted by Nazism and Communism. In Hungary, the memories of both ideologies represented by the prohibited symbols, as well as the sins committed under these symbols, are still alive in the public knowledge and in the communities of those who have survived persecution; these things are not forgotten. The individuals who suffered severely and their relatives live among us. The use of such symbols recalls the recent past, together with the threats of that time, the inhuman sufferings, the deportations and the deadly ideologies.[11]

This shows both how fresh the memory of atrocities still was and how important the legislator deemed the specific historical situation to be in order to justify a limitation of the freedom of expression.

Vajnai took his case to Strasbourg. The arguments of both parties focused on the role of the contested symbols, and specifically the red star, in Hungarian society and the effects of their use. Hungary adduced that

---

[9] *Ibid.*, para. 15.
[10] For this and what follows, see: Constitutional Court, decision no. 14/2000 (V. 12.), as cited in *Vajnai*.
[11] *Ibid.*, para. 17.

the conviction had been necessary both to protect the rights of others and to prevent disorder. It specifically referred to the fear and indignation such a symbol could cause. The applicant emphasised that his party was very small, had never gained seats in parliament and had never been accused of attempting to overthrow the government. More generally, he argued that Hungary as a state, almost twenty years after the fall of communism, had become a stable democracy, embedded in European structures such as the Council of Europe and the European Union. Nevertheless, the Court accepted that the interference could be argued to pursue both the protection of the rights of others and the prevention of disorder.

The problem for Hungary was that the Court did not deem the interference to have been necessary. The arguments used by both parties focused on the connotations and interpretations of the red star symbol and on its use in a political context. The Court first determined that the wearing of the red star by the applicant should be regarded as a political statement – which under the Convention system means that there is little scope for restrictions by the state. The Court delved into three different arguments: the danger for Hungarian democracy, the meaning of the symbol of the red star, and the feelings of past victims of communism and their relatives. Each of these relate directly to issues pertinent to transitions.

On the first argument, the possible dangers for Hungarian democracy, the Court mostly agreed with the applicant and emphasised the lapse of time since the end of the communist regime. Hungary had become a stable democracy and had been integrated into the value system of the ECHR. There was no 'real and present danger' of a restoration of communist dictatorship. It is instructive to see that the Court made reference in this respect to two of its judgments against Lithuania on the dismissal of state employees with a KGB past. In those cases the Court had also stressed the lapse of time since the fall of communism: less than one decade.[12] These judgments and *Vajnai* itself stand in contrast to an earlier judgment concerning Hungary – *Rekvényi*[13] – from which the Court felt bound to distinguish the *Vajnai* case. In *Rekvényi*, on the political rights of Hungarian police officers, the Court found the restrictions imposed by Hungary in 1994 (a mere five years after the end of communism) justified. It emphasised that 'especially against this historical background,

---

[12] ECtHR, *Sidabras and Džiautas v. Lithuania*, 27 July 2004 (Appl. nos. 55480/00 and 59330/00) para. 49; ECtHR, *Rainys and Gasparavičius v. Lithuania*, 7 April 2005 (Appl. nos. 70665/01 and 74345/01) para. 36. See further Chapter 7, this volume.

[13] ECtHR, *Rekvényi v. Hungary* [GC], 20 May 1999 (Appl. no. 25390/94).

the relevant measures taken in Hungary in order to protect the police force from the direct influence of party politics can be seen as answering a "pressing social need" in a democratic society'.[14] One may conclude from these cases that in respect of dangers for democracy, the Court does not allow states to use the argument of the special circumstances of transition for a very long time. Especially, one may add, once the state concerned is firmly entrenched in European structures.

The second argument concerns the specific meaning of the red star. The applicant had argued that the red star represented left-wing movements in general since the nineteenth century and not communism only. Hungary, for its part, put emphasis on the most specific meaning of the star in Hungary: its connection to the previous communist dictatorship. It argued that the wearing of the symbol could be equated with the propagation of totalitarian ideologies. The Court held that the red star had multiple meanings and that Hungarian law did not distinguish satisfactorily between the different meanings of that symbol. The critical point for the Court was that Vajnai had not used the symbol as part of dangerous propaganda. And even if he would have, the Court held, 'the potential propagation of that [totalitarian] ideology, obnoxious as it may be, cannot be the sole reason to limit it by way of a criminal sanction'.[15] On this point, it can be concluded that the Court defended the multi-interpretability of symbols and that the way in which is symbol is used is more relevant than the effect it has, through existing connotations, on others. The Court's position contrasts sharply with a judgment from a non-transitional context. In *Lautsi v. Italy*,[16] the Court had been asked to rule on the obligation for public schools to display the crucifix. A mother of two children had complained that such display involuntarily confronted her children with Christian symbolism. In *Lautsi* it was the state rather than the applicant which emphasised the multi-interpretability of symbols. Italy even argued that the crucifix represented not only a religious symbol, but also humanism as a value at the origins of Italy's democracy.[17] The Court held in that case that 'the crucifix is above all a religious symbol'[18], but left open the possibility that it could also have other connotations. In the particular context of the case, the Grand Chamber – contrary to an earlier Chamber judgment – held that Italy did not violate the ECHR. In contrast to the *Vajnai* case, the main meaning

---

[14] *Vajnai*, para. 48.   [15] *Ibid.*, para. 56.
[16] ECtHR, *Lautsi v. Italy*, 3 November 2009 (Appl. no. 30814/06). The case was referred to the Grand Chamber of the Court, which issued its judgment on 18 March 2011.
[17] *Ibid.*, para. 35.   [18] *Lautsi* [GC], para. 66.

rather than the plurality of possible meanings of a symbol was important. More specifically, the Court found that pluralism in the classroom was not endangered by the display of the crucifix symbol.

The third and final argument related to the feelings of past victims and their relatives. The Court acknowledged that the display of a symbol which was also used by the preceding regime responsible for terror could understandably cause unease or worse. But it held that such feelings were not, by themselves, a sufficient reason to limit the freedom of expression, specifically because the Hungarian state had provided moral, legal and material assurances to the victims. The Court concluded:

> [A] legal system which applies restrictions on human rights in order to satisfy the dictates of public feeling – real or imaginary – cannot be regarded as meeting the pressing social needs recognised in a democratic society, since that society must remain reasonable in its judgment. To hold otherwise would mean that freedom of speech and opinion is subjected to the heckler's veto.[19]

This seems to be completely in line with the case law holding that even opinions which 'shock, offend, or disturb', as the Court famously held in *Handyside* v. *United Kingdom*,[20] should be tolerated. Thus, even victims of previous totalitarian regimes cannot expect to be shielded against the symbols of such regimes. However, to qualify this finding, it should be emphasised that the Court leaves the door open for a different outcome if the state would not protect the interests of such victims in any way, leaving them completely vulnerable. In addition, this statement by the Court is probably closely connected to the multi-interpretability of the red star symbol. Matters may have been different if it had been a case about the display of SS-symbols in a neighbourhood inhabited by Holocaust survivors. In the *Vajnai* judgment, the argument concerning the effect on victims seems to have been an additional, rather than the core, reason in the line of argumentation.

The *Vajnai* judgment shows that in general the Court leaves the states little leeway in using the argument of transition as a reason to interfere with human rights. Only very short periods of transition, in which the threats to the stability of democracy are still considerable and direct, are relevant. In general, the Court's case law on transitions is in line with its broader jurisprudence. Nevertheless, it is clear that the Court's explicit protection of plurality serves to strengthen processes of transition to

---

[19] *Vajnai*, para. 57.
[20] ECtHR, *Handyside* v. *United Kingdom*, 7 December 1976 (Appl. no. 5493/72) para. 49.

democracy. After all, the previous totalitarian governments in Central and Eastern Europe were the very antithesis of such plurality.

Debating history

In 1944, Latvia was in the hands of Nazi Germany. In May of that year, Vassili Makarovich Kononov, with a group of fellow partisans, attacked a village whose inhabitants they suspected of collaborating with the Nazis. During the attack several villagers were killed. After the Second World War, when Latvia had become part of the Soviet Union, Kononov was hailed as a war hero. In the 1990s by contrast, the then newly independent Latvian state prosecuted Kononov for the killings. His once heroic partisan actions were now, in a true reversal of fortune and of views, perceived as war crimes.[21] This example illustrates a more general phenomenon: each transition from a repressive regime to more democratic forms of government has led to new perspectives on a country's history. The power struggle between the new and old powers that be produces different narratives of the oppressor and the oppressed, about the significance of key events and persons and more broadly about right and wrong. History in transitions is even more debated than in ordinary circumstances and often becomes very controversial.[22] Long-silenced voices try to make themselves heard, old controversies re-emerge and taboos are broken.

In periods of transition, politics and history-making remain intertwined, but in very different ways than during an authoritarian regime. Whereas the communist regimes in Middle and Eastern Europe kept a close grip on what the 'right' narrative of historical events was – including their own coming to power – the relation between politics and historical narratives became much more complex during and after the transitions of the late 1980s and early 1990s. New democracies wanted to demarcate a clear divide between themselves and their predecessors. Often such a demarcation was undertaken by claiming continuity with the pre-communist times. Since many countries in the region experienced

---

[21] Kononov brought his case to the European Court of Human Rights on the issue of the retroactive application of criminal sanctions. This resulted in a judgment in which the Court found with a very small margin that the relevant provision of the ECHR, Article 7, had been violated: ECtHR, *Kononov* v. *Latvia*, 24 July 2008 (Appl. no. 36376/04). Subsequently, the case was referred to the Grand Chamber of the Court, which issued its judgment on 17 May 2010 and found no violation.

[22] N. J. Kritz, 'The Dilemmas of Transitional Justice', in N. J. Kritz (ed.) *Transitional Justice*, vol. 1 (Washington, DC: United States Institute of Peace, 1995) xix–xxx, at xxvi.

an occupation by or forged an alliance with Nazi Germany in the period immediately preceding the emergence of communist regimes, this previous history has also often become a bone of contention.

Politicians in the new democratic arena can position themselves in relation to this past. Revisionism occurred both regarding the communist era and regarding the preceding fascist or otherwise Nazi-allied regimes. The difference with these authoritarian periods is that counter-voices could not be stifled as easily. This meant that politicians taking a stance on the past could expect a response from a wide range of historians. In some of these instances, the historical debate ended up in the courtroom. Teitel has argued that legal processes have indeed often been resorted to during transitions to preserve established historical accounts.[23] From a human rights perspective – as opposed to a criminal law one – it can be added that legal processes have an additional function: the preservation of the free exchange of ideas on history. Public debate as such is protected by the freedom of expression. Here, domestic and international courts dealing with human rights issues can emphasise and strengthen the discontinuity between the old regime and the new democracy, not so much by carving new interpretations into stone but by protecting the continuous emergence of new interpretations as such. On this point, not the subject-matter but the process then arguably becomes the core of the new post-authoritarian legal order.

The case of *Karsai* v. *Hungary*[24] before the European Court of Human Rights reflects this phenomenon. In 2004, a public debate took place in the Hungarian media about the country's role in the Second World War and the Holocaust. The specific issue at stake was whether a statue of Pál Teleki should be raised. Teleki had been Hungary's Prime Minister twice, had enacted anti-Semitic laws and had allied Hungary with Nazi Germany at the start of the war. Some political parties of the right strongly identified with this pre-communist Hungarian regime, of which Teleki was the figurehead. In a newspaper article the historian and university professor László Karsai criticised part of the media and several authors, of which he named one in particular – a certain B. T. – for embellishing Teleki's role and for making anti-Semitic statements. B. T. sued Karsai and eventually the latter was ordered to pay compensation for his statements on the former's anti-Semitism, for which the domestic court saw no factual proof, and to publish a rectification.

---

[23] R. Teitel, *Transitional Justice* (Oxford University Press, 2000) 105.

[24] ECtHR, *Karsai* v. *Hungary*, 1 December 2009 (Appl. no. 5380/87).

The European Court found that the domestic courts had gone beyond what was necessary and concluded that Article 10 ECHR had been violated. I will focus here on two arguments in the Court's reasoning which are relevant in a transitional context. The first is that the Court has generally accorded a high level of protection to expressions relating to matters of public interest and to the press as a watchdog of democracy.[25] Thus the contributions of academics to a public debate conducted through the media fall under this protective human rights umbrella.[26] In *Karsai* the Court held that a debate 'concerning the intentions of a country, with episodes of totalitarianism in its history, to come to terms with its past'[27] was such an issue of utmost public interest. The second relevant argument in the Court's reasoning is that the obligation to publish a rectification affected 'his professional credibility as a historian' and could have a chilling effect.[28] The Court also emphasised that B. T. had knowingly exposed himself to public criticism by extensively publishing in the press. All of this taken together points to a strong protection for historic debate in the public sphere concerning key issues of transition.

The fashion of reasoning in *Karsai* is not specific to problems of transition. The Court does not give Hungary more leeway for having to deal with a context of re-assessing a painful past in periods of transition. This becomes even clearer if one compares this case to one in a completely non-transitional context. The case of *Orban and others*[29] dealt with a book on a very sensitive issue of French history: the war of independence in Algeria. The book had been written by a former member of the French secret service active in Algeria in the 1950s and was published in 2001. At the request of a number of French human rights organisations, the state started proceedings against the author and the publishers of the work. National courts fined the author for trying to persuade readers that torture and summary executions had been legitimate and inevitable during the Algerian conflict and they fined the publishers for glorifying the author as a living legend. As in *Karsai* the European Court found a violation of Article 10 ECHR. It noted, amongst others, that the book was part of a debate of public concern and that the author's writings, even though they did not clearly distance themselves from the practice of torture, were clearly a witness account. The protection of public debate on an issue of

---

[25] See, for references, *Karsai*, para. 35.
[26] ECtHR, *Riolo* v. *France*, 17 July 2008 (Appl. no. 42211/07) para. 63.
[27] *Karsai*, para. 35.   [28] *Ibid.*, para. 36.
[29] ECtHR, *Orban and others* v. *France*, 15 January 2009 (Appl. no. 20985/05).

general importance thus received as much protection by the Court in the French case as in the Hungarian one, irrespective of the very different content of the respective publications. One may note that the Court in *Orban and others* concluded that the statements on the war in Algeria were still able to bring back memories of past suffering, even over forty years later. But, crucially, the passing of time meant that such statements should not be judged with the same intensity that could have been reasonable ten or twenty years earlier.[30] The Court referred back to the earlier judgment of *Lehideux and Isorni v. France*. In that case, on publications concerning the collaborating Pétain regime in France during the Second World War, the Court had already indicated that such tolerance to other ideas 'forms part of the efforts that every country must make to debate its own history openly and dispassionately'[31] – a phrase it reiterated in *Orban and others*. The proximity in time of sensitive past events can thus justifiably affect the way in which state parties to the European Convention deal with public debates about these events.[32] However, the Court seems to make no difference in that regard between post-war and post-transition situations.

The transitional context thus does not seem to affect the case law on historical debates. Rather the effect works the other way around: the Court squarely positions such debates under the protective scope – and a high level at that – of the freedom of expression, scrutinises the issue closely and affords protection to those seriously researching the past – in this case academic historians – on a par with the press.[33] This means in practice that the European Convention on Human Rights supports the shift in transitional societies from a single state-directed perspective on the past to a plurality of voices.[34] The debate as such on key issues of a country's past thus receives protection.

[30] *Ibid.*, para. 52.

[31] ECtHR, *Lehideux and Isorni v. France*, 23 September 1998 (Appl. no. 24662/94) para. 55.

[32] A case in which the events were truly recent is that of a cartoon glorifying the September 11 attacks on the World Trade Center, which was published within days after the attacks in a journal in the – itself rather volatile – Basque region: ECtHR, *Leroy v. France*, 2 October 2008 (Appl. no. 36109/03). The Court held that the fine imposed on him, considering the context, did not amount to a violation of Article 10.

[33] There is an outer limit to the protection of Article 10 over historical debates: complaints about being convicted for holocaust denial have been labelled by the Court as an abuse of rights under Article 17 ECHR: ECtHR, *Garaudy v. France* [admissibility], 24 June 2003 (Appl. no. 65831/01).

[34] The contribution of international human rights to such a shift is neither automatic nor easy, as Souillac indicates: G. Souillac, 'From Global Norms to Local Change: Theoretical Perspectives on the Promotion of Human Rights in Societies in Transition', in S. Horowitz

Hate speech in transitions

There may be situations in which the state deems it fit to restrict the range of narratives on history, not out of a totalitarian reflex but rather to entrench certain historical accounts of past human rights violations. This could entail laws prohibiting denial of the Holocaust or of other grave abuses of human rights, but also the prosecution of people who distort accounts of key historical events for political reasons. The issue is a particularly sensitive one, since restrictions on the freedom of speech can easily clash with the liberal order many societies in transition start to espouse.[35]

The Strasbourg approach to such instances of hate speech which are directly related to the re-labelling or denial of important past crimes or human rights abuses, has been mixed. If the disputed expression at issue was held to be inciting hatred against a particular group rather than contributing to historical or public debate, the Court has declared complaints inadmissible with reference to Article 17 ECHR which prohibits the abuse of rights. In the case of *Garaudy* v. *France*, on the conviction of a French academic and politician who denied the Holocaust, the Court held the following:

> Denying crimes against humanity is therefore one of the most serious forms of racial defamation of Jews and of incitement to hatred of them. The denial or rewriting of this type of historical fact undermines the values on which the fight against racism and anti-Semitism are based and constitutes a serious threat to public order. Such acts are incompatible with democracy and human rights because they infringe the rights of others.[36]

It is not entirely clear from the Court's jurisprudence which kinds of denials of crimes against humanity will be dismissed with recourse to Article 17 and which will be assessed under Article 10.[37] Nevertheless, the direct use of Article 17 remains a rare occurrence.[38] The large majority of cases will be decided under Article 10, either on the merits or even in simple admissibility decisions.[39]

---

and A. Schnabel (eds.), *Human Rights and Societies in Transition. Causes, Consequences, Responses* (Tokyo: United Nations Press, 2004) 77–99, at 89.

[35] Teitel, *Transitional Justice*, 108.

[36] ECtHR, *Garaudy* v. *France* [admissibility], 24 June 2003 (Appl. no. 65831/01).

[37] D. J. Harris, M. O'Boyle, E. P. Bates and C. M. Buckley, *Law of the European Convention on Human Rights*, 2nd edn (Oxford University Press, 2009) 451.

[38] A. Weber, *Manual on Hate Speech* (Strasbourg: Council of Europe Publishing, 2009) 27.

[39] As an example of the latter, see: ECtHR, *Le Pen* v. *France* [admissibility], 20 April 2010 (Appl. no. 18788/09), which related to hate speech against Muslims.

The Court's judgment in *Balsytė-Lideikienė* v. *Lithuania*[40] is a case in point of contested hate speech in a society struggling with its past. The applicant in the case was a publisher of the Lithuanian calendar, which appeared yearly and included comments on important dates in the country's history. Several comments in the 2000 edition related to Jews, Poles and Russians in which all these groups were depicted as aggressors, killers and even *génocidaires*. An example of an entry in the calendar is 'The soviet occupying power, with the help of the communist collaborators, among whom, in particular, were many Jews, for half a century ferociously carried out the genocide and colonisation of the Lithuanian nation'.[41] The calendar also included a map which depicted parts of neighbouring Poland, Russia and Belarus as ethnic Lithuanian regions under temporary occupation. After complaints, both from Parliament and neighbouring countries, all copies of the calendar were confiscated by the authorities and the applicant was prosecuted. Eventually, she was convicted under a provision of the Code on Administrative Offences, which prohibited the promotion of national, racial or religious hatred. The conviction consisted of the lowest administrative penalty, a warning, because the domestic court – after seeking expert advice from a psychologist, a historian, a political sciences expert and a library sciences expert – found that the applicant had acted recklessly but not deliberately. Although the court held that the statements were a one-sided depiction of relations between specific groups which 'obstructed the consolidation of civil society and promoted ethnic hatred',[42] it also found that it had not caused any significant harm.

At the European Court of Human Rights, Lithuania defended its interference with the freedom of expression by invoking two aims: the protection of ethnic groups in Lithuania and the safeguarding of the relations of Lithuania with its neighbours, which were endangered by the calendar. The Court accepted these as legitimate aims, but only explicitly mentioned the first one – thereby indicating what, in its view, was the heart of the matter. It concluded that there had been no violation of Article 10 ECHR, since the penalty imposed was proportionate and since the authorities remained within their margin of appreciation in holding that there was a pressing social need. The issue of the 'pressing social need' is the most relevant. Not surprisingly, the Court pointed at Lithuania's international obligations to combat advocacy of national hatred and to protect 'people

---

[40] ECtHR, *Balsytė-Lideikienė* v. *Lithuania*, 4 November 2008 (Appl. no. 72596/01).
[41] *Ibid.*, para. 9.   [42] *Ibid.*, para. 28.

who may be subject to such threats as a result of their ethnic identity'.[43] The Court held that various passages in the calendar's text were expressions of aggressive nationalism and ethnocentrism and incited hatred. In addition, the national courts had considered the reactions in Lithuania itself and of the neighbouring countries and the opinions of a range of experts. One may note here that such experts on the national level are probably better placed, due to their geographical, cultural and temporal proximity to the events at issue, to give their assessment than an international court is. In the context of transitions, the Court specifically took into account that ever since the renewed independence of the Lithuanian state, after many decades of being part of the Soviet Union, 'the question of territorial sovereignty and national minorities were sensitive'.[44] The reactions from Lithuania's three neighbours underlined that point.

What may one conclude on this issue? It is clear that the Court accepted that Lithuania used the argument of transition in assessing the case at the domestic level. The Republic of Lithuania was a new state – or, more precisely a state in its second youth – which included many minorities due to its recent history as a republic of the Soviet Union. Ten years after independence, when the calendar appeared, this was apparently still a valid consideration. However it was not important enough for the Court to explicitly broaden the state's margin of appreciation. And although it was the first consideration the Court mentioned in its assessment of the pressing social need, it was not the only one. The issue seems very particular to the case: Lithuania was not only a state in transition but also a state which re-asserted its independence. Any irredentist claims from one side or another are prone to be very sensitive from that perspective. But this seems to have been an additional argument rather than a crucial one here. Equally important was the protection of incitement of hatred against specific groups – and in that respect the Court's argumentation in this 'transitional' case did not differ significantly from hate speech cases in other contexts.

The effect of the transition may not have been a key point here, but in parallel to other aspects of Article 10 there was an effect the other way around. By supporting the claim of Lithuania that it was important to combat hate speech which endangered social peace, the Court helped to protect the precarious ethnic pluralism in Lithuanian society. One-sided, hateful, and extremely nationalist accounts of history could thus be combated, as long as the existing requirements of the ECHR were met.

---

[43] *Ibid.*, para. 78.   [44] *Ibid.*, para. 78.

Accessing the past

A different aspect related to re-assessing history in the transitional phase and beyond is access to information held by the government. Under a totalitarian or authoritarian system, control over information mostly also entails high discretionary powers for secret services for collecting information about citizens. The boundaries between the private and the public sphere are to a large extent destroyed by the authorities in an effort to control the population as fully as possible. Paradoxically, the boundary remains firmly in place from the citizen's perspective, as a kind of one-way reflecting window: individuals in totalitarian systems do not have any meaningful or non-arbitrary access to the information thus collected by the state, not even when it concerns their own personal files. This has been the experience under many communist regimes in Central and Eastern Europe in the second half of the twentieth century. The transition from such regimes to democratic societies has therefore often been seized as an opportunity to restore a private sphere for citizens by restricting the state's collection of personal data. As a corollary, access to information held by the state is regulated and increased. This represents a crucial and critical step in the construction of more open societies, as Teitel has argued.[45]

The establishment of a new balance between the state's and society's interests concerning information manifests itself in two different dimensions. First, a personal dimension for an individual citizen to gain access to the information collected about him or her during the preceding regime. Second, a public dimension in the sense of accessing state-held information by stakeholders such as the press, non-governmental organisations or academics. In both dimensions this enables a re-construction of the past, either through personal narratives or common ones. In both dimensions access to information also represents a democratic counter-force to closed authoritarian systems. This serves not only the uncovering of the truth about the past, but equally strengthens accountability of the authorities to society in the present and in the future.

How has this played out in the jurisprudence of the European Court? At the outset, it must be noted that Article 10 ECHR does not only protect the freedom of expression, but also the freedom 'to receive and impart information'. This does not amount to a general right for everyone of access to data and documents in the hands of the state.[46] But it does cover a certain

---

[45] Teitel, *Transitional Justice*, 100–102.
[46] ECtHR, *Loiseau* v. *France* [admissibility], 18 November 2003 (Appl. no. 46809/99) page 5.

measure of access. In *TASZ* v. *Hungary*, the Court recognised that not only the press, but also 'social watchdogs', such as in that case an NGO involved in human rights litigation, have a qualified right to access to information held by the authorities. The defining element seems to be that such information serves to create 'a forum for public debate'.[47] Moreover, public figures cannot use arguments of data protection in order to stifle public debate on issues related to themselves by way of denying access to such information.[48]

The link between access to information and historical enquiries into a previous authoritarian regime came to the fore in the case of *Kenedi* v. *Hungary*.[49] The applicant in the case was a historian specialised in the functioning of secret services in totalitarian states. In the context of research into the functioning of the Hungarian State Security Service in the 1960s, he requested access to a number of documents on this from the Ministry of the Interior. Access was denied with reference to a decision less than two weeks earlier, classifying the documents as state secrets. Kenedi obtained several domestic court decisions ordering access to the information at stake, but he was never given full access to them all. The European Court found a violation of Article 10 ECHR. The Hungarian government had contended that the restrictions on access pursued the aim of national security, which is one of the accepted legitimate aims under Article 10. One might question whether the retroactive classification as 'secret' only once someone asks for access is in itself justified. Indeed, at the national level, the courts had already decided that the timing of this classification was contrary to the law. It may be for this reason that the European Court did not go into the argument of national security – and thus the test of whether the state pursued a 'legitimate aim'. Rather it held that the restriction was not 'prescribed by law', since the authorities were repeatedly reluctant to fully execute the judgments of the domestic courts. The Court labelled this attitude as being 'in defiance of domestic law and tantamount to arbitrariness' and as 'essentially obstructive'.[50]

In parallel to the Court's case law on the freedom of expression of historians, the Court's main reasoning here does not as such present us with a *sui generis* example of transitional jurisprudence. This judgment does

---

[47] ECtHR, *Társaság a Szabadságjogokért (TASZ)* v. *Hungary*, 14 April 2009 (Appl. no. 37374/05) para. 27.

[48] *Ibid.*, para. 37.

[49] ECtHR, *Kenedi* v. *Hungary*, 26 May 2009 (Appl. no. 31475/05).

[50] *Ibid.*, para. 45.

not reveal that the particular context of transition affected the case directly. However, the case does obviously arise from a transitional context of historical enquiry into the acts of the former Hungarian communist regime. The mere fact that, almost forty years after the period which Kenedi researched, denial of access was still an issue points to the continuing sensitivity. No closure of the communist past has been reached in that sense. This connects to one of the crucial novelties in the judgment. The Court extended the right to access to information from the press and NGOs to historians by holding that 'access to original documentary sources for legitimate historical research' was an essential part of Kenedi's freedom of expression. Since the Court referred to the *TASZ* case here, one may infer that it considers that serious historians can also function as social watchdogs. By doing so the Court's case law may actually affect transitions in a very distinct way: human rights protection offered by the European Convention – in this case access to state-held information on the pre-transition era – enables the re-construction or re-assessment of the past by actors outside the state. The very fact that this may be done by an indefinite number of watchdogs in itself constitutes a democratisation of information. Post-communist states such as Hungary, through the system of the ECHR, commit themselves to such multi-actor truth-finding. The Court's case law here affirms and strengthens the shift from state-held information monopolies to a more open discussion of the past by society itself. The constructive interplay between national laws on access to information and the European Court thus helps to increase a more accountable government through information-sharing and at the same time enables a more thorough inquiry into a sensitive past. As such, these kinds of judgments serve as judicial markers on the path from authoritarianism to more open societies.

Conclusion

Processes of transition are not only about political or economic change. They touch the core of societies' identities. Yet, trying to find a new idea of the self without imposing a new monolithic image of a state or society is a major challenge. Open discussion with a plurality of voices is necessary but without losing crucial social cohesion. The abolition of censorship, open public debate on issues of general importance and the protection of the freedom of expression more generally are all hallmarks of free societies emerging from dark periods of authoritarianism and dictatorship. In that context, a legal entrenchment of free debate through the human rights norm of the freedom of expression can play an important role. The European Convention of Human Rights, to which most Central and Eastern European countries acceded in the years immediately following the demise of communist regimes, was a crucial signpost on the road to democracy and the rule of law. Nevertheless, the political transitions were rarely easy and in some countries suffered important setbacks or were even temporarily reversed. It is for that very reason that the supervisory machinery of the Convention, with the Court at its core, became so crucial. Its case law served as a recurring reminder for state parties of their initial pledge at the moment of ratification.

In this contribution I have tried to assess how the European Court of Human Rights decided cases on four different aspects of the freedom of expression, protected in Article 10 ECHR, in transitional situations. The general picture that emerged is that state parties to the Convention cannot extensively use the argument of transition to justify far-reaching interferences with human rights or to claim a larger margin of appreciation. Only in a handful of cases (e.g. *Rekvényi, Balsytė-Lideikienė*) has the Court ruled that the immediate years following a change of regime – usually less than a decade – may sometimes serve to widen the margin of appreciation for the state or can be part of the relevant context to be taken into account. The same holds for interfering with sensitive discussions on certain aspects which may be painful for victims of recent human rights abuses: the more time passes, the less relevant such a justification becomes.

Whereas transitions do not often cause the Court to deviate from its established jurisprudence, the Court's judgments on the freedom of expression are of particular salience to transitional processes. This seems to be part of a wider pattern. The Court indeed may have rarely dealt with the argument of transition as such, but it has much more often adjudicated transitional issues[51] – as the other chapters in this book amply testify.

The Court has stressed, in a case of systematic censorship of the media by the authorities (*Manole and others* v. *Romania*), that the state is the 'ultimate guarantor of pluralism'.[52] This protection of pluralism is the

---

[51] D. Kosař, 'Lustration and Lapse of Time: "Dealing with the Past" in the Czech Republic', *European Constitutional Law Review* 4 (2008) 460–487, at 472.

[52] ECtHR, *Manole and others* v. *Moldova*, 17 September 2009 (Appl. no. 13936/02) para. 107.

main principle that emerges from the Court's Article 10 case law in situations of transition. This occurs in a number of ways. The Court protects the process of truth-seeking and history-writing by a multitude of voices in transitional societies. In doing so, it emphasises the watershed between the new democracies and the old monopolies on information, historical narratives and the truth of previous dictatorial regimes. Debates on human rights violations of previous regimes and a society's history more broadly are labelled as matters of public interest which deserve a high level of protection under Article 10. Key actors in such processes, such as the media, NGOs and historians, also benefit from this higher degree of protection in as far as they contribute to such debates of public interest. Minorities who are the victims of hate speech can equally claim protection, but not in an absolute way. And in relation to symbols, the Court explicitly protects the multiple interpretations which can be attached to them, especially the minority views.

The Court's jurisprudence thus strongly espouses processes of information exchange and pluralities of voices. It thereby restores the balance between a society's citizens and the state – a balance completely lost during preceding eras of authoritarian rule. Not a specific truth – although the Court protects some outer limits – but the *process* of seeking and discussing truths (plural) receives protection. This is a genuine contribution of an international institution to open and democratic societies. In doing so, the Court's case law on transitional issues helps states and their societies to get beyond the transition as soon as possible: the European Court of Human Rights as the guardian of democratic normalcy rather than of transitional exceptionalism.

As a final note, the *Castells* case from the introduction offers a good illustration of the Court's possible influence on the domestic legal order in dealing with issues arising from transitions. A year after the judgment of the European Court, Spain's Constitutional Court formally accepted to start using Strasbourg case law as a formal source of interpreting human rights issues. In addition, it held that that jurisprudence was directly applicable in the legal order of Spain.[53] The values of the rule of law and the protection of pluralism in democratic societies thus became firmly anchored at the national level through Strasbourg's protection of the freedom of expression.

---

[53] R. A. Lawson and H. G. Schermers, *Leading Cases of the European Court of Human Rights*, 2nd edn (Nijmegen: Ars Aeqi Libri, 1999) 465–466.

Bibliography

Fein, E., 'Transitional Justice and Democratization in Eastern Europe', in May, R. A. and Milton, A. K. (eds.) *(Un)civil Societies* (Lanham: Lexington Books, 2005) 197–223.

Harris, D. J., O'Boyle, M., Bates, E. P. and Buckley, C. M., *Law of the European Convention on Human Rights*, 2nd edn (Oxford University Press, 2009).

Kosař, D., 'Lustration and Lapse of Time: "Dealing with the Past" in the Czech Republic', *European Constitutional Law Review* 4 (2008) 460–487.

Kritz, N. J., 'The Dilemmas of Transitional Justice', in Kritz, N. J. (ed.) *Transitional Justice*, vol. 1 (Washington, DC: United States Institute of Peace, 1995) xix–xxx.

Lawson, R. A. and Schermers, H. G., *Leading Cases of the European Court of Human Rights*, 2nd edn (Nijmegen: Ars Aeqi Libri, 1999).

Souillac, G., 'From Global Norms to Local Change: Theoretical Perspectives on the Promotion of Human Rights in Societies in Transition', in Horowitz, S. and Schnabel, A. (eds.) *Human Rights and Societies in Transition. Causes, Consequences, Responses* (Tokyo: United Nations Press, 2004) 77–99.

Teitel, R., *Transitional Justice* (Oxford University Press, 2000).

Weber, A., *Manual on Hate Speech* (Strasbourg: Council of Europe Publishing, 2009).

7

Transition, political loyalties and the order of the state

MICHAEL HAMILTON

Introduction

Forty years after the European Convention on Human Rights (ECHR) was drafted, the political climate of the region was transformed. Fledgling democracies in post-communist Eurasia faced many challenges, including the need to earn the political loyalty previously demanded by the so-called Peoples' democracies.[1] Ensuring this loyalty entailed the reconfiguration of the public sphere and, to varying degrees, the selective restriction of core political rights. In turn, this reconfiguration resulted in new dynamics of inclusion and exclusion – the inclusion of those previously prevented from accessing the political domain, and the exclusion of those who would seek a return to the past or might otherwise undermine democratic consolidation. Restrictions upon political rights included the dissolution of successor communist parties and other political associations, lustration laws designed to ensure discontinuity with the prior regime, and the exclusion of certain categories of individuals from running for or holding political office.

Such restrictions most obviously engage the rights to freedom of assembly and association (Article 11 ECHR) and the obligation upon states to hold free elections (Article 3, Protocol 1 ECHR – hereafter, P1–3).[2]

Michael Hamilton, Associate Professor, Legal Studies Department, Central European University, Budapest and Senior Lecturer, Transitional Justice Institute, University of Ulster.

[1] The Soviet-led polities were characterised by the absence of political choice despite maintaining an electoral façade. See, for example, K. L. Scheppele, 'Democracy by Judiciary. Or, Why Courts Can be More Democratic than Parliaments', in A. Czarnota, M. Krygier and W. Sadurski (eds.) *Rethinking the Rule of Law after Communism* (Budapest and New York: CEU Press, 2005) 25–60, 32.

[2] 'The High Contracting Parties undertake to hold free elections at reasonable intervals by secret ballot, under conditions which will ensure the free expression of the opinion of the people in the choice of the legislature.'

Governments have sought to justify interferences with these rights because of a need to foster democratic values in the early years of transition. This chapter examines how the European Court of Human Rights (hereafter the Court) has responded to allegations of *excessive* rights limitation. It argues that the Court has relied on four juridical devices to enable it to take into account the potential risk to democratic stability inherent in different courses of legal action. As discussed below, these four devices are: (first) heightened deference in respect of electoral rights; (second) militant democracy and the abuse of rights prohibition; (third) the margin of appreciation, and; (fourth) proportionality and the passage of time. It is useful, though, to ground this discussion by first examining the concept of 'transition' and the European Convention's underlying premise of an 'effective political democracy'.

Transition, pluralism and loyalty in the public sphere

The concept of 'transition' is used here in the sense of 'a shift in political orders' signalling 'change in a liberalizing direction'.[3] Yet, the transitions that swept East Central Europe in the latter part of the twentieth century raised afresh the very questions about law's role in shaping and constraining politics that prompted the drafting of the Convention itself – the failure to stem the inter-war surge of fascism in Italy and Germany, and the enormity of the Holocaust. Law is often instrumental in the management of political loyalties, but this role is especially pronounced during periods of transition. At such times, law is used to regulate the associational freedoms of those who retain ideological allegiance to the predecessor regime and to determine the employment opportunities or candidature prospects open to those with proven ties to past abuses. Over-extended reliance on such 'belligerent legal measures',[4] however, tends to undermine democratic legitimacy. With the passage of time, law must relinquish its stabilising role, increasingly giving way to plural politics. The challenge for judicial (and particularly supra-national) supervision is in identifying this vertex between coercion and consent (arguably the transition endpoint) after which politics

---

[3] See R. Teitel, *Transitional Justice* (Oxford University Press, 2000) 5.

[4] This is John Borneman's term which he uses to describe the legal measures enacted to criminalise the West German Communist Party in 1956. See J. Borneman, *Settling Accounts: Violence, Justice, and Accountability in Postsocialist Europe* (Princeton University Press, 1997) 53. See further the discussion on 'militant democracy' below.

must become self-legitimating through the open accommodation of divergent loyalties.

Something approximating this political endgame can be inferred from the European Convention's preamble which emphasises the need for an 'effective political democracy' in maintaining fundamental freedoms.[5] Yet this term is undefined in both the Convention and the Strasbourg Court's jurisprudence.[6] 'Effectiveness' might plausibly be viewed as inherently context-dependent – relative to preceding political arrangements – rather than implying an objective litmus test. Nonetheless, several forthright judgments of the European Court of Human Rights relating to freedom of speech, assembly and association strengthen the conclusion that the Court is generally unwilling to allow contextual exceptions where doing so would undermine the protection of fundamental rights. The Court's focus on pluralism has been central to its finding of a violation in a number of Article 11 cases – some of which have clear transitional relevance.[7]

In *Partidul Comunistilor (Nepeceristi) (PCN) and Ungureanu* v. *Romania*,[8] for example, the European Court unanimously found a violation of Article 11 following the refusal of the Bucharest Court of Appeal to register the PCN. While the constitution of the PCN expressly distanced itself from the former Romanian Communist Party,[9] the Bucharest County Court held that its political programme aimed at 'establishing a humane State based on communist doctrine, which would imply that the

---

[5] Noting that Article 31(2) *Vienna Convention on the Law of Treaties* explicitly refers to a treaty's preamble in determining 'the context for the purpose of' its interpretation.

[6] The Court has noted that 'pluralism, tolerance and broadmindedness are hallmarks of a "democratic society"' and that democracy should not be conceived in majoritarian terms: 'a balance must be achieved which ensures the fair and proper treatment of minorities and avoids any abuse of a dominant position'. See ECtHR, *Young, James and Webster* v. *UK*, 13 August 1981 (Appl. no. 7601/76; 7806/77) para. 63.

[7] For example, ECtHR, *Freedom and Democracy Party (Özdep)* v. *Turkey*, 8 December 1999 (Appl. no. 23885/94) para. 41, emphasising that 'it is of the essence of democracy to allow diverse political projects to be proposed and debated, even those that call into question the way a State is currently organised'; ECtHR, *Ouranio Toxo and Others* v. *Greece*, 20 October 2005 (Appl. no. 74989/01) para. 41; ECtHR, *Bączkowski* v. *Poland*, 3 May 2007 (Appl. no. 1543/06) para. 64, describing the state as 'the ultimate guarantor of the principle of pluralism'. See also, ECtHR, *Alekseyev* v. *Russia*, 21 October 2010 (Appl. nos. 4916/07, 25924/08 and 14599/09) para. 70; ECtHR, *Manole and others* v. *Moldova*, 17 September 2009 (Appl. no. 13936/02) para. 107; ECtHR, *Barankevich* v. *Russia*, 26 July 2007 (Appl. no. 10519/03) para. 30, noting that 'the role of the authorities … is not to remove the cause of tension by eliminating pluralism, but to ensure that the competing groups tolerate each other'.

[8] ECtHR, *Partidul Comunistilor (Nepeceristi) and Ungureanu* v. *Romania*, 3 February 2005 (Appl. no. 46626/99).

[9] Article 20 of the PCN's constitution stated that the PCN was 'not the successor of the former Romanian Communist Party'. *Ibid.*, para. 10.

constitutional and legal order in place since 1989 is inhumane and not founded on genuine democracy'. However, rejecting the government's argument that Romania could not allow 'the emergence of a new communist party to form the subject of democratic debate',[10] the European Court strongly suggested that a standard test would (in general) apply to all signatories to the Convention. It stated that political parties play an 'essential role in ensuring pluralism and the proper functioning of democracy'[11] and 'there can be no democracy without pluralism':[12]

> The Court is also prepared to take into account the historical background to cases before it, in this instance Romania's experience of totalitarian communism prior to 1989. However, it observes that context cannot by itself justify the need for the interference, especially as communist parties adhering to Marxist ideology exist in a number of countries that are signatories to the Convention.[13]

Insofar as Article 11 is concerned, therefore, few concessions are made to the transitional dilemma of how best to manage or corral diverse political loyalties. A strikingly different approach arises in the transition case law regarding the right to stand for election under P1–3.

Electoral rights and deference to 'the institutional order of the state'

Given that the Court has considered pluralism to be a fundamental characteristic of democracy, it has found a number of violations of Article 11 where states have refused to register, or have sought the dissolution of, political parties. However, while the Court has also emphasised the centrality to a functioning democracy of the right to stand for election (the passive component of P1–3),[14] it has been more reluctant to find a violation of this provision where individuals have been prevented from standing for election because of their complicity with a predecessor regime.[15]

---

[10] *Ibid.*, para. 55.   [11] *Ibid.*, para. 44.   [12] *Ibid.*, para. 45.

[13] *Ibid.*, para. 58. It is noteworthy that the Court also rejected the need to bring Article 17 ECHR into play (para. 59).

[14] 'The right to stand as a candidate in an election ... is inherent in the concept of a truly democratic regime.' See, inter alia, ECtHR, *Podkolzina* v. *Latvia*, 9 April 2002 (Appl. no. 46726/99) para. 35; ECtHR, *Melnychenko* v. *Ukraine*, 19 October 2004 (Appl. no. 17707/02) para. 59; *Aliyev* v. *Azerbaijan* 8 April 2010 (Appl. no. 18705/06) para. 72.

[15] There are, however, several cases in which the Court has found a violation of P1–3. For example, *Petkov and Others* v. *Bulgaria*, 11 June 2009 (Appl. nos. 77568/01, 178/02 and 505/02) (due, primarily to the failure of the electoral authorities to give effect to a binding

P1–3 has thus been subject to less exacting scrutiny than the qualified rights in Articles 8–11,[16] and its contextual contingency has been repeatedly highlighted by the Court:

> [A]ny electoral legislation must be assessed in the light of the political evolution of the country concerned, so that features that would be unacceptable in the context of one system may be justified in the context of another.[17]

There are two related explanations for this divergence. First, there is an implicit tension between these two Convention rights. This was manifest during the drafting of the ECHR and resulted in the relegation of electoral rights to a separate protocol. Consequently, some of those most closely involved in the drafting process lambasted the Convention as 'watered down'[18] and 'emaciated'.[19] The *travaux preparatoires* reveal that the exclusion of electoral rights from the main body of the Convention was urged on the basis that it was impossible to reach agreement on the fundamental principles of democracy (despite seeming agreement by most members of the Committee of Ministers),[20] and that electoral rights should be distinguished due to their 'constitutional and political character'.[21] Second, the right to free and fair elections differs in structure from the qualified

---

domestic court ruling). Also, *Aziz* v. *Cyprus*, 22 June 2004 (Appl. no. 69949/01) (given the longstanding nature of the situation, see para. 29); and *Sejdić and Finci* v. *Bosnia and Herzegovina*, 22 December 2009 (Appl. nos. 27996/06 and 34836/06), discussed further below (text accompanying notes 79–100).

[16] A number of lustration cases – engaging Article 8 of the Convention – also serve to highlight the distinction between Articles 8–11 and P1–3 (see further below, text accompanying notes 120–25).

[17] See ECtHR, *Podkolzina* v. *Latvia*, 9 April 2002 (Appl. no. 46726/99) para. 33; ECtHR, *Sukhovetskyy* v. *Ukraine*, 28 March 2006 (Appl. no. 13716/02). Also, ECtHR, *Mathieu-Mohin and Clerfayt* v. *Belgium*, 2 March 1987 (Appl. no. 9267/81) para. 54.

[18] European Convention on Human Rights, *Travaux Preparatoires*, P1–3. Available at: www.echr.coe.int/library/DIGDOC/Travaux/ECHRTravaux-P1–3-Cour(86)36-BIL1221606.pdf. See Lord Layton (UK) at 53 [or 111/167].

[19] *Ibid*. See Mr Finan (Ireland) at 54 [or 113/167].

[20] See B. Bowring, 'Negating Pluralist Democracy: The European Court of Human Rights Forgets the Rights of Electors', *KHRP Legal Review* 11 (2007) 67, 74–78.

[21] Opposing a compromise that might have seen the inclusion of electoral rights in the Convention with complaints being passed to the Committee of Ministers as political issues rather than to the Court, the French representative on the Consultative Assembly, Mr Pierre-Henri Teitgen, argued that: '[I]ntervention by the European Court must be possible immediately a totalitarian dictatorship has been set up. It is from the very first day, from the day of the assassination of a Matteotti, from the day of a Reichstag fire, it is from that very moment that it must be able to intervene'. See European Convention on Human Rights, *Travaux Preparatoires*, P1–3. Available at: www.echr.coe.int/library/DIGDOC/Travaux/ECHRTravaux-P1–3-Cour(86)36-BIL1221606.pdf. See 'Consultative

rights in Articles 8–11 of the Convention, operating instead on the basis of 'implied limitations'.

These distinctions between Articles 11 and P1–3 proved decisive in the Grand Chamber's overturning of the Chamber judgment in *Ždanoka v. Latvia*,[22] a case involving restrictions on political rights during Latvia's transition from communist rule and to independence.[23] The applicant, Mrs Tatjana Ždanoka, had been a member of the Communist Party of Latvia (CPL). By virtue of electoral laws enacted in 1995 (and periodically renewed thereafter), she was prevented from standing in parliamentary elections in 1998 and 2002, and in 1999 forfeited her seat as a Riga city councillor. These laws disqualified from standing for office anyone who had 'actively partici-pated' in the CPL after 13 January 1991, when the Soviet army launched a military offensive in Lithuania and the CPL Central Committee called on the Latvian government to resign, culminating in a failed coup in Riga on 15 January (with five fatalities and thirty-four people injured).[24]

The Chamber and Grand Chamber in *Ždanoka* adopted starkly dif-ferent approaches to the interpretation of the right to stand as a candi-date for election. In its Chamber judgment, the Court found that these restrictions violated Mrs Ždanoka's P1–3 right. The Chamber felt bound to 'adhere to the same criteria' permitted by Articles 8–11: 'the only type of necessity capable of justifying an interference with any of those rights is, therefore, one which may claim to spring from "democratic society."'[25] The Grand Chamber, however, reasoned that:

> [W]here an interference with Article 3 of Protocol No. 1 is in issue the Court should not automatically adhere to the same criteria as those applied with regard to the interference permitted by the second para-graphs of Articles 8 to 11 of the Convention … *Because of the relevance of Article 3 of Protocol No. 1 to the institutional order of the State*, this provi-sion is cast in very different terms from Articles 8 to 11 of the Convention … *The standards to be applied for establishing compliance with Article 3 of Protocol No. 1 must therefore be considered to be less stringent than those applied under Articles 8 to 11 of the Convention.*[26]

Assembly sitting on 16 August 1950 (morning): Mr Teitgen (France) (Translation)', at 23 [or 51/167].

[22] ECtHR, *Ždanoka v. Latvia* [GC], 16 March 2006 (Appl. no. 58278/00).

[23] It is noteworthy that the Grand Chamber viewed P1–3 as the *lex specialis*, thus requiring no further examination of the applicant's Article 11 complaint. *Ibid.*, para. 141.

[24] See further the background facts in ECtHR, *Kuolelis, Bartosevicius and Burokevicius v. Lithuania*, 19 February 2008 (Appl. nos. 74357/01, 26764/02 and 27434/02).

[25] ECtHR, *Ždanoka v. Latvia* [Chamber], 17 June 2004 (Appl. no. 58278/00) para. 82.

[26] ECtHR, *Ždanoka v. Latvia* [GC], 16 March 2006 (Appl. no. 58278/00) para. 115(a) [emphasis added].

This implied deference to 'the institutional order of the state' echoes the reference to P1–3's 'constitutional and political character' in the *travaux preparatoires*. It establishes a high supervisory threshold whereby a violation would only be found if procedural deficiencies gave rise to likely arbitrary treatment.[27]

One apparent consequence of the more relaxed scrutiny of P1–3 is that no assessment need be made of extant transitional risks. This again sharpens the contrast with Articles 10 and 11 ECHR which demand attention to the imminence of an evidenced threat. The Chamber in *Ždanoka* regarded the electoral law as being 'firmly focused on the past' and thus not allowing for 'sufficient evaluation of the current threat posed by the persons concerned'.[28] The Chamber was also critical of the fact that the applicant's disqualification was 'based on her previous political involvement rather than on her current conduct' and held that 'her current public activities do not reveal a failure to comply with the fundamental values of the Convention'.[29] The Grand Chamber, in contrast, stated that P1–3 does not exclude that restrictions on electoral rights may be imposed on 'an individual who has, for example, seriously abused a public position or whose conduct threatened to undermine the rule of law or democratic foundations'.[30]

In an apparent U-turn, the Court subsequently found violations of P1–3 in the cases of *Ādamsons* v. *Latvia*[31] (discussed below in relation to the 'passage of time') and in *Tănase* v. *Moldova*.[32] The latter case concerned electoral reforms introduced in Moldova in May 2008 which served to exclude anyone holding dual nationality from political office. The applicant, Alexandru Tănase, was an ethnic Romanian politician in Moldova who sought to challenge the requirement that he renounce his secondary citizenship. The Moldovan government sought to justify the reforms on

---

[27] As was the case in ECtHR, *Podkolzina* v. *Latvia*, 9 April 2002 (Appl. no. 46726/99), and ECtHR, *Melnychenko* v. *Ukraine*, 19 October 2004 (Appl. no. 17707/02). See ECtHR, *Ždanoka* v. *Latvia* [GC], 16 March 2006 (Appl. no. 58278/00) paras. 107–108. Note too the dissenting opinions of Judges Bonello and Levits in the Chamber judgment in *Ždanoka* (2004) para. 33.

[28] *Ždanoka* (2004) para. 97.

[29] The Chamber distinguished *Ždanoka* from both EComHR, *Glimmerveen and Hagenbeek* v. *the Netherlands*, 11 October 1979 (Appl. nos. 8348/78 and 8406/78) and EComHR, *German Communist Party and Others* v. *Germany* [report] 20 July 1957 (Appl. no. 250/57).

[30] See *Ždanoka* [GC, 2006], para. 110, citing *Glimmerveen and Hagenbeek* (ibid.).

[31] ECtHR, *Ādamsons* v. *Latvia*, 24 June 2008 (Appl. no. 3669/03) in French only, extract from Press release issued by the Registrar.

[32] ECtHR, *Tănase* v. *Moldova* [GC], 27 April 2010 (Appl. no. 7/08).

the basis of the need to ensure political loyalty,[33] but this was disputed by both the applicant and the Romanian government (exercising its right to intervene). The latter argued that 'even if a condition of single citizenship could have been justified in the early years following Moldovan independence, with the passage of time and the consolidation of democracy, such a condition could no longer be justified'.[34] The Court seemed convinced by this line of argument, refusing to be swayed by Moldova's particular historico–political situation. The Grand Chamber judgment held that:

> As regards the aim of ensuring loyalty, a concept invoked by all parties in their submissions before the Court ... the Court would distinguish at the outset between loyalty to the State and loyalty to the Government. While the need to ensure loyalty to the State may well constitute a legitimate aim which justifies restrictions on electoral rights, the latter cannot. In a democratic State committed to the rule of law and respect for fundamental rights and freedoms, it is clear that the very role of members of Parliament, and in particular those members from opposition parties, is to represent the electorate by ensuring the accountability of the Government in power and assessing their policies. Further, the pursuit of different, and at times diametrically opposite, goals is not only acceptable but necessary in order to promote pluralism and to give voters choices which reflect their political opinions.[35]

Certainly, the judgments in both *Ādamsons* and *Tănase* suggest a significant narrowing of the gap between Article 11 and P1–3 and a renunciation of the Grand Chamber position in *Ždanoka*. These two cases clearly indicate that loyalty based justifications have a limited shelf-life which must ultimately give way to more untrammelled pluralism. In this light, the Grand Chamber's reasoning in *Ždanoka* can be critiqued for diminishing the protection of passive electoral rights, particularly when the imposition of restrictions due to either past rights abuse or the risk of future abuses could – if necessary – be justified through the application of Article 17 (which prohibits the abuse of rights) or the concept of militant democracy.

Consolidating democracy: militant democracy and past rights abuses

> A certain brand of anti-communism, which claims to fight communism not with democratic methods but with dictatorial methods, sometimes puts in jeopardy the very principles of democracy.[36]

---

[33] *Ibid.*, para. 137.   [34] *Ibid.*, para. 151.   [35] *Ibid.*, paras. 165–166.
[36] First Session of the Consultative Assembly of the Council of Europe, Strasbourg, Preliminary debate, 19th August 1949, M. Teitgen (France). Coll. Ed., I, p.28; or Rep., 1949, II, p.406.

The concept of 'militant democracy' – or 'a democracy capable of defending itself' – underlies many of the justifications advanced for constraining political dissent during times of political flux.[37] While some have questioned whether 'militant democracy' is applicable in contexts where democracy itself is not yet well embedded,[38] others have argued that militant democracy should be understood precisely as belonging to transitional constitutionalism when 'closer judicial vigilance' is warranted given the fragility of democratic institutions.[39]

Drawing upon Lowenstein's emphasis on the threat to democracy posed by emotional populism, András Sajó – now a judge on the European Court of Human Rights – has asserted the need for constitutional democracies to 'be ready and able to confine the politics of emotion'.[40] This is a form of 'precautionary legality'[41] that prioritises self-preservation and risk aversion in the face of potentially cascading anti-democratic harms.[42] Considering the 'special problems' of militant democracy in post-totalitarian and post-communist countries, Sajó observes that, '[t]he inclination to social risk aversion increases where specific historical experiences and reasons dictate precaution. Here even low probabilities of occurrence

---

[37] The seminal text on militant democracy – written in the context of the failure of the Weimar Republic – is K. Loewenstein, 'Militant Democracy and Fundamental Rights', *American Political Science Review* 31 (1937) 417. See also P. Macklem, 'Militant Democracy, Legal Pluralism, and the Paradox of Self-Determination', *International Journal of Constitutional Law* 4(3) (July 2006) 488; A. Sajó, 'Militant Democracy and Transition Towards Democracy', in A. Sajó (ed.) *Militant Democracy* (Utrecht: Eleven International Publishing, 2004) 209–230; P. Harvey, 'Militant Democracy and the European Convention on Human Rights', *European Law Review* 29(3) (2004) 407–420; R. Teitel, 'Militating Democracy: Comparative Constitutional Perspectives', *Michigan Journal of International Law* 29(1) (2007) 49; J. Wise, 'Dissent and the Militant Democracy: The German Constitution and the Banning of the Free German Workers Party', *University of Chicago Roundtable* 5 (1998) 301; J. Vidmar, 'Multiparty Democracy: International and European Human Rights Law Perspectives', *Leiden Journal of International Law* (2010) 209; Bowring, 'Negating Pluralist Democracy'; and R. O'Connell, 'Militant Democracy and Human Rights Principles', *Constitutional Law Review* (a publication of the Georgian Constitutional Court) (2010) 84–91. Available at: http://constcourt.ge/files/SJ-eng.pdf.

[38] Paul Harvey, for example, has argued that '[m]ilitant democracy's ... principal preoccupation is to define when an otherwise liberal constitutional order can take illiberal action'. See Harvey, 'Militant Democracy', 410.

[39] R. Teitel, 'Militating Democracy'. See also C. Horne, 'International Legal Rulings on Lustration Policies in Central and Eastern Europe: Rule of Law in Historical Context', *Law and Social Inquiry* 34(3) (Summer 2009) 713–744, 734.

[40] Sajó, 'Militant Democracy and Transition Towards Democracy', 211.

[41] *Ibid.*, 212.

[42] *Ibid.* See also, M. Hamilton, 'Freedom of Assembly, Consequential Harms and the Rule of Law: Liberty Limiting Principles in the Context of Transition', *Oxford Journal of Legal Studies* 27(1) (2007) 78–81.

of an anti-democratic U-turn are impermissible or at least a matter of pre-cautionary restriction'.[43]

The 'precautionary' measures adopted in post-communist regimes have varied both in scope and severity (often reflecting the nature of the transition itself),[44] and much of the literature focuses on their review by Constitutional Courts.[45] While the European Court has never itself used the term 'militant democracy', several judgments clearly embrace its logic.[46] Moreover, it overlaps with the general 'abuse of rights' provision in Article 17 ECHR which supplements the limiting clauses of Articles 8–11 and the implied limitations of P1-3. Article 17 provides that Convention rights should never be interpreted to imply a right to engage in activities aimed at the destruction of others' rights and freedoms.

Early Article 17 jurisprudence points to its salience in transitional con-texts. Its focus was on the need to protect the free functioning of democratic institutions in the aftermath of abusive regimes (the *German Communist Party* case) and the appropriateness of the state's response in the face of violent resistance (*Lawless* v. *Ireland*).[47] In the *German Communist Party*

---

[43] Sajó, 'Militant Democracy and Transition Towards Democracy', 215.

[44] See J. J. Linz and A. Stepan, 'Varieties of Post-Totalitarian Regimes: Hungary, Czechoslovakia, Bulgaria', in J. J. Linz and A. Stepan, *Problems of Democratic Transition and Consolidation: Southern Europe, South America, and Post-Communist Europe* (Baltimore and London: Johns Hopkins University Press, 1996) 296. See also Jon Elster's discussion of 'emotional decay' caused by the lapse of time after the worst atrocities of Stalinism: J. Elster, *Closing the Books: Transitional Justice in Historical Perspective* (Cambridge University Press, 2004) 223. See also Samuel Huntington's taxonomy of democratization processes (as transformation, transplacement, replacement and inter-vention): S. P. Huntington, *The Third Wave: Democratization in the Late Twentieth Century* (University of Oklahoma Press, 1991) 113–114.

[45] See A. Czarnota, 'Lustration, Decommunisation and the Rule of Law', *Hague Journal on the Rule of Law* 1 (2009) 307–336; R. Uitz, *Constitutions, Courts and History: Historical Narratives in Constitutional Adjudication* (Budapest and New York: CEU Press, 2005) 204–224; R. Uitz, 'Constitutional Courts and the Past in Democratic Transition', in A. Czarnota, M. Krygier and W. Sadurski (eds.) *Rethinking the Rule of Law after Communism* (Budapest and New York: CEU Press, 2005) 235–262; and H. Schwartz, *The Struggle for Constitutional Justice in Post-Communist Europe* (University of Chicago Press, 2000) 102. Also, Sajó, 'Militant Democracy and Transition Towards Democracy', 218–220 and 223–230.

[46] The Court has, for example, accepted loyalty laws in Germany in both *Glasenapp* v. *Germany*, 28 August 1986 (Appl. no. 9228/80) and *Kosiek* v. *Germany*, 28 August 1986 (Appl. no. 9704/82) though cf. *Vogt* v. *Germany*, 26 September 1995 (Appl. no. 7/1994/454/535) in which a 10–9 majority Grand Chamber ruling found a violation of Articles 10 and 11 ECHR.

[47] EComHR, *German Communist Party* v. *Germany* [report], 20 July 1957 (Appl. no. 250/57); ECtHR, *Lawless* v. *Ireland* (No. 3), 1 July 1961 (Appl. no. 332/57). See further Chapter 2 by Fionnuala Ní Aoláin in this volume.

case, the European Commission of Human Rights emphasised that dictatorial regimes were anathema to the effective protection of rights and freedoms, and incompatible with the Convention.[48] The Commission held that the organisation and functioning of the Communist Party of Germany – in seeking to establish a dictatorship of the Proletariat – constituted an activity within the meaning of Article 17 (the party's complaint thus being deemed inadmissible): 'Recourse to dictatorship for the creation of a regime is incompatible with the Convention since it involves the destruction of many of the rights and freedoms protected by the Human Rights Convention.'[49]

The Court has stated that it will first consider whether the restrictions imposed on a particular right were within the range of permissible limitations, and only then decide 'in the light of all the circumstances of the case, whether Article 17 of the Convention should be applied'.[50] Nonetheless, the Court's application of Article 17 has been notoriously haphazard, and Article 17 has rarely factored in the Court's reasoning where states have imposed restrictions on political rights based on an individual's complicity in the rights abuses of prior regimes.[51]

Arguably, the appeal of Article 17's straightforward calculus is limited in cases where the facts or their significance are contested (when the Court may be reluctant to declare unequivocally that an abuse of rights

---

[48] The Commission cited the Convention's *travaux preparatoires*: 'Preparatory Work, Reports of the Consultative Assembly', 1949, 1st Session, pages 1235, 1237, 1239.

[49] EComHR, *German Communist Party* v. *Germany* [report], 20 July 1957 (Appl. no. 250/57). Similarly, in ECtHR, *Lawless* v. *Ireland* (No. 3), 1 July 1961 (Appl. no. 332/57) para. 6. See further, A. M. Williams, 'The European Convention on Human Rights: A New Use', *Texas International Law Journal* 12(1977) 283–284. Williams emphasises the relevance to Article 17 analysis of the *seriousness* and the *duration* of the extant threat (which in ECtHR, *DeBecker* v. *Belgium*, 27 March 1962 (Appl. no. 214/5) was a *past* threat, in contrast to the *continuing* activities of the German Communist Party).

[50] See ECtHR, *United Communist Party of Turkey and Others*, 30 January 1998 (Appl. no. 19392/92) para. 32; ECtHR, *Refah Partisi (The Welfare Party) and Others* v. *Turkey* [GC], 13 February 2003 (Appl. nos. 41340/98, 41342/98, 41343/98 and 41344/98) para. 96. Cf. the joint dissent of Judges Foighel, Loizou and Sir John Freeland in ECtHR, *Lehideux and Isorni* v. *France*, 23 September 1998 (Appl. no. 55/1997/839/1045), arguing that even if Article 17 is deemed inapplicable, 'the principle which underlies Article 17 is a factor which can properly be taken into account in the assessment of the exercise of the margin of appreciation and the existence of necessity'.

[51] For example, the Chamber judgment in *Ždanoka*, with the exception of one passing reference in its analysis of P1–3 to the government's Article 17 claim (para. 84), only assesses the applicability of Article 17 in relation to Article 11. See the government's argument (at para. 105) and the Chamber's finding that Article 17 is not applicable (at para. 109). Cf. the Grand Chamber judgment at paras. 99–100, and see also the dissenting opinion of Judge Zupančič.

has taken place).[52] This is frequently true of transitional cases where there may be particular reason for ambivalence in attributing individual responsibility for past abuses.[53] Furthermore, the facts of a case may render it simply unnecessary for the court to draw upon Article 17 (the limiting clauses being adequate themselves to justify the restrictions imposed). In *Kuolelis, Bartoševičius and Burokevičius* v. *Lithuania*, for example, the transitional context paralleled the concurrent events in *Ždanoka*. Here, the Court found that there had been no violation (of Articles 6, 7, 9, 10, 11 or 14) in relation to the prosecution of the applicants (each of whom occupied executive positions in the Central Committee of the Communist Party of Lithuania) for their involvement in the attempted Soviet-led coup in Lithuania between 11 and 13 January 1991.[54] Given the violent nature of the attempted coup in which thirteen Lithuanians were killed and more than a thousand injured, the Court saw no need to expatiate further on the Lithuanian government's assertion that '[t]he applicants were not prosecuted for their political beliefs or communist party affiliations, but for their anti-state activities, in contravention of Article 17 of the Convention, against which the young democracy of Lithuania had been entitled to defend itself'.[55]

Arguments relating to militant democracy thus appear to have greater purchase in transitional settings than the express application of Article 17. In *Refah Partisi (The Welfare Party) and Others* v. *Turkey* (2003), the Welfare Party's increased democratic mandate was (without irony) relied on to justify its dissolution on militant democracy grounds.[56] The Turkish government, fearing a growing threat of political Islam, successfully argued

---

[52] The Commission's report in the *Lawless* case suggested that it may not be appropriate to apply Article 17 if the Strasbourg institutions were unable to pronounce on a factual dispute closely connected to the merits of the claim. See EComHR, *Lawless* v. *Ireland* [report], 19 December 1959 (Appl. no. 332/57). The factual dispute in *Lawless* concerned whether or not the applicant had ceased to be a member of the Irish Republican Army.

[53] See, for example, ECtHR, *Zickus* v. *Lithuania*, 7 April 2009 (Appl. no. 26652/02), dissenting opinion of Judges Jociene, Tsotsoria and Sajó, para. 3.

[54] ECtHR, *Kuolelis, Bartoševičius and Burokevičius* v. *Lithuania*, 19 February 2008 (Appl. nos. 74357/01, 26764/02 and 27434/02).

[55] At para. 124. Similarly, in ECtHR, *Rufi Osmani and Others* v. *Former Yugoslav Republic of Macedonia* (FYROM) [admissibility], 11 October 2001 (Appl. no. 50841/99), Article 17 was not raised at all – perhaps superfluous to the limiting clauses in Article 10, perhaps because of uncertainty regarding the applicant's personal involvement in organising 'armed shifts'.

[56] The same rationale was applied in both ECtHR, *United Macedonian Organization ILINDEN – PIRIN and others* v. *Bulgaria*, 20 October 2005 (Appl. no. 59489/00) para. 61, and in ECtHR, *Zhechev* v. *Bulgaria*, 21 June 2007 (Appl. no. 57045/00) para. 50, but in both cases reaching the opposite conclusion.

that 'militant democracy required political parties ... to show loyalty to democratic principles, and accordingly to the principle of secularism'.[57] Similarly, in *Ždanoka*, the Latvian government argued that '[t]he new democracies of central and eastern Europe were more sensitive than other European countries to the threat to the democratic regime presented by the resurgence of ideas akin to those espoused by the CPSU and CPL', given that the Soviet communist party controlled not only 'the branches of power but also the "lives and minds" of the people'.[58] Moreover, the government posited that since it was a preventive restriction, no proof of actual undemocratic activities need be provided.[59] The Court broadly accepted these arguments, holding that:

> [I]n order to guarantee the stability and effectiveness of a democratic system, the State may be required to take specific measures to protect itself ... The problem which is then posed is that of achieving a compromise between the requirements of defending democratic society on the one hand and protecting individual rights on the other ... Every time a State intends to rely on the principle of 'a democracy capable of defending itself' in order to justify interference with individual rights, it must carefully evaluate the *scope* and *consequences* of the measure under consideration, to ensure that the aforementioned balance is achieved.[60]

Militant democracy however can cut both ways – it says little of the specific substance of the democracy envisioned or the particular democratic trajectory being consolidated. It remains unclear in what circumstances the Court will accept arguments from militant democracy (and what constitutes a relevant or sufficient threat).[61] Was, for example, the risk in *Ždanoka* that the applicant sought to move Latvia closer to the Commonwealth of Independent States and away from the EU and NATO,[62] or simply that the threat of resurgent communism was a legitimate governmental fear during a period when loyalty to the restored Constitution was precarious? Furthermore, what room is left for legitimate disagreement about what

---

[57] ECtHR, *Refah Partisi (The Welfare Party) and Others* v. *Turkey* [Chamber], 31 July 2001 (Appl. nos. 41340/98, 41342/98, 41343/98 and 41344/98) para. 62, though this argument only succeeded in the Grand Chamber judgment of 13 February 2003. For criticism of the Grand Chamber judgment in *Refah*, see Teitel, 'Militating Democracy', 69. See also Macklem, 'Militant Democracy', 509 and 512; and Chapter 5 by James Sweeney in this volume.

[58] ECtHR, *Ždanoka* [GC, 2006] paras. 95 and 88.

[59] *Ibid.*, para. 86.

[60] *Ždanoka* [2004] para. 80; and [GC, 2006] para. 100 [emphasis added].

[61] See Macklem, 'Militant Democracy', 507 and 513.

[62] *Ždanoka* [2004] para. 74; and [GC, 2006] para. 93.

is in the best interests of democracy?[63] In the context of transition, it is suggested that reliance on the concept of militant democracy ought to entail a detailed assessment of how and why a transitional state's capacity is weakened, as well as the nature and seriousness of the specific threat to the furtherance of democracy.[64]

The margin of appreciation

The doctrine of the margin of appreciation cuts across many of the other interpretative principles relied upon by the Court – including both assessment of the legitimacy of the governmental aim, and the proportionality of the restrictions imposed. It can, however, be difficult to identify precisely at what stage in its reasoning the margin influences the Court's judgment.[65] Moreover, while the breadth of the margin is determined, in part, by the political and historical context, it is difficult to anticipate the extent of this elasticity in particular cases.

Undoubtedly, the margin of appreciation has often diluted the level of scrutiny afforded by the Strasbourg institutions. The Court has evaded contentious issues (relating, for example, to inter-communal relations) by deferring to the assessment of the national authorities.[66] In one example, a Budapest police officer (and Secretary General of the Independent

---

[63] For example, in his dissenting opinion in ECtHR, *Sejdić and Finci* v. *Bosnia and Herzegovina*, 22 December 2009 (Appl. nos. 27996/06 and 34836/06), Judge Bonello argued that it was the Dayton peace accord that 'saved [the State's] democratic existence'. Similarly, the dissenting opinion of Judges Maruste and Jaeger in *Petkov and Others* v. *Bulgaria*, 11 June 2009 (Appl. nos. 77568/01, 178/02 and 505/02). Cf. ECtHR, *Linkov* v. *Czech Republic*, 7 December 2006 (Appl. no. 10504/03) judgment in French only.

[64] See, for example, the Court's analysis of the depth of democratic transition (and the legal, moral and material assurances given by the Hungarian government) in *Vajnai* v. *Hungary*, 8 July 2008 (Appl. no. 33629/06), as discussed in Chapter 6 by Antoine Buyse in this volume.

[65] See further, for example, G. Letsas, *A Theory of Interpretation of the European Convention on Human Rights* (Oxford University Press, 2007) 87–88.

[66] A number of cases relating to the conflict in Northern Ireland are illustrative: EComHR, *Rai, Allmond and 'Negotiate Now'* v. *United Kingdom* [admissibility], 6 April 1995 (Appl. no. 25522/94) – cited by Judge Botoucharova in her dissent in ECtHR, *Stankov and the United Macedonian Organisation ILINDEN* v. *Bulgaria*, 2 October 2001 (Appl. nos. 29221/95 and 29225/95). Also, ECtHR, *Murphy* v. *Ireland*, 10 July 2003 (Appl. no. 44179/98), regarding a broadcasting ban on religious radio advertising; ECtHR, *McGuinness* v. *United Kingdom* [admissibility], 8 June 1999 (Appl. no. 39511/98), regarding the withholding of parliamentary privileges because of a refusal to swear allegiance to the British monarchy; and EComHR, *Purcell* v. *Ireland* [admissibility], 16 April 1991 (Appl. no. 15404/89), and EComHR, *Brind* v. *UK* [admissibility], 9 May 1994 (Appl. no. 18714/91), in relation to broadcasting bans in Ireland and the UK governing interviews

Police Trade Union), László Rekvényi, challenged the prohibition of police officers from joining political parties or pursuing political activities.[67] The Court's judgment found the restrictions to be both necessary and proportionate in order to protect the police from the influence of party politics. The Court referred to the needs of democratic consolidation, and justified its conclusion with reference to the state's margin of appreciation:

> In view of the particular history of some Contracting States, the national authorities of these States may, so as to ensure the consolidation and maintenance of democracy, consider it necessary to have constitutional safeguards to achieve this aim by restricting the freedom of police officers to engage in political activities and, in particular, political debate ... Regard being had to the margin of appreciation left to the national authorities in this area, the Court finds that, especially against this historical background, the relevant measures taken in Hungary in order to protect the police force from the direct influence of party politics can be seen as answering a 'pressing social need' in a democratic society.[68]

In the Chamber judgment in *Ždanoka* v. *Latvia*, Judge Bonello (dissenting) accused the Court of abandoning its 'doctrine of "wide margin of appreciation"' (a point with which Judge Levits, also dissenting, agreed), and of substituting 'a text-book political and historical credo for that of a State that had lost democracy through the proficiency of the likes of the applicant'.[69] Judge Levits similarly argued that the Court 'should not overstep the limits of its explicit and implicit legitimacy and try to rule instead of the people on the constitutional order which this people creates for itself ... The appropriate way out of this dilemma is to use the instrument of the margin of appreciation'. He argued that this meant giving different weight both to the legitimate aim and the proportionality of a restriction, and that if 'restrictions pursue a legitimate aim and are not

---

with spokespersons of Sinn Féin (amongst others). On the latter two cases, see further B. Dickson, *The European Convention on Human Rights and the Conflict in Northern Ireland* (Oxford University Press, 2010) 301–302.

[67] ECtHR, *Rekvényi* v. *Hungary*, 20 May 1999 (Appl. no. 25390/94).

[68] *Ibid.*, paras. 46 and 48. As Jure Vidmar notes, 'If "maintenance of democracy" has been implied in previous cases dealing with the so-called concept of a militant democracy, a reference to the "consolidation of democracy" implied a new approach'. See Vidmar, 'Multiparty Democracy', 209–240 (though note that the discussion of *Ždanoka* in Vidmar's article does not include the 2006 Grand Chamber judgment).

[69] Judge Bonello's dissenting opinion at para. 3.5.

arbitrary, then only in exceptional situations can this restriction be found disproportionate'.[70]

The Grand Chamber in *Ždanoka* (2006) recognised that 'the impugned restriction ... must be assessed with due regard to this very special historico-political context and the resultant wide margin of appreciation enjoyed by the State in this respect'.[71] Again, the case does little to clarify how or when the historical or political context will determine the application of the margin of appreciation (though this weakness is not unique to the Court's transitional case law). It is noteworthy that in an important recent transitional case, *Sejdić and Finci v. Bosnia and Herzegovina* (2009) (discussed in greater detail below), while noting that 'the scope of a Contracting Party's margin of appreciation in this sphere will vary according to the circumstances, the subject matter and the background',[72] the margin of appreciation does not feature in the majority judgment at all. Drawing attention to this fact, the partly concurring and partly dissenting opinion of Judge Mijović (joined by Judge Hajiyev) stated: 'For the sake of the Court's case law, it would have been very interesting to see how far the Court would have interpreted the margin of appreciation left to the State in this case.'

Proportionality

As noted above, the margin of appreciation frequently cuts across the Court's assessment of the proportionality of interferences with Convention rights. This final section examines how questions of context and, in particular, the passage of time affect the proportionality test in transitional cases. Focusing again on electoral rights, and also on the Court's lustration case law, the section examines what might be inferred about the Court's evaluation of transition endpoints, highlighting the importance of individualised assessment as transitional destinies come into view.

The political context

On the one hand, the Court has clearly intimated that states do not have unlimited discretion in responding to transitional problems by

---

[70] Dissenting opinion of Judge Levits, at paras. 17–18.
[71] *Ždanoka* [GC, 2006] at para. 121.
[72] At para. 42, and citing ECtHR, *Andrejeva v. Latvia* [GC], 18 February 2009 (Appl. no. 55707/00) para. 82.

invoking the need to stabilise democratic politics.[73] On the other hand, the Court has recognised that transitional politics may give rise to exigencies in which rule-of-law ideals could not possibly be realised. Illustrative of the latter situation is the case of the *Georgian Labour Party* v. *Georgia* (2008).[74] Here, the Court held that in the aftermath of the *Rose Revolution* of 20–23 November 2003, there had been no violation of the applicant party's right to stand for election on account of the introduction of a new voter registration system in February 2004 (with repeat elections scheduled in only one month's time). This system placed the onus on voters to register and check their own details on the electoral register. In granting the state a wide margin of appreciation,[75] the Court acknowledged that:

> [T]he electoral authorities had the challenge of remedying manifest shortcomings in the electoral rolls within very tight deadlines, in a 'post-revolutionary' political situation ... Consequently, the Court concludes that the unexpected change in the rules on voter registration one month before the repeat parliamentary election of 28 March 2004 was, in the very specific circumstances of the situation, a solution devoid of criticism under Article 3 of Protocol No. 1.[76]

This judgment, however, should not be read as evidence of transitional exceptionalism. The Court only just stopped short of finding that the Georgian Electoral Commission was imbalanced and insufficiently impartial on account of pro-presidential forces having a relative majority on the body. Moreover, the Court did find a violation of P1–3 on the basis of the Electoral Commission's failure to provide adequate reasons in a 'transparent and consistent manner' for annulling election results in two electoral districts (disenfranchising approximately 60,000 voters).[77] As Melissa Marsh concludes, '[h]olding Georgia liable on one, but not all, counts represents the Court's calculated attempt to regulate Georgia's behavior while still fostering the democratic government it seeks to attain'.[78]

---

[73] See, for example, EComHR, *Cyprus* v. *Turkey* [report], 4 June 1999 (Appl. no. 25781/94), and ECtHR, *Cyprus* v. *Turkey*, 10 May 2001 (Appl. no. 25781/94) – the censorship of school books 'far exceeded the limits of confidence-building methods and amounted to a denial of the right to freedom of information'.

[74] ECtHR, *Georgian Labour Party* v. *Georgia*, 8 July 2008 (Appl. no. 9103/04).

[75] *Ibid.*, para. 90.   [76] *Ibid.*, para. 89.   [77] *Ibid.*, para. 141.

[78] See M. D. Marsh, 'Not Back in the USSR: Georgian Labour Party v. Georgia Enforces Free Elections in an Emerging Democracy', *Tulane Journal of International and Comparative Law* 17 (2008–2009) 585, 593–594.

One of the Court's most significant transitional judgments to date is its ruling in *Sejdić and Finci* v. *Bosnia and Herzegovina* (2009).[79] The context of this case was the internationally led effort to bring peace to this war-torn region. The Court was asked to examine the ineligibility of the applicants to stand for election to both the House of Peoples, and to the Presidency, of Bosnia and Herzegovina under the Constitution of Bosnia and Herzegovina as adopted in Annex 4 of the Dayton Peace Agreement (DPA). Their ineligibility arose because they did not self-identify as one of the 'constituent peoples', instead being of Roma and Jewish origins respectively.[80] The Court found a violation of Article 14 in conjunction with P1–3 in relation to their ineligibility to stand for election to the House of Peoples (a majority of 14–3), and a violation of Article 1 of Protocol 12 (the first violation of this Protocol since it came into force) in relation to the Presidency (a majority of 16–1). The Court did not consider whether there had been a violation of P1–3 in its own right (arguably, this being the only deference shown by the Court to the DPA).

The impugned restriction was held to have 'pursued at least one aim which is broadly compatible with the general objectives of the Convention, as reflected in the Preamble to the Convention, namely the restoration of peace',[81] but the Court went on to say that it did not need to decide whether the contested provision 'could be said to serve a 'legitimate aim' since 'the maintenance of the system in any event does not satisfy the requirement of proportionality'.[82] The Court observed that there had been 'significant positive developments'[83] in Bosnia and Herzegovina since Dayton, although progress had not always been consistent and challenges remained. It recognised – relying heavily upon Opinions of the Venice Commission – that there were other safeguards in the power-sharing

---

[79] ECtHR, *Sejdić and Finci* v. *Bosnia and Herzegovina*, 22 December 2009 (Appl. nos. 27996/06 and 34836/06). See also 'Case Comment', *EHRLR* 2 (2010) 235–239.

[80] This has been referred to as a 'double exclusion' (Venice Commission, *Amicus Curiae* in the case of *Sejdić and Finci* v. *Bosnia and Herzegovina*, para. 9). Not only the exclusion of non-constituent peoples (i.e. persons not self-classifying as Bosniac, Croat or Serb) but Bosniacs or Croats residing in the Republika Srpska, or Serbs residing in the Federation of Bosnia and Herzegovina (see Article V of the General Framework Agreement, Annex 4, Constitution of Bosnia and Herzegovina).

[81] *Sejdić and Finci* (2009), para. 45.   [82] *Ibid.*, para. 46.

[83] *Ibid.*, para. 47. The Court cited the fact that the former parties to the conflict surrendered control of the armed forces and transformed them into a small, professional force (2005); Bosnia and Herzegovina jointed NATO's Partnership for Peace (2006), and signed and ratified an EU Stabilization and Association Agreement (2008); amended its constitution for the first time (2009); and elected a member of the UN Security Council (for two years from 1 January 2010).

arrangements that did not automatically exclude representatives of the other communities.[84] This sanguine assessment, however, was not shared by all commentators – amongst other sources on which it cited, the Court pointed to a March 2009 report by International Crisis Group as evidencing that preparations were underway to close the international administration. The same ICG report, though, opens with the following caution:

> While Bosnia and Herzegovina's time as an international protectorate is ending, which is in itself most welcome, now is the wrong time to rush the transition … tensions are currently high and stability is deteriorating, as Bosniaks and Serbs play a zero-sum game to upset the Dayton settlement. Progress toward EU membership is stalled, and requirements set in 2008 for ending the protectorate have not been not met.[85]

Some commentaries on this case have stated that removing the ineligibility of minority groups to stand for election in Bosnia and Herzegovina is entirely uncontroversial (even trivial) – that there is widespread support for such reform (delayed only because of the 'all or nothing' nature of constitutional amendment).[86] Others, though, have suggested that the decision is more significant and 'gives politicians political-cover … by providing a legal reason for change outside the hands of the political process'.[87] Whichever view is preferred, the judgment is highly significant in terms of the Court's perception of its competence and role in consolidating transition. Arguably, it demonstrates that the European Court will purposely seek to facilitate transition, understanding the DPA in terms of the political expedients it navigated rather than as a roadmap for the future,[88] and catalysing upshifting between different phases in the transition process. It rejected the stasis that characterised political life in Bosnia and

---

[84] These safeguards included the 'vital interest' veto, the bicameral system, and the Collective Presidency.

[85] International Crisis Group, *Bosnia's Incomplete Transition: Between Dayton and Europe* (9 March 2009). Available at: www.crisisgroup.org/en/regions/europe/balkans/bosnia-herzegovina/198-bosnias-incomplete-transition-between-dayton-and-europe.aspx.

[86] Clive Baldwin (then a lawyer for the Minority Rights Group, now for Human Rights Watch) who represented Mr Finci at Strasbourg, commented that the result was 'a no-brainer' since 'the Dayton Accords were hardly a recipe for long-term stability and peace'. C. Baldwin, 'Dayton Discord: How the International Community Failed Bosnia', *Foreign Policy*, March/April 2010. Available at: www.foreignpolicy.com/articles/2010/02/22/dayton_discord.

[87] S. P. Rosenberg, Counsel for Jakob Finci, Director, Human Rights and Genocide Clinic Benjamin N. Cardozo School of Law, NY. Available at: www.ejiltalk.org/grand-chamber-judgment-in-sejdic-and-finci-v-bosnia.

[88] See R. Teitel, 'Transitional Jurisprudence: The Role of Law in Political Transformation', *Yale Law Journal* 106 (1996–1997) 2009–2080.

Herzegovina and which was grounded in bargains reached in a fifteen-year-old peace agreement. As Fionnuala Ní Aoláin argued in 1998, '[t]he Bosnia that came into being after the Dayton Agreement was the effective consolidation of division'[89] with 'the potential for the Constitution itself to endanger rights rather than protect them'.[90] Thus, '[t]o view the Dayton Agreement as fixed, is to eschew the possibility of recreating Bosnia as an ethnically mixed, multinational state'.[91] Proposing a middle position, Ní Aoláin argued for a 'corrective process'[92] in which the DPA should be viewed only as 'a transitionary structure'[93] – 'an intermediate stage'[94] – rather than 'fortifying the DPA's divisive structures'.[95] The Court's judgment certainly advances along this track.

An alternative view is presented by the characteristically bold dissent of Judge Bonello (recently retired), echoing his earlier dissent in the Chamber judgment in *Ždanoka*.[96] Judge Bonello rounded on the Court for having 'divorced Bosnia and Herzegovina from the realities of its own recent past' and for telling 'both the former belligerents and the peace-devising do-gooders that they got it all wrong'.[97] He describes the DPA as being 'a most precarious equilibrium ... laboriously reached, resulting in a fragile tripartite symmetry born from mistrust and nourished on suspicion'. Moreover, he viewed the Strasbourg Court's judgment as 'an exercise in star-struck mirage-building which neglects the rivers of blood that fertilised the Dayton Constitution', and positions the Court as 'the uninvited guest in multilateral exercises and treaties that have already been signed, ratified and executed':

---

[89] F. Ní Aoláin, 'The Fractured Soul of the Dayton Peace Agreement: A Legal Analysis', *Michigan Journal of International Law* 19 (1998) 957, 968.

[90] *Ibid.*, 974.   [91] *Ibid.*, 965–966.   [92] *Ibid.*, 961.

[93] *Ibid.*, 965.   [94] *Ibid.*, 966.

[95] Similarly, Paddy Ashdown (former High Representative in BiH): P. Ashdown, *Swords and Ploughshares: Bringing Peace to the 21st Century* (London: Weidenfeld & Nicolson, 2007) 99–102. See also B. Dakin 'The Islamic Community in Bosnia and Herzegovina v. The Republika Srpska: Human Rights in a Multi-Ethnic Bosnia', *Harvard Human Rights Journal* 15 (Spring 2002) 245, 263: 'This system has ... rendered political stalemate inevitable.'

[96] In *Ždanoka* [2004], Judge Bonello argued in dissent (para. 3.3) that 'it was never for the Court to determine such subjective and elusive questions as the one whether in 1998 the transitional period to a new democracy had been fully played out or otherwise ... I fail to see how an international Court is better placed to impose its own value judgments on such evanescent and ephemeral issues as to exactly when a state of emergency or transition is over'.

[97] See further the partly dissenting opinion of Judge Mijović (joined by Judge Hajiyev).

[A] judicial institution so remote from the focus of dissention can hardly be the best judge of this. *In traumatic revolutionary events, it is not for the Court to establish, by a process of divination, when the transitional period is over, or when a state of national emergency is past and everything is now business as usual.* I doubt that the Court is better placed than the national authorities to assess the point in time when previous fractures consolidate, when historical resentments quell and when generational discords harmonise.

In a similar vein, Judges Mijović and Hajiyev (citing *Ždanoka v. Latvia*, 2006) argued that the domestic authorities should be left 'sufficient latitude to assess the needs of their society in building confidence in the new democratic institutions'. Crucially, they ask: 'Is it up to the European Court of Human Rights to determine when the time for change has arrived?' Whilst not giving a definitive answer, they lament the failure of the Court 'to provide more decisive and convincing arguments or at least a ground for comparison with other member States'.

Of course, it also remains to be seen what the impact of the judgment will be on the ground. Will it play into the hands of those seeking to undermine Dayton, given especially that the High Representative has voiced concern about the deteriorating political situation?[98] Or will it, in setting an anti-discrimination high-watermark, enhance Bosnia's constitutional credentials and nudge it towards the prize of EU candidacy?[99] As Louise Arbour stated (in November 2009), preparations must 'include authorizing the state to … implement obligatory EU reforms, including ensuring that the constitution is compliant with the European Convention of Human Rights'.[100] Just as the Court has discounted arguments which fail to acknowledge the transitional dilemmas which constrain decision-making (as in the *Georgian Labour Party* case), it has shown its impatience in *Sejdić and Finci* with arguments that might entrench irresolution in the status quo. This demonstrates a concern on the part of the Court to move the transitional process forward. The question then becomes at what point do arguments from transition cease to have purchase?

---

[98] See High Representative for the Implementation of the Peace Agreement on Bosnia and Herzegovina, *Report to the Secretary-General of the United Nations* S/2009/246 (21 May 2009). Available at: www.ohr.int/other-doc/hr-reports/default. asp?content_id=43537.

[99] *Sejdić and Finci* (2009) para. 43.

[100] See L. Arbour, 'Bosnia's Continuing Chaos', *Foreign Policy* (18 November 2009). Available at: www.foreignpolicy.com/articles/2009/11/18/bosnia_s_continuing_chaos?page=0,1.

The passage of time, transitional endpoints and individualised scrutiny

While the jurisprudence of the Court does not provide a real-time lens through which to focus on post-conflict and post-totalitarian transitions,[101] as is noted elsewhere in this collection, the passage of time has clearly influenced the Court's analysis.[102] It is not, though, necessarily a decisive factor in the Court's reasoning – other signifiers of democratic progress will also be weighted in the assessment of proportionality. In *Yumak and Sadak* v. *Turkey*,[103] for example, the Court accepted that Turkey's 10 per cent electoral threshold (higher than any in Europe)[104] had been enacted in 1983 after a three-year period of military rule 'to avoid excessive parliamentary fragmentation and thus strengthen governmental stability'.[105] While the passage of time between the introduction of the threshold and present day conditions was clearly influential in the joint dissenting opinion,[106] the majority found there to have been no violation of P1–3. The Court reasoned that (in spite of the passage of twenty years) the existence of other democratic safeguards – particularly, the successive reviews by the Turkish Constitutional Court – were an important factor in determining 'the point of equilibrium between the principles of fair

---

[101] At first glance, this would preclude the norms established by the Court from having a guiding or constitutive role in transitional situations, but see, in particular, Chapters 3 and 4 in this volume. See also the expedited hearing in ECtHR, *Christian Democratic People's Party (CDPP)* v. *Moldova*, 14 February 2006 (Appl. no. 28793/02) discussed further in the concluding chapter.

[102] See, for example, Buyse (Chapter 6) in this volume, discussing the cases of *Lehideux and Isorni* v. *France* (1998) and *Orban and others* v. *France* (2009).

[103] ECtHR, *Yumak and Sadak* v. *Turkey*, [GC] 8 July 2008 (Appl. no. 10226/03).

[104] At para. 127. The Council of Europe pointed out that '*in well-established democracies*, there should be no thresholds higher than 3 per cent during the parliamentary elections' [emphasis added], para. 130.

[105] See para. 120 (government) and para. 125 (Court's assessment). Of course, it is questionable whether Turkey's 1983 transition is comparable to the other transitions examined in this chapter. See Huntingdon, *The Third Wave*, at 130 and 176; and Sajó, 'Militant Democracy and Transition', at 221.

[106] Judges Tulkens, Vajić, Jaeger and Šikuta argued that the electoral threshold far exceeded Turkey's margin of appreciation, and quoted Professor Ian Budge: '[w]hat might have been justified then [1983] as an exceptional measure to buttress a still fragile democracy can hardly be justified now when the democracy is considered sufficiently stable and mature to seek membership of the European Union.' See Joint dissenting opinion at para. 5. See also H.-M. ten Napel, 'The European Court of Human Rights and Political Rights: The Need for More Guidance', *European Constitutional Law Review* 5 (2009) 464 at 471.

representation and governmental stability'.[107] Such safeguards served to moderate the intensity of the Court's supervision, leading it to defer to the government's assessment of the need for such a high threshold.

How precisely temporal factors are taken into account says something about how the Court views the depth of a transition, and also reveals how the Court gauges when transitional endpoints – or significant staging posts – have been reached. This is especially important given that parties before the Court often envisage different transitional endpoints, and both thus seek to benefit from transitional posturing.[108] The Court's consideration of protracted peace negotiations provides a useful illustration.

In an important interstate judgment, the Turkish government attempted to argue that ongoing peace negotiations justified the Turkish government's refusal to allow displaced Greek Cypriots to return to their homes in northern Cyprus. However, the European Commission on Human Rights (and subsequently also the Court) found a continuing violation of Article 8 ECHR in the absence of any legal basis for the general exclusion (which was also held to be wholly disproportionate to the claimed security interests). The Commission stated that:

> [T]he inter-communal talks must be seen as an instrument to put an end to such violations as might continue to occur, but the negotiations in themselves, even if they are actively pursued, do not wipe out those violations ... [I]t appears that the process of the inter-communal talks is still very far from reaching any tangible results in this respect.[109]

More recently, however, the Court rejected a similar complaint. The Court charted a number of changes that had occurred regarding the situation in Northern Cyprus (including the 'Annan talks'), observing that there was now legislation which sought to provide a mechanism of redress, and that the political climate had ameliorated, with borders to the north no longer closed:[110]

---

[107] *Ibid.*, para. 146.

[108] In *Ždanoka*, for example, both the Latvian government and the applicant argued that at the material time, the transition was incomplete. The end or culmination of transition was argued by the government to be marked by Latvia's accession to the European Union on 1 May 2004 [2004] para. 50; [GC, 2006] para. 66. The applicant asserted that at the time of events, the transition was incomplete and that the characterisation of the CPL's activities as a *coup d'état* was therefore misplaced [GC, 2006] para. 78 – a coup could only arise where there was an established and stable polity.

[109] EComHR, *Cyprus* v. *Turkey* [report], 4 June 1999 (Appl. no. 25781/94) para. 269; and ECtHR, *Cyprus* v. *Turkey*, 10 May 2001 (Appl. no. 25781/94) para. 169.

[110] *Demopoulos and Others* v. *Turkey* [Admissibility, GC], 1 March 2010 (Appl. nos. 46113/99, 3843/02, 13751/02, 13466/03, 10200/04, 14163/04, 19993/04, 21819/04) paras. 34–38.

> [T]he Court finds itself faced with cases burdened with a political, histor-
> ical and factual complexity flowing from a problem that should have been
> resolved by all parties assuming full responsibility for finding a solution
> on a political level. This reality, as well as the passage of time and the con-
> tinuing evolution of the broader political dispute must inform the Court's
> interpretation and application of the Convention which cannot, if it is to
> be coherent and meaningful, be either static or blind to concrete factual
> circumstances.[111]

The Court's long-term view in these cases is not dissimilar to its conceptualisation of the transition lifespan in its post-communist jurisprudence.
The Court does not confine its assessment of the transition to the period
begun by the Declarations of Independence and ended when the provision declaring an official transition period is repealed.[112] The Court takes
a broader view, narrating the historical background, and citing such factors as the holding of parliamentary elections, the adoption of the restoration constitutions, and the final withdrawal of troops (for example, from
the Baltic states in 1994) as relevant staging posts. The cases of *Kuolelis,
Bartoševičius and Burokevičius* v. *Lithuania* (2008)[113] and *Ždanoka* v.
Latvia (2006) help illustrate the point.

The backdrop to these cases represented a critical moment in the transition to constitutional democracy and independence in the Baltic states
(the period between January and August 1991).[114] As discussed earlier, the
applicants were prosecuted (*Kuolelis*) and prevented from standing for
election (*Ždanoka*) due to their involvement in the Communist Party's
failed coups in their respective countries. The Strasbourg Court refused
to accept Tatjana Ždanoka's argument that this transition period represented a constitutional diarchy, when divergent opinions concerning
Latvia's future political direction should have been protected.[115] However,
while the Court has stated its intention to 'abstain, as far as possible, from
pronouncing on matters of purely historical fact',[116] it was not blind to the

---

[111] *Ibid.*, para. 90.
[112] In Latvia, for example, para. 5 of the Declaration of Independence of 4 May 1990 declared
       a transition period during which institutional links with the USSR would be gradually
       severed. This provision was repealed on 21 August 1991.
[113] ECtHR, *Kuolelis, Bartoševičius and Burokevičius* v. *Lithuania*, 19 February 2008 (Appl.
       nos. 74357/01, 26764/02 and 27434/02).
[114] See Linz and Stepan, *Problems of Democratic Transition*, 406–410; and M. McFaul, 'The
       Fourth Wave of Democracy and Dictatorship: Non Co-operative Transitions in the
       Post-Communist World', *World Politics* 54 (January 2002) 212, 231.
[115] *Ždanoka* [GC, 2006] para. 79
[116] *Ždanoka* [2004] para. 77 and [GC, 2006] para. 96.

contested nature of the events of January 1991 and their implication for law's role in the process of transition. In *Kuolelis*, the Court stated that:

> [T]he historical and political background to the present case is an import-ant element, reflecting as it does a period of tension caused by the tran-sition between two different legal systems after the re-establishment of the independence of the Republic of Lithuania. The period between 24 February 1990 (the date of the parliamentary elections) until August 1991 (the time of the failed coup in Moscow and the recognition of Lithuania's independence by the USSR) was thus one of relative instability in Lithuania, as the new democratic forces sought to establish a firm foot-hold, whilst the previous Soviet regime sought to retain power.[117]

Indeed, commenting on the fact that the Election Acts, which debarred those who had actively participated in the Communist Party from stand-ing for election, were not enacted until 1995, the Grand Chamber in *Ždanoka* stated that 'it is not surprising that a newly established demo-cratic legislature should need time for reflection in a period of political turmoil to enable it to consider what measures were required to sustain its achievements'.[118]

This begs the question of for how long, post-transition, such restrict-ive legislative measures should be permitted in order to 'sustain' tran-sitional achievements – not least because one such 'achievement' might be regarded by the successor government as the exclusion from the pub-lic sphere of those exhibiting loyalty to the predecessor regime.[119] This question is especially pertinent given that several states have 'recently opted for late or renewed lustration policies, arguing there is a need for continued moral cleansing and bureaucratic change in order to address the on-going problems'.[120] A brief examination of the Court's lustration cases shows that the Court has consistently opposed belated lustration programmes which are widely cast or which do not contain adequate pro-cedural safeguards.

---

[117] *Kuolelis* (2008) para. 117. Although this passage appears in the Court's consideration of Article 7, it can also be regarded as relevant to its (rather peremptory) analysis of Articles 9, 10 and 11 given that its conclusion here is based on the 'case viewed as a whole' (para. 126).

[118] *Ždanoka* [GC, 2006] para. 131; also cited in the partly dissenting opinion in *Sejdić and Finci* (2009).

[119] For an interesting comparison, see C. Collins, 'State Terror and the Law: The (Re) judicialization of Human Rights Accountability in Chile and El Salvador', 35(5) *Latin American Perspectives* (2008) 20.

[120] C. Horne, 'Lustration and Trust in Public Institutions. A Retrospective on the State of Trust Building in Central and Eastern Europe', *Sphere of Politics* (*Sfera Politicii*), 142 (2009) 30, 42–43. Available at: www.ceeol.com.

In *Sidabras and Džiautas* v. *Lithuania*[121] the two applicants faced employment restrictions under the 1999 KGB Act because they were deemed, by the Lithuanian State Security Department and the 'Centre for Research into the Genocide and Resistance of the Lithuanian People', to have 'former KGB officer' status. These restrictions prevented them from obtaining employment in various branches of the private sector until 2009. The Court found a violation of Article 14 in conjunction with Article 8, later applying this decision in the similar case of *Rainys and Gasparavičius* v. *Lithuania*.[122] In the latter case, the declaration of 'former KGB officer' status not only limited the applicants' possible employment opportunities, but also led to their actual dismissal as private-sector lawyers. In *Sidabras and Džiautas* (as in *Ždanoka*), the Court considered the timing of the enactment of the KGB Act. In contrast to *Ždanoka*, however, the Court noted that the Act came into force:

> [A]lmost a decade after Lithuania declared its independence on 11 March 1990; in other words, the restrictions on the applicants' professional activities were imposed on them thirteen years and nine years respectively after their departure from the KGB. The fact of the KGB Act's belated timing, although not in itself decisive, may nonetheless be considered relevant to the overall assessment of the proportionality of the measures taken.[123]

Similarly, in *Zickus* v. *Lithuania*,[124] the Court again found a violation of Article 14 in conjunction with Article 8 (albeit here, in a narrow 4–3 majority judgment). Egidijus Žičkus was declared to be a former secret collaborator and was consequently dismissed from his post in the human resources department of the Ministry of Interior. The case focused on the proportionality of the scheme enacted by the 1999 *Law on registering, confession, entry into records and protection of persons who have admitted to secret collaboration with special services of the former USSR*. Under this Act, voluntary confessions of collaboration with the special services of the former USSR were to be classified as state secrets if made within six months of a date determined by the Commission (also established by the Act). The majority argued that the law failed to differentiate between different levels of former KGB involvement, that it was enacted 'almost

---

[121] ECtHR, *Sidabras and Džiautas* v. *Lithuania*, 27 July 2004 (Appl. nos. 55480/00 and 59330/00).
[122] ECtHR, *Rainys and Gasparavičius* v. *Lithuania*, 7 April 2005 (Appl. nos. 70665/01 and 74345/01).
[123] *Sidabras and Džiautas* (2004) at para. 60.
[124] ECtHR, *Zickus* v. *Lithuania*, 7 April 2009 (Appl. no. 26652/02).

a decade after Lithuania had declared its independence', and that the restrictions were imposed on the applicant 'at least a decade after he had ceased collaborating with the KGB'.[125]

These lustration cases confirm that the passage of time is one of several factors considered by the Court in its assessment of proportionality in the context of transition. However, as with the judgment in *Sejdić and Finci* (2009), the findings of a violation do not easily align with the Grand Chamber's conclusion in *Ždanoka* (2006). It is instructive to contrast again the Chamber and Grand Chamber judgments in *Ždanoka*, and to compare these judgments with more recent P1-3 jurisprudence. While the Grand Chamber in *Ždanoka* framed the 'development of democracy' as an issue of proportionality, the proportionality test it applied was strikingly different from that which was central to the Chamber's earlier finding of a violation of P1-3.[126] As explained earlier in this chapter, this is partly due to the Chamber's application of principles deriving from the Court's Articles 8-11 jurisprudence to its assessment of P1-3 (an approach rejected outright by the Grand Chamber). However, a further distinction can be drawn between the Chamber and Grand Chamber's examination of the passage of time (and in particular, its preparedness to consider the extent of the present threat posed by previously 'disloyal' citizens). The Grand Chamber's conclusion is all the more questionable given the Court's ruling only two years later in *Ādamsons* v. *Latvia*.

The premise in *Ždanoka* (2006) – that given the wide margin of appreciation afforded in P1-3 cases, a national parliament may legitimately enact electoral laws requiring the differential treatment of a certain category of individuals '[a]s long as the statutory distinction itself is proportionate' – was confirmed in *Seyidzade* v. *Azerbaijan* (2009).[127] In such cases, 'the task of the domestic authorities may be limited to establishing whether a

---

[125] The joint dissenting opinion of Judges Jočienė, Tsotsoria and Sajó focused on the legitimate purpose of the legislative scheme (inter alia, to offer former collaborators protection against blackmail), the fact that this was a public sector position (thus distinguishing it from both *Sidabras* and *Rainys*), the existence of adequate safeguards, and, in particular, the applicant's own unexplained non-compliance with the scheme.

[126] See 'Elections: former member of Communist Party prevented from standing for parliamentary election – Articles 10 and 11, and Article 3 of Protocol No.1', Case Comment, *E.H.R.L.R.* 4 (2006) 478–481: 'The Grand Chamber's a marked departure from the earlier Chamber judgment as it is based on an opposed approach to the "proportionality" of an interference.'

[127] *Ždanoka* [GC, 2006] paras. 108 and 134–135 and ECtHR, *Seyidzade* v. *Azerbaijan*, 3 December 2009 (Appl. no. 37700/05) para. 30.

particular individual belongs to the impugned statutory category'.[128] The key question for transition cases (including *Ždanoka*) concerns the proportionality of the statutory distinction when the salience of that distinction is itself eroded with the passage of time.[129] The test has essentially two limbs (examined separately below). The first concerns the duration of the provision and the length of time since the occurrence of the events giving rise to the statutory category. The second limb concerns the degree of individualised scrutiny required.

With regard to the duration of the provision, the Chamber in *Ždanoka* held that 'the measure in question must remain temporary in order to be proportionate'[130] whereas the restriction amounted to a 'permanent disqualification'.[131] However, the Grand Chamber, referring to the conclusion reached by the Latvian Constitutional Court in August 2000, merely noted that 'the Latvian parliament must keep the statutory restriction under constant review, with a view to bringing it to an early end'.[132] As Bill Bowring (who represented Mrs Ždanoka at the European Court) justifiably asks, '[w]hy should it be swiftly repealed if it did not in any event violate P1–3?'.[133]

With regard to the factors relevant to the proportionality assessment, the Chamber held that although the restriction might have been proportionate during the first years after the re-establishment of Latvia's independence irrespective of the applicant's individual conduct, '[a]fter a certain time ... this ground is no longer sufficient to justify the preventative aspect of the restriction in question; *it then becomes necessary to establish whether other factors, particularly an individual's personal participation in the disputed events*, continue to justify his or her ineligibility'.[134] The Chamber concluded that although it was clear that the applicant had held an important post within the CPL, 'none of the evidence produced by the Government proves that she herself committed specific acts aimed at destroying the Republic of Latvia or at restoring the former system'.[135] The Grand Chamber, however, held that:

---

[128] *Seyidzade* (2009) para. 30.
[129] This was not the case in *Seyidzade* where the Court found a violation of P1–3 because of the *imprecision* of the relevant statutory category – in this case, 'clergymen' or 'professional religious activity' (see para. 125).
[130] *Ždanoka* [2004] para. 88.   [131] *Ibid.*, para. 99.
[132] *Ždanoka* [GC, 2006] para. 135. See also paras. 62 and 122.
[133] Bowring, 'Negating Pluralist Democracy', 93.
[134] *Ždanoka* [2004] para. 92 [emphasis added].
[135] *Ibid.*, para. 94

There was no obligation under Article 3 of Protocol No.1 for the Latvian
parliament to delegate more extensive jurisdiction to the Latvian courts
to 'fully individualise' the applicant's situation so as to enable them to
establish as a fact whether or not she had done anything which would
justify holding her personally responsible for the CPL's activities ... or to
reassess the actual danger to the democratic process which might have
arisen by allowing her to run for election in view of her past or present
conduct.[136]

The Grand Chamber noted, while the Chamber judgment did not, that
in domestic proceedings against other members of the CPL, some were
found *not* to have been 'active participants' after 13 January 1991 – thus,
a modicum of individual assessment, albeit confined to that historical
moment, was implicit in the impugned statutory distinction.[137] However,
in deciding only to examine the proportionality of the restriction 'from
the standpoint of this provision',[138] the Grand Chamber regarded as irrelevant whether Mrs Ždanoka's loyalties had since moderated, or even the
extent of the anti-democratic threat she might have posed either in 1998
or 2002 when she was prevented from running for parliament. Arguably,
this substitutes a reasonableness test for the assessment of proportionality, and can be contrasted with the case of *Ādamsons* v. *Latvia*.[139]

In *Ādamsons*, the Court found a violation of P1–3 in relation to the disqualification from standing for election in 2002 of a former low-ranking
'serving officer of the KGB Border Guard Forces' (cf. a 'KGB officer' as in
both *Sidabras* and *Rainys*, or a communist party leader associated with
a Soviet-led coup as in *Ždanoka*). In *Ādamsons*, not only did the Court
assess the degree and significance of the particular individual's involvement in the former regime, it also examined the applicant's activities in
the decade following the collapse of communism (and whether he had
demonstrated loyalty to the Latvian state during that time). Crucially, the
Court held the government to a stricter evidential standard:

> The Court considered, in the light of the particular socio-historical back-
> ground to the applicant's case, that during the first years after Latvia had
> regained independence, electoral rights could be substantially restricted
> without thereby infringing Article 3 of Protocol No.1. However, with the

---

[136] *Ždanoka* [GC, 2006] para. 128.
[137] *Ibid.*, para. 45. See also [2004] para. 72 and [GC, 2006] para. 90.
[138] *Ždanoka* [GC, 2006] para. 125.
[139] ECtHR, *Ādamsons* v. *Latvia*, 24 June 2008 (Appl. no. 3669/03), in French only, extract
from Press release issued by the Registrar. See also M. Varju, 'Transition as a Concept
of European Human Rights Law', *European Human Rights Law Review* 170 (2009):
Ādamsons provides 'confirmation that according to the Court of Human Rights the process of democratic transition should have been completed by now'.

passing of time, a mere general suspicion regarding a group of persons no
longer sufficed and the authorities had to provide further arguments and
evidence to justify the measure in question.[140]

This denouement has since been affirmed in the case of *Tănase* v. *Moldova*[141]
in which the Court unanimously found that Moldova had violated P1–3
by prohibiting individuals with dual-citizenship from standing for election 'some seventeen years after Moldova had gained independence and
some five years after it had relaxed its laws to allow dual citizenship':

> [H]istorical considerations could provide justification for restrictions on
> rights intended to protect the integrity of the democratic process by ...
> excluding individuals who had actively participated in attempts to over-
> throw the newly-established democratic regime. However ... such restric-
> tions were unlikely to be compatible if they were still applied many years
> later, at a point where the justification for their application and the threats
> they sought to avoid were no longer relevant. Subsequently, in *Ādamsons*
> v. *Latvia* ... the Court emphasised that with the passage of time, general
> restrictions on electoral rights become more difficult to justify. Instead,
> measures had to be 'individualised' in order to address a real risk posed
> by an identified individual.[142]

Conclusions

The political disorientation experienced during periods of transition is
heightened by anxiety about regressive political loyalties. Transitional
governments 'preoccupied with the threat of authoritarian reversal'[143] have
used 'belligerent'[144] or 'precautionary'[145] legal provisions to minimise the
potential risks to the institutional order of the state and to forge a public
domain absent those who might seek a return to the predecessor regime.
The supervision of these measures has, however, presented uniquely transitional challenges for the European Court of Human Rights. As examined
in this chapter, the Court has principally relied upon four juridical devices
to meet these challenges. Specifically: increased deference in relation to
electoral rights, militant democracy and the abuse of rights doctrine, the
margin of appreciation, and individualised scrutiny commensurate with

---

[140] *Ādamsons, ibid.*
[141] ECtHR, *Tănase* v. *Moldova* [GC], 27 April 2010 (Appl. no. 7/08).
[142] *Ibid.*, para.159 (and para.174). See also, ECtHR, *Republican Party of Russia* v.
       Russia (Appl. no. 12976/07) 12 April 2011, at paras.127–8.
[143] Collins, 'State Terror and the Law', 21.
[144] Borneman, *Settling Accounts*, 53.
[145] Sajó, 'Militant Democracy and Transition Towards Democracy', 212.

the passage of time. These have assisted the Court in gauging the significance properly accorded to a country's transitional narrative.

Through the associational protection afforded by Article 11, the Court
has demonstrated its resolve to foster a robust and inclusive political
sphere, underpinned by the values of pluralism and social cohesion. In
this regard, it has sought to avoid transitional exceptionalism (see, for
example, *Partidul Comunistilor (Nepeceristi) v. Romania*). In contrast,
transitional compromises have been viewed more sympathetically in
the less stringent (implied limitations) framework of P1–3 (for example,
Georgian Labour Party v. Georgia).

The cases of *Ādamsons v. Latvia* and *Tănase v. Moldova* suggest a
narrowing of the gap between Article 11 and P1–3 scrutiny (while still
admitting the passage of time as a relevant factor). However, rather than
maintaining this hierarchy of political rights (most clearly evidenced in
the Grand Chamber judgment in *Ždanoka v. Latvia*), the Court could
develop a more consistent approach to transition cases by expounding
more fully its concept of 'militant democracy' (noting Article 17's inherent transitional limitations). Similarly, as noted in the dissenting opinion in *Sejdić and Finci v. Bosnia and Herzegovina*, more could be done to
explain the operation of the margin (and the role of the Court) in situations of diminished sovereignty. Otherwise, the margin of appreciation
remains an unpredictable factor which stands to undermine the human
rights anchorage provided by regional scrutiny.

Nonetheless, the Court has demonstrated – not least in its *Sejdic and
Finci* judgment – a concern to move transitional processes forward. It
has also developed a nuanced approach to proportionality whereby the
degree of individualisation required is partly contingent on the passage
of time. The latter, though, is not a standalone or linear formula based
only upon years passed. Rather, the passage of time is but one crucial
variable amongst others, including the clarity of the impugned legislation (*Seyidzade v. Azerbaijan*), a state's integration into regional or international organisations (*Yumak v. Turkey* cf. *Sejdić and Finci v. Bosnia and
Herzegovina*), the presence of alternative democratic safeguards such as
Constitutional Court review (*Yumak*; *Ždanoka*), consociational protections (*Sejdić*), privacy guarantees (*Zickus v. Lithuania*, dissent), mechanisms of redress (*Demopoulos v. Turkey*) or other reparative assurances
(*Vajnai v. Hungary*). These cases provide a window to the Court's expanding transitional jurisprudence, and underscore the continuing need for
a highly contextualised approach to the question of what constitutes an
'effective political democracy'.

Bibliography

Arbour, L., 'Bosnia's Continuing Chaos', *Foreign Policy*, (18 November 2009). Available at: www.foreignpolicy.com/articles/2009/11/18/bosnia_s_continuing_chaos? page=0,1.

Ashdown, P., *Swords and Ploughshares: Bringing Peace to the 21st Century* (London: Weidenfeld & Nicolson, 2007).

Baldwin, C., 'Dayton Discord: How the International Community Failed Bosnia', *Foreign Policy*, March/April 2010. Available at: www.foreignpolicy.com/articles/2010/02/22/dayton_discord.

Bell, J. D. (ed.), *Bulgaria in Transition: Politics, Economics, Society and Culture after Communism* (Boulder: Westview Press, 1998).

Borneman, J., *Settling Accounts: Violence, Justice, and Accountability in Postsocialist Europe* (Princeton University Press, 1997).

Bowring, B., 'Negating Pluralist Democracy: The European Court of Human Rights Forgets the Rights of Electors', *KHRP Legal Review* 11 (2007) 67–96.

Collins, C., 'State Terror and the Law: The (Re)judicialization of Human Rights Accountability in Chile and El Salvador', 35(5) *Latin American Perspectives* (2008) 20–37.

Council of Europe, *Restrictions on Political Parties in the Council of Europe Member States* (Political Affairs Committee, Parliamentary Assembly of the Council of Europe, Doc. 9526, 17 July 2002: Rapporteur: Mr Michel Dreyfus-Schmidt). Available at: assembly.coe.int/Documents/WorkingDocs/doc02/EDOC9526.htm#P116_18790.

Threat Posed to Democracy by Extremist Parties and Movements in Europe (Political Affairs Committee, Parliamentary Assembly of the Council of Europe, Doc. 86073 January 2000: Rapporteur: Mr Henning Gjellerod). Available at: assembly.coe.int/Documents/WorkingDocs/doc00/Edoc8607.htm.

Czarnota, A., 'Lustration, Decommunisation and the Rule of Law', *Hague Journal on the Rule of Law* 1 (2009) 307–336.

Czarnota, A., Krygier, M. and Sadurski, W. (eds.), *Rethinking the Rule of Law after Communism* (Budapest and New York: CEU Press, 2005).

Dakin, B. 'The Islamic Community in Bosnia and Herzegovina v. The Republika Srpska: Human Rights in a Multi-Ethnic Bosnia', *Harvard Human Rights Journal* 15 (Spring 2002) 245–267.

Dickson, B. *The European Convention on Human Rights and the Conflict in Northern Ireland* (Oxford University Press, 2010).

Elster, J., *Closing the Books: Transitional Justice in Historical Perspective* (Cambridge University Press, 2004).

Gelazis, N., 'Institutional Engineering in Lithuania: Stability through Compromise', in Zielonka, J. (ed.) *Democratic Consolidation in Eastern Europe, Volume 1: Institutional Engineering* (Oxford University Press, 2001) 165–185.

Goldhaber, M., *A People's History of the European Court of Human Rights* (New Jersey: Rutgers University Press, 2007).

Hamilton, M., 'Freedom of Assembly, Consequential Harms and the Rule of Law: Liberty Limiting Principles in the Context of Transition', *Oxford Journal of Legal Studies* 27(1) (2007) 75–100.

Harvey, P., 'Militant Democracy and the European Convention on Human Rights', *European Law Review* 29(3) (2004) 407–420.

High Representative for the Implementation of the Peace Agreement on Bosnia and Herzegovina, *Report to the Secretary-General of the United Nations* S/2009/246 (21 May 2009). Available at: www.ohr.int/other-doc/hr-reports/default.asp?content_id=43537.

Horne, C., 'International Legal Rulings on Lustration Policies in Central and Eastern Europe: Rule of Law in Historical Context', *Law and Social Inquiry* 34(3) (Summer 2009) 713–744.

'Late Lustration Programs in Romania and Poland: Supporting or Undermining Democratic Transitions?', *Democratization* 16(2) (2009) 344–376.

'Lustration and Trust in Public Institutions. A Retrospective on the State of Trust Building in Central and Eastern Europe', *Sphere of Politics (Sfera Politicii)* 142 (2009) 30. Available at: www.ceeol.com.

Huntington, S. P., *The Third Wave: Democratization in the Late Twentieth Century* (University of Oklahoma Press, 1991).

International Crisis Group, *Bosnia's Incomplete Transition: Between Dayton and Europe* (9 March 2009). Available at: www.crisisgroup.org/en/regions/europe/balkans/bosnia-herzegovina/198-bosnias-incomplete-transition-between-dayton-and-europe.aspx.

Letsas, G., *A Theory of Interpretation of the European Convention on Human Rights* (Oxford University Press, 2007).

Linz, J. J. and Stepan, A., *Problems of Democratic Transition and Consolidation: Southern Europe, South America, and Post-Communist Europe* (Baltimore and London: Johns Hopkins University Press, 1996).

Loewenstein, K., 'Militant Democracy and Fundamental Rights', *American Political Science Review* 31 (1937) 417–432.

McFaul, M., 'The Fourth Wave of Democracy and Dictatorship: Non Co-operative Transitions in the Post-Communist World', *World Politics* 54 (January 2002) 212–244.

Macklem, P., 'Militant Democracy, Legal Pluralism, and the Paradox of Self-Determination', *International Journal of Constitutional Law* 4(3) (July 2006) 488–516.

Marsh, M. D., 'Not Back in the USSR: Georgian Labour Party v. Georgia Enforces Free Elections in an Emerging Democracy', *Tulane Journal of International and Comparative Law* 17 (2008–2009) 585–599.

Napel, H.-M. ten, 'The European Court of Human Rights and Political Rights: The Need for More Guidance', *European Constitutional Law Review* 5 (2009) 464–480.

Ní Aoláin, F., 'The Fractured Soul of the Dayton Peace Agreement: A Legal Analysis', *Michigan Journal of International Law* 19 (1998) 957–1004.

O'Connell, R., 'Militant Democracy and Human Rights Principles', *Constitutional Law Review* (Georgian Constitutional Court, 2010) 84–91. Available at: http://constcourt.ge/files/SJ-eng.pdf.

Rule of Law Program South East Europe, 'Status quo of "Lustration" in South East Europe as of 31 January 2008' (Konrad-Adenauer-Stiftung, 2008). Available at: www.kas.de/wf/doc/kas_13092–544–2–30.pdf.

Sajó, A., 'From Militant Democracy to the Preventive State?', *Cardozo Law Review* 27 (2005–2006) 2255–2294.

'Militant Democracy and Transition Towards Democracy', in Sajó, A. (ed.) *Militant Democracy* (Utrecht: Eleven International Publishing, 2004) 209–230.

Scheppele, K. L., 'Democracy by Judiciary. Or, Why Courts Can be More Democratic than Parliaments', in Czarnota, A., Krygier, M. and Sadurski, W. (eds.) *Rethinking the Rule of Law after Communism* (Budapest and New York: CEU Press, 2005) 25–60.

Schwartz, H., *The Struggle for Constitutional Justice in Post-Communist Europe* (University of Chicago Press, 2000).

Steiner, H., 'Political Participation as a Human Right', *Harvard Human Rights Yearbook* 1 (1988) 77–134.

Sweeney, J., 'Divergence and Diversity in Post-Communist European Human Rights Cases', *Connecticut Journal International Law* 21 (2005–2006) 1–40.

Teitel, R., 'Militating Democracy: Comparative Constitutional Perspectives', *Michigan Journal of International Law* 29(1) (2007) 49–70.

'Transitional Jurisprudence: The Role of Law in Political Transformation', *Yale Law Journal* 106 (1996–1997) 2009–2080.

Transitional Justice (Oxford University Press, 2000).

Uitz, R., 'Constitutional Courts and the Past in Democratic Transition', in Czarnota, A., Krygier, M. and Sadurski, W. (eds.) *Rethinking the Rule of Law after Communism* (Budapest and New York: CEU Press, 2005) 235–264.

Constitutions, Courts and History: Historical Narratives in Constitutional Adjudication (Budapest and New York: CEU Press, 2005).

Varju, M., 'Transition as a Concept of European Human Rights Law', *European Human Rights Law Review* 2 (2009) 170–189.

Vidmar, J., 'Multiparty Democracy: International and European Human Rights Law Perspectives', *Leiden Journal of International Law* 23(1) (2010) 209–240.

Williams, A. M. 'The European Convention on Human Rights: A New Use', *Texas International Law Journal* 12 (1977) 279–292.

Wise, J. 'Dissent and the Militant Democracy: The German Constitution and the Banning of the Free German Workers Party', *University of Chicago Roundtable* 5 (1998) 301–344.

8

Transition, equality and non-discrimination

ANNE SMITH AND RORY O'CONNELL

Introduction

This chapter examines a necessarily select list of Article 14 (the prohibition of discrimination) jurisprudence involving ethnic minorities, most notably the Roma minority in post-Communist countries before the European Court of Human Rights (the Court). The aim is to identify to what extent, if any, have the cases informed the transition processes. The chapter focuses on the Roma because the Roma form a 'special minority group' as they have a 'double minority status': 'They are an ethnic community and most of them belong to the socially disadvantaged groups of society.'[1] While this double discrimination exists throughout Europe, there are particular difficulties during transition processes. First, the end of the Communist regimes raised the spectre of 'old problems of ethno-nationalism … challenging the authority of central governments, threatening the break up of the nation state, raising tensions between neighbouring states and leading to intra- and inter-state conflict'.[2] This prompted the Council of Europe to become more concerned with minorities, adopting treaties on minorities[3] and minority languages.[4] Second, many Communist countries adopted a policy of assimilation towards the Roma.[5] While not unique in the Communist states, it was 'most evident'

Anne Smith is a Lecturer at the Transitional Justice Institute, University of Ulster; Rory O'Connell is a Senior Lecturer at the Human Rights Centre, School of Law, Queen's University Belfast.

[1] Parliamentary Assembly Recommendation no. 1203 (1993) on Gypsies in Europe, quoted in ECtHR, *D.H and Others* v. *Czech Republic*, 13 November 2007 (Appl. no. 57325/00) para. 58, 181.

[2] S. Wheatley, 'Minority Rights and Political Accommodation in the "New" Europe', *European Law Review (Human Rights Survey)* 22 (1997) 63.

[3] Framework Convention for the Protection of National Minorities 1995 ETS no. 157.

[4] European Charter for Regional or Minority Languages 1992 ETS no. 148.

[5] D. Ringold, *Roma and the Transition in Central and Eastern Europe: Trends and Challenges* (Washington, DC: World Bank, 2000) 5.

in them.[6] Third, the Communist regimes provided a level of social and economic security which could not be guaranteed after the transition to a market economy.[7] For the Roma this transition has been difficult[8] and has sometimes meant that they had to migrate to poorer parts of the countries or the cities.[9] Fourth, despite providing some social and economic benefits for Roma, the Communist states tended to sideline them into less skilled labour roles which were not sustainable in a market regime.[10] Fifth, societies emerging from decades of Communism naturally focus on the groups that are relevant to context specific problem, such as a conflict or a history of authoritarian rule. A transition process addressing such problems may focus on specific groups and neglect the interests of other minorities.

The case law of the Court offers a clear example of this last aspect. As noted in other chapters, *Sejdić*[11] focused on the constitutional structure of Bosnia and Herzegovina. The issue in this case was the exclusion of the two applicants (one of Jewish and one of Roma origin) from becoming Members of the Upper House of Parliament as they did not self-identify as one of the 'constituent peoples'.[12] The Court concluded that these provisions were discriminatory under Article 14 (in combination with Article 3 of Protocol 1)[13] and Protocol 12, the free-standing non-discrimination provision (see below) and could not be justified. There were strong dissenting opinions which emphasised the particular circumstances of

---

[6] Minority Rights Group International, *Roma/Gypsies: A European Minority. A Paper by Jean-Pierre Liegeois and Nicolae Gheorghe* (United Kingdom: Minority Rights Group, 1995) 6.

[7] European Union Monitoring Centre for Racism and Xenophobia (EUMC), *Roma and Travellers in Public Education* (Vienna: European Union, 2006) 19 and I. Pogany, 'Minority Rights and the Roma of Central and Eastern Europe', *Human Rights Law Review* 6 (2006) 1–26, 12.

[8] Ringold, *Roma and the Transition in Central and Eastern Europe*, viii, 2.

[9] EUMC, *Roma and Travellers in Public Education*, 54, commenting on Hungary.

[10] Pogany, 'Minority Rights and the Roma of Central and Eastern Europe', 10 and Ringold, *Roma and the Transition in Central and Eastern Europe*, 6.

[11] ECtHR, *Sejdić and Finci* v. *Bosnia and Bosnia and Herzegovina*, 22 December 2009 (Appl. no. 27996/06 and 34836/06). This was the first decision of the Court on Protocol 12 which guarantees a free-standing right to equality (see below).

[12] As part of that power-sharing structure, only persons who self-identified as one of the three groups (termed the 'constituent peoples') could become a member of the three-person Presidency or the upper chamber of the federal Parliament (called the 'House of Peoples of the Parliamentary Assembly'). The 'constituent peoples' included the three communities primarily involved in the conflicts in the Former Yugoslavia: Bosniacs, Croats and Serbs.

[13] The right to regular, free and fair elections.

the Bosnian transition. While *Sejdić* is controversial, it demonstrates the danger that a transition process might include provisions that exacerbate the continuing political exclusion of the most vulnerable.

Discrimination, as this chapter illustrates, is not limited to the political sector. Racial discrimination permeates different fields. As the following discussion demonstrates, such discrimination is either unaddressed by government action and/or inaction. As courts are anti-majoritarian, the option of taking a case before the Court, has, as we will see, become attractive for the Roma minority. However, to what extent, if any, have the Court's 'equality in transition'[14] cases informed and helped the process of transition? Using two selected categories of law, this chapter seeks to address this question.

The categories of cases are, first, racially motivated violence and the subsequent failure to carry out an effective investigation into these incidents;[15] and second, segregation in schools.[16] The continuing discrimination in the two categories of case law highlights specific aspects of the Communist past which need to be addressed if Roma are to be recognised and treated as equals. For example, racial discrimination and segregation of ethnic minorities in social and economic areas including housing and education, prevent Roma exercising their right to adequate housing and the right to education. In so doing, as the case law section illustrates, Roma are denied both the right to 'equality of opportunity' (creating opportunities which enable and empower people to have

[14] This term is borrowed from James Sweeney's chapter in this volume (Chapter 5) but 'religion' is replaced with 'equality'.

[15] The substantive articles in this category are Articles 2 and 3 which guarantee the right to life and the prohibition of inhuman treatment respectively. These rights also give rise to a 'procedural or investigative' aspect. The origins of the procedural aspect were developed in ECtHR, *McCann* v. *United Kingdom*, 27 September 1995 (Appl. no. 18984/91) and consolidated and elaborated in a series of Turkish and United Kingdom cases, most notably: ECtHR, *Jordan, McKerr, Kelly, Shanahan* v. *United Kingdom*. These cases found that an effective, prompt and thorough and independent investigation are key components of the right to life when individuals have been killed as a result of the use of force by state officials. The obligation also applies to other avoidable deaths, such as a killing by a prisoner (ECtHR, *Edwards* v. *United Kingdom*, 22 July 2003 (Appl. no. 39647/98)), suicide in prison (ECtHR, *Keenan* v. *United Kingdom*, 3 April 2001 (Appl. no. 27229/95)), death in a hospital (ECtHR, *Silih* v. *Slovenia*, 9 April 2009 (Appl. no. 71463/01)). Where there have been allegations of torture, the same requirements apply, see ECtHR, *Selmouni* v. *France*, 28 July 1999 (Appl. no. 25803/94).

[16] Article 2 of Protocol 1, the right to education. Constraints of space mitigate against examination of other categories such as forced sterilisation of Roma women; protection from racially insulting speech; and as briefly discussed above, representation of Roma in the electoral system.

options and make choices) and 'equality of results' (aims to ensure an equal and fair distribution of goods and opportunities to economically disadvantaged groups to ensure that the result is equal). Regarding the failure to carry out effective investigations into racially motivated violence by state (and non-state actors), as Bell and Keenan argue, attempts to hold state actors accountable for human rights abuses lie 'at the heart of more paradigmatic "transitional justice" debates over how to deal with the abuses of the past, post-peace agreement and the relationship of justice to peace'.[17]

For conceptual clarity and coherence of argumentation, the chapter first considers what we mean by 'equality' and 'non-discrimination'. It is important to bear in mind that what is being postulated here is not a radical or new way of thinking about these terms. Rather, this discussion is part of a wider debate, offering a more contemporary understanding of equality. Following on from this, the chapter then examines the non-discrimination provision of the European Convention on Human Rights (ECHR), Article 14. Reference will also be made to the evolution and operation of Article 14 which will then be discussed in the case law section. Following an analysis of the two categories of cases, conclusions will be drawn from the findings of the case law determining what role, if any, has the Court's approach contributed and moved the transitional process forward for Roma.

Definitional issues: equality and non-discrimination

Equality is an amorphous concept. Equality proves an 'elusive notion',[18] and 'conceptions of equality are notoriously protean'.[19] Broadly speaking, a distinction is frequently drawn between formal and substantive concepts of equality. Similarly, discrimination, which generally refers to differential treatment on grounds such as sex, race, age and so on resulting in the individual or a group of individuals being disadvantaged, can be divided into formal and substantive categories.

---

[17] C. Bell and J. Keenan, 'Lost on the Way Home? The Right to Life in Northern Ireland', *Journal of Law and Society* 32(1) (2005) 68–89, 71.

[18] N. Bamforth, 'Conceptions of Anti-Discrimination Law', *Oxford Journal of Legal Studies* 24(4) (2004) 693–716, 704.

[19] D. Harris, 'Equality, Equality Rights and Discrimination under the Charter of Rights and Freedoms', *University British Columbia Review* 21 (1987) 389–428, 390.

Formal equality/discrimination

Essentially, formal equality requires that all persons who are in the same situation be accorded the same treatment and that people should not be treated differently because of arbitrary characteristics such as religion, race or gender.[20] Any distinction based on such grounds needs to be rationally justifiable. This formulation resonates with the original Aristotelian conception of equality, that like cases should be treated alike. It is the most widespread and least contentious understanding of equality and forms the conceptual basis of the legal concept 'direct discrimination'.[21] Under this formal notion of discrimination, as long as there is consistency in treatment, there will be no discrimination. This means simply that it is illegal to treat a man worse than a woman or a white person worse than a black person and vice versa. Conversely, if both parties were treated equally badly, then there would be no discrimination as there is consistency in treatment. Thus, as far as direct discrimination is concerned, it does not matter if a person belongs to a disadvantaged or a privileged group: it is a symmetrical concept. Another reason why direct discrimination fits neatly into formal equality is the need for a comparator. The comparator in proving direct discrimination tends to be white, male, able-bodied and heterosexual.[22] Such a narrow approach ignores the array of different identities and lifestyles of different groups in a multicultural society, an approach which can have detrimental implications for the Roma minority. Despite its simplicity, a formal notion of equality therefore equates to fairly limited and reactive discrimination rather than anything more far reaching. These limitations raise serious questions as to the suitability of incorporating such an understanding of equality in addressing Roma inequalities in transition processes.

Substantive equality/discrimination

A substantive notion of equality, in contrast, orients the right to equality from a negatively oriented right of non-discrimination to a positively

---

[20] This version of equality is described by McCrudden as equality as 'individualised justice', C. McCrudden, 'Theorising European Equality Law', in C. Costello and E. Barry (eds.) *Equality in Diversity* (Dublin: Ashfield Publications, 2003) 20–21.

[21] Direct discrimination occurs where a person is disadvantaged simply on the ground of her/his race, sex, gender or some other criterion.

[22] S. Fredman, *Discrimination Law* (Oxford University Press, 2002) 9.

oriented right to substantive equality.[23] It does this by ensuring that laws or policies do not reinforce the subordination of groups already suffering social, political or economic disadvantage. The focus is on the group and on the impact of the law on its social, economic or political conditions. A substantive model is therefore concerned with distinctions or situations that tend to reinforce systemic discrimination. It recognises that sameness of treatment can reinforce inequality and, in certain circumstances, equality (of result) actually requires differential or preferential treatment (positive/affirmative action). This positive and 'thick' concept of equality requires the state to adopt an asymmetrical and substantive approach and to facilitate or provide so as to create 'equality of opportunity' and 'equality of results/outcomes'.[24] With the emphasis on the effect/impact of the law and the move beyond consistency to substance, the different notions of substantive equality are commensurate with the other legal concept of discrimination, namely indirect discrimination. Indirect discrimination occurs when policies are applied which appear to be neutral but have an adverse affect on a disproportionate number of a certain group. Rather than adopting a colour or gender blind approach to discrimination (an approach advocated by formal equality), a substantive model of equality adopts a colour conscious approach. Such an approach is more conducive in maintaining cultural diversity and accommodating and recognising the special needs of minorities. With the emphasis on recognition of difference and not homogeneity, and accommodating special needs of a particular group, such a notion is vital for transitional societies as it helps fulfil four central aims identified by Fredman. These are: breaking the cycle of disadvantage associated with membership of a particular group; promoting respect for equal respect and dignity,[25] thereby reducing stereotypical representation of their own culture; providing positive measures of individuals as members of the group; and facilitating integration and full participation in society.[26] Unfortunately both the formulation of Article 14

---

[23] While the authors acknowledge the different and, at times, competing tenets underpinning a substantive notion of equality, space constraints mitigates addressing this debate. For further information on this debate see A. Smith, 'Constitutionalising Equality: The South African Experience', *International Journal of Discrimination and the Law* 9 (2008) 201–249.

[24] For further discussion on these and other tenets of substantive equality see C. McCrudden, 'Theorising European Equality Law', 19–33.

[25] Though we note that 'dignity' is a potentially controversial and amorphous term itself: R. O'Connell, 'The Role of Dignity in Equality Law: Lessons from Canada and South Africa', *International Journal of Constitutional Law* 6(2) (2008) 267–286.

[26] These aims are borrowed from S. Fredman, *Human Rights Transformed: Positive Rights and Positive Duties* (Oxford University Press, 2008) 179.

and *most* of the Court's equality jurisprudence has tended to favour the traditional Aristotelian thinking instead of the substantive approach to equality. That said, some of the most recent equality jurisprudence suggests that the pendulum may be swaying in the direction of the latter approach. It is to these issues that the chapter now turns.

Concepts of equality and non-discrimination within the framework of the ECHR: Article 14

Article 14 ECHR reads:

> The enjoyment of the rights and freedoms set forth in this Convention shall be secured without discrimination on any ground such as sex, race, colour, language, religion, political or other opinion, national or social origin, association with a national minority, property, birth or other status.

There are a number of concerns about the efficacy of Article 14.[27] In contrast with the extensive equality rights in the South African or Canadian constitutions which provide a free-standing right to equality 'before and under' the law as well as 'equal protection' and 'equal benefit' of the law, the text of Article 14 does not include a comprehensive, independent guarantee of equality. The formulation '[t]he enjoyment of the rights and freedoms set forth in this Convention' enjoin that Article 14 must be linked to another ECHR right/protocol. In other words, Article 14 has to be within the scope of the ECHR which has been referred to as the 'ambit requirement'.[28] Accordingly, Article 14 has been described as a 'parasitic'[29] and a 'Cinderella' provision.[30] Some argue that such descriptions are unjustified as the ambit requirement has been interpreted generously so that even a tenuous link with an ECHR right might be sufficient and therefore does not limit the application of Article 14 to those listed rights/protocols in the European Convention.[31] That said, even those who

---

[27] R. O'Connell, 'Cinderella comes to the Ball: Art 14 and the Right to Non-Discrimination in the ECHR', *Legal Studies* (2009) 1–19 and A. Baker, 'The Enjoyment of Rights and Freedoms: A New Conception of the "Ambit" under Article 14 ECHR', *Modern Law Review* 69(5) (2006) 714–737.

[28] Baker, 'The Enjoyment of Rights and Freedoms', 714–737.

[29] N. Whitty, T. Murphy and S. Livingstone, *Civil Liberties Law: The Human Rights Act Era* (Bath: Butterworths, 2001) 404.

[30] O'Connell, 'Cinderella comes to the Ball', 1–19, at 2.

[31] For example, social security matters have been held to be within the ambit of the right to property, Protocol 1 of Article 1; ECtHR, *Stec* v. *United Kingdom*, 12 April 2006 (Appl. no. 65731/01 and 65900/01). In *Belgian Linguistics*, 23 July 1968 (Appl. no. 1474/62), the first

argue that such descriptions are unjustified and unhelpful, acknowledge that unlike the equality provisions in the South African Bill of Rights and in the Canadian Charter, or Article 26 of the International Covenant on Civil and Political Rights (ICCPR), Article 14 provides no free-standing protection of discrimination.[32] This limitation has been addressed with the introduction of Protocol 12 rendering the non-discrimination clause applicable to 'any right set forth by law' and not only to 'Convention rights'. However, at the time of writing, only eighteen countries have ratified the Protocol.[33]

Although Protocol 12 strengthens Article 14, neither non-discrimination clauses are preceded with a general provision on equality incorporating substantive notions of equality. As was noted earlier, this contrasts with the approach adopted by South Africa and Canada, and by international texts such as Article 26 of the ICCPR and Articles 20 and 21 of the European Union's Charter of Fundamental Rights. Such an approach is important for transitional societies as a general equality provision helps to spell out the objectives of an equality provision, while an accompanying or subsequent discrimination clause helps provide substance to the equality right. Generally, a right to equality is potentially more positive than a prohibition against discrimination as the equality right may require, in appropriate circumstances, government and other actors to act affirmatively, taking positive measures to address pre-existing inequality and disadvantage. On the other hand, a non-discrimination clause is negative as it merely prohibits actions which may have an adverse effect and does not place obligations on governments to take any particular action to address disadvantage or to provide particular benefits. This leaves equality as an issue for the legislature to decide alone. This negative understanding of the right to equality requires only that once governments decide to act, they do so in a non-discriminatory way.[34]

Concerning the non-discrimination clause, this clause highlights the practical reality that individuals and members of particular social groups can often suffer discrimination and need further enhanced equality protection.[35] Equally important for both the general equality provision and

---

equality case, the Court cited examples of how the ambit extends beyond the protective scope of other ECHR rights.

[32] Baker, 'The Enjoyment of Rights and Freedoms', 714–737.

[33] Protocol came into force on the 1 April 2005.

[34] In describing equality and discrimination in this way, the authors do not mean to suggest the 'negative' versus 'positive' rights dichotomy.

[35] For a fuller discussion on the relationship between equality and discrimination see E. Holms, 'Anti-Discrimination Rights Without Equality', *Modern Law Review* 68(2) (2005) 175–194.

the non-discrimination clause, a positive/substantive conceptualisation is integral to adding substance to both concepts of equality and discrimination if past inequalities are to be remedied. Unfortunately, for transitional societies, the Court has adopted primarily, though not exclusively, a formalistic and thin approach to both concepts. Arguably, such a restrictive approach alongside the doctrine of margin of appreciation (see below), is one of the major weaknesses of Article 14. Such a weakness can, as we will see shortly, influence the Court's approach to the right to equality in transition cases.

Discrimination

Until recently the Article 14 case law of the Court focused on the simplest type of discrimination: overt direct discrimination which, as noted earlier, involves an explicit distinction between two groups. According to the case law of the Court, such distinctions are prohibited unless justified. They could be justified if they were shown to have a legitimate aim and bear a reasonable relationship of proportionality to that aim. The justification test operates according to a 'sliding scale' – certain types of distinction are subject to more rigorous scrutiny than others. The most suspect types of distinction are those based on race, nationality, sex, sexual orientation, birth (within/outside marriage) and similar statuses. Less rigorous scrutiny might be applied to distinctions based for instance on residence, or the type of commercial activity being regulated. Further the margin of appreciation doctrine can be brought in to play where the Court judges believe that they, as international judges upholding minimum European standards, are not best placed to assess whether a fair balance has been struck between a legitimate public interest and the individual's rights. The breadth of this margin of appreciation can vary over time. In the 2004 case of *Fretté* v. *France*, the Court accorded a wide margin of appreciation to the case of a gay man wanting permission to adopt a child, finding no violation when the man was denied permission.[36] However, when a very similar case came up four years letter, the margin of appreciation was barely mentioned and a violation was found.[37]

For a long time, the Court did not move beyond the prohibition of direct discrimination. The Court refused to draw inferences from statistical evidence that a facially neutral rule or policy actually had disparate impact on disadvantaged groups. Apart from a reluctance to consider statistical

[36] ECtHR, *Fretté* v. *France*, 26 February 2002 (Appl. no. 36515/97).
[37] ECtHR, *E.B.* v. *France*, 22 January 2008 (Appl. no. 43546/02).

evidence, the Court also declined to find violations in cases where an apparently neutral policy might have a discriminatory effect. For instance the Court did not analyse rules about employees working on a particular day as it might impact on members of particular religions.[38]

Over the last decade the Court has started to address cases other than the simple form of overt direct discrimination. For example, not all discrimination is overt; a party is unlikely to announce it is discriminating. Therefore it is important to be able to draw inferences from some evidence that there is discrimination. The *Baczkowski* case demonstrates this.[39] An elected mayor in a Polish town made a number of derogatory comments about gay men and lesbians. Not long afterwards a public servant in local government made a decision denying permission for a gay pride march. This decision was flawed in a number of ways, but there was no evidence the public official acted from discriminatory motives. However the Court was prepared to infer that there was discrimination because of the likelihood a public servant would be influenced by the views of the mayor.

The possibility to draw inferences enables a court to identify possible cases of covert discrimination. This is important and valuable but still limited. It fails to address problems of indirect discrimination. While the Court has made occasional references over the decades to indirect discrimination, it was only in 2007 that the Grand Chamber clearly announced that indirect discrimination was a violation of the Convention. This was in *DH* v. *Czech Republic*.[40] The Grand Chamber announced a sophisticated position on indirect discrimination. If there was evidence of 'disproportionately prejudicial effects on a particular group' or a 'de facto situation' of inequality, then a prima facie case of discrimination was made out. This need not be established beyond all doubt, but rather can be established by showing facts which allow an inference of discriminatory effects; this may include statistical evidence. Once this is done, the burden switches to the state to justify the situation.[41]

These cases establish a more coherent position on the prohibition of discrimination. However substantive equality requires more than a prohibition of discrimination. It must also include efforts – positive action – to achieve equality in practice. This raises two questions. First, does the ECHR permit such positive action? Second, does the ECHR require positive action?

---

[38] EComHR, *Stedman* v. *United Kingdom*, 9 April 1997 (Appl. no. 29107/95).
[39] ECtHR, *Baczkowski* v. *Poland*, 3 May 2007 (Appl. no 1543/06).
[40] ECtHR, *DH* v. *Czech Republic*, 13 November 2007 (Appl. no. 57325/00).
[41] *Ibid.*, paras. 175–181.

Article 14 is a qualified right. Therefore a prima facie case of discrimination can be compatible with the ECHR if it can be shown to be a proportionate means to achieve a legitimate aim. The Court has confirmed that the realisation of equality in practice is a legitimate aim.[42] So positive action to achieve equality can be justified provided it is proportionate.

That the ECHR permits positive action is important, but probably inadequate to achieve equality. A permissive approach depends on public authorities taking the initiative to adopt positive measures. The ECHR may sometimes go beyond this permissive attitude and require positive action. There are at least two lines of jurisprudence to this effect. First, where there is an allegation of a biased motivation behind the commission of a crime (e.g. racial hatred), then there is a positive obligation to investigate this allegation (see below). Second, there is a line of case law concerning planning decisions made on ostensibly neutral grounds but which impact on Roma, Travellers and other nomads. Here the Court has said that there is a duty to take into account the special needs of nomads as a historically disadvantaged group.[43] The Court has invoked this principle in a very different context, holding that where the Spanish authorities had led a Roma woman to believe that her traditional Roma marriage ceremony would be treated as a valid civil law marriage, then the authorities could not deny her a pension paid to the survivor of a married couple.[44] As we will see, the Court has started to develop some other important notions of positive obligations in Roma cases.

Overview of the two categories of case law

Category one: racially motivated violence and lack of effective investigations

The Court's Article 14 jurisprudence can arguably be described as rudimentary as the first case where a violation of Article 14 with regard to race/ethnic origin was decided, only as late as 2004 in *Nachova*[45] (see below).

---

[42] ECtHR, *Stec v. United Kingdom*, 12 April 2006 (Appl. nos. 65731/01 and 65900/01) para. 61.

[43] ECtHR, *Chapman v. United Kingdom*, 18 January 2001 (Appl. no. 27238/95).

[44] ECtHR, *Munoz Diaz v. Spain*, 8 December 2009 (Appl. no. 49151/07).

[45] ECtHR, *Nachova and Others v. Bulgaria*, 26 February 2004 (Appl. nos. 43577/98 and 43579/98) and [GC] 6 July 2005. Overall, there has been a low success rate: in only 20 cases since 1968 has a violation of Article 14 been found, S. Besson, 'Gender Discrimination under EU and ECHR Law: Never Shall the Twain Meet?', *Human Rights Law Review* 8(4) (2008) 647–682, 656.

This does not mean that the Court has been unaware of the discrimination against Roma. For example, in *Velikova*,[46] a case which concerned the death of a Romany Gypsy while in police custody following his arrest on suspicion of cattle theft, the Court found a violation of Article 2(1) as the state failed 'to provide a plausible explanation'[47] of the events leading to the applicant's death who was in good health when taken into police custody. The Court also held that there had been a violation of the investigative/procedural aspect of Article 2 as the state failed to conduct an effective investigation.[48] Although *Velikova* is important in that the burden of proof was shifted onto the state to provide an explanation refuting the applicant's charges, the Court's approach to equality and subsequently its transitional justice role was disappointing. Despite extensive documentation of instances of racially motivated violence and widespread prejudice against Roma by Bulgarian police officers presented to the Court,[49] the Court unanimously found no violation of Article 14. This was primarily attributable to the Court imposing an onerous evidentiary burden, namely 'beyond reasonable doubt' on the applicant. Requiring such a high standard, akin to criminal trials, the Court concluded that despite acknowledging the seriousness of the applicant's Article 14 arguments:

> The material before it does not enable the Court to conclude beyond reasonable doubt that Mr. Tsonchev's death and the lack of meaningful investigation into it were motivated by racial prejudice.[50]

Imposing such a high and unrealistic burden, the Court misunderstood the purpose and function of international protection of human

---

[46] ECtHR, *Velikova* v. *Bulgaria*, 18 May 2000 (Appl. no. 41488/98).

[47] *Ibid.*, para. 84.

[48] In reaching this decision, the Court referred to unexplained omissions in the investigation, the failure to collect evidence, combined with the failure to provide reasons for failing to investigate, *ibid.*, paras. 77–84. The Court also found a violation of Article 13, the right to an effective remedy, based on the same factors as it relied upon in finding a violation of Article 2. *Ibid.*, paras. 89–90.

[49] For example, the applicant quoted from various intergovernmental organisations on racism against Roma by the police. She referred to the UN Special United Nations' Special Rapporteur on Contemporary Forms of Racism, Racial Discrimination, Xenophobia and Related Intolerance (1999), who had reported that 'police abuse of Roma in custody [was] widespread in Bulgaria … Since 1992, at least fourteen Roma men in Bulgaria have died after having last been seen alive in police custody, or as a result of the unlawful use of firearms by law enforcement officers' and concluded that 'as a rule investigative and judicial remedies are rare'. *Ibid.*, para. 87.

[50] *Ibid.*, para. 94.

rights which was eloquently stated by another regional court, the Inter-American Court of Human Rights:

> The international protection of human rights should not be confused with criminal justice. States do not appear before the Court as defendants in a criminal action. The objective of international human rights law is not to punish those individuals who are guilty of violations but rather to protect the victims and to provide for the reparation of damages resulting from the acts of States responsible.[51]

Not only did the Court's approach demonstrate a lack of understanding of the purpose and function of international protection of human rights, its approach in combating racist discrimination can arguably be described as lacklustre and, thereby, rendering meaningless in Article 14 cases the Court's often cited dictum that the ECHR rights should not be 'theoretical and illusory' but 'practical and effective'.[52] Rather than imposing a positive obligation to investigate allegations of racially motivated violence on the perpetrators (thereby adopting a substantive approach to equality), imposing such difficult procedural and evidentiary obstacles, the Court acted in a reductive, regressive and formalistic manner with negative results for progressing the transitional process. Unfortunately this case is not isolated or unique as even in the most egregious cases of racially motivated violence and/or killings, the Court's failure to develop a substantive conception of equality has prevented the Court from finding a violation of Article 14 in conjunction with Articles 2 and 3.[53] The clearest expression of dissatisfaction of the Court's perfunctory approach was eloquently captured by a powerful, albeit lonely dissenting judgment of Judge Bonello in *Anguelova* v. *Bulgaria*.[54] Bonello found it 'particularly disturbing'[55] that at that time, in the fifty years of the Court's history, the Court had failed to find that the maiming, killing and torture of victims was related to the race, colour or place of origin of the victim.[56] This resulted in 'an exemplary haven of ethnic fraternity'.[57] The root cause for

---

[51] IACtHR, *Velasquez Rodriguez* v. *Honduras*, 29 July 1988 ((Ser. C) no. 4, 1988) para. 134.

[52] ECtHR, *Artico* v. *Italy*, 13 May 1980 (Appl. no. 6694/74) para. 33.

[53] ECtHR, *Tanrikulu* v. *Turkey*, 8 July 1999 (Appl. no. 23763/94) and ECtHR, *Kurt* v. *Turkey*, 25 May 1998 (Appl. no. 24276/94) and ECtHR, *Assenov* v. *Bulgaria*, 28 October 1998 (Appl. no. 24760/94) and ECtHR, *Anguelova* v. *Bulgaria*, 12 June 2002 (Appl. no. 38361/97) and ECtHR, *Notar* v. *Romania*, 20 April 2004 (Appl. no. 42860/98). For further academic commentary on the standard of proof see U. Erdal, 'Burden and Standard of Proof in Proceedings under the European Convention', *European Law Review* 26 (2001) 68–85.

[54] ECtHR, *Anguelova* v. *Bulgaria*, 12 June 2002 (Appl. no. 38361/97).

[55] *Ibid.*, paras. 2–3.   [56] *Ibid.*, para. 3.   [57] *Ibid.*, para. 2.

such a 'haven of ethnic fraternity' was, for the reasons just discussed, the onerous evidentiary burden on the applicant.[58] Judge Bonello warned that such an unrealistic burden of proof meant the Court was only paying 'lip-service' to the ECHR guarantees.[59] The Judge stated that the way forward was to radically and creatively rethink the Court's approach to ensure the Court does not become 'an inept trustee of the Convention'.[60]

Bonello's warning seemed to have been listened to with the landmark Chamber judgment in *Nachova and Others v. Bulgaria*.[61] As noted earlier, for the first time in its history, the Court found both substantive and procedural violations of Article 2 in conjunction with Article 14. Regarding the substantive violation, having examined the evidence including the unnecessary use of firearms and the lack of an appropriate legal and administrative framework to ensure adequate protection of the right to life, coupled with the lack of planning and control of the operation, the Court held the state was responsible for the fatal shooting of the two Romani men.[62] The Court was able to reach this conclusion by modifying the current standard of proof, noting that:

> [W]here the authorities have not pursued lines of inquiry that were clearly warranted in their investigation into acts of violence by State agents and have disregarded evidence of possible discrimination, it may, when examining complaints under Article 14 of the Convention, draw negative inferences or shift the burden of proof to the respondent Government.[63]

In light of the evidence,[64] the Chamber concluded that the government should have the burden of proof to prove that the actions were not racially motivated, a burden which the state failed to discharge.[65] Regarding the procedural violation, the Chamber criticised the Bulgarian investigation as 'flawed'[66] as it failed to comply with the standard required by Article 2. Article 2 imposes a positive obligation to take all possible steps

---

[58] *Ibid.*, paras. 4–11.   [59] *Ibid.*, para. 13.   [60] *Ibid.*, para. 172.

[61] ECtHR, *Nachova and others* v. *Bulgaria*, 26 February 2004 (Appl. nos. 43577/98, 43579/98).

[62] The two men had absconded from compulsory military service and an arrest warrant was subsequently issued. During their arrest, the two unarmed conscripts were fatally wounded by military police officers.

[63] ECtHR, *Nachova and others* v. *Bulgaria*, 26 February 2004 (Appl. nos. 43577/98, 43579/98) para. 169.

[64] The investigating officers had failed to investigate the excessive use of force and the use of racist comments from one of the arresting officers.

[65] ECtHR, *Nachova and others* v. *Bulgaria*, 26 February 2004 (Appl. no. 43577/98, 43579/98) para. 172.

[66] *Ibid.*, para. 128.

to investigate whether or not discrimination may have played a role in the events, which the state failed to do. A striking feature of the judgment was the Court's emphasis on the need to treat racially motivated violence differently than those cases with 'no racist overtones'.[67] Such an approach represents a high water mark in the Court's history in dealing with equality in transition cases as it is a recognition and affirmation of substantive equality. As noted earlier, the accommodation of people's differences is what defines a substantive understanding of equality. Sometimes this will require treating people differently in light of their circumstances rather than treating everyone the same way as formal equality does. In this regard, Judge Bonello's description of the case as a 'giant step forward that does the Court proud'[68] is justified.

However, if the Chamber judgment represents a high water mark and a 'giant step forward' in equality in transition cases, the Grand Chamber's rejection of the Chamber's decision to impose the burden of proof on the state represents a giant step backwards. For the first time, for reasons not clearly stated, the Grand Chamber distinguished between the procedural and substantive aspects of Article 14. The Court upheld the Chamber's finding of a procedural violation of Article 14 in conjunction with Article 2 (which is to be welcomed and commended), however the Court did not find a substantive violation of Article 14 taken together with Article 2. The Court held that it:

> [D]oes not consider that the alleged failure of the authorities to carry out an effective investigation into the supposedly racist motive for the killing should shift the burden of proof to the Government with regard to the alleged violation of Article 14 of the Convention taken in conjunction with the substantive aspect of Article 2.[69]

This raises the question as to when the burden of proof should be transferred onto government. The Grand Chamber hinted that:

> In certain cases of alleged discrimination it may require the respondent Government to disprove an arguable allegation of discrimination and – if they fail to do so – find a violation of Article 14 of the Convention on that

---

[67] Ibid., para. 158.
[68] Ibid., para. 1, concurring opinion of Judge Bonello. In contrast, in ECtHR, *Balogh* v. *Hungary*, 20 July 2004 (Appl. no. 47940/99) para. 79, the Court held although there was a violation of Article 3 regarding the applicant's treatment by the police during an arrest, there was no violation of Article 14 on the basis that unlike in *Nachova* there was 'no substantiation of the applicant's allegation that he was discriminated against'.
[69] Ibid., para. 157.

basis. However, where it is alleged – as here – that a violent act was motivated by racial prejudice, such an approach would amount to requiring
the respondent Government to prove the absence of a particular subjective attitude on the part of the person concerned.[70]

In other words, Bulgaria could not be considered responsible for the
motivations that prompted the state agents. However, unlike the other
aspects of the decisions, this particular judgment was not unanimous
as six judges partly dissented. Their dissent, shared by third party inter-
veners, some activists and academics,[71] was based on the argument that
an holistic approach would have been preferable since it better reflects the
special nature of Article 14, which has no independent existence. The dissent insisted that the factual evidence was enough if the case was taken as
a whole to find a violation of Article 14.[72] The authors echo the dissenting
judgment as it arguably weakens the Court's approach in its fight against
racial discrimination.

The full impact of the Grand Chamber's 'artificial and unhelpful'[73]
approach has been clearly demonstrated in subsequent cases as a substantive violation of Article 14 in conjunction with either Article 2 or 3 is
now difficult to prove.[74] While there was a modicum of hope in *Stoica* v.
Romania,[75] as the Court found a substantive violation of Article 14 taken
together with Article 3, this was short-lived as the Court unanimously
held there was no substantive violation of Article 14 taken together with

---

[70] *Ibid.*, para. 157.
[71] R. Sandland, 'Developing a Jurisprudence of Difference: The Protection of Human Rights
of Travelling Peoples by the European Court of Human Rights', *Human Rights Law Review*
8(3) (2008) 475–516, 514, described the situation as 'anomalous'; another commentary
viewed it as 'lamentable', Case Comment, 'International Law, Human Rights, European
Court of Human Rights finds Bulgaria liable for failure to investigate racially motivated killings- ECtHR', *Nachova and others* v. *Bulgaria*, 6 July 2005 (Appl. no. 43577/98
and 43579/98) *Harvard Law Review* 119 (2006) 1907–1914, 1910. See M. Dembour, 'Still
Silencing the Racism Suffered by Migrants … The Limits of Current Developments under
Article 14 ECHR', *European Journal of Migration and Law* 11 (2009) 221–234.
[72] ECtHR, *Nachova and others* v. *Bulgaria*, 6 July 2005 (Appl. nos. 43577/98 and 43579/98)
Concurring opinion of Judge Sir Nicolas Bratza, Joint partly dissenting opinion of Judges
Casadevall, Hedigan, Mularoni, Fura-Sandstrom, Gyulumyan and Spielmann, para. 17.
[73] *Ibid.*
[74] ECtHR, *Bekos and Koutropoulos* v. *Greece*, 13 March 2006 (Appl. no. 15250/02); ECtHR,
Cobzaru v. *Romania*, 26 July 2007 (Appl. no. 48254/99); ECtHR, *Petropoulou-Tsakiris* v.
Greece, 6 March 2008 (Appl. no. 44803/04); *Vasil Sashov Petrov* v. *Bulgaria*, 10 June 2010
(Appl. no. 63106/00); ECtHR, *Dimitrova and Others* v. *Bulgaria*, 27 January 2011, (Appl. no.
44862/04); and also ECtHR, *Ognyanova and Choban* v. *Bulgaria*, 23 February 2006 (Appl.
no. 46317/99), where the Court failed to find even a procedural violation of Article 14.
[75] ECtHR, *Stoica* v. *Romania*, 4 March 2008 (Appl. no. 42722/02).

Article 3 in *Beganović* v. *Croatia*.[76] The Court reached this finding despite repeating similar dicta from the Chamber's judgment in *Nachova* about the need to take all reasonable steps to detect any racial motivations behind criminal acts.[77] Notably, in this case, unlike *Nachova*, the Court continued to state that such an obligation is not absolute and granted the state authorities a wide margin of appreciation, resulting in a failure to identify and punish killings motivated by racial discrimination.[78] With these recent developments the Court is 'pay[ing] lip-service'[79] to the right guaranteed by Article 14. As noted earlier, while in some cases there have been procedural violations of Article 14 in conjunction with either Articles 2 and/or 3 which the authors fully endorse and support,[80] the bifurcation of Article 14 may well have resulted in the Court being less inclined to find a substantive violation. Procedural violations, while important, arguably do not carry the same weight as a substantive violation.[81] Furthermore, substantive violations need substantive remedies which are arguably more probing and demanding than procedural remedies. The former may require positive action to address and eradicate endemic and institutionalised racial discriminatory practices (action which is essential for transitional processes), whereas, in the latter, the state is responsible, at most, for rectifying the impugned policy/procedure. Fortunately, as the

---

[76] ECtHR, *Beganovic* v. *Croatia*, 25 June 2009 (Appl. no. 46423/06). In the recent case of ECtHR, *Carabulea* v. *Romania*, 13 July 2010 (Appl. no. 45661/99), while the Court found a violation of both Articles 2 and 3, unfortunately for the development of Article 14 jurisprudence in this field, the Court considered it unnecessary to examine Article 14 separately. A concern was expressed by three dissenting judges, two of whom found a procedural violation of Article 14 in conjunction with Articles 2 and 3. While the third, partly dissenting opinion of Judge Ziemele did not expressly state a violation of Article 14, his dissatisfaction was also clear: he 'regretted' the decision of the majority not to investigate the possible racial motives behind the events leading to the death of Mr Carabulea since it 'goes against the Court's own case-law' (para. 5).

[77] *Ibid.*, paras. 93–98. See also the recent case of ECtHR, *Sashov* v. *Bulgaria*, 7 January 2010 (Appl. no. 14383/03). In this case although the Court found a violation of Article 3 both procedurally and substantively regarding the treatment of three Bulgarian nationals of Roma origin during their arrest and detention in police custody, there was no examination of Article 14.

[78] *Ibid.*, para. 93.

[79] ECtHR, *Anguelova* v. *Bulgaria*, 12 June 2002 (Appl. no. 38361/97) para. 13.

[80] Other similar cases are ECtHR, *Šečić* v. *Croatia*, 31 May 2007 (Appl. no. 40116/02) and ECtHR, *Angelova and Iliev* v. *Bulgaria*, 26 July 2007 (Appl. no. 55523/00).

[81] Dissenting opinion in ECtHR, *Labita* v. *Italy*, 6 April 2000 (Appl. no. 26772/95), Jointly dissenting opinion Mr Pastor Ridruejo, Mr Bonello, Mr Makarczyk, Mrs Tulkens, Mrs Strážnická, Mr Butkevych, Mr Casadevall and Mr Zupančič.

following discussion demonstrates, the bifurcation of Article 14 seems to primarily apply to the field of policing.

Category two: education

The right to education has many facets. It is intrinsically important for the individual in providing a rewarding experience. It is socially important as education facilitates social and economic development. It is also important as it facilitates and enhances nearly every other right. For example, education is important in protecting the right to health, in seeking employment, in exercising free expression and for taking part in political affairs.[82] It was not a coincidence that one of the main litigation planks in the African American struggle for equality focused on education.

The education situation of Roma, Travellers and other nomads throughout Europe is dire.[83] Roma face difficulties in terms of enrolment at school, attendance, academic attainment, completion rates, bullying and segregation.[84] The Court had not dealt with such cases until the twenty-first century, but has now addressed the problems in three cases, two of which are from ex-Communist states.[85]

The landmark case is *DH* v. *Czech Republic*.[86] The Czech Republic provided a system of 'special schools' for pupils with 'mental deficiencies'. In some regions, Roma were overrepresented in these schools. In the Ostrava district a Roma pupil was twenty-seven times more likely to be assigned to a special school than a non-Roma child.[87] The applicants in *DH* had been transferred to special schools following psychological tests and with the consent of their parents.[88] The Chamber which initially heard the case concluded by six votes to one that there was no violation.

The Grand Chamber reversed the decision of the Chamber, finding a violation by thirteen votes to four. As noted above, the Grand Chamber adopted a statement on how the Court should approach indirect

---

[82] Committee on Economic, Social and Cultural Rights General Comment 13 on the right to education (Art.13): 08/12/99. E/C.12/1999/10 1999, para. 1.

[83] Commissioner for Human Rights of the Council of Europe, *Final Report on the Human Rights Situation of Roma, Sinti and Travellers*, CommDH, 1 (2006).

[84] European Union Monitoring Centre on Racism and Xenophobia (EUMC now the Fundamental Rights Agency) (Vienna: European Union, 2006), *Roma and Travellers in Public Education* and H. O'Nions, 'Different and Unequal: The Educational Segregation of Roma Pupils in Europe', *Intercultural Education* 21(1) (2010) 1–13.

[85] The third is ECtHR, *Sampanis* v. *Greece*, 5 June 2008 (Appl. no 32526/05).

[86] ECtHR, *DH* v. *Czech Republic*, 13 November 2007 (Appl. no. 57325/00).

[87] *Ibid.*, paras. 16–18.   [88] *Ibid.*, para. 20.

discrimination cases. The Grand Chamber underlined that the Roma were a 'specific type of disadvantaged and vulnerable minority' and so required 'special protection'.[89] In contrast to its approach in *Nachova*, the Grand Chamber relied on statistical evidence, but also the reports of a variety of international organisations on the general position of the Roma in the Czech Republic, to conclude that a prima facie case of discrimination was made out.[90] The Grand Chamber considered that there was no objective and reasonable justification for this. The tests used to allocate the children were not sufficiently reliable and did not take account of the cultural specificities of the Roma children.[91] Parental consent was not relevant – it was not clear that the parents, who were members of a disadvantaged minority, had been given all the information required to give informed consent. In any event, one could not consent to racial discrimination.[92]

The most recent of the desegregation cases is *Oršuš v. Croatia*.[93] The case concerned Roma children in two schools. In one, Podturen, there were forty-seven Roma children, seventeen of whom were in a Roma-only class. In Macinec 142 pupils attended Roma-only classes while fifty-two Roma pupils attended mixed classes.[94] The Chamber found unanimously that there was no violation of the right to education or of Article 14 in combination with the right to education (though it found a violation of the right to a judicial hearing in good time under Article 6).[95] The Grand Chamber disagreed with the Chamber, finding a violation of Article 14 by nine votes to eight. The Grand Chamber reiterated the need to consider that this was a case involving a vulnerable minority which required special protection.[96] Although the statistical evidence did not establish a prima facie case of discrimination, the Grand Chamber noted that the language requirement was only applied to Roma in some schools; further there was evidence from international reports of hostility by non-Roma parents to mixed schools in Croatia.[97]

Therefore the situation called for an objective and reasonable justification from the government. The Grand Chamber accepted that temporarily putting children in special classes due to language problems was justifiable

---

[89] *Ibid.*, para. 182.   [90] *Ibid.*, paras. 191–193.
[91] *Ibid.*, paras. 200–201.   [92] *Ibid.*, paras. 203–204.
[93] ECtHR, *Oršuš and others* v. *Croatia*, 17 July 2008 (Appl. no. 15766/03) and ECtHR, *Oršuš and others* v. *Croatia* [GC], 16 March 2010 (Appl. no. 15766/03).
[94] *Ibid.*, paras. 13–14.   [95] *Ibid.*, paras. 65–69.
[96] *Ibid.*, paras. 147–148.   [97] *Ibid.*, paras. 152–155.

provided – this is the crucial point – there were safeguards.[98] The Grand
Chamber noted that there was no clear legal basis for the measures and
that the allocation decision was not based specifically on *language* tests.[99]
Further, the students were offered an 'adapted curriculum' though it was
not clear what this was. Some, but not all, of the pupils were offered extra
classes in Croatian. This situation did not satisfy the positive obligation
on the state to provide an education, including special language classes
in Croatian, to enable the Roma students to join mixed classes as soon as
possible.[100] There should have been a transparent monitoring procedure
to assess the pupils' competence in Croatian and transfer them to mixed
classes as soon as possible; this did not exist.[101] Concerning the problems
of absenteeism, the Grand Chamber held that there were positive obligations to raise awareness of the importance of education among Roma
parents, to assist the pupils with any difficulties they were having with the
curriculum and to involve the social services in a structured way to consider problems of absenteeism.[102]

These cases are still very recent, and so it is difficult to assess their
effects. There are some welcome aspects. These include the development
of a clear doctrine on indirect discrimination and the identification in
Oršuš of specific positive obligations on state parties, going beyond the
vague generalities about showing special concern for a disadvantaged
minority. Perhaps the most important development is the willingness to
use reports by international organisations to assess the general context in
which the specific individual cases occur.

That said, there are some points for concern. First, there is a genuine
concern that the cases address only one aspect of the problems facing
Roma education, but have not as yet considered the wider problems of
Roma enrolment. One dissenter in *DH* drew attention to the shocking
statistic that in the EU, in 1989, perhaps between 250,000 and 300,000
Roma children had never attended school.[103]

Second, there is the significant problem of the effect of these decisions
on the ground. A report by the European Roma Rights Centre based on
research conducted a year after the Grand Chamber decision in *DH*, noted
that there had been some positive efforts by the Czech government.[104]

---

[98] *Ibid.*, para. 157.   [99] *Ibid.*, paras. 159–160.   [100] *Ibid.*, paras. 164–171.
[101] *Ibid.*, paras. 172–175.   [102] *Ibid.*, para. 177.
[103] ECtHR, *DH* v. *Czech Republic*, 13 November 2007 (Appl. no. 57325/00), dissent of Judge
Jungwiert.
[104] European Roma Rights Centre (ERRC), *Persistent Segregation of Roma in the Czech
Education System* (Budapest: European Roma Rights Centre, 2009).

However it remained the case that education was segregated in practice. The most positive note in the Report was that the Czech government acknowledged that its reforms had failed to end segregation and so new plans were needed.[105] Third, there appears to be considerable and strong disagreement among the judges themselves in these cases. Of the twenty-four judges who considered *DH*, ten concluded there was no violation; even more strikingly, of the twenty-four judges that heard *Oršuš*, fifteen found no violation. The dissents are often expressed very forcefully. In *DH*, Judge Zupančič suggested that the majority were using 'politically charged argumentation' to hide 'ulterior motives'. In the same case Judge Borrego accused the majority of acting as if in an 'ivory tower' and being condescending to the Roma parents and pupils. The joint partly dissenting opinion in *Oršuš* argues that the majority were going beyond the facts of the actual case before them to develop the general law on indirect discrimination.[106]

Conclusion

The aim of this contribution was to answer the question: has the Court's approach in these two areas of law contributed in progressing the transitional process for Roma? The answer is a qualified yes. On the one hand, some of the most positive features of the case law are: the recognition of the need for a sophisticated indirect discrimination doctrine; the ability of the Court to draw inferences as to the existence of discrimination without insisting on proof beyond all doubt; the development of positive obligations, such as the obligation to investigate allegations of racial bias, and the positive obligation to assist children in non-mainstream classes by providing suitable education. Perhaps the most significant step is the reliance in the school desegregation cases on evidence of the general context of discrimination and disadvantage facing Roma.

However, on the other hand, there are also less promising features. In the cases involving allegations of racially motivated violence, the development of a positive obligation to investigate such allegations frequently goes hand in hand with a reluctance to find a substantive violation of Article 14. The reliance on a duty to investigate sees the Court relying on a familiar technique, but one which also allows it to hold back from a

---

[105] *Ibid.*, section 6.
[106] Joint dissenting opinion of Judges Jungwiert, Vajić, Kovler, Gyulumyan, Jaeger, Myjer, Berro-Lefèvre and Vučinić.

formal finding that state agents were racially biased (even if this was not state policy). Further, even with the progressive decisions in the school desegregation cases, there are still problems about implementation on the ground, dissent among the judges and the wider problem as to whether the ECHR and the Court have the tools and ability to tackle some of the major problems facing the Roma.

All of this reflects the fact that international law and an international court are not immune from the difficulties facing national law and judges in transition processes. International judges may be as inclined as national ones to be activist or deferential in the defence of rights in transitional settings. Much will depend on the work of actors beyond the judges – on the activism of litigants and lawyers at one end of the process, and on the willingness of governments to implement decisions at the other. All actors have a shared responsibility in bridging the unacceptable gap that exists not only in these two areas of law, but in all sectors between Roma and the rest of society. Only then will Roma be able to shed their inegalitarian past for a more democratic and equitable future.

Bibliography

Baker, A., 'The Enjoyment of Rights and Freedoms: A New Conception of the "Ambit" under Article 14 ECHR', *Modern Law Review* 69(5) (2006) 714–737.

Bamforth, N., 'Conceptions of Anti-Discrimination Law', *Oxford Journal of Legal Studies* 24(4) (2004) 693–716.

Bell, C. and Keenan, J., 'Lost on the Way Home? The Right to Life in Northern Ireland', *Journal of Law and Society* 32(1) (2005) 68–89.

Besson, S., 'Gender Discrimination under EU and ECHR Law: *Never Shall the Twain Meet?*', *Human Rights Law Review* 8(4) (2008) 647–682.

Dembour, M., 'Still Silencing the Racism Suffered by Migrants … The Limits of Current Developments under Article 14 ECHR', *European Journal of Migration and Law* 11 (2009) 221–234.

Erdal, U., 'Burden and Standard of Proof in Proceedings under the European Convention', *European Law Review* 26 (2001) 68–85.

Harris, D., 'Equality, Equality Rights and Discrimination under the Charter of Rights and Freedoms', *University British Columbia Review* 21 (1987) 389–428.

Fredman, S., *Discrimination Law* (Oxford University Press, 2002).

    Human Rights Transformed: Positive Rights and Positive Duties (Oxford University Press, 2008).

Harvard Law Review, Case Comment, 'International Law, Human Rights, European Court of Human Rights finds Bulgaria liable for failure to investigate racially motivated killings- ECtHR', *Nachova and Others* v. *Bulgaria*, 6 July 2005 (Appl. no. 43577/98 and 43579/98) Grand Chamber, *Harvard Law Review* 119 (2006) 1907–1914.

Holms, E., 'Anti-Discrimination Rights Without Equality', *Modern Law Review* 68(2) (2005) 175–194.

McCrudden, C., 'Theorising European Equality Law', in Costello, C. and Barry, E. (eds.) *Equality in Diversity* (Dublin: Ashfield Publications, 2003).

O'Connell, R., 'Cinderella comes to the Ball: Art 14 and the Right to Non-Discrimination in the ECHR', *Legal Studies* (2009) 1–19.

'The Role of Dignity in Equality Law: Lessons from Canada and South Africa', *International Journal of Constitutional Law* 6(2) (2008) 267–286.

O'Nions, H., 'Different and Unequal: The Educational Segregation of Roma Pupils in Europe', *Intercultural Education* 21(1) (2010) 1–13.

Pogany, I., 'Minority Rights and the Roma of Central and Eastern Europe', *Human Rights Law Review* 6 (2006) 1–26.

Ringold, D., *Roma and the Transition in Central and Eastern Europe: Trends and Challenges* (Washington, DC: World Bank, 2000).

Sandland, R., 'Developing a Jurisprudence of Difference: The Protection of Human Rights of Travelling Peoples by the European Court of Human Rights', *Human Rights Law Review* 8(3) (2008) 475–516.

Smith, A., 'Constitutionalising Equality: The South African Experience', *International Journal of Discrimination and the Law* 9 (2008) 201–249.

Wheatley, S., 'Minority Rights and Political Accommodation in the "New" Europe', *European Law Review (Human Rights Survey)* 22 (1997) 63.

Whitty, N., Murphy, T. and Livingstone, S., *Civil Liberties Law: The Human Rights Act Era* (Bath: Butterworths, 2001).

9

Closing the door on restitution: the European Court of Human Rights

TOM ALLEN AND BENEDICT DOUGLAS

Introduction

Emergence from authoritarian rule is often accompanied by sweeping changes in systems of governance. New institutional structures are put in place to ensure that the rule of law and the protection of human rights acquire a firm foundation. It is the memory of the past that inspires the creation of these new structures, but do they provide closure? Should they provide a continuing forum for individuals to come to terms with the past? Put simply, can a new institutional order secure the rule of law and human rights without giving a voice to individual stories of past injustice?

This chapter focuses on how the European Court of Human Rights deals with these issues in connection with claims for the restitution of property. The focus is on the former communist states that have denied restitution to at least some former owners. In such cases, the state denies that there is any need to correct past injustices by providing individual remedies. The state may argue, of course, that the new regime provides justice for all, and hence everyone is so much better off that no single individual has a cause to demand a remedy for historic injustice. In practice, however, expectations of justice are not always satisfied in this way, and many individuals turn to the Court for a remedy.

At the national level, there has been no uniformity in the approach to restitution, except that no European state has attempted to entitle everyone who unlawfully or unjustly lost property under the old regime to

---

Both authors are from the University of Durham, UK. This chapter is partly based on an article written by the first author, 'Restitution and Transitional Justice in the European Court of Human Rights', *Colum. J. Euro. L.* 13 (2007) 1.

restitution of their property.[1] Some states have resisted restitution: Poland has yet to determine whether, or how, it will provide restitution,[2] and Turkey dragged its feet on implementing judgments of the European Court of Human Rights regarding property in northern Cyprus held by Greek Cypriots who fled after the 1974 conflict. States allowing restitution have varied in the degree of their commitment to their own programmes. In Romania, for example, restitution has proceeded in fits and starts, with the courts and administrative authorities often issuing conflicting orders regarding the same property.[3] Conversely, Czechoslovakia, and the subsequent Czech and Slovak Republics, embarked on an ambitious programme of restitution. However, to make it economically feasible, and to limit restitution to resident citizens, Czechoslovakia imposed restrictions based on nationality, the current use or ownership of the property, and the timing and circumstances of the original loss.[4] Hungary's programme was broader, but it only offered compensation rather than restitution.[5] Other states have provided substitute land as compensation.[6] Germany offered a combination of restitution and compensation, but eventually

---

[1] See generally, M. Heller, and C. Serkin, 'Revaluing Restitution: From the Talmud to Postsocialism', *Michigan Law Review* 97 (1999) 1385, 1404; A. K. Kozminski, 'Restitution of Private Property: Re-Privatization in Central and Eastern Europe', *Communist and Post-Communist Studies* 30 (1997) 95; C. Offe, *Varieties of Transition: The East European and East German Experience* (Cambridge: Polity Press, 1996); I. Pogany, *Righting Wrongs in Eastern Europe* (Manchester University Press, 1997); E. A. Posner and A. Vermeule, 'Transitional Justice as Ordinary Justice', *Harvard Law Review* 117 (2004) 761, 783–792; R. Procházka, *Mission Accomplished: On Founding Constitutional Adjudication in Central Europe* (Budapest: Central European University Press, 2002) 148–151, 166–167, 173–174.

[2] See generally, M. Loś, 'Property Rights, Market and Historical Justice: Legislative Discourses in Poland', *International Journal of the Sociology of Law* 22 (1994) 39; W. R. Youngblood, 'Note and Comment: Poland's Struggle for a Restitution Policy in the 1990s', *Emory International Law Review* 9 (1995) 645; Kozminski, 'Restitution of Private Property', 101–103.

[3] See generally, Kozminski, 'Restitution of Private Property', 104; P. D. Aligica and A. Dabu, 'Land Reform and Agricultural Reform Policies in Romania's Transition to the Market Economy', *Eastern European Economics* 41(5) (2003) 49.

[4] R. Crowder, 'Restitution in the Czech Republic: Problems and Prague-nosis', *Indiana International and Comparative Law Review* 5 (1994) 237; Kozminksi, 'Restitution of Private Property', 99; Offe, *Varieties of Transition*, 105–130; Pogany, *Righting Wrongs*, 150–155.

[5] G. Halmai and K. L. Scheppele, 'Living Well is the Best Revenge: The Hungarian Approach to Judging the Past', in A. J. McAdams (ed.) *Transitional Justice and the Rule of Law in New Democracies* (University of Notre Dame Press, 1997) 155; Kozminksi, 'Restitution of Private Property', 100; Pogany, *Righting Wrongs*, 155–178.

[6] See Kozminski, 'Restitution of Private Property', 104 (Romania).

gave privatization priority over both; in addition, it denied restitution to anyone expropriated during the Soviet occupation of 1945–1949.[7]

The diversity is not surprising, given states' different circumstances. In the ex-communist states, the practical difficulties of restitution depend partly on the extent and depth of nationalization, which varied from state to state.[8] Additionally, post-Second World War resettlements of refugees affected states differently, and these differences have had an impact on restitution policies.[9] In any case, leaving aside these differences, there is no general consensus on the desirability of restitution. It is unclear whether restitution advances or retards economic growth.[10] The effect of restitution on the rule of law is also disputed. Some argue that it demonstrates a commitment to the rule of law, by distinguishing the present regime from its predecessor and by providing a positive signal that property rights will be respected in future;[11] but this is countered by concerns that the rule of law would be undermined by restitution programmes that upset titles acquired in good faith during the pre-transitional era.[12]

There is also no common ground on the possibility of achieving greater justice through restitution. There are ethical arguments that restitution demonstrates a commitment to human rights and property that spans generations,[13] and is necessary to restore the individual's dignity and reinstate them in social and economic life.[14] But even if confiscations and uncompensated takings do infringe human rights, victims of other violations of human rights – such as torture or the denial of freedom of

---

[7] R. Frank, 'Privatization in Eastern Germany: A Comprehensive Study', *Vanderbilt Journal of Transnational* Law 27 (1994) 809; H. M. Stack, 'The "Colonization" of East Germany? A Comparative Analysis of German Privatization', *Duke Law Journal* 46 (1997) 1211.

[8] Nationalization was most extensive in the Soviet Union and Czechoslovakia, and probably least extensive in Poland, Hungary and Yugoslavia. See generally, Kozminski, 'Restitution of Private Property', 95–97; Pogany, *Righting Wrongs*.

[9] See, for example, the background to ECtHR, *Broniowski* v. *Poland*, 22 June 2004 (Appl. no. 31443/96).

[10] See, Heller and Serkin, 'Revaluing Restitution', 1404, for a summary of the competing arguments. See also, Posner and Vermeule, 'Transitional Justice', 788–789.

[11] Heller and Serkin, 'Revaluing Restitution', 1405–1406.

[12] See *Eur. Parl. Ass. Res.* 1096, *On Measures to Dismantle the Heritage of Former Communist Totalitarian Systems*, para. 10 (1996).

[13] J. Thompson, *Taking Responsibility for the Past: Reparation and Historical Justice* (Cambridge: Polity Press, 2002).

[14] Heller and Serkin, 'Revaluing Restitution', 1405. See also S. Leckie, 'New Directions in Housing and Property Restitution', in S. Leckie (ed.) *Returning Home: Housing and Property Restitution Rights of Refugees and Displaced Persons*, 2nd edn (Ardsley: Transnational Publishers Inc., 2003).

religion – generally cannot be fully restored to their pre-injury status, so why should one expect the new institutional order to achieve full restoration with respect to loss of property?[15] There is even a vigorous debate concerning the relevance of principles of 'ordinary' justice to societies emerging from transition. Posner and Vermeule have argued that transitional justice raises no different issues from 'ordinary' justice: liberal democracies regularly manage change, even radical change, during their 'ordinary' lives, and the issues that they confront in managing this change are not different in kind to those of transitional justice.[16] Others argue, however, that transitional justice works in a radically different context; for example, the threat that a carefully-brokered peace may break down presents issues that do not arise in the ordinary situation.[17] They argue that once the full context is considered, the problems of transitional justice take on a different aspect.

These developments have been the subject of many scholarly examinations, but without a focus on their treatment by the Court of Human Rights in Strasbourg.[18] The Court has decided hundreds of cases on different aspects of restitution and transitional justice. A close study of the cases reveals a fundamental conflict between two schools of thought, manifested most clearly in cases where titles held on the date of ratification are subsequently challenged by a former owner.

One school of thought favours the present owner over the former owner. Judges in this school seem to have two main concerns over restitution. The first relates to the rule of law and the value of stability. For these judges, the primary value of the rule of law in post-communist states is the stability of expectations.[19] Accordingly, they doubt the benefit of re-opening old disputes over the legality of confiscations or other takings. The second concerns the relevance of the principles developed in 'ordinary', non-transitional cases in the resolution of cases dealing

---

[15] See Posner and Vermeule, 'Transitional Justice', for a summary of these arguments.

[16] *Ibid.* See also, Heller and Serkin, 'Revaluing Restitution'.

[17] R. G. Teitel, 'Human Rights in Transition: Transitional Justice Genealogy', *Harvard Human Rights Journal* 16 (2003) 93; C. L. Sriram, 'Transitional Justice Comes of Age: Enduring Lessons and Challenges', *Berkeley Journal of International Law* 23 (2005) 506, 512.

[18] Exceptions are: P. Macklem, 'Rybná 9, Praha 1: Restitution and Memory in International Human Rights Law', *European Journal of International Law* 16 (2005) 1; A. M. Gross, 'Reinforcing the New Democracies: The ECHR and the Former Communist Countries', *European Journal of International Law* 7 (1996) 89.

[19] Cf. K. L. Scheppele, 'When the Law Doesn't Count: The 2000 Election and the Failure of the Rule of Law', *University of Pennsylvania Law Review* 149 (2001) 1361.

with transitional issues. This relates to, for example, the level of scrutiny of national decisions relating to social and economic programmes that affect property rights. In 'ordinary' cases, the Court normally defers to the judgments of national authorities; however, the judges who are reluctant to allow restitution often take a different view in transitional cases.

Judges in the opposing school believe that the threat that restitution poses to stability and rule of law is overstated. Indeed, there are a handful of cases that suggest that judges believe that the rule of law is strengthened by using past abuses of power as examples for future standards. These judges are far more willing to apply the principles of 'ordinary' cases to transitional cases; like Posner and Vermeule, they do not accept that the issues are different in kind.

These differences reveal a deeper split in perceptions concerning the Court's role as an institution. The judges in the first school implicitly accept the modernist faith that new institutions and new legal ideas are sufficient to prevent a recurrence of the past. The creation of new institutions, such as the Court, provides closure for the international community, the state itself, and especially for individuals who suffered under the old regime. Individual complaints of past injustice are resolved and remedied by the creation of the new institution. These points are not so readily accepted by other judges. For them, it is neither desirable, nor perhaps even possible, to draw a clear line between the past and future of human rights.

This chapter considers cases where victims of the old regime have attempted to recover property using Convention rights where recovery is not permitted by domestic law. In these cases, the Court has gone out of its way to develop a set of jurisdictional rules that deny the victims a hearing on the merits. The emphasis of the Court in this area is on stability of current entitlements, to the exclusion of complaints concerning injustice in the pre-transitional era. There are other aspects of restitution: for example, the Court has issued a body of judgments on the balancing of interests in national legislation that does require restitution in some cases.[20] However, the jurisdiction cases are especially important because they reveal the Court's position on the most basic issue: does the European human rights system allow victims of past human rights abuses any voice at all? Or does it deny them entry to the Court?

---

[20] See T. Allen, 'Restitution and Transitional Justice in the European Court of Human Rights', *Columbia Journal of European Law* 13 (2007) 1.

The Convention context

Article 1 of the First Protocol to the Convention ('P1–1') contains the key provision relating to restitution. It came into force on 18 May 1954, eight months after the Convention, and states:

> Every natural or legal person is entitled to the peaceful enjoyment of his possessions. No one shall be deprived of his possessions except in the public interest and subject to the conditions provided for by law and by the general principles of international law.
>
> The preceding provisions shall not, however, in any way impair the right of a State to enforce such laws as it deems necessary to control the use of property in accordance with the general interest or to secure the payment of taxes or other contributions or penalties.

The *travaux préparatoires* give little indication that transitional justice raises questions concerning property.[21] This might falsely give the impression that transitional justice became prominent only when ex-communist states joined the Council of Europe. However, the majority of members ratified the Convention after emerging from a period of military conflict or authoritarian government or both. It seems that the states did not believe that the Commission or Court should be required to provide justice to the victims of the abuses of the recent past. Hence, like other Convention rights, P1–1 was not given retroactive effect. As Macklem argued, the Convention is notable for its 'fearlessly modernist focus on the present and future at the expense of the past, and for its optimistic tendency to equate human rights with human progress'.[22] Although the Convention itself was seen as a restoration of the legal traditions of the member states,[23] the drafters' dedication to the rule of law and

---

[21] Council of Europe, *Collected edition of the 'travaux préparatoires' of the European Convention on Human Rights: Recueil des travaux préparatoires de la Convention européenne des droits de l'homme* (Council of Europe, 8 vols, 1975–1985). See generally, T. Allen, *Property and the Human Rights Act 1998* (Oxford and Portland, Oregon: Hart Publishing, 2005) 17–33; A. W. B. Simpson, *Human Rights and the End of Empire: Britain and the Genesis of the European Convention* (Oxford University Press, 2001) chap. 15.

[22] Macklem, 'Rybná 9, Praha 1', at 23. See also, Teitel, 'Human Rights', at 73–74, and M. Koskenniemi, 'By Their Acts You Shall Know Them … (And Not by Their Legal Theories)', *European Journal of International Law* 15 (2004) 839, 840.

[23] E.g., the preamble to the Convention declares that it is intended to provide for the collective enforcement of the rights in the Universal Declaration of Human Rights, GA Res. 217A (III), UN GAOR, 3d Sess., 1st plen. mtg., UN Doc. A/810 (Dec. 12, 1948), but also refers to the founding members' 'common heritage of political traditions, ideals, freedom and the rule of law'.

the protection of human rights did not require the memorialization of specific past injustices in the judgments of the Court.

The role of P1–1 in achieving greater distributive justice was also uncertain.[24] It was widely believed to be technically impossible to draft an agreement that would accurately express a state's obligations to secure a more equitable distribution of property.[25] Instead, most of the energy that went into the drafting of P1–1 focused on protecting the states' power to undertake bold social and economic programmes, which it was feared a right to property might undermine.

Moreover, P1–1 was only intended to prevent state action: it provides no positive right to acquire property or to receive a minimum share in the property distribution.[26] Even so, the second sentence does not appear to provide any guarantee of compensation. The third sentence seems to impose no substantive obligations on the state.[27] As written, P1–1 appears only to require that states follow the rule of law in relation to property. As such, it was less ambitious than the Statute of Europe's declaration that membership in the Council of Europe would be restricted to states that 'accept the principles of the rule of law and of the enjoyment by all persons within its jurisdiction of human rights and fundamental freedoms'.[28] That is, there is an assumption that respect for the rule of law would not, by itself, ensure protection of human rights; arguably, the member states did intend Convention rights (including P1–1) to have a substantive content that is not fully captured by the rule of law, even if it is not obvious from the literal wording of their provisions.

However, it is not clear what the substantive content of P1–1 was intended to be. The *travaux* confirm that the central concern was lawless governmental conduct. For example, one delegate stated that a right to property was necessary to protect individuals from '"arbitrary confiscation", that is to say, from those high-handed administrative or private measures of which all the totalitarian regimes have furnished such sinister examples'.[29] On the face of it, the real concern was with the rule of law; what this left for the substantive content of P1–1 was not stated. However,

---

[24] See Allen, *Property*, and Simpson, *Human Rights*.

[25] See Allen, *Property*, and Simpson, *Human Rights*.

[26] See, for example, ECtHR, *Marckx v. Belgium*, 13 June 1979 (Appl. no. 6833/74); ECtHR, *Sardin v. Russia* [admissibility], 12 February 2004 (Appl. no. 69582/01).

[27] ECtHR, *Sporrong and Lönnroth v. Sweden*, 23 September 1982 (Appl. nos. 7151/75 and 7152/75).

[28] Statute of the Council of Europe, May 5, 1949, Art. 3, 87 U.N.T.S. 103, 106.

[29] Council of Europe, Collected Edition, vol. 6, 74, 116–118 (Bastid).

the Court now interprets P1–1 as requiring substantive fairness, so that an interference with property is justified only if it is both lawful *and* proportionate to a legitimate aim.[30] But this still does not describe the core interests that P1–1 protects beyond those that would be addressed by fidelity to the rule of law. This is particularly important with respect to transitional justice, to the extent that it is argued that restitution has the substantive effect of restoring dignity and reinstating victims as full participants in the social, political and economic life of the community.

The separation of the rule of law and the protection of human rights suggests that there are two distinct frames of analysis for considering claims for restitution of property. In relation to the rule of law, applicants may argue that the state ought to recognize property rights that were never formally extinguished, but which became impossible to exercise under the old regime. In addition, there may have been confiscations that were in accordance with the positive law at the time, but are now challenged on the basis that the confiscation law was so unjust that it should not be treated as having had any legal effect. In such cases, the issue is whether the legality of past acts is relevant to the Court's task of securing the rule of law and the stability of property with prospective effect.

Other issues might be framed in terms of the principle of proportionality. This depends, however, on the identification of the interest that is protected by the right to property. For example, if P1–1, as a human right, is seen as focusing on values of equality, dignity and autonomy, then a claim for restitution might be based on the argument that the property is so closely identified with the applicant's dignity that denying its return would inflict a disproportionate harm.

Superficially, it may appear that the doctrinal principles regarding lawfulness would reflect the values of the rule of law, and the principles regarding proportionality would reflect other values, such as the importance of individual dignity. Since the vast majority of cases where states are found in breach of P1–1 are decided on the basis of proportionality rather than legality, it may appear that the Court is easily satisfied that states respect the values of the rule of law. However, this does not follow so readily from legal theory or the case law.

In terms of legal theory, it is first necessary to identify the function of the rule of law, and the nature of 'law' that states are expected to follow. To return to the example given above, a strict positivist might regard

---

[30] ECtHR, *Sporrong and Lönnroth* v. *Sweden*, 23 September 1982 (Appl. nos. 7151/75 and 7152/75).

some examples of 'high-handed administrative or private measures' as lawful within some systems. Law, for the positivist, does not involve any necessary connection with morals; public officials may act in a lawful but immoral way.[31] A positivist reading of P1–1 that was intended to secure some protection from immoral state conduct would therefore need to read more into the idea of proportionality and the specific language of P1–1; the substantive protection would not come about merely by ensuring that states adhered to positive law.

However, the requirement of lawfulness developed by the Court is not purely formal. Compliance with the rules of national law must satisfy the Court's 'quality of law' criteria. In order to qualify as law under the Convention, rules must be 'sufficiently accessible, precise and foreseeable'.[32] This is close to Lon Fuller's idea of the 'internal morality of law'.[33] Fuller argued that rules that constitute laws satisfy the following criteria: they must be general in nature, publicly proclaimed, prospective, comprehensible, mutually consistent, capable of compliance, constant, and there must be consistency between the law as written and the law as administered.[34] These criteria follow from Fuller's belief that law's function is to impose duties and create order, but not to set aspirations or describe good order. Hence, law constrains personal choice, but at the same time it also enables choice by allowing individuals to plan their own lives according to their own values.

The Court, like Fuller, accepts that legality involves more than the formal structure of national law. Morality does enter the question, and hence some of the work that the positivist would leave to the proportionality test can be done by the legality test. However, Fuller's criteria, like the criteria of the Court's 'quality of law' principle, are not immediately concerned with the substantive content of legal rules.[35] Nevertheless, the emphasis on the procedural aspects of law still puts the emphasis on the rule of law as a guarantee of stability, and the function of stability in securing autonomy and enhancing the possibilities for human flourishing.[36] The rule of

---

[31] See H. L. A. Hart, *The Concept of Law*, 2nd edn (Oxford University Press, 1994) 200–212, 268–269; H. Kelsen, 'Law, State and Justice in the Pure Theory of Law', *Yale Law Journal* 57 (1948) 377, 383–386.

[32] ECtHR, *Carbonara and Ventura* v. *Italy*, 30 May 2000 (Appl. no. 24638/94).

[33] See L. Fuller, *Morality of Law* (New Haven: Yale University Press, 1969, rev. edn) 38–41.

[34] *Ibid.*, 46–94.   [35] *Ibid.*, 153, 168.

[36] *Ibid.*, 5–9. For a recent (non-transitional) application in relation to property, see ECtHR, *Khamidov* v. *Russia*, 15 November 2007 (Appl. no. 72118/01) at para. 143 ('legal provisions, formulated in vague and general terms, cannot serve as a sufficient legal basis for

law and the protection of human rights share the purpose of safeguarding autonomy, but they diverge in their attention to the content of law. The rule of law is not strictly formal, as it does take into account the basic values of accessibility, precision and foreseeability, and it does so in order to ensure that subjects are in a position to plan their own lives. On the other hand, it appears to exclude substantive concerns regarding equality, autonomy, dignity or other liberal values.

It follows that the Court also rejects the approach of Gustav Radbruch. His theory goes beyond Fuller's, as he maintained that rules do not qualify as law if they fail certain substantive standards.[37] For Radbruch, laws must uphold the values of certainty, purposiveness and justice.[38] Of these, justice is paramount, although in practice injustice would rarely feature in a way that would compel a court (or anyone else) to say that a statute did not constitute law. Since every statute furthers the value of certainty to at least some extent, and justice depends to some extent on certainty, the courts ought to apply even an unjust statute as written. The only exception is where the conflict with justice reaches an 'intolerable degree'. Plainly, the distinction between tolerable and intolerable justice may be difficult to identify, but there is one clear difference between them. Justice, for Radbruch, has equality at its core; hence, when the legislator deliberately betrays the value of equality, as Nazi anti-Jewish laws did, the statute 'lacks completely the very nature of law'.[39]

While the Court's extended conception of law demonstrates that it has scope to consider some issues under the legality condition that a positivist might leave to proportionality, it is important to note that the importance of the rule of law is not expressed solely through the doctrine of legality. For example, the Court's temporal jurisdiction may depend on whether a pre-transitional confiscation of property was lawful, and this may make it necessary to determine whether it was done in accordance with 'law'. The issue is not whether post-transition laws satisfy the quality of law criteria, but whether the pre-transition 'law' qualifies as law.

---

such a drastic interference as occupation for a prolonged period of time of an individual's housing and property').

[37] G. Radbruch, *Gesetzliches Unrecht und Übergesetzliches Recht*, 1 *Süddeutsche Juristen-Zeitung* 105 (1946), translated by B. L. Paulson and S. L. Paulson as 'Statutory Lawlessness and Supra-Statutory Law (1946)', *Oxford Journal Legal Studies* 26 (2006) 1; and G. Radbruch, *Fünf Minuten Rechtsphilosophie*, Rhein-Neckar-Zeitung (Heidelberg, 12 September 1945), translated by B. L. Paulson and S. L. Paulson as 'Five Minutes of Legal Philosophy (1945)', *Oxford Journal Legal Studies* 26 (2006) 13.

[38] Radbruch, 'Statutory Lawlessness', 6–8.

[39] *Ibid.*, at 7.

It is also important to note that, where it is clear that the Court does have jurisdiction, it has been very reluctant to find that the legality rule has been violated. Instead, it tends to consider the criteria of accessibility, precision and foreseeability of those laws under the broad test of proportionality. It is a question of degree: for example, a lack of foreseeability may not be severe enough to violate the legality rule, and yet it may be a material factor in persuading the Court that the interference was not proportionate to the aim. For example, in *Beyeler* v. *Italy*, an Italian pre-emption law for the protection of cultural works applied in an unpredictable way, but not to the point of violating the legality condition. However, the Court still found that Italy violated P1–1, in part because 'the element of uncertainty in the statute and the considerable latitude it affords the authorities are material considerations to be taken into account in determining whether the measure complained of struck a fair balance'.[40] Broadly speaking, the criteria that are relevant to the rule of law and the legality condition are also relevant in determining the content of P1–1. To get a sense of the Court's conception of the rule of law, it is necessary to look beyond the legality rule.

Jurisdiction and the recognition of rules as laws

The Court has refused to recognise a 'law' that purported to extinguish property rights in only one set of cases involving transitional justice, and it did so according to a positivist theory of law. The situation involved attempts by Greek Cypriot refugees from northern Cyprus to return to their property, rebuffed by the Turkish Cypriot authorities.[41] The Turkish government argued that the applicant's title had been expropriated by a constitutional declaration of the Turkish Republic of Northern Cyprus (TRNC) in 1985. The TRNC then redistributed much of the property to other private persons, including Turkish Cypriots who had fled from southern Cyprus. The effect of the TRNC declaration was at the core of the case. If it constituted a valid law, the applicant's case would have collapsed.[42] However, the Court held that the TRNC was not a recognized state under international law.[43] The declaration was therefore invalid and had no effect on the applicant's property rights.[44]

---

[40] ECtHR, *Beyeler* v. *Italy*, 5 January 2000 (Appl. no. 33202/96).
[41] ECtHR, *Loizidou* v. *Turkey*, 18 December 1996 (Appl. no. 15318/89).
[42] On jurisdictional grounds: Turkey has only accepted the jurisdiction of the Court with respect to its acts from 22 January 1990. *Ibid.*, at paras. 24–25.
[43] *Ibid.*, at 42–47.   [44] *Ibid.*

The Court held that the TRNC declaration was not law, but not on the basis of its 'quality of law' criteria, or on a variation of Radbruch's idea of extreme injustice. Instead, it regarded the formal rules of international law as the positive law to which it was subject. This was not the end of the inquiry, however. P1–1 is not an absolute guarantee of property, and so Turkey claimed the denial of access to the property was justified by the pressing social need of the necessity to re-house the Turkish Cypriot refugees, and that a judgment against it would interfere with inter-communal talks. The Court however held that Turkey could not justify 'the complete negation of the applicant's property rights in the form of a total and continuous denial of access and a purported expropriation without compensation'.[45] This statement is so brief that it is unclear whether it was the attempt to make the situation permanent that was important, whether it was the ethnic and religious aspect of the refugee situation, or possibly Turkey's disregard for international law that was evident in the creation of the TRNC 'state'.

Nevertheless, there is a concern with the rule of law, which the Court identified with the stability of formal law through the transitional period rather than the stability of the present social situation.[46] This, as we will see, is exceptional. Moreover, the willingness to evaluate pre-transitional conduct against human rights standards is also exceptional, particularly as contrasted with the Court's general willingness to recognize the lawfulness of confiscations that occurred in the communist era. One of the most striking examples actually comes from post-communist Croatia, in the period before P1–1 took effect in 1997. *Blečić* v. *Croatia*[47] concerned Croatian laws allowing the courts to terminate tenancies where the tenants have been absent for more than six months without good reason. During the conflicts in the early 1990s, many refugees fled. There is evidence that the Croatian authorities and courts have been far more inclined to terminate tenancies of ethnic Serbs, as they did in *Blečić*. The applicant argued this breached P1–1. The parallels with *Loizidou* are clear, except that Croatia was a recognized state. But this, it seems, was conclusive: the Court did not suggest that the application of the termination law was open to reproach. It therefore declined to consider the broader context in

---

[45] *Ibid.*, at 64.
[46] This can also be seen in cases concerning the re-opening and quashing of a final judgment ordering restitution of property; the Court has uniformly found this to be a breach of P1–1. See, for example, ECtHR, *Brumărescu* v. *Romania*, 28 October 1999 (Appl. no. 28342/95).
[47] ECtHR, *Blečić* v. *Croatia*, 8 March 2006 (Appl. no. 59532/00).

which this dispute occurred, and its reasoning discloses no hint that ter-minations of this type were often part of ethnic cleansing.[48]

The judgment in *Blečić* is devoid of any consideration of the practical circumstances of the termination. Indeed, it is only in the dissenting opinions in *Loizidou* that we get a clear sense of concerns that seem to influence the Court's judgments in other cases:

> The 'political nature' of the present case is in my view rather related to the place of the courts in general, and of the Strasbourg mechanism in particular, in the scheme of the division and separation of powers ... Courts are adjudicating in individual and in concrete cases according to prescribed legal standards. They are ill-equipped to deal with large-scale and complex issues which as a rule call for normative action and legal reform.[49]

The complexity of the situation plainly influenced the dissenting judges, although it had no obvious bearing on the validity of the TRNC declar-ation or the jurisdiction of the Court. Nevertheless, it is clear that there is doubt that the 'ordinary' principles of justice and human rights are rele-vant in the transitional context. Or, to be more accurate, there is doubt that the Court's institutional role is to consider these issues: its focus must be prospective, and the resolution of old disputes is not within its domain.

Temporal jurisdiction and long-lost property

Another set of cases moves away from positivist theory of law to some-thing closer to Fuller's theory. Here the Court's primary concern is the uncertainty and instability that would arise if the state failed to put limits on the vindication of the property rights that have not been exercised for a lengthy period.

The legal issues are framed in terms of the Court's temporal jurisdic-tion. In a great many cases, former owners have found that their applica-tions are dismissed on the ground that the Court lacks jurisdiction *ratione temporis*. The temporal issues arise because, for all but the original signa-tories, P1–1 takes effect and the Court acquires jurisdiction from the date

---

[48] The Court considered the issue of temporal jurisdiction and decided that the termination of her tenancy was completed in 1996. Since P1–1 did not take effect in Croatia until 1997, the Court declined jurisdiction.

[49] ECtHR, *Loizidou* v. *Turkey*, 18 December 1996 (Appl. no. 15318/89), dissenting opinion of Judge Jambrek, para. 7.

of the deposit of the instrument of ratification. Hence, applicants must be able to identify some post-ratification act or conduct attributable to their state in order to make their case. In many cases, there is such an act, such as the refusal by the courts to order the restoration of property on a request from the former owner. The real issue is whether the continued retention of property is itself an interference with the claim of a previous property right. This would only be the case if the applicant's property rights still existed when P1–1 took effect. If so, the Court would have jurisdiction.

In international law, and under P1–1, these questions turn on the distinction between continuing and completed (or 'instantaneous') acts.[50] The Court has jurisdiction over acts that continue through to the post-ratification period. It is important to note, however, that it is the act that must continue, rather than the effects of the act. For example, in *Ponomarev* v. *Russia*,[51] the Court held that it had no jurisdiction over an Article 3 claim by an applicant that he had contracted tuberculosis while in custody because he initially fell ill before ratification. The effects continued, but not the act of improper custody. Similarly, if property is destroyed before ratification, there is no continuing act that would provide jurisdiction after ratification.[52] With expropriation, of course, the thing itself may continue to exist. However, an expropriation is completed when the owner is lawfully deprived of her property rights. The fact that the state (or its transferee) still has the property is immaterial. It is the date of the violation of the primary obligation that is important, rather than the date of any violation of the secondary obligation to correct the breach.

In numerous cases, the Court has confirmed this as the position under P1–1. An individual cannot raise a complaint regarding possessions that were lawfully taken before P1–1 took effect.[53] Conversely, if the deprivation of property is unlawful under national law, the situation has been treated as a continuing act. Thus in *Papamichalopoulos* v. *Greece* the Court

---

[50] J. Crawford, *The International Law Commission's Articles on State Responsibility: Introduction, Text, and Commentaries* (Cambridge University Press, 2002) 139; J. Pauwelyn, 'The Concept of a "Continuing Violation" of an International Obligation: Selected Problems', *British Yearbook of International Law* 66 (1995) 415, 417; R. Higgins, 'Time and the Law: International Perspectives on an Old Problem', *International and Comparative Law Quarterly* 46 (1997) 501; A. Nissel, 'Continuing Crimes in the Rome Statute', *Michigan Journal of International Law* 25 (2004) 653, 665–668.

[51] ECtHR, *Ponomarev* v. *Russia*, 15 May 2008 (Appl. no. 7672).

[52] See, for example, ECtHR, *Popara* v. *Croatia*, 15 March 2007 (Appl. no. 11072/03).

[53] See, for example, ECtHR, *Blečić* v. *Croatia*, 8 March 2006 (Appl. no. 59532/00).

described the Navy's unlawful occupation of a naval base as 'a continuing situation, which still obtains at the present time'.[54] The Court took a similar view in *Loizidou*.[55] Although Turkey had accepted the jurisdiction of the Court only with respect to its acts from 22 January 1990, the continued existence of the applicant's property rights made the denial of access a continuing act.[56] Yet these cases are exceptional; in most situations, the Court has determinedly avoided jurisdiction. For example, it stated that a pre-ratification act that violates customary international law should not be regarded as an unlawful act under P1–1 if it was lawful under national law.[57] Similarly, it has held that unsatisfied claims for a remedy under customary international law are not themselves possessions for the purposes of P1–1.[58]

The most striking set of cases concerns claimants who found it impossible to exercise rights of property during the pre-transitional period and were still denied the possibility of exercise after the transition. These cases arose frequently in many post-communist states, due to the practical problems caused by the collapse of the administrative structures for governing private property and the resulting loss, destruction, defacement or absence of property records.[59] Consequently, many found it practically impossible to vindicate their rights under the old regime, although the rights were never formally extinguished, or only partly extinguished. However, many post-transition governments have given limited or no recognition to dormant property rights.

Under P1–1, the issue is whether the old property right qualifies as a possession, despite having been impossible to exercise for an extended period. The positivists would hold, as in *Loizidou*, that the rights continue to exist until lawfully extinguished. However, the Court has developed two doctrines that lead it to refuse jurisdiction in such cases.

With the first, it simply holds that the property interest ceased to exist for the purposes of P1–1, irrespective of the position under national law.

---

[54] ECtHR, *Papamichalopoulos and Others* v. *Greece*, 24 June 1993 (Appl. no. 14556/89). The point was not contested by Greece. See also, ECtHR, *Vasilescu* v. *Romania*, 22 May 1998 (Appl. no. 27053/95); noted in S. Djajic, 'The Right to Property and the *Vasilescu* v. *Romania* Case', *Syracuse Journal of International Law and Commerce* 27 (2000) 363.

[55] ECtHR, *Loizidou* v. *Turkey*, 18 December 1996 (Appl. no. 15318/89).

[56] *Ibid.*, at paras. 62–64.

[57] EComHR, *Weidlich* v. *Germany*, 4 March 1996 (Appl. nos. 9048/91, 19049/91, 19342/92, 19549/92, 18890/91).

[58] *Ibid.*

[59] See Kozminski, 'Restitution of Private Property', at 96–97; A. J. McAdams, *Judging the Past in Unified Germany* (Cambridge University Press, 2001) 135.

This began with *Weidlich* v. *Germany*,[60] where the Commission stated that:

> [T]he hope of recognition of the survival of a former property right which has not been susceptible of effective exercise for a long period ... [is] not to be considered as 'possessions' within the meaning of Article 1 of Protocol No 1 (P1–1).[61]

The effect of this statement was uncertain because it had no direct bearing on the case, the Commission having held that the rights in question were extinguished before P1–1 took effect. In any case, the reference to a 'former right' suggests that the Commission was only referring to lost rights. If so, the Commission was only saying that the hope that the state will restore a property right fully extinguished is not itself a P1–1 possession.

The issue was also addressed in *Malhous* v. *The Czech Republic*.[62] Again, the Court held that an old expropriation left the former owner with no subsisting rights to provide the basis for a claim under P1–1. Nevertheless, it stated that 'the hope of recognition of the survival of an old property right which it has long been impossible to exercise effectively cannot be considered as a "possession"'.[63] Here, the reference is to an *old* property right rather than a *former* property right, subsequent cases show that a distinction was intended:

> The hope that a long-extinguished property right may be revived cannot be regarded as a 'possession,' and neither can the hope of recognition of the survival of an old property right which has long been impossible to exercise effectively.[64]

---

[60] EComHR, *Weidlich* v. *Germany*, 4 March 1996 (Appl. nos. 9048/91, 19049/91, 19342/92, 19549/92, 18890/91).

[61] This statement was relied upon in a series of Commission admissibility decisions: EComHR, *H.K.* v. *Germany*, 10 February 1993 (Appl. no. 20931/92); EComHR, *Luck* v. *Germany*, 30 November 1994 (Appl. no. 24928/94); EComHR, *Firma 'Brauerei Feldschlösschen Ferdinand Geidel Kg' Davies* v. *Germany*, 24 February 1997 (Appl. no. 19918/92); EComHR, *Krug Von Nidda und Von Falkenstein* v. *Germany*, 24 February 1997 (Appl. no. 25043/94); EComHR, *Kremer-Viereck* v. *Germany*, 21 May 1998 (Appl. no. 34197/96); EComHR, *Peltzer* v. *Germany*, 21 May 1998 (Appl. no. 35223/97); EComHR, *Heuer* v. *Germany*, 21 May 1998 (Appl. no. 37255/97); and EComHR, *Von Rigal-Von Kriegsheim* v. *Germany*, 21 May 1998 (Appl. no. 37696/97).

[62] ECtHR, *Malhous* v. *the Czech Republic* [admissibility], 13 December 2000 (Appl. no. 33071/96).

[63] *Ibid.*, at 17.

[64] ECtHR, *Myšáková* v. *Czech Republic* [admissibility], 28 March 2006 (Appl. no. 30021/03) and ECtHR, *Nadbiskupija Zagrebacka* v. *Slovenia* [admissibility], 27 May 2004 (Appl. no. 60376/00).

The Court has not indicated how long it takes for property right to be extinguished. In some cases, the owner was unable to exercise the rights for less than a decade.[65] In any event, where the period is even shorter, the Court applies a second doctrine, holding that it has no jurisdiction where post-ratification acts are closely connected with pre-ratification conduct. For example, *Multiplex* v. *Croatia*[66] concerned the seizure of the applicant's vehicle in 1992 by the military police, for use in the war. In 1995, in proceedings brought by the applicant for damages, the Croatian authorities stated that the confiscation was only temporary and the vehicle would be returned after the war. In 1999, the Croatian legislature imposed an indefinite stay on actions for damages arising from the conduct of police officers and soldiers when acting in their official capacity during the war.[67] P1–1 came into effect in Croatia on 5 November 1997, but since the seizure did not extinguish the applicant's property rights, by the reasoning in *Papamichalopoulos* and *Loizidou* it should have been treated as a continuing act; in any case, the 1999 stay did not formally extinguish any rights of property. However, the Court not only held that the seizure was an instantaneous act, but went further by concluding that:

> [A]lthough the legislative interference took place after the Convention entered into force in respect of Croatia it was so closely related to the events that gave rise to the applicant's claim that divorcing the two would amount to giving retroactive effect to the Convention which would be contrary to general principles of international law.[68]

It is clear that the justification for the exclusion is not based on the idea that the injury took place in the remote past, despite the references to property being 'long-lost'. It is doubtful that any credible defence can be built on Fuller's theory or the Court's own 'quality of law' criteria. Indeed, in non-transitional cases, the Court would not accept such short prescriptive periods in national legislation.[69] It is also clear that the Court had no regard for the approach it took in *Loizidou* and the other Cypriot cases.

---

[65] EComHR, *Ivanovic* v. *Slovak Republic* [admissibility], 4 March 1998 (Appl. no. 37892/97).

[66] ECtHR, *Multiplex* v. *Croatia* [admissibility], 26 September 2002 (Appl. no. 58112/00). See also, ECtHR, *Ponomarenko* v. *Ukraine*, 14 June 2007 (Appl. no. 13156/02).

[67] Changes of the Civil Obligations Act, Official Gazette no. 112/1999 (cited in *Multiplex*).

[68] There was a breach of Article 6 (access to a court for the determination of civil rights), due to the length of stay.

[69] See ECtHR, *J.A. Pye (Oxford) Ltd.* v. *United Kingdom* [GC], 30 August 2007 (Appl. no. 44302/02).

To get a better sense of vision of law that the Court applies to these cases, it is necessary to consider how the Court determined the content and effect of the relevant rules of national law. To borrow Manfred Gabriel's terminology, the Court has a choice between adopting the perspective of a participant or an observer when determining the content of national law.[70] It would take the perspective of a participant if it stepped into the shoes of a national court and asked how it would have resolved a dispute. In the context of property restitution, it would ask whether the national courts would have said that the applicant's property rights were lawfully extinguished. In the long-lost property cases, this should require a close examination of (for example) the rules on prescription or adverse possession. This is the Court's usual method in the non-transitional cases, as it normally equates P1-1 possessions with property as it is understood in national law by the national courts. However, the participant perspective is limited: the Court does not resolve disputes over the content of national law. This includes disputes over the existence of property rights. The Court refuses to be a final court of appeal on questions of national law.[71] If the national courts have not provided a definitive ruling on the validity of a claim to property, the Court does not put itself in their place and reach its own conclusions on validity. But if, for example, the national legislature extinguished the claim before the courts could rule on it, the Court may apply the doctrine of the 'autonomous meaning', under which terms that define the scope of Convention rights may be given a meaning that is independent of their content under national law.[72]

The Court developed this doctrine to prevent states from avoiding their obligations by relabelling rights or legal processes that would otherwise come within the scope of a Convention right.[73] The doctrine has been applied to 'possessions', with the result that property rights that are not treated as proprietary interests by the relevant national courts may still

---

[70] M. Gabriel, 'Coming to Terms with the East German Border Guards', *Columbia Journal of Transnational Law* 38 (1999–2000) 375, 387–394.

[71] See, for example, ECtHR, *Iatridis* v. *Greece*, 25 March 1999 (Appl. no. 31107/96).

[72] See generally, T. Allen, 'The Autonomous Meaning of "Possessions" under the European Convention on Human Rights', in E. Cooke (ed.) *Modern Studies in Property Law*, vol. 2 (Oxford and Portland, Oregon: Hart Publishing, 2003); and Allen, *Property*, 42–46. On the doctrine of the autonomous meaning under other Convention rights (and P1–1), see G. Letsas, 'The Truth in Autonomous Concepts', *European Journal of International Law* 15 (2004) 279.

[73] ECtHR, *Öztürk* v. *Germany*, 21 February 1984 (Appl. no. 8544/79).

be protected under P1–1.[74] The idea of an 'autonomous' meaning also suggests that the Court could develop P1–1 to reflect the core individual interests of the Convention; their relationship with others concerning the use or disposition of things being essential to their equality, autonomy or dignity.[75] In practice, however, it is quite limited in scope.

In addition to those cases where the Court has taken the participant perspective or reached its own conclusion using the autonomous meaning doctrine, the Court in other cases has taken the perspective of an observer of the national system. Under this approach, in essence it asks whether the victim has been treated as the owner of property.[76] In *Beyeler* v. *Italy*, for example, the applicant argued the seizure of a painting violated P1–1, but Italy pointed out that the 'contract' under which he had obtained the painting had never come into effect and hence the seizure did not interfere with any of his possessions under P1–1.[77] However, the Court noted that 'on a number of occasions the applicant appears to have been considered de facto by the authorities as having a proprietary interest in the painting, and even as its real owner'.[78] This was enough to persuade the Court that the applicant should be treated as holding possessions for the purposes of P1–1. The result, in the non-transitional cases, is that the Court takes jurisdiction if the national courts have already determined that the applicant has property, and it also takes jurisdiction if the national administrative practice has been to treat the applicant as a property holder. The Court is happy to switch between observer and participant in order to extend its jurisdiction and provide the applicant with a hearing. With transitional cases, however, the Court switches between the two modes to avoid jurisdiction: if the national courts would have decided that the applicant lost property before ratification, the Court accepts it and refuses jurisdiction. Conversely, if the property was not lost under formal law, the Court might still refuse jurisdiction on the grounds that there was an administrative practice of treating the applicant as having lost the property.

The Court's determination to avoid jurisdiction is confirmed by its reluctance to rigorously apply neither the participant nor the observer perspectives. It does not seriously investigate the legal rules of the

---

[74] EctHR, *Gasus Dosier-Und Fördertechnik GmbH* v. *Netherlands*, 23 February 1995 (Appl. no. 15375/89).

[75] See Allen, 'Autonomous Meaning', Allen, *Property*, at 42–46, and Letsas, 'The Truth in Autonomous Concepts'.

[76] See, Gabriel, 'Coming to Terms', at 388.

[77] ECtHR, *Beyeler* v. *Italy*, 5 January 2000 (Appl. no. 33202/96) para. 86.

[78] *Ibid.*, para. 104.

communist era to determine whether a national court would have held that title had been lost; neither does it seriously investigate old administrative or social practices to discover whether the applicant would have been recognized as a (temporarily dispossessed) owner. Indeed, discussion of the facts is often so brief that we cannot know whether the impossibility of exercising rights of property was due to an unstated policy of denying access to property or whether it was simply due to incompetence or local abuses that would have been corrected if the applicant had pursued the issue. The effect is to deny a forum in which individual stories of injustice can be heard.

This demonstrates that the Court's vision of the rule of law in transition cases does not fall easily into any of the theories described above. Whether the Court followed the positivist approach, or the approach of Fuller or even Radbruch, one would expect it would seek to inform itself of the actual circumstances that made it impossible to exercise the rights in question. The breadth and type of the circumstances under consideration would vary, depending on the theory followed, but in any case, we would not expect a blanket rule to the effect that rights of property that were not capable of exercise immediately before the ratification of P1–1 must be treated as having been extinguished.

Temporal jurisdiction and the confiscation of property

As stated above, Radbruch argued that the Nazi statutes aimed at Jews could not be recognised as laws. Thus the courts of the Federal Republic of Germany decided that the confiscatory statutes should be treated as nullities, with no effect on the rights of the property owners. Hence, post-war restitution statutes that required owners to file claims for recovery within a specified time period could not operate so as to leave those who did not file without a right to restitution, because they never lost property in the first place.[79]

A similar situation arose in the Czech Republic, in respect of communist-era convictions for the 'crime' of an unauthorized departure from the state. On conviction, the courts would normally order the confiscation of property. After the fall of communism, Czech legislation reversed the convictions and quashed the confiscation orders. However,

---

[79] See R. Alexy, 'A Defence of Radbruch's Formula', in D. Dyzenhaus (ed.) *Recrafting the Rule of Law: The Limits of Legal Order* (Oxford and Portland, Oregon: Hart Publishing, 1999); F. Haldemann, 'Gustav Radbruch vs. Hans Kelsen: A Debate on Nazi Law', *Ratio Juris* 18 (2005) 162, 175.

the legislation imposed conditions: for example, it restricted restitution to nationals who were also residents of the Czech Republic. In addition, there was no right to recover if the property was held by a natural person who had acquired the property in good faith. Temporal conditions were also imposed: victims had to apply for recovery within six months of the law becoming effective. Applicants before the Court arguing that the exclusion of some victims violates P1–1 have put forward two alternative arguments. Either the original property rights were never extinguished, or the post-transition restitution statutes conferred a new property right, a statutory right to restitution. The Court consistently rejects both arguments holding that neither could be regarded as a 'possession' for the purposes of P1–1.[80]

Obviously, the Court does not believe that the Czech confiscations do not amount to extreme injustice in Radbruch's sense.[81] Nevertheless, it is remarkable that the Court has actually gone to the opposite extreme, especially since the Czech courts had already decided that the applicant held a property interest under Czech law.[82] If it had followed the approach taken in non-transitional cases, it would have held that P1–1 applied.[83] However, it would require the Court to balance the public interest in extinguishing the property rights against the applicant's right to the enjoyment of its possessions.

This distinction between the treatment of transitional and non-transitional cases is also seen in the non-transitional cases on the specific issue of statutory conditions on the vesting of property. In *Polacek*, the Court made much of the failure to satisfy these conditions, but in non-transitional cases, it has not. For example, in *Gaygusuz v. Austria*,[84] the

---

[80] ECtHR, *Polacek v. the Czech Republic*, 10 July 2002 (Appl. no. 38645/97) at para. 62. Note that, if a state decides to confirm the existence of a prior property right, the Court will treat it as a subsisting property right. See, for example, *Broniowski*; see also ECtHR, *Beshiri v. Albania*, 22 August 2008 (Appl. no. 7352/03) and ECtHR, *Bat'a v. Czech Republic*, 24 June 2008 (Appl. no. 43775/05).

[81] In ECtHR, *Maltzan v. Germany*, 2 March 2005 (Appl. nos. 71916/01, 71917/01 and 10260/02) at para. 70, the applicants argued that the expropriations of property that occurred between 1945 and 1949 in the Soviet Occupied Zone of Germany and after 1949 in the German Democratic Republic amounted to 'crimes against humanity'. The Court held that it did not have temporal jurisdiction, without addressing this point. *Ibid.*, at paras. 79–84 and 110–114.

[82] See generally, Procházka, *Mission Accomplished*, 148–151, 166–167, 173–174.

[83] It would not necessarily follow that denying restitution would breach P1–1: it may be possible for the state to justify an extinction of the applicant's property interests without compensation.

[84] ECtHR, *Gaygusuz v. Austria*, 16 September 1996 (Appl. no. 17371/90).

applicant claimed that the failure to recognize a statutory right to emergency welfare assistance was an interference with his possessions. The applicant's claim for assistance was rejected on the sole ground that he was not an Austrian citizen. He fulfilled all the other criteria for assistance, including the payment of regular contributions to the unemployment scheme, but the legislation stated that only citizens were eligible for assistance. The formal reasoning of *Polacek* would suggest that the failure to satisfy the nationality requirement meant that the applicant did not hold possessions under P1–1. However, in *Gaygusuz*, the Court not only found that there were possessions, but also that Austria violated the Convention rules against discrimination, when applied to the right to property. This is the conclusion reached in most of the cases: normally, the Court takes an expansive view of 'possessions' in order to ensure that discriminatory legislation is subject to a human rights review.[85]

These cases confirm *Loizidou* as exceptional, and a general trend against any reopening of disputes arising from pre-transitional conduct. But is it fair to say that they reflect a modernist vision of P1–1, under which the Court acts prospectively, and the rule of law is maintained by upholding the stability of current entitlements at the expense of claims based on old injustices? Arguably, the Court is merely applying general principles of international law; the jurisdiction cases may be restrictive, but they represent the only reasonable interpretation of the jurisdiction provisions of the Convention and Protocol. This point deserves consideration on its own.

The Court of Human Rights and general principles of international law

The European cases on temporal jurisdiction not only reveal a distinction in the treatment of transitional and non-transitional cases, but also between the treatment of transitional cases in the Court and other international tribunals. The European Court has framed its temporal jurisdiction doctrines in a way that suggests that it is merely applying general principles of international law. However, as the Court has noted,[86] the United Nations Human Rights Committee has taken a different view in its interpretation of the prohibition on discrimination contained in Article 26

---

[85] See, for example, ECtHR, *Willis* v. *United Kingdom*, 11 June 2002 (Appl. no. 36042/97); ECtHR, *Koua Poirrez* v. *France*, 30 September 2003 (Appl. no. 40892/98).

[86] ECtHR, *Des Fours Walderode* v. *Czech Republic* [admissibility], 4 March 2003 (Appl. no. 40057/98).

of the International Covenant on Civil and Political Rights (ICCPR).[87] For example, in *Simunek* v. *The Czech Republic*,[88] the UN Committee considered several petitions involving the confiscation and sale of property. As in the European cases, there were temporal issues because the confiscations occurred before the ICCPR Optional Protocol took effect for the Czech Republic.[89] However, this presented no obstacle to the Committee which observed that the complaints concerned the discriminatory effect of limiting the statutory right to restitution to resident nationals.[90] The Committee regarded the restitution law itself as an 'affirmation' of the discriminatory acts of the old regime, and hence it treated the earlier violation of the right against discrimination as a continuing violation.[91]

The Court has noted – but not followed – the UN Committee's approach. Instead, it is suggested that its decisions represent straightforward applications of general principles of international law.[92] However, the are reasons for caution in state-to-state disputes that do not apply in relation to individual petitions to the Court. In particular, in *Phosphates in Morocco*, the Permanent Court stressed the consensual aspect of its jurisdiction: a declaration 'must on no account be interpreted in such a way as to exceed the intention of the states that subscribed to it'.[93] This need to focus on state sovereignty and consent to jurisdiction is less compelling in the Convention rights context. The Court has said that the Convention is intended to create a European public order, where the states' obligation to protect human rights is stressed rather than the protection of their sovereignty.[94] Accordingly, there should be scope to depart from the general principles regarding the interpretation of treaty provisions and state declarations or ratifications relating to temporal jurisdiction.[95] To some

---

[87] International Covenant on Civil and Political Rights, Dec. 19, 1966, 999 U.N.T.S. 171.

[88] *Simunek, Hastings, Tuzilova and Prochazka* v. *The Czech Republic*, Communication No. 516/1992, UN Doc. CCPR/C/54/D/516/1992 (1995). See Macklem, 'Rybná 9, Praha 1', for a full discussion of the UN Committee's decisions on these issues.

[89] The Optional Protocol provides for individual complaints to the Human Rights Committee; Optional Protocol to the International Covenant on Civil and Political Rights, opened for signature 19 December 1966, 999 U.N.T.S. 171, 302 (entered into force 23 March 1976).

[90] *Simunek*, para. 4.3.   [91] *Ibid.*, para. 4.5.

[92] See ECtHR, *Polacek* v. *the Czech Republic*, 10 July 2002 (Appl. no. 38645/97). See also Macklem, 'Rybná 9, Praha 1', 20.

[93] Phosphates in Morocco, 1938 *P.C.I.J.* (ser. A/B) No. 74.

[94] See, for example, ECtHR, *Mamatkulov and Askarov* v. *Turkey*, 4 February 2005 (Appl. nos. 46827/99 and 46951/99) para. 100.

[95] See Pauwelyn, 'The Concept of a "Continuing Violation"'.

extent, the Court departed from the general principles in relation to reservations made by states, but it has not done so in relation to temporal jurisdiction.[96]

The restrictiveness of the current approach is particularly marked where the object of property rights has not been destroyed, as in the case of a de facto deprivation of possessions. The legal notion of property concentrates on the existence of rights rather than the existence of the thing that is the object of those rights, but this is far from the non-legal view of property. Indeed, the Court had implicitly acknowledged this point in some non-transitional cases, where applicants have been found to hold possessions after their property rights were extinguished, but the object of property remained in existence.[97] The Court plainly disregards this approach when dealing with transitional claims.

It is clear that the Court is not following a positivist conception of law in the transitional cases. The Court is also a long way from Radbruch's theory; there is no sensible argument that the revival of property rights would amount to an injustice so extreme that a court should disregard them. Arguably, there is a common theme with Fuller's theory and the Court's own quality of law principles, in the sense that there is a concern with stability. The cases seem to be motivated by a fear that reviving old titles would interfere with reconstruction in a post-transition world. Nevertheless, it is highly doubtful that Fuller would accept the validity of the Court's approach on the facts of the cases that have come before it. Indeed, in the non-transitional cases where the quality of law criteria are examined, the Court is very reluctant to say that the exercise of a power (public or private) over property was so unforeseeable that the state has acted unlawfully.[98] Moreover, it would be unreasonable to allow a state to benefit from its own wrongs. As the UN Committee stated in *Simunek*, the claimants lost their property because the state drove them out of the country; to require them to return would be incompatible with the condemnation of the state's acts.[99]

---

[96] Indeed, in ECtHR, *Blečić v. Croatia*, 8 March 2006 (Appl. no. 59532/00) at para. 57, the applicant appears to have raised this argument, but it was dismissed by the Court, as it relied on the standard jurisprudence (including the judgment in *Phosphates in Morocco*) to restrict the scope of its temporal jurisdiction.

[97] See, for example, ECtHR, *Stretch v. United Kingdom*, 24 June 2003 (Appl. no. 44277/98).

[98] See, for example, ECtHR, *J.A. Pye (Oxford) Ltd and J.A. Pye (Oxford) Land Ltd v. United Kingdom* [Chamber], 15 November 2005 (Appl. no. 44302/02); cf. ECtHR, *J.A. Pye (Oxford) Ltd. v. United Kingdom* [GC], 30 August 2007 (Appl. no. 44302/02).

[99] *Simunek*, at para. 11.6.

But why is the Court so set against restitution that it refuses even to consider these cases on the merits? The dissenting opinion in *Loizidou* illustrates a general view that disputes over transitional justice cannot be resolved within the Court. They are non-justiciable, because they do not raise questions of 'ordinary' justice. Given the complexity of disputes over conflicting claims to property, the rule of law is most likely to be furthered if the Court seeks to preserve the facts on the ground.

The response may also be prudential: the need for reconstruction in many post-transitional states is incontestable, and there is evidence that restitution has interfered with reconstruction in some states and slowed privatization,[100] aggravated housing shortages,[101] and made it more difficult to maintain social cohesion,[102] to give just a few examples.[103] Moreover, there is little evidence that transitional justice helps victims as much as has been claimed. Hence, the refusal to recognize old titles may well be the most prudent policy in at least some circumstances.

But is the Court's response pragmatic or dogmatic? If the judges were reacting to pragmatic concerns over restitution and reconstruction, we would expect to see at least some examination of the practical effects of restitution and the actual circumstances of the parties in the judges' reasoning. Instead of cutting off claims on jurisdictional grounds, we would expect to see the competing interests weighed against each other in the fair balance test, where the Court would decide whether restitution would have an unacceptable impact on reconstruction. Instead, the doctrine is directed towards the exclusion of this kind of investigation. This is a fairly

---

[100] See Crowder, 'Restitution in the Czech Republic', at 262; Frank, 'Privatization in Eastern Germany', and F. H. Foster, 'Restitution of Expropriated Property: Post-Soviet Lessons for Cuba', *Columbia Journal of Transnational Law* 34 (1996) 621, 641–643, 646–648.

[101] See Foster, 'Restitution of Expropriated Property', at 644–646; K. Duffy, *Final Report of the HDSE Project: Opportunity and Risk: Trends of Social Exclusion in Europe* (Council of Europe, 1998); A. Narusk, *HDSE Project Report on Estonia Part IV* (Council of Europe, 1997); Feliciana Rajevska, *HDSE Project Report on Latvia* (Council of Europe, 1997); J. Van Weesep, 'Comment: A Perspective on Housing Privatization in Eastern Europe', *Urban Lawyer* 29 (1997) 595.

[102] See Duffy, *Final Report*; Narusk, *HDSE Report*; Rajevska, *HDSE Report*; A. Juska, A. Poviliunas and R. Pozzuto, 'Resisting Marginalisation: The Rise of the Rural Community Movement in Lithuania', *Sociologia Ruralis* 45 (2005) 3, 8; and I. Tosics and J. Hegadüs, *South East Europe Strategic Review on Social Cohesion: Housing Problems in South East Europe* (2001), for the proposition that restitution caused uncertainty in the land markets in Bulgaria, Romania, Albania and, ultimately, in combination with other factors, made housing less affordable for low income households.

[103] Aligica and Dabu, 'Land Reform', at 66, stating that the restitution programme has been a cause of the failure of Romanian agriculture reform, partly because the precollectivization structure of land holdings produced 'an extreme parcelization of land'.

radical approach. Even if one accepts that the recognition of the old property rights would present real problems for the post-transitional state,
and hence that states would normally be justified in refusing restitution,
it does not follow that the Court proactively seek to find that the property rights were extinguished. P1–1 was drafted to allow states to redis-
tribute property in pursuit of social justice and economic restructuring.
Finding that property was not extinguished would not end the judicial
inquiry; there should be a further investigation of the proportionality of
the refusal of the present regime to recognize that property interest. If the
jurisdiction cases reflected prudential concerns over the desirability of
restitution, we would see less reliance on jurisdiction tests and more on
the proportionality analysis.

These beliefs are compatible with dogmatic modernism that holds that
the risk of an abuse of power can be controlled by improving the institutional order and that the practical successes of the new order will provide adequate compensation for those who suffered in the past.[104] With the
former communist states, the market economy would provide the opportunity to recover the material wealth to replace what was lost when property was confiscated, and the new democratic structures would ensure that
the oppression of the past would not recur. The new institutional order
may be a response to memory of the injustices of the past, but there is still
a very strong sense of doubt that individual stories of past injustices have
any useful place in the new order. Hence, for those who subscribe to this
view, transitional justice is fundamentally different from non-transitional
justice. Specifically, restitution is incompatible with the restructuring of
the new market order and the certainty of title that it requires.

Conclusions

One could argue that the European Court of Human Rights has taken a
perverse view of its own function in resolving issues of transitional justice and property. If it took a more robust approach in requiring states to
correct the abuses of human rights that occurred in the past, it could send
out a powerful signal to all governments that it would not permit similar
abuses in the future. Moreover, by supporting victims of past abuses in
their quest to recover their property, the Court would help them regain
their personal sense of their equal status as subjects of the 'new' state
and ease their reinstatement into the social world from which they were

---

[104] See also, Macklem, 'Rybná 9, Praha 1'.

once excluded. Instead, we find that the Court seems to take little interest
in these matters, apparently in the name of the rule of law and the all-
important value of maintaining the stability of property relations. Cases
are decided by rules that take little account of the actual circumstances at
the time of the original loss of property or the subsequent claim for restitution. Even where it seems that the Court may have responded to serious
injustice, it has been anxious to avoid saying so.[105]

It is clear that there is a strong (though not universal) belief that there
is little to be gained by investigating the stories of victims. The function of
the Court and Convention is not to make justice available to all victims of
abuses of power, but more narrowly to secure the rule of law and the protection of human rights prospectively. The Statute of Europe declares that
the protection of human rights will secure the conditions necessary for
democracy to flourish, and it seems that this can be done without addressing the injustices of the past. But this view is becoming anachronistic. In
addition to the UN Committee's jurisprudence, we can point to the rise of
truth commissions, the International Criminal Court, and prosecutions
of human rights violators in national courts as evidence of a growing belief
that the re-examination of the past is essential in establishing the foundation on which new institutional structures can operate.[106] In relation
to property, there is an increasing emphasis on the right of refugees and
internally displaced persons to return to their homes after armed conflict,
even where this necessitates the removal of secondary occupants.[107] There
is a growing belief that institutions function better where victims of past
injustices are given a forum in which to be heard.

Arguably, in this area, there is no 'transitional jurisprudence', in
the sense that the Court does not feel that the Convention allows it to
evaluate pre-ratification acts, or even the post-ratification responses to
pre-ratification acts. Of course, one might argue that silence is its own
statement. There may be very little in the way of a transitional jurisprudence of restitution, but there is a kind of transitional *justice* of property. However, it is a distributive rather than a corrective form of justice
that is in evidence. For example, the lack of a human rights evaluation of
pre-ratification expropriations and confiscations suggests that they are
regarded as the products of poor economic policies. This is especially
true of the former communist states: the failure of economic policies does

---

[105] E.g., *Loizidou*.
[106] See generally, Teitel, 'Human Rights'.
[107] Leckie, 'New Directions', at 47–48.

not mean that individual rights were violated in a manner that demands action in the post-transition world. The confiscations and expropriations were a little like bad weather: victims of a hurricane may have a claim for support from their government, but those claims are based on a theory of distributive justice rather than corrective justice. Undoubtedly, many of those who were convicted *in absentia* after fleeing their former home would not share the belief that the loss of property was not attributable to deliberate and wrongful acts of their own state, and that the responsibility for correcting these wrongs does not lie with the current government. Plainly, this view was also shared by the UN Committee in *Simunek*,[108] but the Court of Human Rights is more doubtful. In *Blečić*, for example, the Court did not question the finding of the Croatian courts that 'there had been no justified reason for the applicant not to return' to her home, despite the fact that she was an ethnic Serb-Montenegrin and lived in an area where armed conflict had broken out and anti-Serb violence was occurring.[109]

It is ironic that the focus remains resolutely fixed on prospective justice, especially in the states that went through communism, because there is a parallel in the communist treatment of the Holocaust. There was a faith that the new order would make it unnecessary to address the past, or, to put it more accurately, there was a faith that the creation of the new order would provide a complete answer to individual claims for redress.[110] We now see the same pattern being repeated, using the new market economy. The Court of Human Rights has not seriously questioned this faith in the new order. Perhaps time will prove it right: perhaps economic growth will be so strong that we will all agree one day that living well really was the best revenge, and the stories of the unsatisfied victims will die with them. But the line that demarcates the present and future from the past is frustratingly unclear. The promise of a better future for all does not satisfy everyone who suffered injustice. Victims continue to tell their stories of abuse and harm and old disputes do not simply disappear.

---

[108] Communication No. 516/1992.

[109] See ECtHR, *Blečić* v. *Croatia*, 8 March 2006 (Appl. no. 59532/00). See generally, J. Martin, M. Scully and B. Levitt, 'Injustice and the Legitimation of Revolution: Damning the Past, Excusing the Present, and Neglecting the Future', *Journal of Personality and Social Psychology* 59 (1990) 281; M. Wenzel, 'Justice and Identity', *Personality and Social Psychology Bulletin* 26 (2000); and M. Wenzel with G. Mikula, 'Justice and Social Conflict', *International Journal of Psychology* 35 (2000) 157.

[110] I. Markovits, 'Reconcilable Differences: On Peter Quint's *The Imperfect Union*', *American Journal of Comparative Law* 47 (1999) 189, 195–196.

Bibliography

Alexy, R., 'A Defence of Radbruch's Formula', in Dyzenhaus, D. (ed.) *Recrafting the Rule of Law: The Limits of Legal Order* (Oxford and Portland, Oregon: Hart Publishing, 1999).

Aligica, P. D. and Dabu, A., 'Land Reform and Agricultural Reform Policies in Romania's Transition to the Market Economy', *Eastern European Economics* 41(5) (2003) 49.

Allen, T., 'The Autonomous Meaning of "Possessions" under the European Convention on Human Rights', in Cooke, E. (ed.) *Modern Studies in Property Law*, vol. 2 (Oxford and Portland, Oregon: Hart Publishing, 2003).

  Property and the Human Rights Act 1998 (Oxford and Portland, Oregon: Hart Publishing, 2005).

  'Restitution and Transitional Justice in the European Court of Human Rights', *Columbia Journal of European Law* 13 (2007), 1.

Council of Europe, *Collected edition of the 'travaux préparatoires' of the European Convention on Human Rights: Recueil des travaux préparatoires de la Convention européenne des droits de l'homme* (Council of Europe, 8 vols, 1975–1985).

Crawford, J., *The International Law Commission's Articles on State Responsibility: Introduction, Text, and Commentaries* (Cambridge University Press, 2002).

Crowder, R., 'Restitution in the Czech Republic: Problems and Prague-nosis', *Indiana International and Comparative Law Review* 5 (1994) 237.

Djajic, S., 'The Right to Property and the *Vasilescu* v. *Romania* Case', *Syracuse Journal of International Law and Commerce* 27 (2000) 363.

Duffy, K., *Final Report of the HDSE Project: Opportunity and Risk: Trends of Social Exclusion in Europe* (Council of Europe, 1998).

Foster, F. H., 'Restitution of Expropriated Property: Post-Soviet Lessons for Cuba', *Columbia Journal of Transnational Law* 34 (1996) 621.

Frank, R., 'Privatization in Eastern Germany: A Comprehensive Study', *Vanderbilt Journal of Transnational Law* 27 (1994) 809.

Fuller, L., *Morality of Law* (New Haven: Yale University Press, 1969, rev. edn).

Gabriel, M., 'Coming to Terms with the East German Border Guards', *Columbia Journal of Transnational Law* 38 (1999–2000) 375.

Gross, A. M., 'Reinforcing the New Democracies: The ECHR and the Former Communist Countries', *European Journal of International Law* 7 (1996) 89.

Haldemann, F., 'Gustav Radbruch vs. Hans Kelsen: A Debate on Nazi Law', *Ratio Juris* 18 (2005) 162.

Halmai, G. and Scheppele, K. L., 'Living Well is the Best Revenge: The Hungarian Approach to Judging the Past', in McAdams, A. J. (ed.) *Transitional Justice and the Rule of Law in New Democracies* (University of Notre Dame Press, 1997).

Hart, H. L. A., *The Concept of Law*, 2nd edn (Oxford University Press, 1994).

Heller, M. and Serkin, C., 'Revaluing Restitution: From the Talmud to Postsocialism', *Michigan Law Review* 97 (1999) 1385.

Higgins, R., 'Time and the Law: International Perspectives on an Old Problem', *International and Comparative Law Quarterly* 46 (1997) 501.

Juska, A., Poviliunas, A. and Pozzuto, R., 'Resisting Marginalisation: The Rise of the Rural Community Movement in Lithuania', *Sociologia Ruralis* 45 (2005) 3.

Kelsen, H., 'Law, State and Justice in the Pure Theory of Law', *Yale Law Journal* 57 (1948) 377.

Koskenniemi, M., 'By Their Acts You Shall Know Them ... (And Not by Their Legal Theories)', *European Journal of International Law* 15 (2004) 839.

Kozminski, A. K., 'Restitution of Private Property: Re-Privatization in Central and Eastern Europe', *Communist and Post-Communist Studies* 30 (1997) 95.

Leckie, S., 'New Directions in Housing and Property Restitution', in Leckie, S. (ed.) *Returning Home: Housing and Property Restitution Rights of Refugees and Displaced Persons*, 2nd edn (Ardsley: Transnational Publishers Inc., 2003).

Letsas, G., 'The Truth in Autonomous Concepts', *European Journal of International Law* 15 (2004) 279.

Loś, M., 'Property Rights, Market and Historical Justice: Legislative Discourses in Poland', *International Journal of the Sociology of Law* 22 (1994) 39.

McAdams, A. J., *Judging the Past in Unified Germany* (Cambridge University Press, 2001).

Macklem, P., 'Rybná 9, Praha 1: Restitution and Memory in International Human Rights Law', *European Journal of International Law* 16 (2005) 1.

Markovits, I., 'Reconcilable Differences: On Peter Quint's *The Imperfect Union*', *American Journal of Comparative Law* 47 (1999) 189.

Martin, J., Scully, M. and Levitt, B., 'Injustice and the Legitimation of Revolution: Damning the Past, Excusing the Present, and Neglecting the Future', *Journal of Personality and Social Psychology* 59 (1990) 281.

Narusk, A., *Human Dignity and Social Exclusion (HDSE) Project Report on Estonia Part IV* (Council of Europe, 1997).

Nissel, A., 'Continuing Crimes in the Rome Statute', *Michigan Journal of International Law* 25 (2004) 653.

Offe, C., *Varieties of Transition: The East European and East German Experience* (Cambridge: Polity Press, 1996).

Pauwelyn, J., 'The Concept of a "Continuing Violation" of an International Obligation: Selected Problems', *British Yearbook of International Law* 66 (1995) 415.

Pogany, I., *Righting Wrongs in Eastern Europe* (Manchester University Press, 1997).

Posner, E. A. and Vermeule, A., 'Transitional Justice as Ordinary Justice', *Harvard Law Review* 117 (2004) 761.

Procházka, R., *Mission Accomplished: On Founding Constitutional Adjudication in Central Europe* (Budapest: Central European University Press, 2002).

Radbruch, G., *Fünf Minuten Rechtsphilosophie*, Rhein-Neckar-Zeitung (Heidelberg, 12 September 1945), translated by Paulson, B. L. and Paulson, S. L. as 'Five Minutes of Legal Philosophy (1945)', *Oxford Journal Legal Studies* 26 (2006) 13.

Gesetzliches Unrecht und Übergesetzliches Recht, 1 *Süddeutsche Juristen-Zeitung* 105 (1946), translated by Paulson, B.L. and Paulson, S. L. as 'Statutory Lawlessness and Supra-Statutory Law (1946)', *Oxford Journal Legal Studies* 26 (2006) 1.

Rajevska, F., *Human Dignity and Social Exclusion (HDSE) Project Report on Latvia* (Council of Europe, 1997).

Scheppele, K. L., 'When the Law Doesn't Count: The 2000 Election and the Failure of the Rule of Law', *University of Pennsylvania Law Review* 149 (2001) 1361.

Simpson, A. W. B., *Human Rights and the End of Empire: Britain and the Genesis of the European Convention* (Oxford University Press, 2001).

Sriram, C. L., 'Transitional Justice Comes of Age: Enduring Lessons and Challenges', *Berkeley Journal of International Law* 23 (2005) 506.

Stack, H. M., 'The "Colonization" of East Germany? A Comparative Analysis of German Privatization', *Duke Law Journal* 46 (1997) 1211.

Teitel, R. G., 'Human Rights in Transition: Transitional Justice Genealogy', *Harvard Human Rights Journal* 16 (2003) 69.

Thompson, J., *Taking Responsibility for the Past: Reparation and Historical Justice* (Cambridge: Polity Press, 2002).

Tosics, I. and Hegadüs, J., *South East Europe Strategic Review on Social Cohesion: Housing Problems in South East Europe* (2001), available at: www.coe.int/T/E/Social_cohesion/Strategic_review/Publications/Housing_Network/EHousingProblemsSEER%282001%291.asp.

Van Weesep, J., 'Comment: A Perspective on Housing Privatization in Eastern Europe', *Urban Lawyer* 29 (1997) 595.

Wenzel, M., 'Justice and Identity', *Personality and Social Psychology Bulletin* 26 (2000) 157.

Wenzel, M. with Mikula, G., 'Justice and Social Conflict', *International Journal of Psychology* 35 (2000) 126.

Youngblood, W. R., 'Note and Comment: Poland's Struggle for a Restitution Policy in the 1990s', *Emory International Law Review* 9 (1995) 645.

10

The Inter-American human rights system
and transitional processes

DIEGO RODRÍGUEZ-PINZÓN

Introduction

The notion of 'transitional justice' in the Inter-American system has been traditionally associated with the fight against impunity. Due to the sad and long history of gross and systematic violations of human rights in the Americas, whether under authoritarian regimes or democratically elected despots,[1] the Inter-American Commission on Human Rights (hereinafter 'Inter-American Commission' or 'Commission') and the Inter-American Court on Human Rights (hereinafter 'Inter-American Court' or 'Court') have extensive case law and jurisprudence dealing with the intricacies of transitional processes and the affirmation of fundamental human rights. This 'hemispheric laboratory' effectively allows the review of situations

Diego Rodríguez-Pinzón (JD, LLM, SJD) is Co-Director of the Academy on Human Rights and Humanitarian Law and Professorial Lecturer in Residence at the Washington College of Law, American University. The author gratefully acknowledges the research and editing assistance provided by Luiza Di Giovanni, a law student at the Washington College of Law and editor at the Academy on Human Rights and Humanitarian Law. This chapter was finalised in August 2010. As such, it does not take into account the Inter-American Court's amnesty judgment concerning Brazil: IACtHR, *Gomes Lund et al.* v. *Brazil*, 24 November 2010 (Series C No. 21) (though for background, see text accompanying notes 20-21 below).

[1] The struggle against gross and systematic violations of human rights has marked most of the institutional history of the Inter-American system. There have been two distinct phases in dealing with gross and systematic violations. The first phase regards dictatorships with no functional rule of law and a complete lack of democratic institutions. The second phase occurred in the 1990s, after most American States had transitioned to democracies. During this period the system had to confront 'authoritarian democracies' (i.e. refined forms of authoritarianism), which perpetrated and/or tolerated gross human rights violations. The distinction being that 'dictatorships' are classic military governments, while 'authoritarian democracies' are weak civilian governments supported by strong military institutions (see R. K. Goldman, 'History and Action: The Inter-American Human Rights System and the Role of the Inter-American Commission', *Human Rights Quarterly* 31/4 (2009) 856–887).

such as the dictatorships in the southern cone, the civil wars in Central America, the 'democratic' dictatorship of the Fujimori regime, and the protracted war still affecting Colombia.

The Inter-American system also allows for analysis of several legal–technical issues in transitional situations. The system, for instance, exercises a narrow level of deference to national processes when it comes to gross and systematic human rights violations. This chapter discusses deference doctrines such as the Fourth Instance Formula developed by the Inter-American Commission for certain cases. It further describes how the Inter-American bodies have exercised their supervisory and remedial powers when dealing with cases of gross violations of human rights as well as national transitional processes.

Finally, this chapter analyses the different methods in which these regional human rights mechanisms have facilitated in the transitioning processes, especially with respect to impunity for gross human rights violations. In addition, the analysis includes how the decisions of the Court and the Commission are integrated into the legal dialogue among national and international tribunals.

General description of the Inter-American human rights system

The Inter-American Commission is composed of seven members elected as 'independent experts'. The OAS General Assembly choose the elected members from a list of candidates proposed by Member States.[2] Commission members are elected for a term of four years and may be re-elected once.[3] The Secretariat of the Inter-American Commission is located in Washington, DC, where the headquarters of the OAS are based.[4] The Statute of the Inter-American Commission enumerates the powers of the Commission with regard to OAS Member States that have

---

[2] Statute of the Inter-American Commission of Human Rights (IAComHR) art. 3, OAS Res 447 (IX-0/79), available in 'basic documents pertaining to human rights in the Inter-American System' at www.cidh.oas.org.

[3] *Ibid.*, art. 4; American Convention on Human Rights (ACHR) art. 37 (22 November 1969) 1144 UNTS 123, entered into force 18 July 1978, available in 'basic documents pertaining to human rights in the Inter-American System' at www.cidh.oas.org.

[4] The Commission's authority arises from its dual nature: (1) it is an organ of the OAS Charter with a statutory mandate authorizing it to supervise compliance by OAS member States with the American Declaration of the Rights and Duties of Man ('American Declaration' or 'Declaration') and (2) it is also a supervisory organ of the American Convention on Human Rights ('American Convention' or 'Convention'). The powers and functions of the Commission regarding each State vary depending on whether the State has ratified the Convention and accepted the Court's contentious jurisdiction.

not yet ratified the American Convention.[5] These powers include an individual complaint procedure against all OAS Member States for alleged violations of the Declaration in individual cases, which provides standing to individuals in such international proceedings.

The Inter-American Court is 'an autonomous judicial institution' entrusted with 'the application and interpretation of the American Convention'.[6] It is composed of seven members who serve in their individual capacities, not representing any State. States Parties to the American Convention elect these members from a panel of candidates nominated by those States.[7] The Inter-American Court of Human Rights is located in San José, Costa Rica. The judges of the Court are elected for six years and may be re-elected once.[8]

These Inter-American supervisory organs have exerted their corresponding mandates by resorting to a variety of tools. The Commission's supervisory powers include political supervision through on-site visits and reporting on either a country's general human rights situation or a human rights issue of regional significance. Both the Commission and the Court exercise adjudicatory powers in individual cases and can issue orders for interim measures of protection in particular situations.[9]

The Inter-American system on transitional situations in the Americas

Amnesty laws

One of the major areas in which the Inter-American system has developed very significant standards related with massive violations of

---

[5] IACHR Statute, arts. 18, 20.

[6] Statute of the Inter-American Court on Human Rights (IACtHR) art. 1, OAS Res 448 (IX-0/79), www.corteidh.or.ce/estatuto.cfm.

[7] *Ibid.*, arts. 6–7; ACHR, arts. 52–53.

[8] IACtHR Statute, art. 5; ACHR, art. 54. The Inter-American Court has two distinct jurisdictions: contentious jurisdiction and advisory jurisdiction (see ACHR, arts. 62, 64.) It is the only judicial organ of the Inter-American human rights system; as such its adjudicatory functions are characterised by binding decisions. In addition, its advisory jurisdiction provides for ample powers to interpret *in abstracto* the human rights obligations of states based on the American Convention.

[9] The Inter-American system has denounced gross and systematic violations; documented individual violations; empowered and protected national actors and victims; outlawed amnesty laws; monitored political agreements to ensure that human rights laws are respected; promoted the prosecution of perpetrators of gross violations and contributed to the development and protection of human rights through many other actions. These supervisory functions have directly and indirectly impacted subsequent transitional processes in several of these countries.

human rights is that of amnesty laws. Many authoritarian regimes in the Americas recurrently resorted to amnesty laws as a way to escape prosecution when stepping down and/or transitioning to democracy. This practice had multiple effects regarding the rights of victims under international and national law, by depriving them from individual remedies and reparations and curtailing other rights that were subsequently recognised by the Inter-American system and some national tribunals and/or commissions.

In the last two decades, the Inter-American Commission and the Inter-American Court have been called to deal with complex situations in several States that adopted amnesty laws in the framework of transitional processes. Their involvement resulted in well-developed international standards that severely restrict the validity of such laws in a wide variety of situations where crimes against humanity or war crimes were committed. These standards have since been developed in the context of transitions from dictatorial regimes to democracies.

This is evidenced in the case of Argentina, where the new democratic government adopted the *Ley de Obediencia Debida* (Due Obedience Law) and the *Ley de Punto Final* (Final Stop Law) to benefit military operatives that perpetrated crimes against humanity.[10] In a landmark decision in 1992, the Commission found these laws to be incompatible with the American Convention and American Declaration.[11] The main rationale behind this decision explained that the rights of victims had been violated because the amnesty scheme 'denied the victims their right to obtain a judicial investigation in a court of criminal law to determine those responsible for the crimes committed and punish them accordingly'.[12] It is notable that the Commission recognised that Argentina had adopted several reparatory measures, such as the creation of an official national commission (CONADEP) 'that investigated and documented the disappearances that occurred during the so-called "dirty war" in its historic report *"Nunca Más"* as well as the allocation of "pension equal to 75% of the minimum lifetime salary to the next-of-kin of the disappeared"

---

[10] Among the many human rights violations committed, the Argentinean military systematically disappeared thousands of persons, executing and torturing most of them. See B. D. Tittemore, 'Ending Impunity in the Americas: The Role of the Inter-American Human Rights System in Advancing Accountability for Serious Crimes Under International Law', *SouthWestern Journal of Law and Trade in the Americas* 12/429 (2006) 450–455.

[11] IAComHR, *Herrera et. al.* v. *Argentina*, 2 October 1992 (No. 28/29, Cases 10.147, 10.181, 10.240, 10.262, 10.309 and 10.311), Annual Report 1992–93. All IACHR cases are available under 'Annual Reports' at www.cidh.oas.org.

[12] *Ibid.*, para. 50.

and "a pension to persons who, during the previous dictatorship, were arrested on orders from the National Executive Power".[13]

That same year, the Commission also released a similar decision outlawing the Uruguayan amnesty (i.e. *Ley de Caducidad* (Caducity Law)),[14] which was adopted by the new democratic government and approved by a referendum adopted by a significant majority of Uruguayan voters.[15] Unlike the Argentinean amnesty, Uruguay had not implemented a truth commission or other significant reparation programmes.[16] Additionally, in 1992 the Commission also declared that the Amnesty Law of El Salvador in *Las Hojas Massacre* v. *El Salvador* was incompatible with the American Convention.[17] Later, in 1996, the Commission also issued a decision against the Chilean 'self-amnesty' adopted by the authoritarian regime of Augusto Pinochet when it was about to hand over power to civilian democratic rule.[18]

The cases mentioned were never filed before the Inter-American Court and thus remained the only decisions on amnesty laws for several years. During those years those respective States did not comply with the recommendations of the Commission and continued to apply such amnesties. Nevertheless, these international decisions continued to empower victims in seeking justice. For instance, pursuing alternative judicial actions on matters that were not safeguarded under amnesties – as occurred in Argentina. It was not until 2001, in *Barrios Altos* v. *Peru*,[19] that the Inter-American Court issued its first decision on amnesties. This seminal

---

[13] *Ibid.*, paras. 42–46.

[14] IAComHR, *Hugo Leonardo de los Santos Mendoza et. al.* v. *Uruguay*, 2 October 1992 (No. 29/92, Cases 10.029, 10.036, 10.145, 10.305, 10.372, 10.373, 10.374 and 10.375) Annual Report 1992–93.

[15] The Commission indicated regarding the Caducity Law adopted by referendum that the 'application of the Convention and examination of the legal effects of a legislative measure, either judicial or of any other nature, insofar as it has effects incompatible with the rights and guarantees embodied in the Convention or the American Declaration, are within the Commission's competence'. *Ibid.*, para. 31.

[16] Only until 2003 the *Comisión para la Paz* (Commission for Peace) of Uruguay would issue the *Informe Final de la Comisión para la Paz.*

[17] IAComHR, *Las Hojas Massacre* v. *El Salvador*, 24 September 1992 (No. 26/92, Case 10.147) Annual Report 1992–93. The Commission would also follow the same approach in subsequent cases indicating that El Salvador should 'render null and void the General Amnesty Law' (see IAComHR, *Ignacio Ellacuría, S.J. et. al.* v. *El Salvador*, 22 December 1999 (No. 136/99, Case 10.488) Annual Report 1999; IAComHR, *Monsignor Oscar Romero* v. *El Salvador*, 13 April 2000 (No. 37/00, Case 11.481) Annual Report 1999).

[18] IAComHR, *Hector Marcial Garay Hermosilla et. al.* v. *Chile*, 15 October 1996 (No. 36/96, Case 10.843) Annual Report 1996.

[19] IACtHR, *Case of Barrios Altos* v. *Peru*, 14 March 2001 (Series C No. 75).

decision regarding Peru's amnesty law, adopted during the Fujimori regime, has served as a basis for further national action – not only in Peru but in other countries as well (discussed further below).

Subsequently in 2009, the Commission filed an application before the Inter-American Court against Brazil, in the *Araguaia Guerrilla Movement* case,[20] for adopting and applying its Amnesty Law (Law No. 6.683/79) in violation of the American Convention. This case has significant implications considering that the President Lula is currently facing a dilemma posed by his government's initiative to establish a truth commission and the vehement opposition of high-ranking military officers that threatened to quit their posts if such initiative is implemented.[21].

Generally speaking, the Commission and the Court have exercised close scrutiny of amnesty laws applicable to crimes against humanity or war crimes. The system has increasingly expanded the legal effects of its decisions. This is apparent in decisions, such as *Barrios Altos* v. *Peru*, where the Inter-American Court had the authority to declare the incompatibility of the Peruvian Amnesty Law and its 'lack of legal effect'.[22] This is a significant legal step towards a monist approach in regional international law. The Court appears to consider that the Inter-American system's current stage of development permits an intense relationship between the Court's decisions and national constitutional structures, which consequently limits States' options in their transition processes.

The expanding body of decisions of the Inter-American system may be the result of civil society's continuous struggle to achieve justice. For example, victims and non-governmental organisations in Argentina have played a critical role in keeping the claim alive within the national public opinion.[23] The consolidation of the modern notion of 'rule of law' in the

---

[20] IAComHR, *Araguaia Guerrilla Movement (Gomes Lund et. al. v. Brazil)*, 26 March 2009 (No. 33/01, Case 11.552), Petition filed before the IACtHR. Demanda ante la Corte Interamericana de Derechos Humanos, en el caso de *Gomes Lund y Otros (Guerrilha do Araguaia)* (Caso 11.552) contra la Republica Federativa de Brasil, 26 March 2009 (Application filed by the Inter-American Commission against Brazil before the Inter-American Court). As noted at the outset, the Court's judgment of 24 November 2010 was delivered after the finalisation of this chapter, and so is not covered here.

[21] G. Duffy, 'Brazil Truth Commission Arouses Military Opposition', *BBC* (London: 11 January 2010), news.bbc.co.uk/2/hi/8451109.stm.

[22] The Court stated in the *Barrios Altos Case* that 'amnesty laws No. 26479 and No. 26492 are incompatible with the American Convention on Human Rights and, consequently, lack legal effect' (see *Barrios Altos Case*).

[23] This may be compounded by the fact that Argentina's social structure is very homogenous, with a quite significant middle class to which many of the victims belong.

Americas, after most of the countries in the region underwent a democratic transition, also likely empowered individual victims and other civil society actors to claim their rights through the legal process, both at the national and international level.

The consequences of this very strict approach on limiting the effect of amnesty laws in the Americas are also being felt in Colombia. Local actors appear to implicitly acknowledge that amnesty measures will not be possible in this country. The demobilisation of paramilitary groups has not been subject to a classical amnesty measure. National legislators crafted a demobilisation law (*Ley de Justicia y Paz*) that resembles a plea bargain structure used in other States around the world to confront organised criminal structures and convict perpetrators. Under this normative structure, paramilitary groups and individuals have begun to demobilise.[24] However, the implementation of such law has been subject to criticism from many observers as its effects appear to be closely related to those of an impunity or amnesty law.[25] Petitions have been filed claiming that the law's adoption and implementation violates the Convention, but the Inter-American Court has declined to issue judgment on this matter.[26]

In El Salvador, the reaction to the Commission's decisions declaring the General Amnesty Law incompatible with the Convention has been less evident. Notwithstanding the statement released on 16 January 2010 by the administration of President Funes, during the eighteenth anniversary of the Peace Accords, indicating that the State of El Salvador recognised the responsibility of State agents (armed forces, public security groups, and their proxies) 'for having committed grave human rights violations during the country's armed conflict (1980–1992), and asked the victims

---

[24] It is important to mention that the case of the State of Colombia can shed some light on how the evolving Inter-American standards regarding the obligation to prosecute and punish perpetrators of grave human rights violations has had a significant impact in modifying the conduct of such a State. This has special importance due to the fact that it is an ongoing armed conflict in which actors are now acting and reacting on the basis of the significant developments in international human rights law. This modified conduct of the State was expressed through the actions of the Colombian Congress and the executive branch in its implementation of the Peace and Justice Law, with the subsequent intervention of the Constitutional Court of Colombia, which adjusted the bill to existing international human rights standards.

[25] Human Rights Watch, *Paramilitaries' Heirs: The New Face of Violence in Colombia*, 3 February 2010, www.hrw.org/node/88060.

[26] IACtHR, *Rochela Massacre v. Colombia*, 11 May 2007 (Series C No. 163) para. 190–198. All IACtHR cases are available under 'Jurisprudence' at www.corteidh.or.cr/index.cfm.

and their relatives for forgiveness'.[27] It is interesting to observe how, after almost two decades since the Peace Agreements, there is still a need to seek justice in El Salvador. Notably, despite the fact that two decades have passed since the Commission's first amnesty case, El Salvador has yet to implement such decisions.

Overall, the Inter-American system's response to transitional proc-esses that have adopted amnesty laws varies. States are more likely to implement the decisions of the Commission and the Court after signifi-cant time has passed since the adoption of such amnesties. Yet, the Inter-American system does not appear to modify its jurisprudential approach to amnesties on the basis of temporal proximity to the events. In fact, the system appears to react strongly when facing the possible adoption of an impunity law, as is currently evident in Colombia.[28]

The Inter-American system and truth commissions

The Inter-American system and truth commissions have a close relation-ship. The Commission has often referred to the findings of truth com-missions in its decisions. Similarly, the decisions of the Commission and Court have informed and empowered the truth commissions. Both regimes coexist and empower each other, even though there are times when tensions may arise between them.

Regarding the relevance of truth commissions and the international human rights obligations of States, the Inter-American Commission has expressly recognised the relevance and importance of such com-missions in guaranteeing the *right to truth* and affording reparations, even if other aspects of such institutions may not sufficiently secure vic-tims' human rights or ensure that States fulfil all their duties under the American Convention.[29] Referring to the National Commission for Truth and Reconciliation (NCTR) in Chile, the Commission noted that 'the

---

[27] IACHR, 'IACHR Welcomes El Salvador's Recognition of Responsibility and Apology for Grave Human Rights Violations During the Armed Conflict', 21 January 2010, Press Release, No. 6/10, www.cidh.oas.org/Comunicados/English/2010/4–10eng.htm. President Funes referred to 'massacres, arbitrary executions, forced disappearances, acts of torture, sexual abuses, arbitrary deprivations of liberty, and various acts of repression. The majority of all these abuses were executed against defenseless civilians who were not involved in the conflict'.

[28] The Inter-American Commission has been closely following the implementation of the 'Justice and Peace Law' using its general reporting powers.

[29] IAComHR, *Hector Marcial Garay Hermosilla et. al.* v. *Chile*, 15 October 1996 (No. 36/96, Case 10.843) Annual Report 1996, para. 74.

investigations conducted by that Commission into cases of violation of the right to life, the victims of other violations, including torture, were deprived of any legal recourse and of any other type of compensation'. It further stated that the NCTR 'was not a judicial body and its work was limited to establishing the identity of the victims whose right to life had been violated. Under the terms of its mandate, the Commission was not empowered to publish the names of those who had committed the crimes, or to impose any type of sanction on them. For this reason, despite its important role in establishing the facts and granting compensation, the Truth Commission cannot be regarded as an adequate substitute for the judicial process'.[30]

The existence of truth commissions has not precluded the exercise of jurisdiction by the Commission in related cases. In *Comadres* v. *El Salvador*,[31] for instance, the Commission took notice of the Truth Commission's report on this case. The Commission considered that that the Truth Commission could not substitute a regular judicial process in light of the requirements of the American Convention. However, the Commission did support several of its findings of violations of the Convention on evidence gathered and assessed by the Truth Commission.[32] Similarly, in *Parada Cea et. al.* v. *El Salvador*,[33] the Commission emphasised the fact that the Salvadoran Truth Commission was not a jurisdictional mechanism.

The Inter-American Court has followed the same line of analysis when referring other truth commissions.[34] It has clarified the scope and relevance of such truth commissions under the American Convention by stating:

> The Court deems that the establishment of a Truth Commission – depending on its object, proceedings, structure and purposes – can contribute

[30] *Ibid.*, para. 75.
[31] IAComHR, *Comadres* v. *El Salvador*, 1 March 1996 (No. 13/96, Case 10.948) Annual Report 1996.
[32] *Ibid.*, para. 24.12. For example, the Inter-American Commission stated that it 'agrees with the conclusions of the Truth Commission for El Salvador, which determined in its report that there was "ample proof that the Salvadoran Government has not fulfilled its duty to guarantee the human rights" of COMADRES members, and that there is "substantial proof that the competent officials of El Salvador did not conduct a complete and impartial investigation" of the attack against the COMADRES headquarters'.
[33] IAComHR, *Lucio Parada Cea et. al.* v. *El Salvador*, 27 January 1999 (No. 1/99, Case 10.480) Annual Report 1999, 27 January 1999.
[34] IACtHR, *'Las Dos Erres' Massacre* v. *Guatemala*, 24 November 2009 (Series C No. 211) para. 232. See also IACtHR, *Almonacid Arellano et. al.* v. *Chile*, 26 September 2006 (Series C No. 154) para. 150 and IACtHR, *Anzualdo Castro* v. *Peru*, 22 September 2009 (Series C No. 202) para. 180.

to build and safeguard historical memory, to clarify the events and to determine institutional, social and political responsibilities in certain periods of time of a society. The recognition of historical truths through this mechanism should not be understood as a substitute to the obligation of the State to ensure the judicial determination of individual and state responsibilities through the corresponding jurisdictional means, or as a substitute to the determination, by this Court, of any international responsibility. Both are about determinations of the truth which are complementary between themselves, since they all have their own meaning and scope, as well as particular potentialities and limits, which depend on the context in which they take place and on the cases and particular circumstances object of their analysis. In fact, the Court has granted a special value to reports of Truth Commissions as relevant evidence in the determination of the facts and of the international responsibility of the States in various cases which has been submitted before it.[35]

The Commission's general reports have also called on States to adopt this line of reasoning and implement truth commissions as part of their Inter-American human rights commitments.[36] The mutual recognition between the Commission and the Court not only strengthens their authority, but also further empowers truth commissions. Similarly, Truth Commission reports have also referred to the reports of the Inter-American Commission and to the decisions of the Inter-American Court. The Truth and Reconciliation Commission of Peru made extensive references to cases and general reports of the Inter-American system.[37] Some referred to cases decided against Peru and others were broader references to cases or reports regarding other States (e.g. Honduras, Haiti).[38]

Truth commissions continue to be implemented in several States of the Americas long after the conflict situations or authoritarian regimes have ended.[39] This suggests that consolidating democracies seek to 'revisit' the

---

[35] IACtHR, *Zambrano Vélez et. al.* v. *Ecuador*, 4 July 2007 (Series C No. 166) para. 128.

[36] The Commission indicated to El Salvador 'that compliance with the recommendations on human rights made by various international governmental agencies that have acted in the framework of the Peace Agreements would represent a major step in consolidating and improving democracy in El Salvador' (see IAComHR, 'El Salvador', Annual Report of the IACHR 1994, Chapter IV, www.cidh.oas.org/annualrep/94eng/chap.4b.htm). For further discussion see L. J. Laplante and K. Theidon, 'Truth with Consequences: Justice and Reparation in Post-Truth Commission Peru', *Human Rights Quarterly* 29 (2007) 228.

[37] Peru's *Comisión de la Verdad y Reconciliación* (Truth and Reconciliation Commission), 28 August 2003, www.cverdad.org.pe/ifinal/index.php.

[38] Peru appears to follow a similar approach to that of the Argentinean Supreme Court in the *Simon case* (see below).

[39] Ecuador's *Comisión de la Verdad para Impedir la Impunidad* (Truth Commission to Impede Impunity) (2008); Paraguay's *Comisión de Verdad y Justicia* (Truth and Justice

past in order to complete such transitional processes, even if revisiting the past is no longer a formal precondition for such a transition. Truth commissions, however, are conducive to the development of democratic societies – specifically because of their role in responding to victims' claims. Furthermore, they may prove useful in pursuing judicial action against the perpetrators of atrocities.[40]

Other rights in transitional situations

The Commission and the Court have also handled other rights under the American Convention that are not necessarily related with traditional paradigmatic transitional issues. These bodies have dealt with the right to property in the context of civil strife and official repression. In *Plan de Sánchez Massacre* v. *Guatemala* the Court reviewed the 1982 massacre perpetrated by Guatemalan military in collaboration with paramilitary patrols (so-called 'PAC') against Mayan indigenous communities. The Court recognised that the right to property recognised under Article 21 of the ACHR was affected when the population abandoned their traditional lands and their belongings due to the massacre.[41] The Court ordered the State to pay compensatory damages to each person affected by the dispossession,[42] and, additionally, to implement a housing programme for the victims.[43] These reparations generally reflect some aspects of the Peace Agreements that directly benefited some of the inhabitants of Plan de Sánchez.[44] To a certain extent, the local transitional processes in Guatemala gave the Court authority to require the State to provide individual reparations and implement collective programmes that would adequately ensure the right to property. Similarly, the Court

---

Commission) (2008); Uruguay's *Informe Final de la Comisión para la Paz* (Final Report of the Commission for Peace) (2003). As mentioned, truth commissions in Brazil and Colombia are still being debated.

[40] For example, the Peruvian Truth Commission does not preclude further judicial action against the perpetrators. This is still an ongoing process in Peru.

[41] IACtHR, *Plan de Sánchez Massacre* v. *Guatemala*, 19 November 2004 (Series C No. 116) Reparations and Costs.

[42] *Ibid.*, para. 74.

[43] The Court indicated: 'Since the inhabitants of Plan de Sánchez lost their homes as a result of the facts of this case … the Court considers that the State must implement a housing program to provide adequate housing to the surviving victims who live in that village … and who require it. The State must implement this program within five years of notification of this judgment.' *Ibid.*, para. 105.

[44] *Ibid.*, para. 38.

has recognised the right to property in other similar situations, specifically issues regarding internally displaced persons in Colombia whom are
denied their right to return home and recoup their possessions.[45]

Another critical case concerning the legacy of the transitional process
is *Aylwin Azocar et. al. v. Chile*.[46] This case referred to the Chilean constitutional provision by which General Augusto Pinochet, among others,
was designated as senator-for-life. The Commission reviewed the case in
lieu of Article 23 (the right to participate in government) and Article 24
(equal protection under the law) of the American Convention. Under very
strict scrutiny, the Commission found that such constitutional provisions
were incompatible with the Convention; thus, no level of deference was
granted to the State and its transitional process. In its dissenting opinion, Commissioner Goldman considered that a certain level of deference
should be afforded when reviewing cases under Article 23 given the great
diversity of democratic systems recognised under different constitutional
arrangements and the complex historical, political and social realities.[47]

In an alternate case, *Carranza v. Argentina*,[48] the Commission found
that the refusal of the Argentinean courts to hear the case in the merits
violated several provisions of the American Convention. Accordingly, a
former judge claimed the illegality of his dismissal as judge during the de
facto military regime. The Superior Chubut Court found the claim 'non-
justiciable' based on the inappropriate application of the 'political question doctrine'. The case was then filed in 'extraordinary appeal' before the
Supreme Court of Argentina (a recourse similar to the US Supreme Court
certiorari) and this court rejected hearing the case. The Commission contended that the lack of review of the case in the merits is a violation of the
right to an effective remedy of the Convention. Typically the Commission
does not have the authority to pass judgment on the wisdom or efficacy
of a judicial doctrine per se, unless the claim arose from a violation of
any right protected under the American Convention. The Commission
indicated that the effect of the political question doctrine has been to preclude petitioners' claims regarding decisions on the merits and attested
that such preclusion violates the Convention. The Commission further

---

[45] IACtHR, *Pueblo Bello Massacre v. Colombia*, 31 January 2006 (Series C No. 140) para.
275–276.
[46] IAComHR, *Aylwin Azocar et al. v. Chile*, 27 December 1999 (No. 137/99, Case 11.863)
Annual Report 1999.
[47] *Ibid.*
[48] IAComHR, *Carranza v. Argentina*, 30 September 1997 (No. 30/97, Case 10.087) Annual
Report 1997.

noted that the removal of magistrates by order of the competent body and in accordance with constitutional law is one thing, but the 'dismissal of a magistrate' by an illegitimate authority was quite another. Once again, the Commission exercised a very strict scrutiny on a case that emerged from illegitimate authorities under the de facto regime.

Other mechanisms of supervision

On-site visits and general reports

The Inter-American system can further engage in transitional situations through other modalities. Since its founding, the Commission was immediately called upon to intervene in situations that had transitional characteristics; whereby it mainly resorted to its political supervisory powers through on-site visits and issuing general reports on country situations. The most notable example of its early work was the Commission's deployment to the Dominican Republic in 1965. After the OAS sent an Inter-American Peace Force to that country to secure peace and democracy, the OAS Secretary General asked the Commission to perform an on-site visit to investigate alleged human rights.[49] Thereafter, the Provisional Government invited the Commission to remain in the country and to observe and report on the elections in mid-June of 1966.[50] This visit marked the most prominent and successful intervention of the Commission, which strengthened its political powers to confront large-scale violations and contribute to restoring democracy.

Later regarding El Salvador, the Commission issued in 1994 its *Special Report on the Situation of Human Rights in El Salvador*,[51] which analysed in detail the evolving situation of its human rights while national negotiations and agreements were being finalised.[52] The following year, the Commission released its general report on El Salvador as a follow-up mechanism to the Special Report, which reiterated the State's duty to investigate and punish those responsible for the atrocities.[53] The report further indicated that the transition to a peaceful democracy would

[49] Goldman, 'History and Action', 870.
[50] *Ibid.*
[51] IAComHR, 'Report on the Situation of Human Rights in El Salvador', 11 February 1994, www.cidh.oas.org/countryrep/ElSalvador94eng/toc.htm.
[52] The Commission indicated in such report, among other matters, that the Amnesty Law was incompatible with the American Convention, which created a legal impasse that still exists.
[53] IAComHR, 'El Salvador'.

require more than just peace agreements. As such, the report emphasised critical measures like the implementation of land reform and the
improvement of public security to prevent possible spikes in crime stemming from demobilised paramilitary operatives (which, unfortunately,
proved to be true in subsequent years).

The Commission produced another emblematic report in 1980 with
regards to the human rights situation in Argentina.[54] After performing
an on-site visit to Argentina in September 1979, the Commission documented the human rights situation for its report. Up to that point, there
was no official confirmation that the de facto regime was engaged in a
systematic practice of forced disappearances of persons, among other
very serious violations of human rights. The report served as an official
confirmation of the existing situation and triggered international action
led by the US Carter administration. Soon after, forced disappearance
of persons ceased, but the official story would mark the long transitional
process that presently continues with the prosecution of several officials after the Supreme Court declared the amnesty unconstitutional.
The evidence gathered during on-site visits is crucial in establishing
core indicators on patterns and practices of massive and gross violations that may subsequently be used in ascertaining other cases emerging from similar situations. Arguably, such findings could prove to be
relevant even for other international adjudicatory mechanisms, such
as the International Criminal Tribunal, whereby the Statute of Rome
stipulates that crimes against humanity must show an existence of a
'systematic' element in the prosecutable offence. The application of such
indicators remains to be tested in other international forums that are
allowed jurisdiction over certain cases that emanate from the States of
the Americas.

The Commission also had an influential role in Peru during its transition from the Fujimori regime.[55] The Commission released a pivotal special report in 2000, as a result of an on-site visit performed in 1998, which
played a key role in documenting how the regime progressively destroyed
the Peruvian rule of law. The Report was released during the General
Assembly and proved instrumental in triggering collective action at the
OAS, which subsequently influenced Fujimori's decision to resign.[56]

---

[54] IAComHR, 'Report on the Situation of Human Rights in Argentina', 11 April 1980, www.
cidh.oas.org/countryrep/Argentina80eng/toc.htm.
[55] Goldman, 'History and Action', 856–887.
[56] *Ibid.*, 878.

The Court and the Commission have also played a very interesting and creative role regarding the process currently taking place in Colombia under the so-called *Ley Justicia y Paz* (Peace and Justice Law). The Commission has been supervising the implementation of the OEA-MAPP agreement signed between the OAS and the Government of Colombia[57] regarding the demobilisation process of paramilitary groups in Colombia. These groups are accused of having committed war crimes and crimes against humanity. The Commission's supervisory role seeks to guarantee that measures adopted in the framework of OAS-MAPP do not violate Inter-American human rights standards. As such, the Commission has issued several reports raising awareness of the potential violations of the American Convention that may occur due to the demobilisation process; in particular, the negative effects that may ensue during the pursuit and punishment of perpetrators as well as the implementation of other measures to efficiently repair victims.[58]

The Commission's supervisory role with respect to transitions, at first, was marginal – as evident in Argentina. In subsequent cases, like those in Peru, their supervisory role developed substantially. Currently, this role has gained much visibility and importance in settings where transitional processes are still taking place, like in Colombia. This could be attributed, among other factors, to the fact that the Inter-American Court strengthened its jurisdiction through its proactive jurisprudence, which has increased awareness of its powers and mechanisms of redress to individuals in many countries.

Interim measures and friendly settlements

The Commission may adopt preventive measures or protective 'precautionary measures in serious and urgent cases to prevent irreparable harm to persons'. The Court can issue 'provisional measures' in similar circumstances, to preserve the status quo or prevent a serious violation

---

[57] Mission to Support the Peace Process in Colombia, OEA-MAPP agreement, signed on 23 January 2004, www.mapp-oea.org. The agreement creates an OAS Mission in Colombia of the demobilisation efforts.

[58] This matter created much tension within the OAS regarding how international institutions should contribute in such situations. For instance, the OAS was very willing to engage in Colombia by signing an agreement to create a special mission (OAS MAPP) to accompany the demobilisation process. Yet, it took civil society to pressure the OAS to include the Inter-American Commission in the agreement as a guarantor to ensure that human rights standards would be respected.

from occurring. Due to their nature, these interim measures allow the Commission and the Court to react immediately to an event occurring in the jurisdiction of a State. Therefore, in theory, such measures are applicable in situations whereby certain national policies directed to secure a transitional process may seriously infringe on basic rights.[59] The System has yet to issue interim measures in such a scenario; possibly because, inter alia, the Court found that it should refrain from issuing provisional measures if it implies a prejudgment on the merits of a case.[60]

Another important aspect of the proceedings before the Commission and the Court is the possibility of reaching a friendly settlement. This friendly settlement process is intended to give the parties the opportunity to settle through negotiation, thus closing the case in advance. The process is structured in a manner that gives the parties considerable latitude to present proposals for a solution without it implicating the acceptance of responsibility or other legal concessions. It may be characterised as a form of 'political space' for negotiation that allows the parties to reach an agreement in which the State's consent is offered without imposing external views in very complex local political environments, such as those related with transitional issues. For example, in the *Compliance Agreement* case (*Carmelo Soria* v. *Chile*),[61] the parties were allowed to determine how a previous decision of the Commission should be implemented in their case. The family of Mr Soria, who disappeared during the dictatorship while he was an international officer for CELADE/ECLAC (an international organisation part of the UN System), agreed to terminate a civil suit filed before national courts. The State agreed to compensate the family (1.5 million dollars), and make public statements recognising the violation, including a monument in remembrance of Mr Soria in Santiago, Chile. Furthermore, the State agreed to request the judiciary to reopen the criminal case against the perpetrators of the crime.

Similarly, in *Aguiar de Lapaco* v. *Argentina*[62] the State agreed to recognise that the right to truth compelled the authorities to exhaust all available means to determine the whereabouts of Alejandra Lapaco who

---

[59] This could be the hypothetical situation of imminent adoption of a final decision by a national tribunal that could have the absolute effect of preventing investigation and prosecution of a perpetrator of serious human rights violations.

[60] IACtHR, *Constitutional Court* v. *Peru Case*, 7 April 2000, para. 12.

[61] IAComHR, *Compliance Agreement (Soria Espinoza* v. *Chile)*, 6 March 2003 (No. 19/03, Case 11.725) Annual Report 2003.

[62] IAComHR, *Aguiar de Lapaco* v. *Argentina*, 29 February 2000 (No. 21/00, Case 12.059) Annual Report 2000.

disappeared in 1977. Furthermore, the State agreed to adopt legislation that would federalise all criminal cases that occurred before 1983 and would establish an ad hoc group of prosecutors dedicated to establish the whereabouts of disappeared persons. Evidently the friendly settlement went beyond the reparations required in the specific case and was able to trigger Argentina's consent to adopt measures to adequately deal with all other similar cases.

Narrow deference to States on gross and systematic violations of human rights

The Inter-American system has been very cautious in granting States some level of deference when exercising its supervisory functions, especially in situations of gross and massive violations of human rights. The Court has refused to develop any doctrine that may allow States a *margin of appreciation* in specific cases.[63] In fact, since the landmark *Velasquez-Rodríguez* case, the Court expanded its evidentiary powers in cases dealing with victims of gross and systematic violations, such as forced disappearance of persons.[64] This tribunal has acted with deliberate care in confronting perverse practices that could, by eliminating any vestige of evidence in a case, defeat international supervision. Arguably, this necessarily requires restricting the latitude that may otherwise be afforded to States under other less serious circumstances.

The Commission has followed a similar approach in cases claiming serious violations of core rights. But unlike the Court, it has developed a Fourth Instance Formula that defers on decisions of national tribunals in cases that do not involve violations of the rights to life, personal integrity and non-discrimination, among other serious violations.[65] Additionally, the Commission has resorted to its political powers, such as the possibility of issuing reports regarding the general human rights situation of a country, to confront gross and systematic violations of human rights.

---

[63] The Court has only referred to such notion in Advisory Opinion OC-4/84 when dealing with naturalisation provision in Costa Rica's Constitution, but has not subsequently applied such notion in later opinions. (See *Proposed Amendments of the Naturalization Provisions of the Constitution of Costa Rica*, 19 January 1984, IACtHR, Series A No. 4, Advisory Opinion OC-4/84, para. 58).

[64] IACtHR, *Velazquez-Rodriguez v. Honduras*, 29 July 1988 (Series C No. 4).

[65] See D. Rodríguez-Pinzón, 'The "Victim" Requirement, the Fourth Instance Formula and the Notion of "Person" in the Individual Complaint Procedure of the Inter-American Human Rights System', *ILSA Journal of International and Comparative Law* 7 (2001) 373 (discussing in detail the Fourth Instance Formula).

These powers have allowed the Commission to closely follow evolving transitional processes almost in 'real time', which ordinarily is one of the limitations of case law supervision. Therefore, it affords a certain degree of latitude to States in developing national political and legal processes; while simultaneously supervising over the processes taking note of any indicators that may jeopardise or violate Inter-American standards.

In 1992, Argentina and Uruguay amnesty decisions clearly suggested that the Commission would have little deference with States when assessing the compatibility of such amnesty laws with the regional human rights instruments. The States themselves advanced the argument that the Commission should consider that internationally recognised rights might be subject to permissible restrictions; that such legitimate laws should pursue a valid aim (national reconciliation and the return to democracy) and that States should be deferred on matters related to 'the political context of the reconciliation'.[66] The Commission rejected such argument and strictly applied the notion that the 'effects' of any national law on the rights of victims was the issue assessed, which implicitly suggests that no deference is granted in such situations. The Commission confirmed this approach in subsequent amnesty cases, as did the Court in the *Barrios Altos* case.[67]

Impact of the Inter-American system

The Inter-American system has come a long way since the creation of the Commission in 1959. During the first years of existence, the States of the Americas gave little recognition to the Commission. Many governments did not engage with the Commission or even respond to its communications. However, it increasingly gained legitimacy throughout the region, especially in democratic environments, such as democratic States or civil society advocates on democracy. Similarly, the Inter-American Court established in 1980 was only able to adjudicate its first case by the end of that decade and has slowly been able to consolidate its jurisdiction with a steady flow of cases. Its judicial nature has positioned this organ as an important reference for national tribunals of Latin-American countries.[68]

---

[66] *Hugo Leonardo de los Santos Mendoza et al. v. Uruguay*, para. 22.
[67] See text accompanying notes 10–28 above.
[68] The jurisdiction of the Court has been accepted by twenty-two State Parties to the American Convention, most of them from Latin America. In some instances, the Commission and the Court have played the role of ultimate safeguards of democracy in the face of authoritarian measures that threatened to undermine the rule of law. A clear

It is not possible to establish clear lines of direct and unique impact of the Inter-American system and national transitional processes. There are many variables that interact in such situations, which mutually reinforce their impact. However, it is possible to identify several modalities of interaction through, for example, the legal references among tribunals to their mutual opinions or the adoption of legislation that expedites implementation of international decisions.

A first interesting example is the multiple effects that the robust body of amnesty case law has had in the Americas. In Argentina a first notable interaction between the Commission's cases and the national process could be seen in the immediate effect that the simple act of filing an international petition before this body had. The Commission indicated in *Alicia Consuelo Herrera et. al. v. Argentina* that two executive decrees 'benefited only a certain number of victims who, after having filed an action for economic compensation – without success – in the domestic courts, filed a complaint with the Commission'.[69] These modest measures are significant in showing how the mere fact of submitting an international complaint before the Commission can trigger actions by the national authorities that, in this case, benefited several victims that were being denied justice in the national level. The strong presence of the Inter-American system may be an important variable in the national equation when 'negotiating' the rights of individuals.

Another very important effect is the increasingly intense and implicit dialogue between the Inter-American system and the national tribunals. After most countries in the Americas transitioned into democratic systems, with precarious separation of powers and functional judiciaries, national tribunals naturally assumed the role of guarantors of individual rights and freedoms. This created an immediate 'harmonic resonance' between these national courts and the international adjudicatory jurisdiction of the Commission and the Court.

This could explain, to a certain extent, why the Supreme Court of Argentina in 2005 issued its historic decision by which it declared the unconstitutionality of amnesty laws.[70] One of the most significant aspects

example occurred in Peru during the Fujimori regime in which the Inter-American system protected the Constitutional Court of that country which was facing a direct threat from the executive branch (IACtHR, *Constitutional Court* v. *Peru*, 31 January 2001 (Series C No. 71)).

[69] *Herrera et al.* v. *Argentina*, para. 47.

[70] Corte Suprema de Justicia de la Nación (Supreme Court of Argentina), S. 1767, XXXVIII Recurso de Hecho, *Simon, Julio Hector y Otros*, s/ privación ilegitima de la libertad, etc. causa 17.768 (14 June 2005).

of that decision was the fact that the tribunal relied, not only on the Commission's 1992 decision, but also more importantly on the *Barrios Altos* case which dealt with Peru's amnesty.[71] In short, the Supreme Court of Argentina considered that the standard set by the Inter-American Court had practical effects beyond the *Barrios Altos* case and that all State Parties to the American Convention were bound to apply such standards in their domestic systems.

This approach, of course, has created a ripple effect that is significant in Colombia's constitutional system. Colombia's Constitutional Court had previously recognised the notion of the 'constitutional block' that 'domesticates' the human rights treaties of which it is a State Party and incorporates them into the Colombian Constitution. In other words, the standards set by the Inter-American Court have constitutional status in that country. Therefore, the domestic Colombian political and legal institutions no longer control part of their constitutional standard setting process. This may also explain why it was not possible for Colombia to craft a *Ley de Justicia y Paz* that was stereotypical of other amnesty laws.[72]

In Colombia, the effects of applying the Inter-American system's very strict standards to the demobilisation process of the paramilitary groups remain to be seen. Until now, the process continues under the safeguards incorporated by the Constitutional Court to the *Ley de Justicia y Paz*. However, criticism from nongovernmental organisations, among others, as well as the end of President Uribe's administration may modify the dynamics of such process.

Another important development relevant to situations where impunity reigns, particularly situations of gross violations of human rights, is the emergence of national legislation that gives effect to the decisions

---

[71] International law establishes that the decisions of tribunals such as those of the Inter-American Court do not have *erga omnes* effect, and are only binding upon the parties to the case. However, the Argentinean Supreme Court has gone beyond this purely formalistic analysis to understand further the nature and purpose of an international human rights regime.

[72] Corte Constitucional de Colombia, sala plena (Constitutional Court of Colombia), C-370 del 2006, 18 May 2006. This decision regarding the Constitutionality of the *Ley de Justicia y Paz* (Justice and Peace Law) by the Constitutional Court of Colombia makes specific references to several decisions of the Inter-American Court, including the *Barrios Altos* case, among many others, to articulate the main rationale of the decision regarding obligation to investigate and prosecute perpetrators and provide for adequate reparations for the victims. This decision, in practice, incorporated international human rights standards into the interpretation of the Law with the intent of adequately demobilising perpetrators of human rights and war crimes.

of international human rights organs at the national level. Colombia has moved to implement national legislation conducive to human rights standards and international decisions. The Constitutional Court of Colombia issued a decision in 2003 (C-04/03) that triggered the reformation of the Criminal Procedural Code. The Code was amended to allow reopening cases in which perpetrators of gross abuses had been unlawfully acquitted, so long as the acquittal is based on a declaration of international responsibility of Colombia in a case before the Inter-American Commission or Court. Notably, this mechanism severely limited one of the modalities used by perpetrators seeking to shield themselves from further criminal prosecutions.[73] Similarly, Peru adopted Law 27775 of 27 June 2002 that allows decisions of the Inter-American Court, with respect to compensation for victims and other forms of reparations, to be implemented, which would presumably include reopening cases or adopting measures that the Court requested in its reparatory orders.

The extradition and prosecution of former Peruvian President Alberto Fujimori is another most significant event that demonstrates how the Inter-American system has served as a basis to bring to justice the leading perpetrators of atrocities in the framework of broad transitional process to democracy. The Peruvian authorities' request that President Fujimori be extradited from Chile to Peru was grounded on national criminal cases as well as the decisions of the Inter-American system, especially the *Barrios Altos* and *Cantuta* cases of the Inter-American Court. The Chilean Supreme Court had few options given the fact that both Chile and Peru are State Parties to the American Convention. The highest jurisdictional organ under the Convention had already rendered a decision regarding those cases and the extradition was the only action possible so that Peru could comply with the order of the Court to prosecute those responsible. Soon after the extradition, the Peruvian Courts convicted Fujimori on 17 April 2009 in what became one of the most pivotal decisions in contemporary human rights law in the fight against impunity in the Americas.[74] Peru continues to be an evolving democracy and a clear example of how accountability for serious violations of human rights is an important part of a solid transition to the rule of law.

---

[73] Colombia also adopted Law 288 of 1996 that requires the implementation of an expeditious national compensatory mechanism to ensure that decisions of the Commission with respect to compensating victims are enforced.

[74] Fujimori case: 'Sentencia de la Sala Penal Especial en el Expediente N° AV 19–2001 (acumulado), del siete de abril de 2009. Casos Barrios Altos, La Cantuta y sótanos SIE.'

Reparations for gross violations

The reparations afforded by the Court and the Commission also contributes to the significant development of the system. This is an area in which the Commission and especially the Court have shown little deference with States when redressing gross and systematic violations of human rights. The detailed orders on compensatory damages, specifically reparatory measures of broader legal, social and political impact, have compelled States to adopt measures that, in many instances, are an integral part of the national transition to democracy.[75]

The Commission has also developed a similar approach in seeking reparations in certain cases regarding serious violations of human rights, but it is not yet a uniform practice. One notable example is the *Maria Maia da Penha* v. *Brazil* case, whereby the Commission ordered the State to adopt very specific remedial measures to prosecute perpetrators of violence against women and implement State policies that strengthen judicial proceedings and police capacity in order to prevent domestic violence.[76]

---

[75] See, for example, *Constitutional Court* v. *Peru*, analysing the impact that the *Barrios Altos* and *Cantuta* cases had in Peru's prosecution of former President Alberto Fujimori.

[76] The Commission recommended to the Brazilian State that: '1. Complete, rapidly and effectively, criminal proceedings against the person responsible for the assault and attempted murder of Mrs. Maria da Penha Fernandes Maia. 2. In addition, conduct a serious, impartial, and exhaustive investigation to determine responsibility for the irregularities or unwarranted delays that prevented rapid and effective prosecution of the perpetrator, and implement the appropriate administrative, legislative, and judicial measures. 3. Adopt, without prejudice to possible civil proceedings against the perpetrator, the measures necessary for the State to grant the victim appropriate symbolic and actual compensation for the violence established herein, in particular for its failure to provide rapid and effective remedies, for the impunity that has surrounded the case for more than 15 years, and for making it impossible, as a result of that delay, to institute timely proceedings for redress and compensation in the civil sphere. 4. Continue and expand the reform process that will put an end to the condoning by the State of domestic violence against women in Brazil and discrimination in the handling thereof. In particular, the Commission recommends: a. Measures to train and raise the awareness of officials of the judiciary and specialised police so that they may understand the importance of not condoning domestic violence. b. The simplification of criminal judicial proceedings so that the time taken for proceedings can be reduced, without affecting the rights and guarantees related to due process. c. The establishment of mechanisms that serve as alternatives to judicial mechanisms, which resolve domestic conflict in a prompt and effective manner and create awareness regarding its serious nature and associated criminal consequences. d. An increase in the number of special police stations to address the rights of women and to provide them with the special resources needed for the effective processing and investigation of all complaints related to domestic violence, as well as resources and assistance from the Office of the Public Prosecutor in preparing their judicial reports. e. The inclusion in teaching curriculums of units aimed at providing an understanding of the importance of respecting

Colombia provides the most relevant examples of the far-reaching implications that cases brought to the Inter-American system have in national transitional processes given that it is one of the few countries in the Americas in which these types of violations still persist. The case of Colombia allows for some practical insight on how the Inter-American human rights mechanisms try to respond to challenges posed by gross and systematic human rights violations. Specifically, it can help us illustrate how the Inter-American Commission and the Court have dealt with the issue of reparations when facing the massacres perpetrated by the State or its proxies. Designing adequate reparations for gross and systematic violations can be a particularly difficult task in contemporary international law, and some useful lessons can be extracted from the Inter-American experience in confronting the current situation in Colombia. These lessons are especially important for transitional situations whereby the main challenge is to craft national measures in a lawful manner when dealing with war crimes and crimes against humanity.

The Inter-American system's first examples of reparations, implemented in Colombia during the late 1990s, demonstrates the practice that is later reflected in the jurisprudence of the Inter-American Court in cases against that country. The experience of the Commission and the Court regarding the Colombian 'massacre cases' appears to suggest that there is a direct relationship between the first Colombian cases during the 1990s Commission proceedings and the judgments of the Inter-American Court regarding Colombia in the last decade.[77] While not necessarily a deliberate relationship, the Commission's cases may have allowed the Court to explore the reparatory measures and the remedies that Colombian institutions were able or willing to accept regarding potential reparations in these types of cases.

In the 1990s, under the Commission's auspices, very significant events occurred in the context of several friendly settlement discussions in cases of massacres perpetrated by Colombian state agents. Among the

women and their rights recognised in the Convention of Belém do Pará, as well as the handling of domestic conflict' (IAComHR, *Maria da Penha* v. *Brazil*, 16 April 2001 (No. 54/01, Case No. 12.051) Annual Report 2000).

[77] This suggests that there is a relationship between the initial steps taken by the Commission in the 1990s and the latest cases of the Court. The 'voluntariness' of friendly settlement procedures enables the State to negotiate with the petitioners regarding the possibility of agreeing to provide extensive reparations, under the auspices of the Commission. Consequently, the State was able to accept appropriate and progressive reparations, which would later be used and expanded by the Court in its own judicial decisions.

most notable cases, *'Los Uvos' Massacre* v. *Colombia*,[78] *'Caloto' Massacre* v. *Colombia*[79] and *Villatina Massacre* v. *Colombia*[80] were all being processed in the individual complaint system of the Commission. In a hearing held in 1995, the government agreed to initiate friendly settlement discussions for those events.[81] The government indicated its willingness to adopt several types of reparations seeking to remedy these egregious human rights violations. As part of those agreements, on 29 July 1998, Colombia's President, Ernesto Samper, publicly stated that government forces were internationally responsible under the American Convention for the violations committed in the massacres of *Los Uvos*, *Caloto* and *Villatina*. This landmark event had structural importance in Colombia with extensive political and social repercussions. A significant effect, among other critical outcomes, was the validation of human rights norms as a legitimate issue and a positive force within the conflict in Colombia. The public acknowledgment of Colombia's President declaring that, in lieu of international laws, the actions by the Colombian security forces violated basic human rights, significantly empowered an important constituency of human rights defenders and victims, among other actors.[82]

Subsequently, the Commission filed the following massacre cases against Colombia before the Inter-American Court:[83] *Mapiripan Massacre*

---

[78] IAComHR, *Los Uvos Massacre* v. *Colombia*, 13 April 2000 (No. 35/00, Case 11.020) Annual Reports 1999, para. 446.

[79] IAComHR, *Caloto Massacre* v. *Colombia*, 13 April 2000 (No. 36/00, Case 11.101) Annual Reports 1999.

[80] IAComHR, *Villatina Massacre* v. *Colombia*, 27 October 2005, Friendly Settlement (No. 105/05, Case 11.141) Annual Reports 2005.

[81] The friendly settlement in the *Villatina Massacre* case was successful, however, eventually failed in the *Los Uvos Massacre* case because of a lack of full compliance with the agreement – particularly regarding the issues of prosecuting those responsible.

[82] It is worth mentioning that the government, in the context of the mentioned massacre cases, also agreed to several other types of reparatory measures. These included, among others, compensating the victims, establishing symbolic reparations, such as monuments and plaques in public places in remembrance of the massacres, as well as 'formulating or implementing, as appropriate, the pending social compensation projects for attending to the displaced families and individuals, health, education, electric power, the Piedrasentada – Los Uvos road, and job creation' (*Los Uvos Massacre* v. *Colombia*, para. 446, quoting the Report of the Coordinating Committee for following up on the recommendations of the *Comité de Impulso* for the incidents of *Los Uvos*, *Caloto* and *Villatina*). All these 'enhanced' reparatory measures were developed in the context of international and national negotiations in cases pending before the Commission.

[83] IACtHR, *Las Palmeras* v. *Colombia*, 6 December 2001 (Series C No. 90) was the first massacre case filed before the Court against Colombia. This case had very tentative results in

v. *Colombia*;[84] *19 Tradesmen* v. *Colombia*;[85] *Pueblo Bello Massacre* v. *Colombia*;[86] *Ituango Massacres* v. *Colombia*[87] and *Rochela Massacre* v. *Colombia*.[88] These cases are dramatic examples where the Court has been required to provide judicial redress for massive violations of the most basic rights. The reparations afforded in those cases appear to reflect the earlier work of the Commission in the other Colombian massacres.[89]

As part of such reparations, in addition to monetary compensation, the Court in all the massacre cases mentioned reaffirmed the duty to investigate, prosecute and punish perpetrators of gross and systematic violations of human rights. The Inter-American system is especially oriented to confront impunity for serious violations. The system has consistently ordered States to prosecute and punish those responsible for massacres and other crimes against humanity and/or war crimes. As noted before, the Court has declared that domestic legislation, such as amnesties or a statute of limitations, cannot be an obstacle for prosecuting perpetrators of serious human rights violations.

Another important notion that has significant implications regarding reparations in certain cases, in particular, with respect to reparatory modalities, such as 'guarantees of non-repetition' as well as 'satisfaction', is the right to truth.[90] In this regard it is important to

---

many legal questions, including reparations, and does not reflect the settled practice that the Court subsequently established in other cases.

[84] IACtHR, *Mapiripan Massacre* v. *Colombia*, 7 March 2005, Preliminary Objections (Series C No. 122).

[85] IACtHR, *19 Tradesmen* v. *Colombia*, 5 July 2004 (Series C No. 109).

[86] IACtHR, *Pueblo Bello Massacre* v. *Colombia*, 25 November 2006 (Series C No. 159).

[87] IACtHR, *Ituango Massacres* v. *Colombia*, 1 July 2006 (Series C No. 148).

[88] IACtHR, *Rochela Massacre* v. *Colombia*, 11 May 2007 (Series C No. 163).

[89] The Court continues to monitor Colombia's compliance with the reparation orders in several cases, thus implies an ongoing dialogue with the State, the victims and the Commission in issues that also have national relevance in the local negotiations to demobilise the paramilitary groups (IACtHR, *Las Palmeras* v. *Colombia*, 3 January 2010, Monitoring Compliance with Judgment, available only in Spanish at www.corteidh.or.cr).

[90] The duty to investigate serious violations necessarily implies the right of the victims and their relatives to know what happened. The right to truth can be adequately addressed in different ways: the criminal investigation in a case can shed light about what really occurred; the State can establish ad hoc truth commissions with a mandate to find the truth in specific cases or specific periods of time in the history of a country; other judicial mechanisms could play such a role, as may happen with civil liability remedies and the State can acknowledge the truth publicly through official statements, monuments or plaques. Additionally, the decisions of both the Court and the Commission can in and of themselves play this role by officially recognising violations.

recall *Mapiripan Massacre* v. *Colombia*.[91] This case addressed the forced disappearance of persons in the framework of these horrible massacres. In the reparations judgment, the Court ordered the state of Colombia to publish extensively, on television, in newspapers, and on radio, information about the case and the need to find other persons that were affected so that they could benefit from the reparations ordered. This is significant because, even though the Court focused the decision on forty-nine victims that were identified then, it allowed subsequent identification of additional victims. The Court specifically ordered the State to take certain measures to establish the whereabouts of the disappeared persons, including the identification of victims by using DNA testing.

There have also been some important measures related to social and institutional reparations in the framework of these cases. For example, forced displacement of persons is one of the most dramatic human rights situations in Colombia. In this regard, the Court has ordered that the State implement special measures to secure adequate housing programmes and ensure the safe and dignified return of individuals or families displaced by the massacres (entire villages were emptied). This is another structural problem that is intrinsically linked with the internal armed conflict; therefore, such measures will, in all likelihood, always be part of Colombia's transitional processes.

Finally, regarding the notion of 'compensation' with respect to the reparations ordered by the Court, there is pending controversy as to the nature of such compensation in several massacre cases. According to the International Law Commission's (ILC) 'Articles on Responsibility of States for International Wrongful Acts',[92] reparations in international law mainly seek restitution, compensation and satisfaction. The compensation required, according to the ILC articles, must strictly respond to the notion of 'proportionality'. The ILC rejected the idea of non-proportional reparations even though its draft articles considered the possibility that so-called 'international crimes' of States could give rise to non-proportional reparations and that certain measures could be the

---

[91] See *Mapiripan Massacre* v. *Colombia*.
[92] Articles on Responsibility of States for Internationally Wrongful Acts, 2001, GA Res 56/83, Annex, UN Doc. A/56/10, 12 December 2001, http://untreaty.un.org/ilc/texts/instruments/English/draft%20articles/9_6_2001.pdf.

equivalent of 'punitive' damages.[93] The Inter-American Court has not explicitly recognised 'punitive' damages.[94]

However, the Court's assessment of compensation in the Colombian cases appears to have taken into account the grave and systematic nature of these violations and imposes cumbersome payment amounts in favour of the victims. It is, of course, difficult to determine what would be proportional compensation in cases of massacres and massive forced disappearances and when such compensation should be 'punitive'. Notably, when confronting gross and systematic violations, reason and justice will leave no alternative for the international community and international human rights bodies but to increasingly recognise the need for appropriate 'enhanced' compensation in these types of cases.

Conclusions

The Commission and the Court have played an important role in the fight against impunity for gross violations of human rights. Their impact on transitional processes has been significant, particularly in facilitating the crafting of remedies for victims, the development of institutional transformations and the implementation of efficient mechanisms to prosecute perpetrators of human rights atrocities. Moreover, their broad powers have enabled them to respond to transitional situations in extraordinary ways. The Commission's political supervisory mechanisms, for instance, enable it to address transitional processes in 'real time' with events currently occurring in a given State. As noted, being able to supervise cases in real time has significant importance in seeking to prevent human rights violations. Likewise, the idiosyncratic methods of both organs are apparent in their ability to resort to individual complaints and adjudicatory jurisdiction in order to review legal implications of national measures.

Although the Inter-American system has taken the lead in developing these processes, remarkably, national tribunals have assumed much of this responsibility and are currently some of the most notable actors in the consolidation and expansion of Inter-American human rights law. Such achievements would have been impossible without the active and

---

[93] Draft Articles on State Responsibility With Commentaries Thereto Adopted by the International Law Commission in First Reading, January 1997, arts. 45, 51–52, www.untreaty.un.org/ilc/texts/instruments/english/commentaries/9_6_1996.pdf.

[94] See *Mapiripan Massacre* v. *Colombia* (Trindade, A., concurring) (asserting the need to examine this notion of punitive damages in the jurisprudence of the Court).

focused work of non-governmental organisations, associations of victims, journalists and other democratic actors that have consistently challenged these institutions, forcing them to embrace their historic role.

To a certain extent, the recent history of the Americas shows us that many of the transitional processes are still, after decades of the initial steps, coming to terms with a tragic past. As democratic values consolidate in many of these societies, they are realising that such transition will only be achieved when accountability for unspeakable crimes is accomplished. Victims, as part of such societies, have found in these vibrant democratic values, embodied in the decisions of national courts or international bodies, that they have the right to claim justice. Not only for their loved ones, but also for the societies they live in. Only then those that exercise power will realise that justice has a long arm. Only then we will be able to say 'Nunca Más'.

Bibliography

Duffy, G., 'Brazil Truth Commission Arouses Military Opposition', *BBC* (London: 11 January 2010). Available at: news.bbc.co.uk/2/hi/8451109.stm.

Goldman, R. K., 'History and Action: The Inter-American Human Rights System and the Role of the Inter-American Commission', *Human Rights Quarterly* 31 (2009) 856.

Human Rights Watch, *Paramilitaries' Heirs: The New Face of Violence in Colombia*, 3 February 2010. Available at: www.hrw.org/node/88060.

Laplante, L. J. and Theidon, K., 'Truth with Consequences: Justice and Reparation in Post-Truth Commission Peru', *Human Rights Quarterly* 29 (2007) 228.

Rodríguez-Pinzón, D., 'The "Victim" Requirement, the Fourth Instance Formula and the Notion of "Person" in the Individual Complaint Procedure of the Inter-American Human Rights System', *ILSA Journal of International and Comparative Law* 7 (2001) 373.

Tittemore, B. D., 'Ending Impunity in the Americas: The Role of the Inter-American Human Rights System in Advancing Accountability for Serious Crimes Under International Law', *SouthWestern Journal of Law and Trade in the Americas* 12 (2006) 429.

11

The 'transitional' jurisprudence of the African Commission on Human and Peoples' Rights

GINA BEKKER

Introduction

The 1990s saw a wave of protests sweep across the African continent in the wake of the fall of the Soviet Union, ultimately leading to substantial political reforms, including the holding in many instances of the first competitive elections in decades and the installation of democratic or nominally democratic regimes in almost half of the fifty-three member states of the Organisation of African Unity (OAU).[1] Simultaneous to these events, the African Commission on Human and Peoples' Rights (the African Commission), which started operating in 1987 and which has a broad mandate in terms of the African Charter on Human and Peoples' Rights (the African Charter) to promote as well as protect human rights on the continent, began to receive its first cases.[2] This chapter considers the manner in which the African Commission has dealt with cases involving countries in conflict or transition as well as the extent to which the

Gina Bekker is Lecturer in Law, University of Ulster. This chapter was finalised in August 2010. As such, it does not take into account the country specific resolutions adopted by the African Commission at its 9th Extra-ordinary Session in February/March 2011 in respect of the human rights situation in Algeria, Egypt, Libya or Tunisia or the more general resolution on Electoral Processes and Participatory Governance in Africa. It also does not deal with Application No. 004/2011: African Commission on *Human and Peoples' Rights* v. *Great Socialist People's Libyan Arab Jamahiriya*, in which the African Court ordered provisional measures against Libya in light of the violent response by the authorities to calls for reform.

[1] For a comprehensive overview of regime change on the continent between 1989 and 1994, see M. Bratton and N. Van de Walle, *Democratic Experiments in Africa: Regime Transitions in Comparative Perspective* (Cambridge University Press, 1997). Note that with the adoption of the Constitutive Act of the African Union in July 2000 by the Assembly of Heads of State and Government of the OAU and the ratification of the instrument by two-thirds of the member states of the OAU less than a year later, the Organisation of African Unity ceased to exist and was replaced by the African Union.

[2] The Commission's mandate is detailed in Article 45 of the African Charter.

Commission has either in its case law or in terms of its promotional mandate addressed 'transitional' issues. The degree to which domestic actors have resorted to the African Charter and the jurisprudence of the African Commission in order to advance reform in situations of conflict or transition will also be considered. In the final instance, the potential of the newly created African Court on Human and Peoples' Rights to address such matters, particularly in light of developments which would have the jurisdiction of the Court expanded to include the trying of international crimes such as genocide, war crimes and crimes against humanity, will also be examined.

The anatomy of the African human rights system

The African human rights system formally came into being in 1981 with the adoption by the Assembly of Heads of State and Government of the OAU of the African Charter.[3] This instrument remained the sole human rights treaty within the framework of the OAU for almost a decade, until the adoption in 1990 of the African Charter on the Rights and Welfare of the Child[4] as a complementary instrument to the United Nations Convention on the Rights of the Child. Subsequently, the OAU adopted a Protocol to the African Charter on Human and Peoples' Rights on the Establishment of an African Court on Human and Peoples' Rights (the Protocol Establishing an African Court). Three years after the adoption of the Constitutive Act of the African Union of 2000,[5] which transformed the OAU into the African Union (AU), a further treaty was adopted, namely the Protocol to the African Charter on Human and Peoples' Rights on the Rights of Women in Africa,[6] to augment the provisions of the African Charter in respect of women.

Whilst the vast majority of the provisions contained in the African Charter, in particular the catalogue of civil and political rights, mirror those found in other human rights instruments such as the Universal Declaration on Human Rights and the two International Covenants, as well as the European and American Conventions on Human Rights, there

---

[3] See OAU/CAB/LEG/67/3/Rev 5, 17 June 1981, 1520 UNTS 217.
[4] The African Charter on the Rights and Welfare of the Child, CAB/LEG/24.9/49, July 1990, reprinted in C. Heyns (ed.), *Human Rights Law in Africa* (The Hague: Kluwer Law International, 2004) 143.
[5] CAB/LEG/23.15, 11 July 2000, 2158 UNTS 3.
[6] CAB/LEG/66.6, 11 July 2003, available at: www.africa-union.org/root/au/Documents/ Treaties/Text/Protocol%20on%20the%20Rights%20of%20Women.pdf.

are nonetheless distinct differences, a number of which have the potential to influence the manner in which transitions are approached.[7] The two features most often singled out as being unique to the African human rights system are the incorporation of individual duties and peoples' rights in the Charter.[8] In this regard, peoples' rights, which may be said to be reflective of an African conception of rights with an emphasis on the community as opposed to the atomised individual, could arguably be used to balance interests of the individual for redress against the broader interests of the community in a transitional scenario.[9] The notion of peoples' rights can also be used as occurred in the case of *Sudan Human Rights Organisation and Centre on Housing Rights and Evictions* v. *the Sudan*,[10] to argue for an acceptance of diversity in societies where difference is the cause of conflict. A situation may also be imagined in which individual duties to family, community, society and the state may be utilised in an attempt to assist the state in the difficult transitional period, though from the outset, the potential dangers inherent in an overemphasis on duties to the exclusion of

---

[7] The Charter recognises the following civil and political rights: the prohibition of discrimination (Article 2); equality (Article 3); bodily integrity and the right to life (Article 4); dignity and prohibition against all forms of exploitation and degradation including slavery and torture and inhuman treatment (Article 5); liberty and security of the person (Article 6); fair trial (Article 7); freedom of conscience (Article 8); information and freedom of expression (Article 9); freedom of association (Article 10); assembly (Article 11); freedom of movement (Article 12); political participation (Article 13); property (Article 14); and independence of the courts (Article 26). Notably absent from this list is the right to privacy.

[8] See W. Benedek, 'Peoples' Rights and Individuals' Duties as Special Features of the African Charter on Human and Peoples' Rights', in P. Kunig, W. Benedek and C. R. Mahalu (eds.) *Regional Protection of Human Rights by International Law: The Emerging African System* (Baden-Baden: Nomos Verlagsgesellschaft, 1985) 59, and R. D'Sa, 'Human and Peoples' Rights: Distinctive Features of the African Charter', *Journal of African Law* 29(1) (1985) 72. On duties in general, see M. Wa Mutua, 'The Banjul Charter and the African Cultural Fingerprint: An Evaluation of the Language of Duties', *Virginia Journal of International Law* 35 (1995) 339. On peoples' rights, see R. N. Kiwanuka, 'Note: The Meaning of "Peoples" in the African Charter on Human and Peoples' Rights', *American Journal of International Law* 82 (1988) 80.

[9] Peoples' rights to be equal (Article 19); to existence and self-determination (Article 20); to freely dispose of their wealth and natural resources (Article 21); to economic, social and cultural development (Article 22); to peace and security (Article 23); and to a satisfactory environment (Article 24) are all recognised in the Charter. In spite of the recognition of the collective, the Charter as a whole still has an 'individualistic ring to it', with 'individuals' or 'every person' characterised as rights bearers (see, in this regard, F. Viljoen, 'The African Charter on Human and Peoples' Rights / The Travaux Préparatoires in the Light of Subsequent Practice', *Human Rights Law Journal* 25 (2004) 313, 314).

[10] 279/03, 296/05, (28th Activity Report, November 2009-May 2010, Annex V).

rights need to be acknowledged.[11] The inclusion of economic and social as well as civil and political rights, the absence of a general derogations clause and the inclusion of 'clawback' clauses are also all seen as distinguishing the Charter from other human rights instruments and these provisions may also impact on transitional cases brought before the Commission.[12]

The supervisory mechanism provided for in the Charter – the African Commission – though theoretically independent, was never intended to be free from the vagaries of the political machinery of the OAU, as is evidenced in particular by Article 59 of the African Charter, which provides that all measures taken by the Commission are to 'remain confidential until the Assembly of Heads of State and Government shall otherwise decide'.[13] The upshot of this provision is that no decisions, resolutions and reports adopted by the Commission are made public until such time as the Assembly has approved them. Whilst this has generally proven to be unproblematic, with the Assembly routinely and unquestioningly 'rubber stamping' the Commission's decisions, the entire matter was brought to a head at the 3rd AU Summit held in July 2004 in Addis Ababa, Ethiopia. Thus, on the basis of objections raised by the Zimbabwean government, the Assembly failed to approve a critical report by the Commission on its 2002 visit to Zimbabwe, in which recommendations were made addressing issues such as the need for dialogue and reconciliation; the creation of an environment conductive to democracy and human rights; the establishment of independent and credible national institutions to monitor and prevent human rights violations; the need to safeguard the independence of the judiciary; the need for a professional police service and the need to create a climate conducive to free expression.[14]

---

[11] For an enumeration of duties in the Charter, see Article 27(1), 28 and 29. To date, the Commission has not dealt with a case involving individual duties.

[12] Though much is often made of the inclusion of socio-economic rights in the Charter, only a limited number of rights are in fact provided for, namely: the right to work 'under equitable and satisfactory conditions' and equal pay for equal work (Article 15); the right to health (Article 16) and the right to education (Article 17).

[13] This state of affairs can be explained by the fact that the African Charter was adopted and the Commission created largely in order to deflect external pressure at the failure of African governments to address the human rights situation on the continent, than out of a genuine concern for human rights. For a general discussion on the use of human rights instruments and institutions by African states in order to safeguard their own interests, see G. Bekker, 'The African Court on Human and Peoples' Rights: Safeguarding the Interests of African States', *Journal of African Law* 51 (2007) 151.

[14] See 'Decision on the 17th Activity Report, African Commission on Human and Peoples' Rights (ACHPR)', Assembly/AU/Dec. 49 (III), paras. 4–5. Subsequently, it also failed to authorise publication of resolutions on Eritrea, Ethiopia, the Sudan, Uganda and Zimbabwe ('Decision on the 19th Activity Report, ACHPR', Assembly/AU/Dec. 101

In spite of these limitations, the Commission has over time utilised, often extremely creatively, its broad mandate to both promote as well as protect human rights. In this regard, the Commission's most important promotional activities include the examination of state party reports,[15] the work of Special Rapporteurs and Working Groups[16] and the adoption of country specific as well as thematic resolutions in response to issues of particular concern. In terms of its protective mandate, the examination of individual as well as inter-state communications represents the Commission's primary activity, though it has also in fulfilment of this aspect of its mandate conducted a handful of on-site country visits.[17] Whilst the African Commission has considered almost 400 cases since its inception, its ability to do anything meaningful about the human rights situation on the continent has been hampered in no small measure by the absence of a specific provision in the Charter compelling states to comply with its recommendations.[18]

(VI)). Most recently the Executive Council has prevented publication of a decision by the Commission on Zimbabwe ('Decision on the 20th Activity Report, ACHPR', EX. CL/Dec. 310 (IX)). A copy of the Executive Summary of the Report of the Fact-Finding Mission to Zimbabwe, 24 to 28 June 2002, as well as the comments by the Zimbabwean government to the report, can be found at: www.achpr.org/english/Mission_reports/ Zimbabwe/ factfinding%20mission%20to%20Zimbabwe.pdf.

[15] See Article 62 of the African Charter as well as Chapter XV of the Rules of Procedure, ACHPR, 6 October 1995. It should be noted that the fact that the concluding observations in respect of these reports are not made public make this largely a paper exercise, with limited impact on state behaviour.

[16] In spite of not having a specific Charter mandate in this regard, the Commission began the practice of appointing Special Rapporteurs in 1994.

[17] With regards to on-site visits, see R. Murray, 'Evidence and Fact-finding by the African Commission', in M. Evans and R. Murray (eds.) *The African Charter on Human and Peoples' Rights: The System in Practice 1986–2006*, 2nd edn (Cambridge University Press, 2008) 139. See Articles 47–59 of the African Charter as well as Rules 88–120 of the Commission's Rules of Procedure in respect of communications. It should be noted that, to date, only one inter-state communication has been brought before the Commission, 227/1999, *Democratic Republic of the Congo* v. *Burundi, Rwanda and Uganda*, 20th Activity Report of the African Commission, January–June 2006, Annex IV.

[18] The Commission itself has stated in this regard that the lack of such a provision means that 'the … victims [of violations of the Charter] find themselves without any remedy' (see *Non-Compliance of State Parties to Adopted Recommendations of the African Commission: A Legal Approach*, 24th Ordinary Session, Banjul, 22–31 October 1998, DOC/OS/50b (XXIV), para. 6). This lack of a legally enforceable remedy was to prove key to calls for the judicial enforcement of rights and ultimately the adoption of the Protocol establishing an African Court. Other factors limiting the ability of the Commission to promote and protect rights in Africa include the lack of political will on the part of states as well as the lack of a Commission-led mechanism to follow-up on recommendations, leaving it largely up to the good will of violating states to comply.

The African Charter and the jurisprudence of the Commission in respect of situations of authoritarian or neo-authoritarian rule: a catalyst for reform?

Whilst the 1990s ostensibly ushered in a new era in African politics, in a large number of countries authoritarian rule continued unabated or was simply replaced by forms of what might be termed neo-authoritarian rule, characterised by a limited opening up of the political process. This state of affairs combined with the fact that, by 1999, all fifty-three member states of the OAU had ratified the African Charter, has meant that the African Commission has had ample opportunity to hold such regimes to the provisions of the Charter. The Commission has, for example, made plain that the trying of civilians by Special Military Tribunals, precluding the jurisdiction of the ordinary courts and the ousting of domestic courts' jurisdiction by means of Military Decree – both measures utilised by the military government in Nigeria in the 1990s – constituted clear violations of the Charter.[19] With regards to Eritrea, it dismissed the submission by the government in *Article 19* v. *the State of Eritrea*,[20] that the incommunicado detention without trial of eleven political dissidents and eighteen journalists and the banning of private newspapers were undertaken 'against a backdrop of war when the very existence of the nation was threatened' in which the authorities were 'duty bound to take necessary precautionary measures (and even suspend certain rights)'.[21] The Commission further, clearly and unequivocally held that the African Charter does not

---

[19] In respect of trial by Military Tribunals, see *Civil Liberties Organisation* v. *Nigeria*, 151/96 (13th Activity Report, ACHPR 1999–2000, Annex V); *Centre For Free Speech* v. *Nigeria*, 206/97 (13th Activity Report, ACHPR 1999–2000, Annex V). With regards to the ouster of the domestic courts' jurisdiction in Nigeria see *Civil Liberties Organization in respect of the Nigerian Bar Association* v. *Nigeria*, 101/93 (8th Activity Report, ACHPR 1994–1995, Annex VI); *Civil Liberties Organization* v. *Nigeria*, 129/94 (9th Activity Report, ACHPR 1995–1996, Annex VIII); *Media Rights Agenda, Constitutional Rights Project, Media Rights Agenda and Constitutional Rights Project* v. *Nigeria*, 105/93, 128/94, 130/94 and 152/96 (12th Activity Report, ACHPR 1998–1999, Annex V); *Constitutional Rights Project, Civil Liberties Organisation and Media Rights Agenda* v. *Nigeria*, 140/94, 141/94 and 145/95 (13th Activity Report, ACHPR 1999–2000, Annex V); *Constitutional Rights Project* v. *Nigeria*, 148/96 (13th Activity Report, ACHPR 1999–2000, Annex V); *Civil Liberties Organisation* v. *Nigeria*, 151/96 (13th Activity Report, ACHPR 1999–2000, Annex V); *Centre for Free Speech* v. *Nigeria*, 206/97 (13th Activity Report, ACHPR 1999–2000, Annex V); *Media Rights Agenda* v. *Nigeria*, 224/98 (14th Activity Report, ACHPR 2000–2001, Annex V); *Huri-Laws* v. *Nigeria*, 225/98 (14th Activity Report, ACHPR 2000–2001, Annex V).

[20] 275/2003 (22nd Activity Report, ACHPR, November 2006 – May 2007, Annex II).

[21] See para. 87.

allow states parties to derogate from it in times of war or other emergency and the existence therefore of 'war, international or civil, or other emergency situation within the territory of a state party cannot therefore be used to justify violation of any of the rights set out in the Charter'.[22] The Commission has also held in respect of Swaziland, that the Proclamation of 1973 by which King Sobhuza I repealed the Constitution of Swaziland of 1968 and by which he declared that he had assumed supreme power in the Kingdom of Swaziland and that all legislative, executive and judicial power vested in him as well as the subsequent Decree No. 3/2001, which ousted the jurisdiction of the Courts, violated a number of provisions of the Charter.[23] The Commission in this case went even further than in the Nigerian and Eritrean cases cited above, recommending inter alia that the state 'engages with other stakeholders, including members of civil society in the conception and drafting of the new Constitution'.[24]

Countries that had made some shift towards more inclusive forms of government, but that largely maintained authoritarian rule, have not escaped scrutiny either. In *Mouvement Burkinabé des Droits de l'Homme et des Peuples* v. *Burkina Faso*,[25] which concerned violations committed prior to the introduction of a new Constitution in 1991 as well as abuses committed thereafter, including arbitrary killings and disappearances, the Commission found the Republic of Burkina Faso in violation of the equality and equal protection clause of the Charter, the right to life, the prohibition against torture, cruel, inhuman or degrading treatment, the right to liberty and security of the person, the right to a fair trial and the right to leave any country and to return to one's own country. The Commission therefore enjoined the authorities to identify and take to court those responsible for human rights violations, accelerate the judicial process in respect of cases still pending before the courts and – without specifying how this ought to occur – compensate the victims of the human rights violations.[26]

Whilst these decisions are important insofar as they reinforce the importance of rights in times of crisis, the impact of these decisions is

---

[22] *Ibid.*

[23] See, *Lawyers for Human Rights* v. *Swaziland*, 251/2002 (18th Activity Report, ACHPR 2004–2005, Annex III) in which it was held that the Proclamation and Decree violated Articles 1, 7, 10, 11, 13 and 26 of the Charter.

[24] *Ibid.* In spite of the Commission's recommendations in this regard, a new Constitution was adopted a mere two months after the Commission's decision, with no engagement of civil society in the process.

[25] 204/97 (14th Activity Report, ACHPR 2000–2001, Annex V).

[26] *Ibid.* See the recommendations made by the Commission in this decision.

greatly tempered by the lack of enforceability of the Commission's recommendations. The degree to which the Charter has therefore directly been
relied upon by domestic actors in order to affect change is therefore perhaps a better measure of success. Thus, for example, in respect of Nigeria,
the African Charter was used to protect rights in situations where the
judiciary's ability to review executive action had been ousted by Military
Decrees.[27] For example, Aderemi JCA of the Nigerian Court of Appeal,
in *Comptroller Nigerian Prisons* v. *Dr. Femi Adekanye and Twenty-six
Others*,[28] boldly made use of the Charter in order to subvert executive
action which allowed for the ousting of the Court's jurisdiction, stating
that:

> In the instant case, with disturbing facts staring one in the face it will be a
> tragedy to the society for a Judge to demonstrate timidity under the muni-
> cipal law and thereby in cheap obedience to its wordings refuse to assume
> jurisdiction when faced with the provisions of the African Charter.[29]

Similarly, in *Chima Ubani* v. *Director of State Security Services and
Attorney-General*,[30] Ogauntade JCA of the Court of Appeal held that:

> It is a clear manifestation of gallantry and judicial innovativeness to be
> able to assert jurisdiction over matters which the military rulers tried to
> shield the judiciary away from.[31]

Situations of 'conflict or transition': from deference to the state to reverence of the African Charter

The first case to directly address issues relating to conflict or transitions in the African human rights system was *Jean Yakovi Degli (au nom*

---

[27] The Nigerian position is somewhat unique in that it is the only 'dualist' African state to
have incorporated the African Charter on Human and Peoples' Rights into domestic law.
See in this regard the African Charter on Human and Peoples' Rights (Ratification and
Enforcement) Act, (Chapter 10 LFN 1990) (No. 2 of 1983), Laws of the Federation of Nigeria,
1990. See in particular Article 1 which provides that: 'As from the commencement of this
Act, the Provisions of the African Charter on Human and Peoples' Rights ... shall ... have
the force of law in Nigeria and shall be given full recognition and effect and shall be applied
by all authorities and persons exercising legislative, executive or judicial power in Nigeria.'

[28] (1999) 10 NWLR 400, as cited in O. C. Okafor, *The African Human Rights System, Activist
Forces and International Institutions* (Cambridge University Press, 2007) 109. Note the
Nigerian Court of Appeal is second only to the Supreme Court in hierarchy.

[29] *Ibid.*

[30] (1999) 11 NWLR 120, as cited in Okafor, *The African Human Rights System*, 112.

[31] *Ibid.*

du Caporal N. Bikagni), Union Interafricaine des Droits de l'Homme, Commission International de Juristes v. *Togo,*[32] in which it was alleged that 'grave and massive violations' had been committed in Togo between October 1992 and January 1993. The African Commission, showing a great deal of deference to the state, adduced on the basis of a visit by a delegation of the Commission, that acts complained of in the communication, which included the torture and maltreatment of a military officer accused of planning a coup, the attempt on the life of an opposition leader, the assassination of the Prime Minister's driver, extortions and killings in the north of the country as well as two shooting incidents resulting in close on twenty deaths, the discovery of fifteen 'mutilated and bound' bodies in the waters around Lomé as well as the killing of twenty peaceful demonstrators by the military and more generally the breakdown in law and order resulting in 40,000 Togolese fleeing the country, had been committed 'under a previous administration'. Thus, the Commission held, without elaborating on the specific measures taken by the state to address the violations complained of, that it was satisfied that this new administration had dealt satisfactorily with the issues.[33] Unlike decisions of the European Court and Inter-American Commission, which justify deference to domestic authorities by reference to the margin of appreciation, the decisions of the African Commission provide no insight into the reasons for deferring to the state.

This highly deferential approach taken by the Commission in respect of the Togolese case is also to be found in a handful of decisions by the Commission in respect of Zimbabwe, with the Commission initially reluctant to engage with potential violations in the country, perhaps as its Mission Report to Zimbabwe undertaken in 2002, which had been highly critical of the situation in the country, had been censured by the AU Assembly.[34] Thus, the case of *Mr Obert Chinhamo* v. *Zimbabwe,*[35] in which it was alleged that agents of the Zimbabwean government had violated the rights of Mr Chinhamo (an employee of the Zimbabwe section of Amnesty International), causing him to seek asylum in South Africa, was

---

[32] 83/92, 88/93, 91/93 (8th Activity Report, ACHPR 1994–1995, Annex VI).
[33] See para. 5. Whilst elections did take place in August 1993 as a result of the Ougagdougou Accord, these elections were marred by controversy, including the boycott by opposition candidates, thus resulting in a victory margin of just over 96 per cent for General Gnassingbé Eyadéma, with less than 40 per cent of the electorate participating in voting.
[34] See further 'Decision on the 17th Activity Report, ACHPR', Assembly/AU/Dec. 49 (III), paras. 4–5.
[35] 307/2005 (23rd and 24th Activity Reports, ACHPR May 2007–May 2008, Annex III).

found to be inadmissible due to the non-exhaustion of domestic remedies. This, in spite of the fact that the Commission had in an earlier case, *Sir
Dawda K. Jawara* v. *the Gambia*,[36] in circumstances where the complainant had fled the Gambia, held that it would be 'an affront to common sense
and logic to require the complainant to return to his country to exhaust
local remedies'.[37] Similarly, the Commission also found inadmissible (due
to a non-exhaustion of domestic remedies) the case of *Michael Majuru*
v. *Zimbabwe*.[38] In this case, Mr Majura, a Zimbabwean judge living in
exile in South Africa, alleged interference committed by the Minister
of Justice, Legal and Parliamentary Affairs and the Central Intelligence
Organisations (CIO) under the Office of the President and Cabinet in the
judicial process in respect of a case in which he was involved as presiding
judge.[39] In particular, the Commission held that as Zimbabwean law does
not require individuals to be physically present in the country to access
local remedies, that the complainant could therefore not claim that local
remedies were not available to him.[40] With regards to the contention by
the complainant that the 'State has the tendency of ignoring rulings taken
against it', thus obviating the need for the exhaustion of domestic remedies, the Commission held that the complainant failed to utilise available
domestic remedies, which 'might have yielded some satisfactory resolution of the complaint'.[41] In the case of *Zimbabwe Lawyers for Human
Rights and the Institute for Human Rights and Development* v. *Republic of
Zimbabwe*,[42] which related the alleged failure of the Zimbabwean courts
to deal expeditiously with election petitions and more generally alleged
violations of the right to participate in government emanating from the
2000 Zimbabwean General Elections the Commission held the case to

[36] 147/95 and 149/96 (13th Activity Report, ACHPR 1999–2000, Annex V).
[37] See para. 36. It might be argued that the circumstances of this case differ from the case
of Mr Chinhamo (the complainant was a former Head of State who had been overthrown by the military, tried *in absentia* and whose political contemporaries had been
detained).
[38] 308/2005 (25th Activity Report, ACHPR May–November 2008, Annex IV). The
Commission further held that the submission of the communication in this case was
unduly delayed and therefore did not comply with the requirements of Article 56(6) (see
para. 110).
[39] The case pertained to a challenge by a publishing house – the Associated Newspaper
Group of Zimbabwe (ANZ) – which sought to challenge the state's act of the banning of
its two newspapers, the *Daily News* and the *Daily News on Sunday*.
[40] Para. 100.   [41] See paras. 101 and 103.
[42] 293/2004 (23rd and 24th Activity Reports, ACHPR May 2007–May 2008, Annex II).

be admissible on the basis of the exception to the exhaustion of domestic remedies rule, given that:

> More than four years after the election petitions were submitted, the Respondent State's courts have failed to dispose of them and the positions which the victims are contesting are occupied and the term of office has almost come to an end.

The Commission, however, went on to hold that there had been no violations of any of the provisions of the African Charter. Thus, with respect to the allegation that there had been a violation of the non-discrimination provision of the Charter, the Commission held that the complainants failed to 'set forth with clarity any particular instance in which they were denied the enjoyment of any of the Charter rights by virtue of the reasons set forth in Article 2'.[43] With respect to the allegation of the violation of the equality provisions of the Charter, the Commission held that the complainants failed to demonstrate the extent to which the Courts treated the petitioners differently from the Respondent State.[44] In respect of allegations pertaining to the violation of due process rights, the Commission appears to have wholeheartedly accepted the contention by the State that it had ensured that the petitioners had the right to be heard by impartial courts or tribunals within a reasonable time.[45] Furthermore, the Commission appears to have based its decision in this regard almost entirely on the basis that the respondent state was able to point to eight named cases out of a total of forty, in which the complainants were to blame for failing to pursue matters or having withdrawn their cases.[46] With regards to the alleged lack of the independence of the judiciary, the Commission held that attributing the resignation of judges to political pressure amounted to mere speculation, this in spite of the fact that the Commission itself had noted a few years earlier in respect of the Zimbabwean judiciary that 'their conditions of service do not protect them from political pressure'.[47] Finally, in relation to allegations by the complainant that the failure to make timely judgments rendered the right to vote meaningless, since this would allow candidates to sit in Parliament whilst the challenge was pending, the Commission also seemingly unquestioningly accepted the version of events presented by the Zimbabwean authorities, who pointed to little than a handful of cases which had been dealt with in around six months within the

---

[43] Para. 122.   [44] Para. 128.
[45] See para. 132.   [46] See paras. 96 and 98.
[47] 'Decision on the 17th Activity Report, ACHPR', Assembly/AU/Dec. 49 (III), paras. 4–5.

filing of the petition, this in spite of the fact, as noted above, that there were a total of forty constituencies in which the election results were challenged.[48]

Whereas the aforementioned decisions highlight a reluctance on the part of the Commission to engage with states in conflict or transition, a distinct shift in attitude is to be detected subsequent to the adoption by the Commission in 2008 of its *Resolution on Elections in Africa*.[49] This document saw the Commission taking a bold, unambiguous stance in respect of the establishment of national unity governments, noting that such forms of government can 'in certain cases legitimise undemocratic elections'. Thereafter, the reticence of the Commission to find violations in respect of the Zimbabwean cases before it appears to have dissipated, with the Commission subsequently finding the Zimbabwean authorities in violation of Charter provisions, in particular those guaranteeing respect for the right to freedom of expression. Thus, in *Zimbabwe Lawyers for Human Rights and Associated Newspapers of Zimbabwe (ANZ) v. Republic of Zimbabwe*,[50] the Commission held that provisions of the Access to Information and Protection of Privacy Act (2002), which provided for the prohibition of 'mass media services' from operating until they had registered with the Media and Information Commission, violated amongst other Charter provisions, the right to freedom of expression.[51] Similarly, the Commission also held in *Scanlen and Holderness v. Zimbabwe*,[52] that provisions of the Access to Information and Protection of Privacy Act which required the accreditation of all journalists by the Media and Information Commission and which additionally provided that a journalist found guilty of abusing journalistic privilege was liable to a fine or a period of imprisonment not exceeding two years, also amounted to a violation of the right to freedom of expression. Finally, in *Zimbabwe Lawyers for Human Rights and the Institute for Human Rights and Development (on behalf of Andrew Barclay Meldrum) v. Republic Of Zimbabwe*,[53] the Commission held that the conduct of the government of Zimbabwe brought the communication within the scope of the

---

[48] See para. 137. With regards to the cases cited in support of the contention that matters were resolved within six months of their filing, see para. 95.

[49] ACHPR/Res.133 (XXXXIIII) 08.

[50] 284/2003 (26th Activity Report, ACHPR, December 2008–June 2009, Annex III).

[51] Other provisions found to have been violated are Articles 1, 14 and 15 of the Charter.

[52] 297/2005 (26th Activity Report, ACHPR December 2008–June 2009, Annex III).

[53] 294/2004 (26th Activity Report, ACHPR, December 2008–June 2009, Annex III).

constructive exhaustion of remedies principle.[54] It therefore found that there had been violations of the general obligations, non-discrimination and equality provisions of the Charter; provisions relating to having one's cause heard and the independence of the judiciary as well as the right to freedom of expression and provisions specifying that non-nationals legally admitted may only be expelled by virtue of a decision 'in accordance with the law'. These decisions are broadly in accordance with the Commission's Resolution on Freedom of Expression[55] adopted in May 2001, the Declaration of Principles on Freedom of Expression in Africa[56] adopted by the Commission in October 2002 as well as the work of the Special Rapporteur on Freedom of Expression[57] appointed in December 2004, all of which emphasise the importance of this right as both a tool to ensure the creation and maintenance of democracy and as a means of ensuring respect for all rights and freedoms.

In *Sudan Human Rights Organisation and Centre on Housing Rights and Evictions* v. *the Sudan*,[58] in which it was alleged that gross, massive and systematic violations of human rights had been committed by the Republic of Sudan against the indigenous Black African population in the Darfur region, the Commission demonstrated that, regardless of political sensitivities, it is no longer prepared to defer to the state in cases of conflict or transition. Instead, the Commission made plain its unwavering adherence to the letter and spirit of the Charter, asserting that:

> It is the primary duty and responsibility of the Respondent State to establish conditions, as well as provide the means, to ensure the protection of both life and property, during peace time and in times of disturbances and armed conflicts.[59]

The Commission subsequently went on to hold that there had been violations of the general obligations provisions of the Charter, the rights to life, dignity, liberty and security of the person, the right to a hearing, freedom of movement, the right to property, the right to the best attainable physical

---

[54] Para. 55. The fact that the complainant had been deported notwithstanding a court decision acquitting him of charges of 'publishing a falsehood' as well as a decision preventing his deportation, made the exhaustion of domestic remedies unnecessary.

[55] ACHPR/Res.54 (XXIX)01: *Resolution on Freedom of Expression.*

[56] ACHPR/Res.62 (XXXII)02: *Resolution on the Adoption of the Declaration of Principles on Freedom of Expression in Africa.*

[57] See ACHPR/Res.71 (XXXVI)04: *Resolution On The Mandate And Appointment Of A Special Rapporteur On Freedom Of Expression In Africa.*

[58] 279/03, 296/05 (28th Activity Report, November 2009–May 2010, Annex V).

[59] Para. 201.

and mental health, the duties incumbent on the state with respect to the protection of families, and the right to development. It recommended that 'all necessary and urgent measures to ensure protection of victims of human rights violations in the Darfur Region' be taken. These measures included the conducting of investigations committed by both members of the military as well as Janjaweed militia; the reform of legislative and judicial frameworks so as to allow for the handling of 'cases of serious and massive human rights violations'; taking steps to prosecute those responsible for the human rights violations; ensuring that victims are accorded effective remedies; and the rehabilitation of economic and social infrastructure, thus, allowing IDPs and refugees to return. Importantly for purposes of distilling a 'transitional' jurisprudence, the Commission also recommended that a National Reconciliation Forum be established to 'address the long-term sources of conflict, equitable allocation of national resources to the various provinces, including affirmative action for Darfur, resolve issues of land, grazing and water rights, including destocking of livestock'.[60] Finally, the Commission also recommended that the government of Sudan desist from adopting amnesty laws and that pending Peace Agreements be consolidated and finalised.[61]

Application of the principle state continuity in post-authoritarian and post-conflict societies

In situations where there has been a genuine, clear break with the past and where regime change or transition is perceived as being 'complete', the Commission has strictly adhered to the principle of the continuity of the state. Thus, in spite of recognising the difficulties which post-authoritarian or post-conflict governments may labour under, the Commission has, uniformly in such situations, held that a new government inherits a previous government's obligations in respect of human rights abuses.

The case of *Achutan (on behalf of Banda) and Amnesty International (on behalf of Orton and Vera Chirwa) v. Malawi*[62] related to abuses committed under the one-party, autocratic rule of President Banda of Malawi.[63] These

---

[60] Para. 229(f).   [61] Para. 229(g) and (f).

[62] 64/92, 68/92 and 78/92 (8th Activity Report, ACHPR 1994–1995, Annex VI).

[63] Hastings Kamuzu Banda ruled Malawi first as Prime Minister and later as its first President. In 1971 he was declared President for Life. In 1993, Banda's one-party state effectively came to an end, with Malawians deciding by referendum to introduce a multi-party political system. Though he did participate as a candidate in elections in 1994, he was defeated by Bakili Muluzi.

abuses included the detention without charge or trial of a political opponent, Aleka Banda, for twelve years; the maltreatment in prison of Orton and Vera Chirwa; the arrest and maltreatment in prison of office workers who had been arrested in 1992 on suspicion that their computers and fax machines could be used to disseminate 'propaganda' for the pro-democracy movement; and the detention and intimidation of Roman Catholic bishops, the imprisonment of trade union leaders, the arrest and torture of students and the killing of striking workers. The Commission held that whilst Malawi had undergone important changes since the filing of the complaint, in particular the holding of multi-party elections, resulting in a new government:

> Principles of international law stipulate, however, that a new government inherits the previous government's international obligations, including the responsibility for the previous government's mismanagement. The change of government in Malawi does not extinguish the present claim before the Commission. Although the present government of Malawi did not commit the human rights abuses complained of, it is responsible for the reparation of these abuses.[64]

Having determined that the new democratic Malawian government was responsible for abuses committed by the former government, the Commission held that there had been violations of the right to life, the prohibition against torture, cruel, inhuman or degrading treatment, the right to liberty and security of the person and the right to a fair trial. Although it is not possible to ascertain the immediate effect this decision may have had on the political situation in Malawi, in the long term, it may be viewed as having reinforced the rule of law.

Similarly in *Organisation Mondiale Contre La Torture and Association Internationale des Juristes Democrates) Commission Internationale des Juristes (C.I.J) Union Interafricaine des Droits de l'Homme* v. *Rwanda*,[65] which concerned the expulsion without a hearing of Burundian refugees as well as the widespread massacres, arbitrary arrests and summary executions against Tutsis between 1990 and 1992, the Commission also held that whilst the situation in Rwanda had undergone 'dramatic change in the years since the communications were introduced' it was nevertheless obliged to 'rule on the facts which were submitted to it'.[66] Furthermore, in the absence of the new Rwandan government engaging with the Commission in respect of these communications, the Commission held

---

[64] See paras. 11 and 12.
[65] 27/89, 46/91, 49/91 and 99/93 (10th Activity Report, ACHPR 1996–1997, Annex X).
[66] Para. 36.

that it had to consider the case, 'regrettably on the basis of facts and opinions submitted by only one of the parties'.[67] After consideration of this information, the Commission found by way of a simple declaratory judgment, that there had been serious or massive violations of the right to life, the prohibition against torture, cruel, inhuman or degrading treatment, the right to liberty and security of the person, the right to a fair trial, in particular the right to appeal, the right to asylum, the procedural rights of non-nationals who were being expelled as well as the prohibition against mass expulsion of non-nationals.

In *Media Rights Agenda* v. *Nigeria*[68] the Nigerian government averred that the law under which the trial by Military Tribunal of Niran Malaoulu, the editor of independent Nigerian daily newspaper *The Diet*, for his alleged involvement in a coup, was conducted under a law validly enacted by the competent authority at the time.[69] By way of further expounding on this point, the Nigerian government in its response to the communication noted that:

> [T]he whole episode took place during a prolonged military regime. It is well known all over the world that military regimes are abnormal regimes and a painful aberration. There was no way of controlling any wanton acts of abuse of fundamental rights by a military junta determined to stay in power at all costs, no matter whose ox was gored.[70]

It also highlighted that the 'obnoxious enactment' at the centre of the complaint had been repealed.[71] Rejecting the government's argument in respect of the fact that the law was validly enacted, the Commission noted that it was not enough for a state to 'plead the existence of a law, it has to go further to show that such a law falls within the permissible restrictions under the Charter and therefore in conformity with its Charter obligation'.[72] The Commission further made plain that the principle of the continuity of the state prevailed, stating that:

> Although not an issue, the Commission notes that the alleged violations took place during a prolonged military rule and that such regimes, as rightly pointed out by the Government are abnormal … The Commission sympathises with the Government of Nigeria over this awkward situation but however asserts that this does not in any way diminish its obligations under the Charter, nor the violations committed prior to its coming into office.[73]

---

[67] Para. 21.
[68] 224/98 (14th Activity Report, ACHPR 2000–2001, Annex V).
[69] See para. 30.   [70] Para. 32.
[71] Para. 35.   [72] Para. 75.   [73] Para. 73.

The Commission therefore found Nigeria in violation of the equal protection provision of the Charter, the prohibition against torture, cruel, inhuman or degrading treatment, the right to liberty and security of the person, the right to a fair trial, freedom of expression, and the duty to safeguard the independence of the courts. By way of remedies, the Commission simply urged the Republic of Nigeria to 'bring its laws in conformity with the provisions of the Charter'.

Accountability for abuses committed by previous regimes has not been limited solely to civil and political rights. In *The Social and Economic Rights Action Center and the Center for Economic and Social Rights v. Nigeria*[74] it was averred that the Nigerian military government had been involved in the environmental degradation and resultant health problems amongst the Ogoni people as well as the destruction of their housing and food sources, through uncontrolled and irresponsible oil production by the state oil company (a majority shareholder in a consortium of oil companies), as well as the ruthless actions of the military in support thereof. In spite of taking note of measures to address the abuses committed by the previous military administration, including the establishment of a Federal Ministry of Environment, the enactment into law of the Niger Delta Development Commission to address environmental issues in the Niger Delta area and the inauguration of the Judicial Commission of Inquiry, the Commission nevertheless found the Federal Republic of Nigeria in violation of a number of provisions of the Charter.[75] In particular, the Commission held that there had been violations of the non-discrimination provisions of the Charter, the right to life, the right to housing and shelter (as read into provisions dealing with the right to highest attainable physical and mental health, property and family provisions of the Charter), the right to food (by reading this into the rights to life, health and economic and social development as provided for in the Charter), the right to freely dispose of natural resources and the right to health and healthy environment.

Challenges and future prospects: the African Court on Human and Peoples' Rights

The Protocol Establishing an African Court on Human and Peoples' Rights as noted at the outset of this chapter was adopted in 1998, the

---

[74] 155/96 (15th Activity Report, ACHPR 2001–2002, Annex V).
[75] See paras. 30 and 69.

election of judges to the bench took place in 2006 and the Court handed down its first judgment in the case of *Michelot Yogogombaye* v. *Republic of Senegal* in December 2009.[76] This case, in which the Court held that it lacked jurisdiction to consider the matter, due to the fact that Senegal had not made the requisite declaration in terms of Article 34(6) of the Protocol, accepting individual petitions, nevertheless raised important issues surrounding transitions. Thus, the applicant advanced arguments that proceedings against Hissène Habré ought to be suspended and that the establishment of a Truth, Justice, Reparations and Reconciliation Commission for Chad, along the lines of the South African Truth and Reconciliation Commission, be ordered by the Court.[77] Much was also made by the applicant of the fact that an 'African solution inspired by African tradition, such as the use of the "Ubuntu" institution (reconciliation through dialogue, truth and reparations)', should have been pursued in this case.[78]

Whilst the institution of the Court has gotten off to a slow start, its first case, the Commission's 'transitional' jurisprudence and the ever shifting political landscape in Africa point to the fact that it is likely to be faced by transitional issues in the future. It remains to be seen how it will deal with these issues, particularly in view of the fact that its jurisdiction encompasses not only the African Charter, but any other human rights instrument ratified by the state party concerned and in all likelihood will be extended to include international crimes such as genocide, war crimes and crimes against humanity.[79]

Conclusion

Although the African Commission has not made explicit reference to the term transition or transitional justice, it has nevertheless developed a distinctive jurisprudence around these issues. It has on a number of occasions made very strong pronouncements condemning aspects of authoritarian rule and has firmly held that post-conflict or post-authoritarian governments are responsible for violations committed by a previous regime. In respect of societies embroiled in conflict or engaged in transition, the Commission's jurisprudence has evolved from an initial approach which appeared to have granted a great deal of leeway to these

---

[76] 001/2008. Available at www.african-court.org/en/cases/latest-judgments.
[77] See para. 23(10).   [78] Para. 22.
[79] See in this regard Assembly/AU/Dec. 213 (XII) and Assembly/AU/Dec. 245 (XIII).

states, to an approach in which states are always to be held accountable for human rights abuses, regardless of domestic or even regional political sensitivities.

Bibliography

Bekker, G., 'The African Court on Human and Peoples' Rights: Safeguarding the Interests of African States', *Journal of African Law* 51 (2007) 151.

Benedek, W., 'Peoples' Rights and Individuals' Duties as Special Features of the African Charter on Human and Peoples' Rights', in Kunig, P., Benedek W. and Mahalu C. R. (eds.) *Regional Protection of Human Rights by International Law: The Emerging African System* (Baden-Baden: Nomos Verlagsgesellschaft, 1985) 59.

Bratton, M. and Van de Walle, N., *Democratic Experiments in Africa: Regime Transitions in Comparative Perspective* (Cambridge University Press, 1997).

D'Sa, R., 'Human and Peoples' Rights: Distinctive Features of the African Charter', *Journal of African Law* 29(1) (1985) 72.

Heyns, C. (ed.), *Human Rights Law in Africa* (The Hague: Kluwer Law International, 2004).

Kiwanuka, R. N., 'Note: The Meaning of "Peoples" in the African Charter on Human and Peoples' Rights', *American Journal of International Law* 82 (1988) 80.

Murray, R., 'Evidence and Fact-finding by the African Commission', in Evans, M. and Murray, R. (eds.) *The African Charter on Human and Peoples' Rights: The System in Practice 1986–2006*, 2nd edn (Cambridge University Press, 2008).

Okafor, O. C., *The African Human Rights System, Activist Forces and International Institutions* (Cambridge University Press, 2007).

Viljoen, F., 'The African Charter on Human and Peoples' Rights / The Travaux Préparatoires in the Light of Subsequent Practice', *Human Rights Law Journal* 25 (2004) 313.

Wa Mutua, M., 'The Banjul Charter and the African Cultural Fingerprint: An Evaluation of the Language of Duties', *Virginia Journal of International Law* 35 (1995) 339.

12

Conclusions

ANTOINE BUYSE AND MICHAEL HAMILTON

> In traumatic revolutionary events, it is not for the Court to establish, by a
> process of divination, when the transitional period is over, or when a state
> of national emergency is past and everything is now business as usual.[1]

This assertion from the dissenting opinion of Judge Bonello in the
Sejdić and Finci case of 2009 illustrates that there is discussion within
the European Court of Human Rights on the Court's role in transitions.
Obviously, the situation at hand – the continuously tense aftermath of the
bloody and traumatic war in Bosnia and Herzegovina – might be a very
extreme example, but the wider salience of Judge Bonello's remark should
not be ignored. This book set out to question and analyse to what extent
the European Court has developed a specific transitional jurisprudence.
By looking at a broad range of issues – from freedom of religion to property rights and from the right to free elections to freedom of expression – a
diversified picture emerges. This chapter draws together common threads
from the preceding contributions and overviews the different settings in
which arguments from transition have been permitted or denied.

The European Convention and transitions

Transitions from armed conflict or authoritarian rule to peace, democracy
and the rule of law rarely follow the same path. Many societies undergo
subsequent transitions (as the history of Europe in the twentieth century
amply shows), and some states continuously oscillate between conflict and
peace. Even the waves of democratisation that swept Southern Europe in
the 1970s and Central and Eastern Europe in the 1990s do not guarantee
arrival at the final station of pluralist democracy.

Nevertheless, parallel developments can be observed in many transitional contexts. One example is that the transitions from war or

[1] Dissenting Opinion of Judge Bonello in ECtHR, *Sejdić and Finci v. Bosnia and Herzegovina*,
22 December 2009 (Appl. nos. 27996/06 and 34836/06).

authoritarianism to more peaceful and democratic societies were very often accompanied by gradual inclusion in European regional organisations, such as the Council of Europe, NATO and the European Union. To different degrees, accession requirements (especially of the EU) engendered change in many fields of state governance. These changes may have served as a safety valve against return to dictatorship, although they never function as absolute guarantees against new forms of authoritarianism.[2]

The accession to regional organisations and the ratification of treaties, including the European Convention on Human Rights, have a specific function. They are symbolic and legal markers which reflect key steps in a transition process. The reasons to ratify may vary significantly. For some states, ratification of the ECHR served as a true milestone of adhering to European values, for others it may have been a necessary and strategic step in order to achieve other goals, such as international recognition and the possibility to enter other regional institutions, as the example of Croatia shows. For many states a combination of reasons undoubtedly played a role. What is crucial, however, is that ratification served to frame subsequent steps in transitions. In many ways, ranging from vetting and lustration exercises for civil servants to policies of property restitution, the ECHR as a normative umbrella limited the policy options of states. A clear example is the emphasis which the European Court placed on the rule of law in many of its judgments. Accession to the Council of Europe and ratification of the Convention in that sense were both markers *of* transition and markers *in* transition. Nonetheless, the supervisory mechanisms in Strasbourg were confronted with the question of whether processes of transition required an exceptional interpretation of the Convention's provisions. Before addressing this question further, we will first pinpoint a key feature of the Strasbourg system: its relative detachment from the transitions themselves.

Lack of proximity in time and space

Regional human rights mechanisms such as the European Court of Human Rights are detached from the events on the ground to a much larger degree than national courts. This plays out in two dimensions:

---

[2] See, for example, W. Sadurski, 'Partnering with Strasbourg', *Human Rights Law Review* 9(3) (2009) 397 at 435.

temporal and cultural-spatial proximity. The Court itself is very aware of this, and has emphasised time and again that it does not strive to be a court of third or fourth instance.[3]

Concerning the temporal detachment of the Court, its work is hampered to a certain extent by the fact that it normally deals with cases years after the facts. The enormous backlog on the Strasbourg docket does not bode well for the future in that respect, in spite of reforms undertaken under Protocol 14 to the ECHR and the Interlaken process initiated in 2010. The only exception to such temporal detachment is the issuing of interim measures by the Court.

In general, this temporal detachment affords the Strasbourg Court a degree of hindsight not enjoyed by domestic authorities. On the one hand, this exempts the Court from having to decide fractious issues in close proximity to the particular conflict. On the other hand, however, such delay precludes the emergence of a real-time transitional jurisprudence at the regional level. The rare use of Article 52 of the Convention is noteworthy in this regard. Article 52 enables the Secretary-General of the Council of Europe to request a High Contracting Party to provide an explanation of the manner in which its internal law ensures the effective implementation of any Convention provisions. Such a request could have significant import in transitional situations. In one of the very few cases where such a request has been made, for example, an inquiry by the Secretary General prompted the Moldovan Ministry of Justice to lift a one-month suspension of the opposition Christian Democratic Peoples' Party (imposed for alleged violations of the law on public demonstrations) prior to local elections.[4]

The Court is also geographically and culturally detached from the cases brought before it. It is composed of judges from different cultural, national and legal traditions. It is therefore not surprising that the Court has time and again repeated its mantra that 'national authorities, who by reason of their direct and continuous contact with the vital forces of their countries are in principle better placed than an international court to evaluate local

---

[3] See further below.
[4] See ECtHR, *Christian Democratic People's Party (CDPP)* v. *Moldova*, 14 February 2006 (Appl. no. 28793/02). See further, Klaus Brummer, 'Enhancing Intergovernmentalism: the Council of Europe and Human Rights', *International Journal on Human Rights* (2010) 1–20; *Report by the Secretary General on the use of his powers under Article 52 of the European Convention on Human Rights in respect of Moldova*, Information Document 20, 6 May 2002. See also ECtHR, *Rosca, Secareanu and Others* v. *Moldova* (adm.decision), 27 March 2008 (Appl. nos. 25230/02, 25203/02, 27642/02, 25234/02 and 25235/02).

needs and conditions'.[5] This reasoning has been used to justify a certain 'margin of appreciation' to states, allowing particular circumstances and histories to guide the choices made. Yet, in the context of transition, a particular question arises in relation to the appropriate level of deference afforded to national authorities. This is one of the key issues addressed in the book: whether transitional cases merit an extra degree of deference or whether they simply ought to be accommodated within Strasbourg's existing doctrine. We address this question in the following section.

Exceptionality and degrees of deference

To what extent do transitions represent an exception to Strasbourg's business as usual? Put differently, does this category of cases reflect a special, *sui generis* jurisprudence? First off, it seems difficult to make a distinction between human rights complaints directly connected to transitions on the one hand and human rights violations which coincide with transitions on the other hand. An example of the former would be a complaint by a civil servant dismissed for allegiance to a former regime. An example of the latter would be a complaint of someone whose trial took too long. Such distinctions are to a large extent artificial. Many problems of societies in transition can be explained by that transition or are exacerbated by it. Even what might at first sight appear to be a de-politicised matter such as an overly lengthy trial can often be explained by backlogs in the judicial system caused by a massive flood of post-conflict or post-authoritarian court applications combined with a partly decimated or poorly trained or disorganised judiciary. The very example of the *Sejdić and Finci* case with which this concluding chapter opened is a case in point. Although the applicants in the case identified themselves as belonging to minorities (Roma and Jews) not involved as one of the key parties in the preceding armed conflict, the peace treaty that formally marked an end to that conflict was based on a power-sharing deal between the three main warring factions (Serbs, Croats and Bosniaks) to the exclusion of other groups in Bosnia and Herzegovina. The deadlock in reforming the constitution because of lack of consensus between those three factions worked to the detriment of people belonging to other minority groups. The same can be said of Roma discrimination in many post-communist states: segregation in schools or ethnically motivated violence by the police against

---

[5] See, for example, ECtHR, *Handyside* v. *the United Kingdom*, 7 December 1976 (Appl. no. 5493/72) para. 48.

Roma does not seem specifically or uniquely related to transition. But as Smith and O'Connell have shown, the interests of vulnerable groups such as the Roma may be sidelined socially and politically, even worsening their situation when compared to the pre-transition period. The difficulty of distinguishing between cases with direct links to transitions and those with more indirect links may be one of the reasons why the approach of Strasbourg to transitions has not been uniform.

To the extent that the transitional context can be seen as an exceptional situation, it can be compared to that other exceptional situation with which the Strasbourg system has extensive experience: emergencies. Article 15 ECHR provides for the possibility to derogate from a number of rights in the Convention during times of war or public emergency. As Ní Aoláin has indicated, the derogation clause was meant to cover temporary situations, but in some states derogations recur and coincide with protracted transitional processes. The danger is that a return to normalcy in a transition can be undercut by such reiterated use of derogations. Although the text of Article 15 provides that such derogatory measures may only be taken when 'strictly required', the intensity of scrutiny by the Court and the leeway left to states has varied. In situations where reversion to authoritarian rule is deemed to be a real possibility – a situation which one might tag 'reverse transition' – the Court has been very strict. But in most other circumstances, the Court's approach has been more equivocal.

The degree of deference accorded to states does not only manifest itself through derogations. The more common way is by assessing whether interferences with human rights are justified under the Convention. In that context, the margin of appreciation, which we address below, plays a role. But there is also another way which de facto defers to the state concerned. This happens when the Court declares an application inadmissible for lack of jurisdiction. In the transitional context this may happen when the complaint concerns rights which are not included in the Convention or its protocols. But more importantly, in transitions the Court can also decline jurisdiction for temporal reasons: if the alleged violation took place before the entry into force of the ECHR for the state concerned and the violation is not continuing, the Court will decline to rule on the merits. This seemingly purely procedural matter has had a large impact on the Court's practice in transitional situations, since many states ratified the Convention after democracy had been re-installed. This means, for example, that killings or enforced disappearances by a previous authoritarian regime, or confiscation of property by way of nationalisation under communism, very often escaped scrutiny by the Convention's machinery. After the demise of communism, Central and Eastern European states, as Allen and Douglas have pointed out, dealt with loss of property in highly divergent ways: some states undertook large-scale restitution processes, others created a right to partial compensation, and some offered no relief to victims of property confiscations at all. In general, the Court's position has been to favour current property entitlements over earlier property claims. When a state chooses to restore property, the Court does test, broadly, the due process and legal safeguard aspects, but a state is not obliged under the Convention to choose restitution of pre-ratification property takings. Although there is still discussion about this within the Court, this seems to be the predominant opinion. Underlying this stance may be a desire to promote stability and the rule of law rather than to function as a mechanism to provide historic justice. The Court's role, in that perspective, fits in a clear break-with-the-past approach. Institutions are meant to uphold human rights now and in the future rather than to look back too far in history. In this sense, the Court does not fit in the broader international trend with its emphasis on restitution, truth commissions and memorialisation.

As indicated, the main issues relating to deference become pertinent in the assessment of the merits of complaints. Most of the rights in the European Convention are not absolute and thus require an analysis of a state's interference with them. Usually this entails the famous three-step test in which the Court scrutinises whether an interference was legal, served a legitimate aim, and was 'necessary in a democratic society'. This last test includes a proportionality assessment. In each of the three phases arguments of transition could surface, but it is important to note that the test itself remains in place in 'transitional cases'.

The first phase of the test offers little leeway for transitional arguments as the Court has rarely recognised that legislation in societies in transition could be much less accessible or foreseeable than in ordinary circumstances. Under the second test, the Court assesses whether the goal of the interference as brought forward by the state can be subsumed by one of the enumerated legitimate aims mentioned in the Convention article at stake. Thus in some freedom of religion cases the stabilisation of society has been accepted as an aim, as Sweeney notes in Chapter 5. And in freedom of expression cases the protection of minorities in difficult and recent processes of state formation has been considered relevant. But by far most discussions of the transitional context in the Court's jurisprudence have taken place in the assessment of the necessity and proportionality of a state's interference with rights.

The usual factors playing a role in the width of the margin of appreciation are: the nature of the legitimate aim invoked, the nature of the individual's interest, the nature of the right at stake and finally the degree of consensus or divergence on a certain matter within Europe.[6] If the aim is closely connected to national security, a broader margin is usually left to the state. The broad overview of cases of transition in this book has shown that the Court was most deferential on issues directly related to the democratic and security core of government, but less so on other matters. If the newly established post-conflict or post-authoritarian state is directly endangered, then the Court might take more distance. But as soon as the link between the interference and the democratic core becomes more tenuous – the arrest of someone for wearing a communist symbol – the Court applies its normal scrutiny. Thus, more deference is applied when the right to elections under Article 3 of Protocol 1 is at stake – because of the close connection to the institutional order of the state – than when the freedom of association under Article 11 is at the core of the complaint, although (as Hamilton argues) the gap between the two approaches has been narrowing over time. In addition, particular transitional elements, such as the stability of democracy, symbolic acts related to the former regime, and the feelings of victims of past abuses may play a role, but again do not automatically lead to a wider margin of appreciation.

The passage of time since the change of regime also influences the level of deference, but not in a completely linear way. Whereas in the immediate aftermath of a change of regime, broad and sweeping measures may be allowed, the more time elapses, the more individualised the assessment of interferences with people's rights should be. In that context, the availability of safeguard measures against abuse on the national level gain in relevance: for example, constitutional review, the degree of thorough legislative evaluation of a measure, and redress and remedial opportunities.

What transpires from the above is that while Court does take arguments of transition seriously, its approach sometimes lacks consistency. The most nuanced approach, which both permits an assessment on the

---

[6] See, for example, D. J. Harris, M. O'Boyle, E. P. Bates and C. M. Buckley, *Harris, O'Boyle and Warbrick: Law of the European Convention on Human Rights*, 2nd edn (Oxford University Press, 2009) at 13; J. Sweeney, 'Margins of Appreciation: Cultural Relativity and the European Court of Human Rights in the Post-Cold War Era', 54 *ICLQ* (April 2005) 459–474; J, Schokkenbroek, 'The Basis, Nature and Application of the Margin of Appreciation Doctrine in the Case law of the European Court of Human Rights', *Human Rights Law Journal* 19(1) (April 1998) 30–36; T. A. O'Donnell, 'The Margin of Appreciation Doctrine Standards in the Jurisprudence of the European Court of Human Rights', *Human Rights Quarterly* 4(4) (1982) 479–493.

merits and a careful contextual scrutiny, would require mainly dealing with arguments of transition in the last phase of assessment: the necessity and proportionality test. In general the Court applies the normal tools and interpretation methods and does not simply give way to state discretion as soon as a complaint relates to issues of transition. In that sense 'transition' is certainly not a trump card which overrules existing human rights norms. The margin of appreciation thus does not automatically become wider once a country finds itself in a situation of transition, but the specific transitional context of the case at hand may influence the extent of the margin. Whenever the state argues that situations of transition necessitate certain measures, the Court is generally careful in its examination of such arguments. Interestingly, it seems to acknowledge in some cases that the mere context of transition is not as such sufficient to justify the need to interfere with human rights.[7] Whereas a transitional jurisprudence in Strasbourg certainly exists, in the sense of case law addressing problems and arguments directly arising from transitions, it has not led to a consistent transitional approach *sui generis* of such issues.

It is clear that states do struggle with great challenges in times of transition. They face issues which, in both scale and sensitivity, deviate from ordinary justice. Thus, a context-sensitive approach – within its existing system of interpretation – is called for. At times the Court has shown a great awareness in this respect, in other cases the peculiar difficulties of either state or victims linked to transition have barely played a role. This is a challenge for the Court to take up, especially in adjudicating on the necessity and proportionality of interferences with human rights. But the way in which this challenge is taken up also depends on the work of actors beyond the Court itself: the information provided by litigants, their lawyers, governments and intervening third parties may all help to elucidate the pertinence of the transitional context at stake.

The effects of transitional jurisprudence

The transitional jurisprudence of international human rights institutions is one among a myriad of factors affecting transitions on the national level. As noted by Sweeney, many developments are internal to the country concerned. Given the limits of courts and constitutionalism, it is not evident that law – least of all regional supervision – could achieve a lot in

---

[7] ECtHR, *Partidul Comunistilor (Nepeceristi) and Ungureanu* v. *Romania*, 3 February 2005 (Appl. no. 46626/99). See also Chapter 7, this volume.

the fraught context of transition. Nevertheless, such jurisprudence can have effects in three different ways: (1) directly, in the execution of judgments; (2) indirectly, but more broadly, as an element in power struggles and transitions within countries; and (3) symbolically, in becoming part of the process of social memory formation.

The first effect is most closely associated with the classic legal process. Once the European Court pronounces its judgment, it is for the state to implement the outcome. Usually, this entails paying compensation to the victim. Thus, for the victims of human rights violations in transitions, the judgments and their follow-up may bring direct relief and recognition of the harm done. But very often more wide-ranging state action is required. If the dispossession of property or failures in a restitution process in an individual case can be traced to flawed legislation, then legislative changes are called for. If legal proceedings were unfair or took too long, reform in the justice system may be required. And if interferences with religious groups or with public debate were overly intrusive and disproportionate, a more tolerant state policy may be crucial. The judging of individual cases in Strasbourg can thus, with the help of supervision by the Council of Europe's Committee of Ministers, instigate broader reforms which directly flow from the judgments in those cases. Especially when the European Court of Human Rights issues pilot judgments these broader repercussions become explicit. In a pilot judgment the Court specifically addresses structural and large-scale human rights problems underlying the individual case at hand, connecting the specific to the general.[8]

The second effect extends beyond the direct procedural realm of Strasbourg's judgments. The case law of the European Court can affect national power struggles in situations of transition or even fill jurisprudential gaps and thereby become a more direct actor in national processes. The latter occurs, for example, when the justice system is severely flawed and the Court, in spite of its own assertion that it is not a court of 'fourth instance',[9] de facto functions as such, as Lamont indicates happened in Croatia. This does not entail that the Court revises or overturns national court judgments – since that would truly be a fourth instance function – but that it indicates to the executive where human rights are violated when national courts fail to fulfil this balancing function. But the Court can also function as an ally of national (highest) courts in struggles with the legislative or the executive. Sometimes the

---

[8] See, for example, ECtHR, *Broniowski* v. *Poland*, 22 June 2004 (Appl. no. 31443/96).

[9] See, for example, ECtHR, *Zičkus* v. *Lithuania*, 7 April 2009 (Appl. no. 26652/02) para. 42.

Court explicitly backs the findings of national courts relating to human rights on executive action and thereby strengthens their position as national watchdogs of citizens' interests. The positions of citizens and of the voices of civil society are also strengthened by the Court's jurisprudence which functions as a safeguard for public debate and plurality concerning the press, academics and civil society organisations. As we alluded in our introductory chapter, regional human rights courts can create structural openings and legal opportunities that shape the strategic choices of those seeking justice in the context of transition. The jurisprudence serves to protect people against excessive political cleansing and exclusionary processes concerning political rights, since in transition minorities of all kinds may be particularly vulnerable. It helps to rebuild a sphere distinct from the formerly authoritarian state by upholding privacy rights. And finally, in the broadest sense, it functions as a catalyst in rebuilding the rule of law, by emphasising the necessity of accessible and foreseeable rules and due legal process and a pluralist, inclusive democracy. It thereby helps to orient transitions in a specific direction. With all its flaws and limitations, the work of the European Court thus engenders a renewed belief in legal processes as opposed to violent armed struggle or revolution, while at the same time binding down the Gulliver of authoritarianism with strong ropes so that society does not revert to dictatorship. This remains a constant struggle as neo-authoritarian impulses in some parts of Europe show.

The third possible effect of transitional jurisprudence of regional human rights institutions is on social memory in a society. Each society struggling with a violent or authoritarian past seeks to give that past a place, even if such choice entails silence. Through political debate, the media, history teaching, and public discussion in the broadest sense, social memories of events are shaped. Processes of transition often offer a chance to re-evaluate the past, to give new meaning, and to label actors as victims or perpetrators. In such reshaping of a social memory law can play an important role. Very often, this is associated with criminal procedures in which the quest for culpability and guilt of individual perpetrators takes the lead. But human rights adjudication, both on the national and the international level, can be equally important. It functions in at least two ways. First, human rights law focuses on the responsibility of the main institutional actor, the state, and its various branches. In doing so it allocates responsibility and indicates whether and to what extent legal boundaries have been transgressed. Second, it starts from the individual's perspective – the applicant in a particular case – and not only recognises or denies the victimhood of a person in a particular situation, but also has a levelling effect by emphasising that all transitional actors are endowed with certain fundamental rights, irrespective of their pasts. Human rights jurisprudence can thus serve to legitimise or de-legitimise state action and recognise the humanity of those targeted by the state. As shown by Kris Brown in Chapter 3 on the armed struggle in Northern Ireland, the judgments of the European Court can become a formidable tool for those seeking to challenge powerful states. The judgments of a court located far from the conflict became building blocks in the construction of a self-image for parties in the conflict and influenced public discussions more broadly. In the Baltic states, judgments which either favoured the majority or the Russian minority also helped to shape the debate about the past. And in the Balkans, Strasbourg's jurisprudence helped to de-legitimise the acts and shortcomings of the (neo-)authoritarian regimes of the 1990s. In all these situations, the case law from the European Court became part of the 'meta-conflict' on the meaning of past struggles and events. As an actor located outside and above the state, its assessment could be used to provide an objectified yardstick for internal matters. While it constitutes only one of many tools of memory construction, the Court's jurisprudence has been used selectively by different groups to re-present and re-shape dominant narratives of the past.

Regional comparisons

Thomas Buergenthal tells the story of the Inter-American Court of Human Rights visiting Strasbourg and being present at the public hearing of the *Campbell* case which involved a claim that the practice of corporal punishment in British schools violated the European Convention. At one point during the argument one of his Latin American colleagues whispered to him, 'If the time ever comes when we have these problems to worry about we will have solved our human rights problems'.[10]

The human rights systems in Africa and the Americas had to address the challenges of societies which experienced protracted ethnic conflicts or endured long periods of oppressive rule. By contrast, the initial signatories to the European Convention on Human Rights comprised a relatively stable group of democracies. Indeed, notwithstanding the expansion of the Council of Europe and some notable European exceptions (the Northern

---

[10] David Seymour, 'The Extension of the European Convention on Human Rights to Central and Eastern Europe: Prospects and Risks', 8 *Conn. J. Int'L*. 243 (1993) at 260–261.

Irish and Turkish-Cypriot situations, the conflicts in the Balkans and the Caucasus), the upheavals during the last three decades in Africa and Latin America have been more severe. Armed conflict has been more pervasive, gross and systemic violations of human rights have been more extensive, and the states in general have been weaker. In this context, two fledgling regional human rights systems, the African and the Inter-American systems, have had to find their place.

The Inter-American system, in its first decades, functioned in a region characterised by military dictatorship rather than democracy. Only in the 1980s, with the transitions to democracy in a number of countries, did this situation change. These countries were faced with an ongoing struggle to deal with a very violent recent history. Some states have subsequently reverted to forms of authoritarianism to a greater or lesser extent. The Inter-American system, though, has amassed a broad-ranging jurisprudence on issues of transitional justice.

The African system was still very young when in the 1990s, in parallel to the transformations in Europe as a result of the end of the Cold War, new democracies were established. Thus, the practical functioning of the African Commission started in the very period of transformation in which the Commission itself was still searching for its own precise role. As in Latin America, the move to democracy was not secure. In several instances young democracies underwent a transformation into new forms of authoritarianism. Under such circumstances, regional human rights supervision became all the more important.

With much smaller financial means than their European counterpart, the Inter-American and African human rights protection systems have found creative ways to deal with human rights in transitions. The first striking feature is that they have used their powers to issue recommendations and to conduct on-the-spot visits which enabled them to monitor human rights developments much more in 'real time' than the European Court. This practice has narrowed both the temporal and geographical gap that regional human rights mechanisms often face. With the exception of the use of interim measures and very rarely used investigation visits, such possibilities are not open to the Court in Strasbourg which is much more institutionally restrained in that respect.

One can also see this creative use of larger mandates – as compared to the European system – in the field of reparations. The Inter-American Court, in its quest to confront impunity, has ordered states to prosecute and punish perpetrators of human rights violations, has indicated reparation measures for victims that went beyond mere compensation, has declared overly broad amnesty laws contrary to human rights, and has even required memory rituals or monuments for the deceased to be set up by the state. In parallel, the African Commission has called for reconciliation bodies and the consolidation of peace agreements.

These aspects may, from a more pessimistic perspective, merely function as legal window-dressing in regional systems which have, in general, been assessed to be weaker than the European model. Nevertheless, the creative engagement of the African and Inter-American systems with transitions means that they connect to the issue at hand not just at the moment of issuing a judgment or recommendation, but also before and after. This may play out beyond the purely legal sphere. The work of regional systems may tip the balance in local and national struggles to claim rights. For example, in Latin America there seems to be a very strong interaction between national constitutional courts and national truth commissions on the one hand and between national courts and the Inter-American Commission and Court on the other hand. This harmonic resonance, as Rodríguez-Pinzón dubs it, strengthens the regional system, which simultaneously cites and inspires the work of national courts. The presence of a regional human rights Court underpinned the position of new or re-established constitutional courts on that national level. In this sense, the experience can be compared to the role of the European Court, whose work has also served as a tipping point in strengthening the position of constitutional courts in Central and Eastern Europe. But the presence of regional human rights mechanisms, as we have emphasised, does not only buttress local courts, it can also empower civil society groups, citizens and other non-state actors to fight for their rights through legal processes. Again, the parallel with Europe, such as with the turn to legal rather than violent struggle of Northern Irish Republicans, is striking – though, of course, it should not be overstated.

The issue of deference plays out very differently from the European system. This is due to a difference in procedural means and to a different approach – both structure and institutional culture thus play a role. The Inter-American Court has generally exercised close scrutiny of state practice in situations of transition. It has not left much room for deference to the state and has even refused to develop anything resembling a margin of appreciation doctrine. To a very large extent, this can be explained by the gravity of human rights violations, including mass killings, enforced disappearances, and torture with which the Court was confronted. Such matters of life and death do not allow for deference. Thus the very subject-matter of the complaints reaching the Court has influenced its position in this respect.

The African system contains no derogations clause or anything comparable. Exceptional situations thus do not permit for differential supervision of human rights issues. Nevertheless, as Bekker argues in her analysis of the practice of the African Commission, it has long been unduly deferential to governments. In the absence of a derogations clause or the adoption of a systematic margin of appreciation doctrine, this was achieved in the early years of the Commission by a very strict application of the admissibility criteria, effectively killing off applications before consideration of their merits. In the last few years, however, a more robust stance has surfaced, with an emphasis on the responsibility of new rulers for the human rights abuses of past regimes. In this way, the Commission clarified that a clean slate approach by states in transition did not free them from obligations to the victims of past abuse. Rather, respect for human rights required that such abuses were addressed.

The extensive experience of these regional peers may serve as an example for European human rights supervision. The practice of the Inter-American and African protection systems in dealing with failed or reverse transitions is undoubtedly salient in the context of an expanding Europe. Given the increasing number of cases dealing with the aftermath, or ongoing occurrence, of armed conflict, and also the resurgence of new forms of (semi-)authoritarian tendencies in some of the European Convention's state parties, a more intense engagement of the European Court of Human Rights with transition (and with the interplay between humanitarian and human rights law norms) is called for. Just as the Strasbourg Court has been stricter on issues of derogations in states where the rule of law was less certain, it should be vigilant in situations in which transitions stagnate or where there is a risk of regression. While the European Court is bound by its different institutional set-up, which permits less flexibility and less scope for broad-ranging reparations, even within those limits the experience gained in other regions is valuable for the Court's own work in addressing transitions.

Looking forward or looking back?

Transitional justice reflects the legal ways in which societies attempt to shift from periods of authoritarianism and armed conflict to democracy based on the rule of law. Inevitably such attempts have a dual character. On the one hand they face the past, by prosecuting perpetrators of past crimes and by undertaking reparations ranging from apologies to full restitution. On the other hand they are future-oriented by setting up new democratic institutions and judicial mechanism built on respect for human rights. How does the European Court fit into this equation? As a human rights court it is an accountability mechanism for states. The past which the Court addresses thus usually concerns the recent past in which a state violated human rights. But there is one crucial element in the context of most transitions that the Court has dealt with: most states ratified the Convention during or after transition. This means that the Court has scrutinised the way in which states currently deal with the abuses of a previous regime (rather than scrutinising those past abuses themselves). This was the case for judgments concerning most of the newly acceding states in Central and Eastern Europe in the 1990s and 2000s. In that sense, the Court used the Convention as a yardstick for present state behaviour rather than for the further past. The focus lies on the functioning of the rule of law and the democratic credentials of a state in or after a transition. The Court's case law looks forward rather than back. As indicated above, this is one of the ways in which the European practice of human rights protection can be distinguished from other regions. One can conclude that the Court does not itself provide transitional justice, but rather that it sets out the legal limits within which states and societies can address problems of transition.

Even if in its judicial reasoning the European Court shows no uniform approach to the issue of transitional justice, the effects of its judgments clearly point towards the future. They restrict the political leeway of states to manage transition as they wish by outlining clear human rights based limits. Through its jurisprudence and its ripple effects, the Court fosters the values of democracy, plurality, openness and the rule of law. In doing so, it maps the transitional goals to be pursued and helps societies, through the interplay with national institutions and civil society actors, in addressing current and future threats to democracy and human rights.

INDEX

*Achutan (on behalf of Banda) and
   Amnesty International (on behalf
   of Orton and Vera Chirwa)* v.
   Malawi (1995), 280–281
Adams, Gerry, 59
Ādamsons v. *Latvia* (2008), 157, 158,
   179–180, 181
Aderemi JCA, 274
African Charter on Human and Peoples'
   Rights ('African Charter,' ACHPR)
   and the African Commission,
      278–280
   and authoritarian rule, 272–274
   coherence of transitional
      jurisprudence, 2–3
   composition of, 268–270
   derogation, use of, 121
   individual duties, 270
   limitations on rights, 106
   margin of appreciation, 125n.81
   people's rights, 269–270
   Protocols, 268
   religious freedom, 104
   responsibility for actions of previous
      regimes, 280–283
   self-defending democracy, 124
   transition role, 3–4, 267–268, 284–285
African Charter on the Rights and
   Welfare of the Child, 268
African Commission on Human
   and Peoples' Rights ('African
   Commission')
   and the African Charter, 278–280
   and authoritarian rule, 272–274, 297
   deference to States, 274–280, 298–299
   margin of appreciation, 125n.81, 275
   reconciliation, call for, 298

responsibility for actions of previous
   regimes, 280–283
role of, 270–271
transition role, 267–268, 284–285,
   296–299
African Court on Human and Peoples'
   Rights, 268, 283–284
African Union (AU), 267n.1, 268, 270
Aguiar de Lapaco v. *Argentina* (2000),
   254–255
Aksoy v. *Turkey* (1995), 39–40
Albania, 232n.102
Algeria, 140–141
Alicia Consuelo Herrera et. al. v.
   Argentina (1993), 257
Allen, Tom, 2, 7, 12, 14, 90n.37, 291
Al-Nashif v. *Bulgaria* (2002), 107–108,
   116, 123, 126, 127
American Convention on Human
   Rights (ACHR), 104, 106, 121,
   125n.81, 249–250
American Declaration of the Rights
   and Duties of Man (American
   Declaration), 104, 106
amnesty laws, 10n.31, 241–246, 256,
   257–258
Anguelova v. *Bulgaria* (2002), 197–198
Araguaia Guerrilla Movement case
   (*Gomes Lund et. al.* v. *Brazil*
   (2009)), 244
Arai-Takahashi, Y., 115, 120n.67
Arbour, Louise, 171
Argentina
   Aguiar de Lapaco v. *Argentina*
      (2000), 254–255
   Alicia Consuelo Herrera et. al. v.
      Argentina (1993), 257

Argentina (*cont.*)
  amnesty laws, 242–243, 244–245,
    256, 257–258
  Carranza v. *Argentina* (1997),
    250–251
  friendly settlements, 254–255
  IACHR visit and report, 252, 253
  transitional legacy cases, 250–251
Arrowsmith v. *United Kingdom* (1977),
    104–105
Arthur, P., 26, 27n.9
Article 2 (right to life), 60–65, 195–202
Article 3 (prohibition of torture),
    200–202
Article 6 (right to a fair trial), 95n.55,
    95n.56, 96
Article 8 (respect for private and family
    life), 107–108, 176–177
Article 9 (freedom of thought,
    conscience and religion), 103,
    104–107, 120–121
Article 10 (freedom of expression)
  hate speech, 142–144
  information, access to, 145–147
  narratives, 138–141
  symbols, use of, 133–138
  and transition, 131–133, 147–149
Article 11 (freedom of assembly)
  and Article 9 (freedom of thought,
    conscience and religion), 105
  and electoral rights, 154–158
  and Protocol 1, Article 3 (elections),
    154–158
  and transition, 151–154, 180–181
  see also association, right to
    (freedom of assembly and)
Article 14 (prohibition of
    discrimination)
  concept of equality, 191–193
  Irish Republican narratives, 72
  racially motivated violence cases,
    195–202
  Roma, transitional difficulties of,
    185–188, 205–206
  Sejdić and Finci v. *Bosnia and
    Herzegovina* (2009), 168
  Sidabras and Džiautas v. *Lithuania*
    (2004), 176–177
  see also non-discrimination

Article 15 (derogation), 43, 120–121,
    290 *see also* derogation
Article 17 (abuse of rights), 142,
    160–164
Article 19 v. *the State of Eritrea* (2007),
    272–273
Article 52 (inquiries by the Secretary
    General), 288
*Asociación de Aviadores de la
    Republica* v. *Spain* (1985), 10n.31
association, right to (freedom of
    assembly and)
  and electoral rights, 154–158
  margin of appreciation, 164–166,
    181, 292
  militant democracy, 158–164
  proportionality of interference with
    rights, 166–180, 181
  and transition, 151–154, 180–181
Austria, 228–229
authoritarianism
  African Commission jurisprudence,
    272–274, 297
  authoritarian democracies in the
    Americas, 239n.1
  IACHR jurisprudence, 297
  judicial system in post-Yugoslav
    states, 86–90
  presidential authoritarianism,
    86–88
autonomous meaning, 225–226
Aylwin Azocar et. al. v. *Chile* (1999),
    250
Azerbaijan, 177–178

Bączkowski and Others v. *Poland
    (2007)*, 153n.7, 194
Baldwin, Clive, 169n.86
Balogh v. *Hungary* (2004), 199n.68
Balsytė-Lideikienė v. *Lithuania* (2008),
    13n.40, 143–144
Barankevich v. *Russia* (2007),
    153n.7
Bárd, Károly, 6–7
Barrios Altos v. *Peru* (2001), 17,
    243–244, 256, 257–258
Beganović v. *Coatia* (2009), 200–201
Bekker, Gina, 3, 9–10, 13, 299
Belarus, Republic of, 41n.48

Bell, Christine, 10, 77, 188
Berman, Paul Schiff, 5
Beyeler v. *Italy* (2000), 218, 226
Blečić v. *Croatia* (2006), 90, 90n.37, 219–220, 231n.96, 235
Blitz, B.K., 98
Bonello J., 126, 164n.63, 165, 170–171, 197–198, 199, 286
Borneman, John, 152n.4
Borrego J., 205
Bosnia and Herzegovina, 81n.1, 83, 86, 91, 168–171, 289 *see also Sejdić and Finci* v. *Bosnia and Herzegovina* (2009c)
Bowring, Bill, 178
Brannigan and McBride v. *United Kingdom* (1993), 33, 37
Brazil, 244, 260
Brecknell v. *United Kingdom* (2007), 71
Brems, E., 27
Britain *see* United Kingdom (UK)
Brogan and Others v. *United Kingdom* (1988), 37
Brown, Kris, 4–5, 19, 296
Buergenthal, Thomas, 296
Bulgaria
  Al-Nashif v. *Bulgaria* (2002), 107–108, 116, 123, 126, 127
  Anguelova v. *Bulgaria* (2002), 197–198
  Dimitrova and Others v. *Bulgaria* (2011), 200n.74
  Hasan and Chaush v. *Bulgaria* (2000), 113–114, 116–117
  Holy Synod of the Bulgarian Orthodox Church (Metropolitan Inokentiy) and Others v. *Bulgaria* (2009), 112–114, 119, 123, 126, 127
  Nachova and Others v. *Bulgaria* (2004), 195, 198–200
  religion in transition, 107–108, 112–114
  restitution of property, 232n.102
  Sashov v. *Bulgaria* (2010), 201n.77
  Stankov and the United Macedonian Organisation Ilinden v. *Bulgaria* (2001), 8n.23

Vasil Sashov Petrov v. *Bulgaria* (2010), 200n.74
Velikova v. *Bulgaria* (2000), 196–198
Velikovi and Others v. *Bulgaria* (2007), 9, 9n.28
burden of proof, 196–202
Burkina Faso, 273
Buyse, Antoine, 5, 6, 10, 13, 14, 18

'*Caloto' Massacre* v. *Colombia* (2000), 261–262
Campbell, C., 27, 48
Canada, 191, 192
Carabulea v. *Romania* (2010), 201n.76
Carmelo Soria Espinoza v. *Chile* (2003) (*Compliance Agreement* case), 254
Carranza v. *Argentina* (1997), 250–251
case load, effects of, 19, 94–98, 287–288
Castells v. *Spain* (1991), 131–132, 149
Cermak, Ivan, 89n.32
Chapman, A., 15
Charter of Fundamental Rights (European Union), 192
Chechnya, 43–44
Chile, 246–247, 250, 254, 259
Chima Ubani v. *Director of State Security Services and Attorney-General* (1999), 274
collective memory
  commemoration, role of, 55–57
  ECtHR jurisprudence, effect of, 59–65, 295–296
  Irish Republicanism, 54–57, 73–77
  and law, 53–54
  and legitimacy, 57–59, 69–72
  and transitional jurisprudence, 52–53, 77–78
Colombia
  '*Caloto' Massacre* v. *Colombia* (2000), 261–262
  constitutional courts, 258–259
  demobilization law, 245, 258
  IACHR, impact of, 258–259
  IACHR visit and report, 253
  Ituango Massacres v. *Colombia* (2006), 262–263
  Las Palmeras v. *Colombia* (2001), 262–263n.83

Colombia (*cont.*)
  'Los Uvos' Massacre v. *Colombia*
    (2000), 261–262
  Mapiripan Massacre v. *Colombia*
    (2005), 262–264, 265n.94
  Pueblo Bello Massacre v. *Colombia*
    (2006), 262–263
  reparations, 261–265
  Rochela Massacre v. *Colombia*
    (2007), 262–263
  Tradesmen v. *Colombia* (2004),
    262–263
  Villatina Massacre v. *Colombia*
    (2005), 261–262
Comadres v. *El Salvador* (1996), 247
commemoration, 55–59, 73–77
Communist totalitarian systems
  see post-Communist states
compensation, 264–265
Compliance Agreement case (*Carmelo
  Soria Espinoza* v. *Chile* (2003)),
  254
Comptroller Nigerian Prisons v. *Dr.
  Femi Adekanye and Twenty-six
  Others* (1999), 274
Connolly, I., 48
constitutional courts
  Colombia, 258–259
  Croatia, 85n.15, 85–86, 87, 96–99
  and the ECtHR, 298
  Hungary, 134
  and the IACtHR, 257–259, 298
  Peru, 256–257n.68
  Serbia, 85n.15, 85–86
  Yugoslavia, 84–86
Council of Europe
  advice on transition for totalitarian
    systems, 108–111, 118–119
  Article 52 of ECHR, 288
  Bosnia and Herzegovina's accession
    to, 81n.1
  Croatia's accession to, 81n.2, 81–84,
    91–94
  and ECtHR jurisprudence, 294
  Macedonia's accession to, 81n.1,
    81n.2
  margin of appreciation, 125
  Montenegro's accession to, 81n.1

rule of law and human rights, 214
and Russia, 108–109
Serbia's accession to, 81n.1
Slovenia's accession to, 81n.1
Turkey's accession, 122
counter-terrorism legislation, 48
Crnic, Jadranko, 87
Croatia
  Blečić v. *Croatia* (2006), 90, 90n.37,
    219–220, 231n.96, 235
  constitutional courts, 85n.15, 85–86,
    87, 96–99
  Council of Europe, accession to,
    81n.2, 81–84, 91–94
  Debelić v. *Croatia* (2005), 96, 97
  and the ECHR, 82–83, 92, 94, 287
  and the ECtHR, 83, 90, 94–101, 294
  and the European Union (EU), 90,
    91, 99–100
  Jelavić-Mitrović v. *Croatia* (2005),
    95–96
  judicial system, effect of conflict,
    86–90
  Kutić v. *Croatia* (2002), 95
  military courts, 87n.22
  Multiplex v. *Croatia* (2002), 224
  narratives of transitional
    jurisprudence, 7
  Oršuš v. *Croatia* (2010), 14, 15,
    203–204, 205
  Pavlinović and Tonić v. *Croatia*
    (2009), 9n.28
  Pibernik v. *Croatia* (2004), 94–95
  presidential authoritarianism, 86–88
  property rights restrictions, 89–90
  Radanović v. *Croatia* (2006), 90n.37
  transitional jurisprudence in,
    94–100
  transitions, 83
  violent conflict, effects of, 86,
    88–90
Croatian Serb Republic of Krajina
  (RSK), 88–89
Cyprus, 167n.73, 173–174, 218–219
Cyprus v. *Turkey* (2001), 167n.73, 173
Czech Republic
  DH v. *Czech Republic* (2008), 18–19,
    194, 202–203, 205

education of Roma, 202–203,
204–205
Malhous v. *The Czech Republic*
(2000), 223
Polacek v. *The Czech Republic* (2002),
228, 229
restitution of property, 209, 227–228
*Simunek, Hastings, Tuzilova and
Prochazka* v. *The Czech Republic*
(1995), 230, 231, 235
Czechoslovakia, 209, 210n.8

Dayton Peace Agreement (DPA),
168–171
Debelić v. *Croatia* (2005), 96, 97
deference to states
African Commission on Human
and Peoples' Rights ('African
Commission'), 274–280, 298–299
Inter-American Commission
on Human Rights (IACHR),
255–256, 298
Inter-American Court of Human
Rights (IACtHR), 255
margin of appreciation, 255
transition, influence of, 289–293
see also states
democracy
African Commission jurisprudence,
297
and associative rights, 153–154
and derogation, 34–42
elections and 'institutional order,'
154–158
as goal of transitional jurisprudence,
12–14
IACHR jurisprudence, 297
and margin of appreciation, 292
militant democracy, 121–124,
158–164
pluralism, protection of, 148–149,
153–154
and religion, 104–108, 118–119
self-defending democracy, 121–124,
158–164
and Sharia law, 108n.19, 122,
123n.78
symbols, use of, 135–136

and transition, 27
Demopoulos and Others v. *Turkey*
(2010), 173–174
derogation
and democracy, 34–42
and emergency, 24–25, 29–42,
49–50
Eritrea, 272–273
geographical scope, 40–41
Northern Ireland, 46–49
oversight, 29
religion in transition, 120–121
and transition, 24–25, 28–29, 49–50,
290
DH v. *Czech Republic* (2008), 18–19,
194, 202–203, 205
dictatorships, 239n.1
Dimitrova and Others v. *Bulgaria*
(2011), 200n.74
discrimination
in Article 14, 191–193
direct discrimination, 189, 192–194
in ECtHR jurisprudence, 193–195
education cases, 202–205
formal discrimination, 188–189,
192–194
Protocol 12, Article 1
(discrimination), 168, 186–187,
192
racially motivated violence cases,
195–202
substantive discrimination,
189–191, 194–195, 197–202,
202–205
and transition, 185–188, 205–206
and transitional jurisprudence,
13–14, 193–195
see also Article 14 (prohibition of
discrimination)
Dominican Republic, 251
Douglas, Benedict, 2, 7, 12, 14, 291

E.B. v. *France* (2008), 193
education, 187–188, 202–205
El Salvador
amnesty laws, 243, 245–246
Comadres v. *El Salvador* (1996), 247
IACHR visit and report, 251–252

El Salvador (*cont.*)
  Las Hojas Massacre v. *El Salvador*
    (1992), 243
  Parada Cea et. al. v. *El Salvador*
    (1999), 247
  truth commissions, 247, 248n.36
electoral rights
  elections (free), 151–158, 180–181
  margin of appreciation, 164–166,
    181, 292
  militant democracy, 158–164
  proportionality of interference with
    rights, 166–180, 181
  and transition, 151–154, 180–181
  see also Protocol 1, Article 3 (elections)
emergency
  concept of, 27–29, 31–33
  derogation, use of, 24–25, 29–42,
    49–50
  frequency of, 28
  humanitarian law and human
    rights, 42–46
  Northern Ireland, use of derogation,
    46–49
  and transition, 29–42, 290
equality
  in Article 14, 191–193
  in ECtHR jurisprudence, 193–195
  in education, 202–205
  formal equality, 188–189, 192–194
  racially motivated violence cases,
    195–202
  substantive equality, 189–191,
    194–195, 197–202, 202–205
  in transition, 13–14, 185–188,
    205–206
Eritrea, 272–273
ethnic minorities, 185–188, 205–206
European Commission of Human
    Rights
  Castells v. *Spain* (1991), 132
  emergency and transition overlaps,
    30–31, 32–33
  Greek derogation (1967), 34–36
  life, right to, 60–61
  margin of appreciation, 32–33
  religion, freedom of, 104–105
  Turkish derogation, 39–40

European Convention on Human
    Rights (ECHR)
  Article 11 vs. Protocol 1–3, 155–156
  Article 52, 288
  associative rights, 153
  comparison with other regional
    systems, 296–297, 299
  derogation, 24, 29, 46–49
  emergency and transition overlaps,
    29–42
  humanitarian law and human
    rights, 42–46
  ratification by Croatia, 82–83, 92, 94
  religion, freedom of, 103
  restitution of property, 213–218
  transition role, 1–2, 26, 286–287
European Court of Human Rights
    (ECtHR)
  associative rights, 152, 153–154,
    180–181
  autonomous meaning, 225–226
  case load, 19, 94–98, 287–288
  case merits test, 291
  coherence of transitional
    jurisprudence, 2–3, 14–15
  and constitutional courts, 298
  contours of transitional
    jurisprudence, 8–12
  and the Council of Europe, 294
  as court of 'fourth instance,' 3–4, 83,
    94–101, 294
  democracy, need for, 121–124
  derogation, use of, 24–25, 46–50,
    120–121
  discrimination, interpretations of,
    193–195
  education cases, 202–205
  elections (free), 154–158
  emergency and transition overlaps,
    29–42
  forward-looking role, 299–300
  and freedom of expression, 131–133,
    147–149
  geographical distance from cases,
    288–289
  goals of transitional jurisprudence,
    12–14
  hate speech, 142–144

humanitarian law and human rights, 42–46, 49–50
inconsistency of approach, 292–293
information, access to, 145–147
and international law on restitution, 229–233
Irish Republican narratives, 59–65, 69–72, 74–75
Irish Republican use of, 52–53, 65–67
jurisdiction, 290–291
and Macedonia, 95n.56
margin of appreciation, 32–33, 164–166, 181
memory, effect on, 59–65, 295–296
militant democracy, 158–164
narratives, 4–7, 59–65, 69–72, 74–75, 138–141, 295–296
as observer in relation to national law, 225–227
as participant in relation to national law, 225–227
pluralism, protection of, 148–149, 153–158
proportionality of interference with rights, 166–180, 181
racially motivated violence cases, 195–202
regional comparisons, 296–299
religion, freedom of, 104, 107–108
religion in transition cases, 111–120, 124–128
restitution and Protocol 1, Article 1 (property), 213–218
restitution of property jurisprudence, 15, 211–212, 218–229, 230–235, 291
symbols, use of, 133–138
terminology in judgments, 72–73
transition role, 15–20, 29–42, 286
UK reaction to *McCann* judgment, 67–69
European Union (EU), 86n.20, 90, 91, 99–100, 192
exceptionality, 28–29, 31–33
expression, freedom of *see* freedom of expression
external research, 18–19

fact-finding, 18–19, 35–36, 251–253, 297
fair trial, right to, 95n.55, 95n.56, 96
family life, 107–108, 176–177
Farrell, Mairéad, 77
fascism, symbols of, 133–138
Fein, Elke, 133
Finci, Jakob, 16–17
Finland, 125n.81
Finucane v. *United Kingdom* (2003), 71
Fourth Instance Formula, 17, 255–256
France
    E.B. v. *France* (2008), 193
    Fretté v. *France* (2008), 193
    Garaudy v. *France* (2003), 142
    Lehideux and Isorni v. *France* (1998), 141, 161n.50
    Orban and others v. *France* (2009), 140–141
    Vo v. *France* (2004), 125–126n.83
Fredman, S., 190
Freedom and Democracy Party (Özdep) v. *Turkey* (1999), 153n.7
freedom of expression
    and the African Commission, 278–279
    and the ECtHR, 131–133, 147–149
    hate speech, 142–144
    information, access to, 145–147
    narratives, 138–141
    symbols, use of, 133–138
Fretté v. *France* (2008), 193
friendly settlements, 254–255
Fujimori, Alberto, 259
Fuller, Lon, 216, 231
Funes, Mauricio, 246n.27

Gabriel, Manfred, 225
Gambia, 276
Garaudy v. *France* (2003), 142
Gaygusuz v. *Austria* (1996), 228–229
Georgia, 41, 167
Georgian Labour Party v. *Georgia* (2008), 167
German Communist Party v. *Germany* (1957), 160–161
Germany
    German Communist Party v. *Germany* (1957), 160–161

Germany (*cont.*)
  Glasenapp v. *Germany* (1986),
    161n.46
  Kosiek v. *Germany* (1986), 161n.46
  Maltzan v. *Germany* (2005), 228n.81
  restitution of property, 209–210, 227
  Streletz, Kessler and Krenz v.
    Germany (2001), 6n.16, 11n.34
  Vogt v. *Germany* (1995), 161n.46
  Weidlich v. *Germany* (1996), 223
Getter, M., 86n.20
Gib, A Modest Exposure (Mitchell), 76
Gibraltar killing of IRA activists
    see McCann v. *United Kingdom*
    (1995)
Glasenapp v. *Germany* (1986), 161n.46
Gotovina, Ante, 89n.31, 89n.32
Granic, Mate, 82
Greece, 32n.25, 34–36, 221–222
Greece v. *United Kingdom* (1958),
    32n.25
Grover, Sonja, 18
Guatemala, 249–250

Hajiyev, J., 171
Hamilton, Michael, 13, 14–15, 16, 18
Handyside v. *United Kingdom* (1976),
    137
Harvey, Paul, 159n.38
Hasan and Chaush v. *Bulgaria* (2000),
    113–114, 116–117
hate speech, 142–144
*Hertzberg, Mansson, Nikula and
    Putkonen* v. *Finland* (1982),
    125n.81
Heseltine, Michael, 68
*Holy Synod of the Bulgarian Orthodox
    Church (Metropolitan Inokentiy)
    and Others* v. *Bulgaria* (2009),
    112–114, 119, 123, 126, 127
Honduras, 255
human rights
  Croatia's accession to Council of
    Europe, 82–83
  and humanitarian law, 42–46,
    49–50
  limitations on (legitimate aims),
    105–106

proportionality of interference with,
    166–180, 215
  and restitution of property, 234
  and the rule of law, 213–218
  and transitional jurisprudence, 1–4,
    124–128, 289–290, 293–296
humanitarian law, and human rights,
    42–46, 49–50
Hungary
  Balogh v. *Hungary* (2004), 199n.68
  constitutional courts, 134
  Karsai v. *Hungary* (2009), 139–140
  Kenedi v. *Hungary* (2009), 10,
    146–147
  Korbely v. *Hungary* (2008), 6n.16, 18,
    44–45
  nationalisation, 210n.8
  Rekvényi v. *Hungary* (1999),
    135–136, 164–165
  restitution of property, 209
  TASZ v. *Hungary* (2009), 146, 147
  Vajnai v. *Hungary* (2008), 133–138

indirect discrimination, 190–191,
    194–195, 197–202, 202–205
individual duties, 269–270
information, access to, 145–147
Inter-American Commission on
    Human Rights (IACHR)
  amnesty laws, 241–246, 256,
    257–258
  composition of, 240–241
  deference to States, 255–256, 298
  fact-finding, 19
  Fourth Instance Formula, 17,
    255–256
  friendly settlements, 254–255
  reparations, 260–265
  reports, 251–253
  role of, 19, 196–197
  self-defending democracy, 123–124
  site visits, 251–253
  and transition, 239–240, 256–259,
    265–266
  transitional legacy cases, 250–251
  truth commissions, 246–247, 248
Inter-American Court of Human
    Rights (IACtHR)

amnesty laws, 242, 243–246, 256, 257–258
coherence of transitional jurisprudence, 2–3
composition of, 240–241
deference to States, 255
interim measures, 253–254
margin of appreciation, 255, 298
and national courts, 257–259, 298
property rights, 249–250
reparations, 260–265, 297–298
transition role, 3–4, 256–259, 265–266, 296–299
truth commissions, 246, 247–248
interim measures, 253–254
International Covenant on Civil and Political Rights (ICCPR)
derogations, 28, 121
equality in, 192
limitations on rights, 106
margin of appreciation, 125n.81
religion, freedom of, 104
restitution of property, 229–230
Socialist Federal Republic of Yugoslavia (SFRJ), 85n.16
International Covenant on Economic, Social and Cultural Rights (ICESCR), 85n.16
International Criminal Tribunal for the Former Yugoslavia (ICTY), 89n.32
international criminal tribunals, 252
International Crisis Group (ICG), 169
International Law Commission (ILC), 264–265
Ireland, Republic of, 29–33, 162n.52
Irish Republicanism
commemoration, use of, 55–57, 73–77
ECtHR jurisprudence, 52–53, 59–65, 72–73
law, use of, 52–53, 65–67
legitimacy of armed struggle, 57–59, 65–67, 69–72
memory, role of, 54–57, 77–78
memory practices, 73–77
narratives, 54–57, 59–65, 296
UK reaction to McCann judgment, 67–69

Italy, 127, 136–137, 218, 226
Ituango Massacres v. Colombia (2006), 262–263

Jean Yakovi Degli (au non du Caporal N. Bikagni), Union Interafricaine des Droits de l'Homme, Commission International de Juristes v. Togo (1994), 274–275
Jelavić-Mitrović v. Croatia (2005), 95–96
Jordan, Hugh, 67, 70
Jordan v. United Kingdom (2001), 63, 187n.15

Karsai v. Hungary (2009), 139–140
Keenan, Brian, 74
Keenan, J., 188
Keller, Helen, 19
Kelly, Máiréad, 67, 70
Kelly and others v. United Kingdom (2001)
ECtHR judgment, 52–53, 59–60, 62–65, 72–73
Irish Republican narrative, 72
law, use of, 67
legitimacy of armed struggle, 69–71
memory, role of, 78
memory practices, 73–77
Kenedi v. Hungary (2009), 10, 146–147
Kertzer, D.I., 57
Khamidov v. Russia (2007), 216–217n.36
King, R., 52–53, 53–54, 65
Kononov v. Latvia (2010), 5–7, 138
Korbely v. Hungary (2008), 6n.16, 18, 44–45
Kosiek v. Germany (1986), 161n.46
Kosovo, 83
Krasner, S.D., 16
Kuolelis, Bartoševičius and Burokevičius v. Lithuania (2008), 162, 174–175
Kutić v. Croatia (2002), 95

Lamont, Christopher, 7, 11, 14, 294
language, 72–73

Länsman et al v. *Finland* (1996),
    125n.81
Las Hojas Massacre v. *El Salvador*
    (1992), 243
Las Palmeras v. *Colombia* (2001),
    262–263n.83
Latvia
    Ādamsons v. *Latvia* (2008), 157, 158,
        179–180, 181
    Kononov v. *Latvia* (2010), 5–7, 138
    period of transition, 174n.112
    Ždanoka v. *Latvia* (2006), 8n.22, 123,
        156–157, 158, 161n.51, 163–164,
        165–166, 173n.108, 174–175,
        177–179
Lautsi v. *Italy* (2009 and 2011), 103, 127,
    136–137
law
    ECtHR jurisprudence, effect of,
        294–295
    and memory, 53–54
    observation by ECtHR, 225–227
    participation by ECtHR, 225–227
    use of, 65–67
lawfulness assessed in restitution cases
    confiscated property, 227–229
    ECtHR jurisprudence, 211–212,
        230–235
    international law, 229–233
    long-lost property, 220–227
    Protocol 1, Article 1 (property) on
        restitution, 213–218
    recognition of, 218–220
Lawless v. *Ireland* (1961), 29–33,
    162n.52
legitimacy
    Croatia's accession to Council of
        Europe, 92
    Irish Republicanism, 57–59, 65–67,
        69–72
    and memory, 57–59, 69–72
    religion in transition cases, 113,
        114–116, 117, 124–126
    and transitional jurisprudence,
        52–53
legitimate aims, 105–106
Lehideux and Isorni v. *France* (1998),
    141, 161n.50
length of proceedings, 94–98

Leuprecht, Peter, 108–109
Levits, J., 165–166
Ley de Caducidad (Caducity Law), 243
Ley de Justicia y Paz (Peace and Justice
    Law), 245, 253, 258
Ley de Obediencia Debida (Due
    Obediencia Law), 242–243
Ley de Punto Final (Final Stop Law),
    242–243
life, right to *see* right to life
limitations on rights, 105–106
Lithuania
    Balsytė-Lideikienė v. *Lithuania*
        (2008), 13n.40, 143–144
    *Kuolelis, Bartoševičius and
        Burokevičius* v. *Lithuania* (2008),
        162, 174–175
    Padalevičius v. *Lithuania* (2009),
        9n.28
    Rainys and Gasparavièius v.
        Lithuania (2005), 176
    Sidabras and Džiautas v. *Lithuania*
        (2004), 176
    time elapsed since communism, 135
    Zickus v. *Lithuania* (2009), 176–177
Little, David, 110–111
Loizidou v. *Turkey* (1996), 218–219,
    222, 229, 232
'Los Uvos' Massacre* v. *Colombia* (2000),
    261–262
Loughgall killing of IRA activists
    see *Kelly and others* v. *United
    Kingdom* (2001)
lustration, 175–177

Macedonia, 81n.1, 81n.2, 95n.56
Macklem, P., 213
Malawi, 280–281
Malhous v. *The Czech Republic* (2000),
    223
Maltzan v. *Germany* (2005), 228n.81
Mapiripan Massacre v. *Colombia*
    (2005), 262–264, 265n.94
margin of appreciation
    African Commission, 125n.81, 275
    Balsytė-Lideikienė v. *Lithuania*
        (2008), 143–144
    and discrimination, 193
    freedom of expression, 132

IACtHR deference to States, 255, 298
influencing factors, 292
political loyalties, 164–166, 181
recognition of, 125n.81
religion in transition cases, 113,
    114–120, 124–128
and transition, 32–33, 164–166, 181,
    292
Maria da Penha Maia Fernades v.
    Brazil (2001), 260
Markac, Mladen, 89n.32
Marsh, Melissa, 167
McAdams, James, 20
McCann v. *United Kingdom* (1995)
    ECtHR judgment, 52–53, 59–62,
        187n.15
    Irish Republican narrative, 72
    legitimacy of armed struggle, 69–71
    memory, role of, 78
    memory practices, 73–77
    Republican utilisation of, 66–67
    terminology in ECtHR judgments,
        72–73
    UK reaction to judgment, 67–69
McCrudden, C., 189n.20
McEvoy, K., 53, 65–66
McGuinness, Martin, 57
McIlduff, Barry, 68
McKerr v. *United Kingdom* (2001), 63,
    187n.15
media freedom, 91–92, 93, 139–140
Media Rights Agenda v. *Nigeria* (2000),
    282–283
memorialisation, 55–59, 73–77
memory
    commemoration, role of, 55–57
    ECtHR jurisprudence, effect of,
        59–65, 295–296
    Irish Republicanism, 54–57, 73–77
    and law, 53–54
    and legitimacy, 57–59, 69–72
    and transitional jurisprudence,
        52–53, 77–78
Merry, S. Engle, 53
Metress, E., 57
Metress, S., 57
Metropolitan Church of Bessarabia v.
    Moldova (2001), 111–112, 123,
    126, 127

Michael Majuru v. *Zimbabwe* (2008), 276
Michelot Yogogombaye v. *Republic of
    Senegal* (2009), 284
Mijović, J., 171
militant democracy, 121–124, 158–164
military courts, 87n.22
Milošević, Slobodan, 86
mis-rule of law, 64, 66–67, 69–71, 78
Moldova
    Metropolitan Church of Bessarabia
        v. *Moldova* (2001), 111–112, 123,
        126, 127
    Tănase v. *Moldova* (2010), 157–158,
        180, 181
    use of Article 52, 288
Montenegro, 81n.1
*Mouvement Burkinabé des Droits de
    l'Homme et des Peuples* v. *Burkina
    Faso* (2001), 273
Mr Obert Chinhamo v. *Zimbabwe*
    (2007), 275–276
Multiplex v. *Croatia* (2002), 224
Munoz Diaz v. *Spain* (2009), 195

Nachova and Others v. *Bulgaria* (2004),
    195, 198–200
narratives
    ECtHR jurisprudence, effect of, 4–7,
        138–141, 295–296
    Irish Republicanism, 54–57, 59–65,
        296
    new perspectives on history, 138–141
    public widening of, 64, 66–67,
        75–76, 78
    transitional jurisprudence, 2, 4–7
National Commission for Truth and
    Reconciliation (NCTR), Chile,
    246–247
national courts, and international
    courts, 257–259, 298
NATO (North Atlantic Treaty
    Organization), 91
necessity
    freedom of expression, 139–140
    religion in transition cases, 113,
        114–116, 117–120, 124–126
    symbols, use of, 135–138
Ní Aoláin, Fionnuala, 1–2, 10–11, 13,
    18, 63, 64–65, 77, 170, 290

Nicaragua, 124
Nigeria
  African Charter, influence of, 274
  and the African Commission, 12,
    272, 282–283
  Comptroller Nigerian Prisons v. *Dr.*
    Femi Adekanye and Twenty-six
    Others (1999), 274
  Media Rights Agenda v. *Nigeria*
    (2000), 282–283
  The Social and Economic Rights
    Action Center and the Center for
    Economic and Social Rights v.
    Nigeria (2001), 283
non-discrimination
  in Article 14, 191–193
  direct discrimination, 189, 192–194
  in ECtHR jurisprudence, 193–195
  education cases, 202–205
  formal discrimination, 188–189,
    192–194
  Protocol 12, Article 1
    (discrimination), 168, 186–187,
    192
  racially motivated violence cases,
    195–202
  substantive discrimination, 189–191,
    194–195, 197–202, 202–205
  and transition, 185–188, 205–206
  and transitional jurisprudence,
    13–14, 193–195
  see also Article 14 (prohibition of
    discrimination)
Northern Ireland, 4–5, 46–49, 296
  see also Irish Republicanism
Northern Ireland Human Rights
  Commission, 48–49

O Caoláin, Caoimhghín, 55–56
O'Connell, Rory, 4, 13–14, 15, 18–19, 290
OEA-MAPP agreement, 253
Ogauntade JCA, 274
Orban and others v. *France* (2009),
  140–141
Organisation Mondiale Contre
  La Torture and Association
  Internationale des Juristes
  Democrates Commission

Internationale des Juristes (C.I.J)
  Union Interafricaine des Droits
  de l'Homme v. *Rwanda* (1996),
  281–282
Organisation of African Unity (OAU),
  267, 267n.1, 268, 270
Organization of American States
  (OAS), 251, 252
Oršuš v. *Croatia* (2010), 14, 15,
  203–204, 205

Padalevičius v. *Lithuania* (2009), 9n.28
Papamichalopoulos and Others v.
  Greece (1993), 221–222
Parada Cea et. al. v. *El Salvador* (1999),
  247
Partidul Comunistilor (Nepeceristi)
  (PCN) and Ungureanu v. *Romania*
  (2005), 153–154
Patterson, Henry, 55
Pavlinović and Tonić v. *Croatia* (2009),
  9n.28
peoples' rights, 269–270
Peru
  Barrios Altos v. *Peru* (2001), 17,
    243–244, 256, 257–258
  constitutional court, 256–257n.68
  Fujimori extradition, 259
  IACHR, impact of, 259
  IACHR visit and report, 252,
    253
  truth commissions, 248
Pevehouse, J., 122n.72
Phosphates in Morocco (1938), 230
Pibernik v. *Croatia* (2004), 94–95
Pinochet, Augusto, 250
Plan de Sánchez Massacre v.
  Guatemala (2004), 249–250
pluralism, protection of, 148–149,
  153–158
Polacek v. *The Czech Republic* (2002),
  228, 229
Poland, 153n.7, 194, 209, 210n.8
policing, 195–202
political loyalties
  and electoral rights, 154–158
  margin of appreciation, 164–166,
    181

militant democracy, 158–164
proportionality of interference with
    rights, 166–180, 181
and transition, 151–154, 180–181
Ponomarev v. *Russia* (2008), 221
Posner, Eric, 7, 211
post-Communist states
    education cases, 202–205
    equality and transition, 185–188
    information, access to, 145–147
    memory, 296
    narratives, 138–140
    racially motivated violence cases,
        195–202
    restitution of property, 208–210
    Roma, transitional difficulties of,
        185–186, 205–206
    symbols, use of, 133–138
    time elapsed, 135, 174–180
    transition guidance from Council of
        Europe, 108–111, 118–119
post-Yugoslav states, 81n.1, 81–84,
    86–90, 94–101
property rights, 89–90, 249–250
    see also restitution of property
proportionality, 166–180, 215
Protocol 1, Article 1 (property)
    confiscated property, 227–229
    lawfulness assessed in restitution
        cases, 218–220
    long-lost property, 220–227
    on restitution, 213–218
Protocol 1, Article 3 (elections)
    and Article 11 (freedom of
        assembly), 154–158
    discrimination, 186–187
    ECtHR jurisprudence, 154–158
    margin of appreciation, 292
    proportionality of interference with
        rights, 166–168
    time elapsed, 172–173, 177–180
    and transition, 151–154, 180–181
    see also electoral rights
Protocol 12, Article 1 (discrimination),
    168, 186–187, 192
public debate, 139–140
Pueblo Bello Massacre v. *Colombia*
    (2006), 262–263

racial segregation, 187–188
racially motivated violence, 188,
    195–202
Radanović v. *Croatia* (2006), 90n.37
Radbruch, Gustav, 216–217, 227, 231
Rainys and Gasparavièius v. *Lithuania*
    (2005), 176
Refah Partisi v. *Turkey* (2001), 108n.19,
    122, 123, 123n.78, 162–163
Rekvényi v. *Hungary* (1999), 135–136,
    164–165
religion, freedom of
    and democracy, 104–108, 118–119
    derogation, use of, 120–121
    ECtHR transition cases, 111–120,
        124–128
    self-defending democracy, 121–124
    and transitional jurisprudence,
        103–104, 107–108, 111–120,
        124–128
    and universality of human rights,
        124–128
reparations, 260–265, 280–283,
    297–298
Reporters Without Borders, 82
Resolution on Elections in Africa, 278
restitution of property
    confiscated property, 227–229
    ECtHR jurisprudence, 15, 211–212,
        218–229, 230–235, 291
    international law, 229–233
    lawfulness assessed by ECtHR,
        218–220
    long-lost property, 220–227
    in post-Communist states, 208–210
    property rights, 89–90, 249–250
    Protocol 1, Article 1 (property),
        213–218
    role of, 210–211
right to life, 60–65, 125–126n.83,
    195–202
Rochela Massacre v. *Colombia* (2007),
    262–263
Rodriguez-Pinzon, Diego, 3, 7, 10, 13,
    17, 19, 125n.81, 298
Roma
    coherence of jurisprudence, 15
    difficulties of transition, 185–186

Roma (*cont.*)
  education cases, 202–205
  goals of transitional jurisprudence, 14
  Munoz Diaz v. *Spain* (2009), 195
  racially motivated violence cases,
    195–202
  transition, effects of, 289–290
  transitional jurisprudence relating
    to, 185–188, 205–206
Romania, 153–154, 200, 209, 232n.102
  Carabulea v. *Romania* (2010),
    201n.76
rule of law
  confiscated property, 227–229
  international law on restitution,
    229–233
  lawfulness assessed in restitution
    cases, 218–220
  long-lost property, 220–227
  Protocol 1, Article 1 (property) on
    restitution, 213–218
  religion in transition cases, 116–117
  and restitution of property, 211–212,
    230–235
  transition guidance from Council of
    Europe, 118–119
Russia, 41–42, 43–44, 108–109, 153n.7,
    216–217n.36, 221
  Republican Party of Russia v. *Russia*
    (2011), 180n.142
Rwanda, 281–282

Sadurski, Wojciech, 16, 16n.54, 17
Safjan, M., 16
Sahin v. *Turkey* (2005), 127
Sajó, András, 159–160
Sakik and Others v. *Turkey* (1997),
    40–41
Samper, Ernesto, 262
Sashov v. *Bulgaria* (2010), 201n.77
Savelsberg, J., 52–53, 53–54, 65
Scanlen and Holderness v. *Zimbabwe*
    (2009), 278
segregation in schools, 187–188
Sejdić and Finci v. *Bosnia and*
    Herzegovina (2009)
  discrimination under Article 14,
    186–187

dissenting opinion, 126, 164n.63
margin of appreciation, 166
proportionality, 168–171, 177, 181
role of the ECtHR, 16–17, 286
transition, effects of, 289
self-defending democracy, 121–124,
    158–164
Senegal, 284
Serbia
  conflict, effects of, 86
  constitutional courts, 85n.15, 85–86
  Council of Europe, accession to,
    81n.1
  and the ECtHR, 94, 96–97
  narratives of transitional
    jurisprudence, 7
  transitional jurisprudence in, 94,
    96–97
  transitions, 83, 83n.9
Seyidzade v. *Azerbaijan* (2009),
    177–178
Seymour, David, 296
Shanaghan v. *United Kingdom* (2001),
    63, 187n.15
Sharia law, 108n.19, 122, 123n.78
Sidabras and Džiautas v. *Lithuania*
    (2004), 176
Simunek, Hastings, Tuzilova and
    Prochazka v. *The Czech Republic*
    (1995), 230, 231, 235
Sinn Féin, 54–59 *see also* Irish
    Republicanism
Sir Dawda K. Jawara v. *the Gambia*
    (2000), 276
site visits, 251–253, 297
Slovak Republic, 209
Slovenia, 81n.1, 86
Smith, Anne, 4, 13–14, 15, 18–19, 290
social need, 143–144
Socialist Federal Republic of
    Yugoslavia (SFRJ), 84–86
  see also post-Yugoslav states
South Africa, 191, 192
Soviet Union, 210n.8
Spain, 10n.31, 131–132, 149, 195
Stankov and the United Macedonian
    Organisation Ilinden v. *Bulgaria*
    (2001), 8n.23

states
  African Commission and, 274–280
  burden of proof, 196–202
  critical examination of, 65, 78
  elections and 'institutional order,'
    154–158
  information, access to, 145–147
  Inter-American Human Rights
    System, 255–256
  mis-rule of law, 64, 66–67
  responsibility for actions of previous
    regimes, 280–283
  transitional jurisprudence, effects
    of, 293–296
  see also deference to states
Stoica v. *Romania* (2008), 200
Stone Sweet, Alec, 19
Streletz, Kessler and Krenz v. *Germany*
  (2001), 6n.16, 11n.34
Sudan, 9–10, 269, 279–280
Sudan Human Rights Organisation
  and Centre on Housing Rights and
  Evictions v. *the Sudan* (2009), 269,
  279–280
Sunday Times v. *United Kingdom*
  (1979), 113n.46
Swaziland, 273
Sweeney, James, 4, 9, 10, 16, 18, 291
symbols, and freedom of expression,
  133–138

Tănase v. *Moldova* (2010), 157–158,
  180, 181
TASZ v. *Hungary* (2009), 146, 147
Teitel, R., 11–12, 110, 115n.52, 127, 139,
  145
Teitgen, Pierre-Henri, 155–156n.21
Teleki, Pál, 139
terminology, 72–73
The Social and Economic Rights
  Action Center and the Center for
  Economic and Social Rights v.
  Nigeria (2001), 283
third-party evidence, 18–19
time elapsed
  deference to States, 292
  ECtHR case load, 19, 287–288
  length of proceedings, 94–98

post-Communist states, 135,
  174–180
proportionality of interference with
  rights, 172–180, 181
site visits, role of, 297
Togo, 274–275
torture, 200–202
totalitarian systems *see* post-
  Communist states
Tradesmen v. *Colombia* (2004), 262–263
transition
  in Africa, 267–268, 284–285
  in the Americas, 239–240, 256–259,
    265–266
  and associative rights, 151–154,
    180–181
  concept of, 25–29
  deference to States, influence on,
    289–293
  and derogation, 24–25, 28–29,
    49–50, 290
  and discrimination, 185–188,
    205–206
  ECHR role, 1–2, 26, 286–287
  ECtHR role, 29–42, 286
  electoral rights, 151–158, 180–181
  and emergency, 29–42, 290
  equality in, 185–188, 205–206
  freedom of expression, 131–133,
    147–149
  hate speech in, 142–144
  IACtHR role, 3–4, 256–259,
    265–266, 296–299
  information, access to, 145–147
  margin of appreciation, 32–33,
    164–166, 181
  meaning of, 152
  militant democracy, 121–124,
    158–164
  narratives, 138–141
  Northern Ireland, 46–49
  post-Communist states, 108–111,
    118–119
  post-Yugoslav states, 81–84, 86–90
  process, 286–287
  proportionality of interference with
    rights, 166–180, 181
  symbols, use of, 133–138

transitional jurisprudence
  coherence of, 2–3, 14–15
  contours of, 8–12
  discrimination, 13–14, 193–195
  effects of, 293–296
  ethnic minorities, 185–188, 205–206
  forward- and backward-looking
    roles, 299–300
  goals of, 12–14
  and human rights, 1–4, 124–128,
    289–290, 293–296
  humanitarian law and human
    rights, 42–46, 49–50
  jurisdiction, 290–291
  and legitimacy, 52–53
  meaning of, 110
  and memory, 52–53, 77–78
  narratives of, 2, 4–7
  post-Yugoslav states, 189.7081–84,
    94–101
  regional courts, legacy of, 20–21
  regional courts, role of, 3–4, 15–20
  religion, freedom of, 103–104,
    107–108, 111–120, 124–128
  restitution of property, 15, 211–212,
    230–235, 291
trial, right to fair, 95n.55, 95n.56, 96
Trimble, David, 58
Truth and Reconciliation Commission
  of Peru, 248
truth commissions, 246–249
Tudjman, Franjo, 81–83, 86, 92–94
Turkey
  Aksoy v. Turkey (1995), 39–40
  and Cyprus, 173–174
  Cyprus v. Turkey (2001), 167n.73, 173
  democracy in, 108n.19, 122, 123n.78
  Demopoulos and Others v. Turkey
    (2010), 173–174
  derogation, use of, 38–41
  Freedom and Democracy Party
    (Özdep) v. Turkey (1999), 153n.7
  Loizidou v. Turkey (1996), 218–219,
    222, 229, 232
  Refah Partisi v. Turkey (2001),
    108n.19, 122, 123, 123n.78,
    162–163
  restitution of property, 209

  Sahin v. Turkey (2005), 127
  Sakik and Others v. Turkey (1997),
    40–41
  Yumak and Sadak v. Turkey (2008),
    172–173

United Kingdom (UK)
  Arrowsmith v. United Kingdom
    (1977), 104–105
  Brannigan and McBride v. United
    Kingdom (1993), 33, 37
  Brecknell v. United Kingdom (2007),
    71
  Brogan and Others v. United
    Kingdom (1988), 37
  derogation, use of, 38
  Finucane v. United Kingdom (2003),
    71
  Greece v. United Kingdom (1958),
    32n.25
  Handyside v. United Kingdom (1976),
    137
  Irish Republican use of law, 65–67
  and Irish Republicanism, 59–65
  Jordan v. United Kingdom (2001), 63,
    187n.15
  Kelly and others v. United Kingdom
    (2001), 52–53, 59–60, 62–65, 67,
    69–71, 72–77, 78
  McCann v. United Kingdom (1995),
    52–53, 59–62, 66–71, 72–77, 78,
    187n.15
  McKerr v. United Kingdom (2001),
    63, 187n.15
  reaction to McCann judgment,
    67–69
  Shanaghan v. United Kingdom
    (2001), 63, 187n.15
  Sunday Times v. United Kingdom
    (1979), 113n.46
United Nations (UN) see International
  Covenant on Civil and Political
  Rights (ICCPR)
United States (US), 93
Universal Declaration of Human
  Rights (UDHR), 104, 105–106
Uruguay, 243, 256
Uzelac, Alan, 88

Vajnai v. *Hungary* (2008), 133–138
Varju, Marton, 8–9
Vasil Sashov Petrov v. *Bulgaria* (2010), 200n.74
Velasquez-Rodríguez v. *Honduras* (1988), 255
Velikova v. *Bulgaria* (2000), 196–198
Velikovi and Others v. *Bulgaria* (2007), 9, 9n.28
Vermeule, Adrian, 7, 211
Viaene, L., 27
victimhood
  equality of, 64–65, 78
  Irish Republican use of law, 65–67
  and memory, 57–59
  and transitional jurisprudence, 52–53
victims' feelings, 137
Vidmar, Jure, 165n.68
Vienna Convention on the Law of Treaties (1969), 153n.5
Villatina Massacre v. *Colombia* (2005), 261–262
violence, 86, 88–90, 188, 195–202
Vo v. *France* (2004), 125–126n.83
Vogt v. *Germany* (1995), 161n.46
Vukovic, Milan, 87

war, 43
Weidlich v. *Germany* (1996), 223
women, 77

Yatama v. *Nicaragua* (2005), 124

Yugoslavia, 81–90, 86n.20, 210n.8
  see also post-Yugoslav states
Yumak and Sadak v. *Turkey* (2008), 172–173

Ždanoka v. *Latvia* (2006)
  Article 17, 161n.51
  'institutional order' and elections, 156–157, 158, 163–164, 165–166
  proportionality of interference with rights, 174–175
  self-defending democracy, 123
  time elapsed, 177–179
  transition, duration of, 8n.22, 173n.108
Zickus v. *Lithuania* (2009), 176–177
Zimbabwe, 270, 275–279
Zimbabwe Lawyers for Human Rights and Associated Newspapers of Zimbabwe (ANZ) v. *Republic of Zimbabwe* (2009), 278
Zimbabwe Lawyers for Human Rights and the Institute for Human Rights and Development (on behalf of Andrew Barclay Meldrum) v. *Republic Of Zimbabwe* (2009), 278–279
Zimbabwe Lawyers for Human Rights and the Institute for Human Rights and Development v. *Republic of Zimbabwe* (2008), 276–278
Zupančič, J., 205